The Fundamentals of a Recovering Fundamentalist

"Fundamentalists have not gone away—they are still part of various segments in the Christian community. Rather than dismissing or disregarding their claims, this book aims to shed light on the reasons behind their beliefs and offers guidance on how to critically examine their ideas. The reader is left with a better understanding and ability to respond to the perils of Fundamentalism. This is a must-read for those who feel trapped in this movement."

—**Rodolfo Galvan Estrada III**, assistant professor of New Testament, Vanguard University

"This book reflects on core Christian commitments by drawing on a diverse array of Christian sources, both geographically and historically. In so doing, this text offers a lamentably rare theological discussion that draws on a more full sampling of the global body of Christ. Given the era of social, political, and theological fragmentation in which we live, this book offers timely and constructive steps on how to enter into the process of construction, de-construction and re-construction."

—**Vince Bantu**, assistant professor of church history and black church studies, Fuller Seminary

"Gabriel Gordon's searing—and occasionally compassionate—critique of American and Northern European Fundamentalism and progressivism reveals his heartfelt journey into pre-enlightenment Christian theology and orthopraxy. Most significantly, he argues that the Jewish roots of Christianity must be reaffirmed and reincorporated into the church's spirituality in conversation with Jewish disciples of Yeshua. As a Jewish evangelical, I may not agree with all he asserts, but his arguments are challenging and worthy of deep reflection."

—**Lee Spitzer**, historian, Baptist World Alliance

"In Gabriel Gordon's book, *The Fundamentals of a Recovering Fundamentalists*, he serves up a thoughtful and scholarly feast for us all. Gordon takes us back to the very core of understanding Jesus, the Jewish Messiah and the role of his faithful followers. Anyone interested in finding a challenging new way to understand an ancient faith, should be reading this great work!"

—**RANDY WOODLEY**, author of *Indigenous Theology and the Western Worldview*

"In *The Fundamentals of a Recovering Fundamentalist*, Gabriel Gordon invites us into the often painful and difficult journey of shedding the Fundamentalist ideology that many of us grew up in and that has caused a great deal of confusion, disorientation, and, at times, damage, in the world of faith. The journey we are invited into leads us to become more aware of, and engage with, a wide diversity of voices in the Christian world."

—**JARED KING**, lead pastor, Missio Church

"Over the years I have known Gabriel Gordon, we have had innumerable theological conversations, whether he was my teaching assistant or we were simply dialoguing as friends. I have had a front-row seat to significant aspects of his 'recovery' from Fundamentalism. He has always made me think and reflect on what I believe. His passion and transparency are heartfelt and contagious. I am thrilled that he has put into writing where his journey has taken him—thus far. I pray you find challenge and hope for your own journey of discipleship with Jesus of Nazareth."

—**DANIEL L. BRUNNER**, professor emeritus of Christian history and formation, Portland Seminary

"Gabriel Gordon takes readers on a fascinating journey to rediscover the beauty, Jewishness, and radical love of the Christian faith. This journey is historical, as Gordon engages many early Christian writers. The journey is thoughtful, as Gordon interacts with contemporary thinkers on a variety of topics. The journey is also deeply personal, as Gordon shares not only what he has learned but how he learned it. There will be much to ponder and discuss upon engaging with Gabriel Gordon's work, and we will be better for it."

—**Dennis R. Edwards**, dean, North Park Theological Seminary

"Gabriel Gordon's book is a courageous and daringly self-revealing witness to the way the God of Israel is still taking hold of the world, even in the twilight of our present culture. It's a young book: fresh, filled with clear images, riven by the internal combat of someone seeking the truth of God, and, through all kinds of struggles, reveling in the God who has first sought him. We should thankfully read Gordon's story because, in a basic way, it is all of ours in its promise and wonder."

—**Ephraim Radner**, professor of historical theology, Wycliffe College, University of Toronto

"Gabriel Gordon admits he doesn't know what kind of book he has written here. I confess that, having got to the end, I'm not exactly sure either. This book recklessly trespasses the boundaries of spiritual biography, theological treatise, socio-cultural analysis, and prophetic proclamation. Yet what I do know is that, if we are on the verge of one of those every five-hundred-year revolutions in thought and society that he predicts, and if we are to avoid therein worsening the already dire effects of modernity (and the "endarkenment") on Christian faith and life, we desperately need the themes broached and questions raised by this book. Highly recommended."

—**Geoffrey Ready**, director of Orthodox Christian Studies at Trinity College, University of Toronto

The Fundamentals of a Recovering Fundamentalist

Reorienting Towards the True, Good, and Beautiful

Gabriel Gordon

Foreword by Thomas Dahlman

WIPF & STOCK · Eugene, Oregon

THE FUNDAMENTALS OF A RECOVERING FUNDAMENTALIST
Reorienting Towards the True, Good, and Beautiful

Copyright © 2024 Gabriel Gordon. All rights reserved. Except for brief quotations in critical publications or reviews, no part of this book may be reproduced in any manner without prior written permission from the publisher. Write: Permissions, Wipf and Stock Publishers, 199 W. 8th Ave., Suite 3, Eugene, OR 97401.

Wipf & Stock
An Imprint of Wipf and Stock Publishers
199 W. 8th Ave., Suite 3
Eugene, OR 97401

www.wipfandstock.com

PAPERBACK ISBN: 978-1-6667-8568-5
HARDCOVER ISBN: 978-1-6667-8569-2
EBOOK ISBN: 978-1-6667-8570-8

VERSION NUMBER 06/07/24

Unless otherwise stated, all Scripture quotations are from the *Syriac-English New Testament: The Traditional Syriac Peshitta Text and the Antioch Bible English Translation*, copyright © 2020 by Gorgias Press LLC. Used with permission of Gorgias Press LLC, 954 River Road, Piscataway, NJ, 08854, USA. All rights reserved.

Quotations marked NETS are taken from the New English Translation of the Septuagint, copyright © 2007 the International Organization for Septuagint and Cognate Studies, Inc. Used by permission of Oxford University Press. All rights reserved.

© Origen, Origen: On First Principles: A Reader's Edition. Oxford, UK: Oxford University Press, 2019. Reproduced with permission of the Licensor through PLSclear.

© Ware, Kallistos. The Orthodox Way. Yonkers, NY: St Vladimir's Seminary Press, 2018. Reproduced with permission of St Vladimir's Seminary Press.

© Isaac of Nineveh. On Ascetical Life. Crestwood, NY: St Vladimir's Seminary Press, 1989. Reproduced with permission of St Vladimir's Seminary Press.

Do not have lots of teachers among you, my brothers and sisters. You should realize that we teachers will incur severer judgement, for we all make many mistakes.

—James 3:1–2 (Judean Jew)

When I err, my error infects every one who believes me. When I sin publicly, every spectator either condones it, thus sharing my guilt, or condemns it with imminent danger to his charity [love] and humility.

—C. S. Lewis (from Ireland, ethnically Welsh and Irish)

Lord Jesus Christ Son of God, have mercy on me, a sinner.

—Jesus Prayer (unknown)

Contents

Foreword by Thomas Dahlman | ix
Preface: A Better Path to Recovery | xiii
Acknowledgments | xvii
Introduction | xxi

1 Prophecy, Pineapples, and Baptists | 1
2 Fundamentalism, Evangelicalism, and Historical Christianity | 17
3 Principles and Practices for Recovering Fundamentalists/Evangelicals | 57
4 Orthodoxy and Orthopraxy | 87
5 What Do I Do with the Bible? | 109
6 The Gnostic Heresy | 140
7 The Gospel | 162
8 The Church | 199

Conclusion: How Then Shall We Live? | 240
Recommended Resources | 247
Bibliography | 253

Foreword

Lord, you now have set your servant free. To go in peace as you have promised. For these eyes of mine have seen the Savior whom you have prepared for all the world to see. A Light to enlighten the nations and the glory of your people Israel.

SIMEON IS AN OLD man. He has been waiting and praying in the temple night and day for the Messiah. One day Mary and Joseph arrive for the presentation of their new baby in the temple as prescribed by the Law. When Simeon sees Jesus with his own eyes—filled with the Holy Spirit— he greets him with a joyful song. At last, he sees the Savior! At last, he sees the light and desire of the nations. Simeon gives thanks that he can now depart in peace. Like Anna, who also waited, Simeon's patient faith is rewarded with sight.

In the Episcopal Church (and all the Anglican Communion) the song Song of Simeon plays a key role in worship. From *1549 onwards*, it has been part of Daily Evening Prayer in every edition of the *Book of Common Prayer*. Its use in the daily prayers of monastics is of course much older.

What is it about the Song of Simeon that endures between centuries and cultures? Why has this simple song remained so important to communities of worship? There are many songs in Scripture we seldom consider, but this one (along with a few others) continues to inspire.

Perhaps it is because like Simeon we need to be able to articulate who we are and what we are doing. Like Simeon, we need dedication to our purpose that lasts beyond a season. Like Simeon, we need to dedicate our lives to pursuits that really matter. Most of all, we need to rediscover the simple passion and vulnerability of this old prophet who sang with joy when he met the One.

In our jaded culture, recovering the spirit of Simeon is not an easy task for one person, to say nothing of an entire fellowship or the church in general. Given Christianity's incredible variety of opinions and approaches, it seems unlikely a critical mass of us could recapture Simeon's beautiful and profound faith. Despite this, I cannot think of a better place to begin than with Simeon in the temple courts. This is the place to be set free and find peace.

As I read Gabriel's story, I was reminded of Simeon patiently waiting in the temple. Be warned, however; the first chapter is full of pain. If you have walked a similar path, you may struggle with Gabe's openness and honesty. Most of us would have quit after the first church, the second church, the abandonment, the third church, the divorce, the abuse, or the excommunication. Most of us did.

This story is not typical. This book will take you on a journey, a search motivated by the need to see the Light to enlighten the nations. Gabriel shows the patience of Simeon in his willingness to keep searching, and in his compassion for those of us who would have given up on faith altogether. Gabriel, as Simeon's time in the temple attests, also points us to the ancient practice and prayers of God's people to avoid dead ends.

I also found the joy and wonder of Simeon in these pages. I know Gabriel. I was with him as he questioned, considered, debated, and discovered. Because I had seen it myself, I could picture the work and the wonder apparent in this thought: "The problem . . . was . . . defining humanity based on us, rather than Yeshua, the only one who reveals both what it is to be God and what it truly is to be human."

My advice to prospective readers is do not read this book if you don't want to be challenged by someone who is clearly young and obviously smart. Time spent in Gabriel's head will only benefit those who are sure they don't have faith figured out and who have the humility to reconsider some ideas they have abandoned.

This book is partially written for people who have faith stories like Gabriel. The problem with most of us is that we are jaded. Most of us have given up. We have understandably lost patience. It is hard for some of us with difficult faith stories to wrap our minds around the idea that others had much rougher roads but still held on to joyful, open, and honest faith through many painful detours. We wonder, how he was able to wait in the temple so long? How did he maintain joy, his passion?

This book may be best for the Simeons and Annas of the world, who have been patiently waiting for Jesus to show up in husbands, wives, friends, children, and family who have given up on God. In these pages you might find the answers to questions you have been asking for a long time. At the very least you will see faith through the eyes of someone who knows what it means to wait in the temple.

Thomas Dahlman

Preface

A Better Path to Recovery

When I first started getting serious about my faith as a teenager living in Bangkok, I found myself praying this simple prayer each day: "God help me to become who you want me to become." As I got older and more educated, I "advanced" to more serious and complex prayers. But God has been active in showing me that education and more complex prayers isn't always a good thing. Sometimes being more "advanced" is actually being further behind in the way of Yeshua (Jesus).[1] Afterall, Messiah says in order to enter the kingdom of God, one needs to have faith like a child. Maybe, as a recovering fundamentalist, I need to get back to that simple prayer. Maybe many of us need to reclaim a certain kind of simplicity that comes with the faith of a child.

Over the last few years I've felt a prompting from the Spirit to write this book, a book for former fundamentalists who have either gone through deconstruction, are currently going through it, or are about to. Having been a part of these circles myself, I have become aware of various depths of hurt and confusion among this group. When we're hurt and confused, we can react in a few different ways: we can shut down; we can sin in our anger; or we can, while refraining from sin, be propelled by our righteous anger to seek healing and to strive to make our own lives and

---

1. Throughout the book I will use the Hebrew term *Yeshua* instead of the English translation, "Jesus," unless I am quoting someone who does. I do this 1) because I'm Jewish, 2) because I'm trying to emphasis the Jewishness of Yeshua, and 3) because I want to highlight the foreignness of Yeshua to the broader gentile world, and particularly his foreignness to the Western world.

those of our fundamentalist world more true, more beautiful, and more good. As a result of our sinning in anger, we often respond in unhealthy ways. We throw the baby out with the bath water. We choose to exclude or avoid those from our background. We read merely in order to critique and degrade, rather than to build or restore. In summary, we often deconstruct badly. That's not to say deconstruction in and of itself is bad, or questions in and of themselves are bad. It is questions and deconstruction that have led me to write this book.

Yet we can become critics for the sake of criticism, but criticism of the other for their guilt-ridden action of demonizing the other is fraught with a high degree of contagion. Without careful intentionality, the evil that our prophetic rebuke is directed toward will become our own. We all need a devil. *So, we former fundamentalists* make devils out of those who make others into devils. Russian-American and Foursquare Scholar A. J. Swoboda captures this perfectly when he writes,

> Whenever we talk about racism—and I see this in myself—it is always *someone else* who is racist. We rail against racism but only in others. It is never us. No one ever says, "Hey, there's this big problem of racism, and it's me!" It is always other people. Other people are sexist. Other people are homophobic. Other people are Islamophobic. It is never, ever me. The echo reverberates: evil is all "out there." And we won't let evil in here.[2]

Oftentimes our own self-righteous criticism is, whether consciously or not, a veil of distraction from that which is wrong in ourselves. Without an awareness of our own sin and evil, we quickly devolve into self-righteous prophets who become just as guilty of the sin that we have been sent to judge, and we become even more blind to the evil that has and continues to makes its home in us. I once met a pastor of a progressive church, who, like myself, came from a Southern Baptist background. When I pointed this connection out for the purpose of developing some rapport with him, rather than for the purpose of ranting, his response was rather telling: "Well, we've evolved." Given his theological context and the tone of his voice, it was clear he was expressing the arrogant and superior attitude of the Enlightenment. But saints are not saints because they are holier or more evolved than everyone else, but because when the lights are turned on in their life they see how messy and sinful they actually are, and thus are humbled.

---

2. Swoboda, *After Doubt*, 136–37.

Preface

In writing this book as a criticism of this phenomenon, I ironically am in danger of doing the exact same thing—of arrogantly seeing myself as more evolved, as if the sin and evil is out there somewhere external to myself. Which it's not. It's also inside me. The Lord instructs us by the hand of Evagrios, the fourth-century monk from Asia Minor, when he writes, "There is scarcely any other virtue which the demons fear as much as gentleness."[3] Until we learn such gentleness, we are in danger of being handed swords while we are still people of wrath. "We must not hand a dangerous sword to those too readily incensed to wrath, for it often happens that people become excessively worked up for quite trivial reasons."[4] Too often we former, or better yet, recovering fundamentalists are "too readily incensed to wrath," because we have yet to do the hard work on ourselves necessary to cease from our *unrighteous* anger and wrath. There is indeed a time for *righteous* anger, as we see from Yeshua's overturning of the money changer's tables in the temple. Yet many of us haven't yet started the hard work of learning to be angry for the right reasons and allowing that anger to lead us to make things better. Anger and wrath are two characteristics that when applied to God cause many of us to be offended. We try to get rid of any anger in God as if injustice doesn't anger a good, loving, and just God. Yet when it comes to us, we are more than comfortable being angry and wrathful. We need to learn there is a kind of righteous anger found in God, which is rooted in the non-coercive love of God.

Nonetheless, before many of us learn this we are given "dangerous swords," platforms to speak, teach, and write. The pen is indeed a dangerous sword, depending on who is writing with it, and who is reading the work produced by it. To borrow from the *Philokalia*, a collection of monastic writings from the fourth to the seventeenth centuries, we former fundamentalists should "stay in bed until [our sickness] is completely recovered and [should] not act like disobedient patients who, before they are fully cured of their disease, start taking baths and so fall sick again. Let us sit still and keep our attention fixed within ourselves, so that we advance in holiness and resist vice more strongly."[5] While we are still sick, hardly able to walk, we leave the hospital against medical advice.

Only after we have done much of the inner work, after we have become gentle and bold, can we then be handed a sword, which in our

---

3. Evagrios, "Texts on Discrimination," 46.
4. Evagrios, "Texts on Discrimination," 41.
5. Evagrios, "Texts on Discrimination," 47.

hands becomes transformed into a scalpel, able to remove cancerous tumors through the hands of mercy and virtue in order to heal and bind rather than divide, hurt, and tear down. Unrighteous anger is of little profit but righteous anger positively directed can kindle the birth of new creation and bring healing. Those of us who come from fundamentalism, if I may say so, bear a sickness and are in need of healing from that sickness. Before we are adequately cured, we must avoid speaking, writing publicly, and so forth. We must have a season of some healing, a time to do the inner work that needs to happen. We must be cured of our fundamentalism. As of now, many of us are still sick. We have yet to go through the actual process of leaving fundamentalism.

Euro-American Wendell Berry once wrote, "The only defense against the worst is a knowledge of the best."[6] In my mind, one of the main problems among us former fundamentalists is the reality that we are often unaware of, and woefully so, of the best of the Christian tradition, especially its depth, breadth, and diversity. We were introduced to a very narrow piece of the Christian pie, so that when we came to reject that narrow bit of Christianity, being unaware of just how truly big the faith is, we unknowingly threw out the whole pie. And sometimes that narrow piece of pie, which we were taught was the whole of Christianity, was in many cases not even part of the Christian pie, but a totally different pie. If we wish to recover from our sickness, we must learn from the best of the Christian tradition and that takes practice, patience, and time, years even. In a culture of instant gratification, this does not come easy or natural to us.

But there's a better way, one that doesn't run from deconstruction or shy away from critiquing what must be criticized, but one that does so out of love and mercy for our brothers and sisters and strives to be faithful to divine Truth. Not truth in the dry modern sense of propositional statements, but *the Truth*, who is the person of Yeshua Messiah. In short, this book is written for former fundamentalists recovering from their fundamentalism, and, as we will see, fundamentalists still suffering from their current fundamentalism. I hope to provide some helpful guidance in doing deconstruction and reconstruction well, a journey of recovery I myself have been on for the past decade. My hope and prayer is this may be useful. What is not helpful, because it is not true, good, and beautiful and therefore not of God, discard through the virtue of bold gentleness.

---

6. Berry, "In Defense of Literacy," 292–95.

Acknowledgments

I WOULD LIKE TO give a special thanks to Christ Community Church in Oklahoma City, Oklahoma. It might seem a bit ironic that in a book addressed to the deconstructionist community and written as a critique of modernist Christianity I would highlight, with particular gratitude, my deep indebtedness to a Southern Baptist church. Yet I think such irony is a profound witness to the comedic nature of God. Hopefully it exhibits some of my own healing from being a jaded former fundamentalist, or as I will so fondly call myself in this book, a recovering fundamentalist, or maybe a recovering modernist, who's hopefully found sobriety. Regardless, this thriving, close-knit Southern Baptist community, for whom I have the utmost respect, did something that would profoundly shape my journey. They gave me a book. That book was Athanasius's *On the Incarnation*, translated by English Eastern Orthodox priest and patristics scholar Father John Behr. My turn away from modernity started with this gift. Such a small moment can have unintended immense consequences. This book, which I hope is saturated with the church fathers, owes its thanks to that gift.

In the light of appreciating my Southern Baptist comrades of old, I dedicate this book to all the people in my life who are in one way or another fundamentalists or evangelicals, many of whom are Southern Baptists. The following people to whom I dedicate this book are in ways I am not always aware of responsible for who I have become today. I learned to read at the comprehension of someone my own age because of Carrie Chappell, her friend who tested my reading skills, and Kannon

Dayton. I fell in love with the Gospels read and preached on Sunday morning through the pastoral work of Martin Chappell. A special thanks to Dr. Bruce Carlton, who taught me the importance of being on mission for the kingdom of God and in surprising ways is continuing to teach me, though he is far away. To Dr. Alan Bandy, whose encouraging and almost prophetic words have served as perpetual guideposts. To Christ Community Church, who shared and lived with me the importance of community. To Paul and Ruth Stevens, who showed and taught me the importance of being known for what we are for, rather than for merely what we are against. To my former boss, Aaron Hembree, who showed me love and acceptance, despite the fact I had rejected my former fundamentalist theology and gave me a job when my wife and I needed it most.

To all those people who showed me the love of Yeshua and provided me with extravagant evidence that not all fundamentalists or evangelicals are assholes. Despite the terribly sad injustices that the Southern Baptist Convention has been guilty of perpetrating, there are lights in those dark moments serving as living witnesses to the goodness of Yeshua, witnesses lit with the fire of the Holy Spirit burning in their denomination. While I'm not uncritical, as you will see below, of fundamentalism, or liberal Protestantism more generally, I am who I am because of the wonderful people I've dedicated this book to.

I also want to acknowledge the profound influence of three of my seminary professors, who if they look carefully will see their fingerprints throughout much of this book: Keetoowah Cherokee farmer and missiologist Dr. Randy Woodley, Indonesian New Testament and postcolonial scholar Dr. Ekaputra Tupamahu, and Swedish-American church historian and spiritual formation professor Daniel Brunner. I'm not quite sure how much of what I say in this book they will agree with, but nevertheless they have provided mentorship, co-learning, and the birthing of critical thinking and embodiment in me to such an extent that without them this book would simply not be possible. Thank you all for your faithful guidance.

I would like to highlight a few friends whom I have to some extent, at some point wrestled with and engaged in thoughtful reflection, without which I would not have had the ability to write this book: Adam D'Achille, a faithful companion and thoughtful, kind dueler; Cameron French, without whom my connection between orthodoxy and orthopraxy would have been severely malnourished; Jon Boss, who was right to point out when I was being unnecessarily unkind in my writing style;

Acknowledgments

Colt Meyer, my best friend, whom I've known since we were teenagers in the youth group—you have been a constant companion throughout our deconstruction; and Derek Lofing, who was one of my main conversation partners during the writing of this book and whose insight was almost always helpful.

To John Hatch, who as a communication scholar kindly offered his services and giftings, reading through the entire manuscript and providing extensive feedback. While at times I argued with John's feedback, such argument for the sake of heaven only served to make the manuscript better. To all those who read some portion and version of the book during its production: my Sunday school group, especially but not limited to Karen and Joel; Rob Christ, who read an early draft of the book; Eric Sears, who read an early draft of chapter 5, and later talked through it. To be frank, when it comes to writing narrative I have a lot of room for improvement; my special thanks to friend and fellow writer Joanna Mumford, who read through chapter 1 (which is essentially all narrative) and made many stylistic suggestions that greatly improved the first chapter. If chapter 1 is not well written, it's much better due to her. Anything left that still needs approvement is of course due to my own lack of writing skills and should not be imputed to her own writing ability.

My special thanks to Ryan Hunziker for emotional and financial support. Your support has not gone unnoticed or unfelt. To my friend and fellow wanderer Josh Patterson, many thanks for your friendship despite our mutually exclusive theological worldviews. Our civil arguments have of course been for the sake of heaven, and I'm sure have been influential on this project. You may be a process theologian, but you're my process theologian. To my friend, and in many ways, mentor Tom Oord, my many thanks for all of your encouragement and support in my writing and theological endeavors over the years. This certainly would not be the book on deconstruction and reconstruction you would write but in many ways I am the theologian I am because of your positive influence in my life. And like Josh, you may be an open theist and process theologian, but you're my open theist and process theologian. Special thanks to Daniel Edwards for reviewing my section on the myth of Christianity's Hellenization. Your scholarship and friendship is always appreciated. Madison Horton and her husband, Chase, also graciously read early portions of the book, for which I give thanks.

Special thanks to Jennifer Rosner, who brought me into Yachad BeYeshua at a crucial moment in my life. My life has forever been changed due to your tireless efforts on behalf of Yachad. To Mark Kinzer and Antoine Levy, who saw the need and had the foresight to create Yachad BeYeshua and bring together Jewish disciples of Yeshua, both Jewish Christians and Messianic Jews, into the same fellowship. This in itself I can't help but believe is a miracle of God. To Ephraim Radner, who has given me a listening ear, deep-seated wisdom, and encouragement as I have journeyed deeper into my Jewish Episcopalianism. To Jeremy Beck and Julia Salkind, whose Jewish friendship and advice have been more helpful than they probably realize.

Louie Hogan helped me finish the last part of chapter 5 when I was completely stumped. Dr. Dennis R Edwards, while not hugely influential on the book as a whole, was in ways I'm sure he is unaware of a word of encouragement that has kept me going throughout the revising and finalizing process of the manuscript. I'd also like to thank Chris Thrutchley, who kindly offered his services to help me with the final read-through of the book. To Karl Barth, my faithful dog and brother, who is always keen to remind me to stop and smell the roses, and to make time to play. And of course to all those whom by faulty memory I am somehow forgetting. You'll have to forgive my selective memory; there is only so much I can hold. It takes a village to write a book, and mine was no different. It also takes land, otherwise I would have nothing under my feet to support me while I wrote. Land, people, and theology are deeply interconnected, and it was while I lived in the Ute people's land in Grand Junction, Colorado that I wrote this book. That land both was shaped by them and in turn they were shaped by it. This book is as it is because of my time being shaped by the Ute people's land. I am grateful.

I would be remiss if I failed to express abundant gratitude for my songbird, my wife, Hannah. She has spent countless hours and days enduring the dull, over-expressive broken record that has been my mouth throughout the writing of this book. As the person who is around me (an external processor) the most, she has suffered greatly in my long lectures about this or that aspect of my book during the process of writing. She is also one of the most faithful people I know, in her walk both with Yeshua (although she doesn't always know it) and with me. The kindness, compassion, and fidelity she exudes is a clear picture of the Messiah incarnated within her.

Introduction

Creator of all things,
true Source of light and wisdom,
lofty origin of all being,
graciously let a ray of Your brilliance
penetrate into the darkness of my understanding
and take from me the double darkness
in which I have been born,
an obscurity of both sin and ignorance.
Give me a sharp sense of understanding,
a retentive memory,
and the ability to grasp things correctly and fundamentally.
Grant me the talent of being exact in my explanations,
and the ability to express myself with thoroughness and charm.
Point out the beginning,
direct the progress,
and help in completion;
through Christ our Lord.[1]

—St. Thomas Aquinas (Italian Roman Catholic
theologian, thirteenth century)

---

1. Thomas Aquinas, "Prayer before Study," quoted in "Prayers of St. Thomas Aquinas."

EVEN AS I STRUGGLE to write these words and sentences, all in the effort to construct this book before you, something deep within, an intuition, says this book is needed. I have no idea what exactly this book is yet, although I have a very rough idea of where I would like to take it (or maybe where the Holy Spirit would like to take it). It seems to me we stand at the precipice, but of what I'm not quite sure. It certainly can be felt, like when a room is filled with so much awkward tension it can almost be cut with a butter knife. Whatever it is, it's thick, filled with substance, like it's at the tip of our tongue. Like that smell that seems familiar, but you can't quite place it—or even tell if it's good or bad. It is simply the reality of change; what may come might be good, bad, or a mixture of both. Phyllis Tickle is famous for suggesting roughly every five hundred years a seismic change takes places in our culture and world. The last culturally shifting event that took place, at least in the West, was the Protestant Reformation, five hundred years ago. If she was right, it would seem in the West we're due for something big.

But what honestly scares me, if I can be honest with you, is the reality that what might occur in our own time may not be better than what happened five hundred years ago. I would do no one any kind of service if I overlooked the reality that I'm inclined to see the Protestant Reformation in a rather poor light. I may have just offended a lot of people, which isn't my intention, but I'd rather be honest with you. It's important for me to recognize that I'm also deeply appreciative of my Protestant brothers and sisters. I am who I am, and for that matter all of us in the West are who we are, because of the Protestant Reformation. Indeed, most of my mentors have been Protestants of one stripe or another. Some of the people I most deeply respect are some kind of Protestant. I even attended a broadly evangelical seminary.

While I may not be Protestant and I may see the Reformation as being more bad than good, I am deeply indebted to my Protestant family, who has shaped me in ways I am sure I am unaware of. As with several movements, this one is a mix of good and bad. And God has squeezed a lot of good out of the bad. I give God praise for that! I would be wrong if I thought God could not use the Protestant tradition, that it was empty of all goodness or totally lacked the presence of the Holy Spirit. A lot of good has come from Martin Luther nailing his Ninety-Five Theses to that door all those years ago. I just tend to think more bad than good has come from it and I reject some of the foundational doctrines that make Protestantism unique. I see the Reformation, right or wrong, as a general orientation and move away from the great tradition towards novelty, and as an intensification of Europe's anti-Judaism. And like the Catholics, I share a view of tradition and Scripture as intimately connected, and like the Orthodox I tend to see Scripture as part of tradition rather than a distinct entity. In short, I believe the Reformation truly saw that something in the Western church needed reforming, but they went wrong in how they did so.

I'm fairly convinced at this point in my life that the way forward for us coming out of fundamentalism isn't forward, so to speak, but backward. Not towards novelty, but back towards the tradition. The reformers also held this perspective and saw themselves as doing exactly that. But in retrospect I'm not sure they did and that should give me and others who share my perspective pause. Erasmus, the Dutch Roman Catholic reformer, a contemporary of the German Protestant reformer Martin Luther, was often accused *of laying the egg that Luther hatched*. Whether or not that's true (the historians can argue about that), it should give us (and I include myself and this book in this) pause about the possible consequences our work may have. We need to be careful of the kinds of eggs we're laying.

What we think we're doing may very well not be what we're actually doing or may have unintended negative consequences. We may be the blind leading the blind, and only the perspective of time will tell. Reminiscent of the Danish philosopher Soren Kierkegaard, Jewish rabbi Jonathan Sacks writes, "We live life forwards, but we understand it only looking back."[2] Keetoowah Cherokee Randy Woodley, in speaking about the Native orientation to the past, writes, "My Mi'kmaq friend Terry LeBlanc tells the story of his grandfather taking him deep into the woods when he was younger. His grandfather told him to look twice as much at the scenery behind him as he moved forward, because if he did not recognize where he had been, he would never find his way out of those woods."[3] In line with Rabbi Sacks, and with Randy's description of the Indigenous orientation, I want to suggest for us former fundamentalists and any kind of modernist progressive Christianity that to live our lives forward we are going to have to *understand life backward*, to see our roots and be utterly shaped by them, to be fully immersed (baptized) in them. My perspective on the way forward for the deconstructionist movement,

---

2. Sacks, *Essays on Ethics*, 39.
3. Woodley, *Shalom and the Community of Creation*, 118.

and other forms of modernist and Western Christianity, can be summed up in the words of former fundamentalist and Euro-Canadian Eastern Orthodox Brad Jersak. We need to be drawn "down [into] the trunk of the historic church and [drawn] deep into the roots of apostolic Christianity as taught by the early mothers and fathers of our faith."[4] This is what I hope to move us toward in this book.

One thing we should keep at the forefront of our minds is that modernist versions of Christianity, whatever the adjective (progressive, fundamentalist, deconstructionist) are white[5] theological movements arising out of the broader adoption of the Northern European Enlightenment over the last couple of centuries. Since Protestant fundamentalism is a white theological tradition, those coming from this tradition in the deconstructionist movement, even if not white, have been profoundly shaped by a white worldview with all the assumptions and categories that stem from that. White groups usually don't think of themselves as white, but this is because of white supremacy, which centers whiteness as the norm.

Because white supremacy can include people who believe the "white race" is superior in explicit ways, such that this term conjures up common images of Nazis or Ku Klux Klan members, I will often use the term "white normativity" in order to capture situations in which people are simply or seemingly oblivious to the assumptions and ways in which whiteness assumes a colonizing superior-ness, normalcy, and centering in everyday life. Many seemingly well-meaning people, who at least outwardly proclaim they genuinely want to combat racism, are nonetheless still unconsciously assuming some level of this white normativity.

---

4. Jersak, *A More Christlike Word*, 54.

5. When I use the term "white," as in terms like "white people," "white culture," "white theology," etc., I am by no means using it as an interchangeable term with "European," nor do I simply mean someone with pale skin color. "White" as I am defining it refers to Northern European Germanic ethnicities, and the culture and worldview that grew from and among those ethnicities during modernity. While Celtic and Slavic peoples are considered white today, there was a time when they were considered racially inferior, and certainly not considered white. My use of this term includes the feature of pale skin, but is not limited to it, and indeed pale skin by itself is not what I have in reference when I say "white." Lastly, when I utilize the term "white," I am referring to the modern construct of whiteness rooted in the universalizing principle of the Enlightenment that deprives people with pale skin color, Northern Europeans or Europeans more generally, of their ethnic particularity and replaces it with this construct, which, like sin, is a deprivation of something, rather than something that has any real substance in itself. "White" as I'm using it did not exist before modernity and is a matrix of power and control rather than something real rooted in real people's cultural and ethnic genetic makeup.

Introduction

This is why everything that isn't white gets labeled with an adjective, but whiteness simply is the norm and is thus seen as having no need for an adjective.

Take fundamentalist or progressive Protestantism as an example. It may be "progressive" theology, but it's not "white theology"; it's just theology that doesn't get an ethnic or racial adjective. But if its theology being done by a Native American or a Black person, particularly if that person refuses to operate within the fundamentalist or progressive Protestant worldview, it gets labeled with an adjective such as "Native theology" or "Black theology." Since the deconstructionist movement and more generally modernist Christianity is a white movement, coming out of the white tradition of fundamentalism and the broader Protestant adoption of the Northern European Enlightenment, we have to be on guard against any modernist tendencies white culture has for colonizing—a tendency for colonizing we have in our theological DNA, and yet may be utterly unaware of. Whatever it is I'm intuiting that's on its way, I think this is somehow part of the equation, at least something we have to take account for.

But I want to make clear from the beginning, even as I critique Western and Northern European peoples and their cultures over the last few centuries, *I am not suggesting* these peoples are inherently evil, colonial, generally racist, or specifically anti-Jewish. *What I am suggesting* is they have often failed to express the image of God inherent in themselves and have instead frequently rejected their God-given call to express God's image in a unique way only they can do. While we must, in the words of Lakota theologian Richard Twiss, "genuinely appreciate all cultures as being capable of reflecting biblical faith,"[6] we cannot assume all cultures, especially the Enlightenment culture, have done so; and indeed in order to help them do so, light must be shed on the ways in which they have failed and the ways in which they need to repent in order to reflect that true faith. The image of God is inalienable in all of us and we all are able to live into the true self that God has called us to be. Indeed, the very fact I am critiquing Northern European modernity at all implies I don't think colonialism and anti-Judaism are part of their true nature, and I believe and hope that they can change.

So the question for us (particularly for those who at some level are connected with the deconstruction movement)—the one we must

---

6. Twiss, *Rescuing the Gospel from the Cowboys*, 16.

answer if we want to avoid repeating the mistakes of history, if we actually want whatever is around the corner to be better than what came before—is: What is the right way of doing deconstruction, and therefore the right way of doing reconstruction? "The right way"?! Yes, this statement makes many of us bristle, a result of our deeply modernist[7] and post-modernist rather than Christian assumptions. "How can there be a right way?" While we may converse on what that right way is, we cannot deny that there is indeed a right way(s), *because we know there certainly are wrong ways*. The moral relativism of Western culture, an aspect of white privilege, needs to be put in check. There is right and wrong, and the only ones who can really deny this reality are privileged white people. The slave being whipped in the cotton fields or, closer to home, the Jew being led to a concentration camp does not have the luxury to live under such delusions.[8]

The title of this book, *The Fundamentals of a Recovering Fundamentalist*, is a tribute to my own recovery not just as a recovering fundamentalist, but as a recovering sex addict, specifically a porn addict. In *recovery* those who are experienced, both in relapse and recovery, will tell you there may be many right ways to work on your recovery from addiction, but their certainly are wrong ways! Swapping porn for prostitutes is certainly the wrong way to seek recovery from sex addiction! There are also many right ways to seek recovery, such as: getting a sponsor who's further along the journey of recovery than you are to walk with you in your own recovery, getting blocking and accountability software on your phone and laptop, not having access to wi-fi, and so forth. My point being: while there are many ways to seek healing, there are also many ways to do so very poorly, ways that further solidify our addictions rather than doing any good for our recovery journey. Addicts tend to be self-deluded and we are great at convincing ourselves we're no longer operating out of our addictions. I use a personal example that is so serious and depraved because I believe that the contemporary theological condition is equally grave.

We're great at convincing ourselves we've left our fundamentalism behind, and that we're in recovery. There may be a few good paths to take, but some are better than others and some are just disastrous for your journey of recovery. I've seen a lot of recovering fundamentalists simply swap their metaphorical porn for sex with a prostitute. Meaning,

---

7. We should note that modernist/Enlightenment values came from Northern Europe.

8. As the reader will discover in the first chapter, I am a Jew of mixed blood.

Introduction

they never actually leave the fundamentalist way of being. If they come from a group of fundamentalists who were intent on being right and excluding people based on correct doctrine and practice—say, belief in the inerrancy of Scripture and the Jewish stance on homosexuality—then instead of becoming the sort of persons who welcome everyone, they still exclude people based on correct doctrine and practice. They may now welcome those from the LGBT community, and those who don't believe that Scripture is without error, but now they exclude a different group of people—those who believe in inerrancy and have a Jewish view of sexuality![9] Instead of swapping the bigotry of their past, which they find so unappealing, with the radical welcoming embrace of Yeshua for everyone,[10] they have merely substituted it with a bigotry based on different theologies and perspectives than they had grown up with.

Rather than learning to be nuanced,[11] some within the deconstruction movement have retained the dualism of their fundamentalist background, the all-or-nothing attitude, and have begun the process of throwing the baby out with the bathwater, of rejecting everything they were once taught. The voices they listen to are leading them down a path of perpetual deconstruction that leads to further bigotry (just underground), more black-and-white thinking, more divisions, more jadedness, and eventually despair. It's in the air and it's suffocating us. As recovering fundamentalists, we have an incredible opportunity before us. We can seek to better the whole one, holy, catholic, and apostolic church, including the fundamentalist tradition, or we can be the perpetual thorn in the side of the body of Messiah that ends up causing an infection that kills and destroys rather than builds and breathes life.

9. It pains me to see a demonizing of the LGBT community but it also more personally pains me to see a demonizing of the traditional sexual ethic, or said another way, the Jewish sexual ethic. One of the only stipulations the council of Jerusalem gave to gentile followers of Yeshua was to abandon the Greco-Roman sexual ethic and adopt the Jewish sexual ethic, which in the church was only recently rejected, first by white Northern European churches that were ridding themselves of anything Jewish about Christianity. White dualistic culture says there are only two options: hate LGBT people and hold to the Jewish sexual ethic, or love LGBT people and reject the Jewish sexual ethic. But I don't think those are the only two options, nor do I think modernism has the right to serve as the judge over the Jewish ethic.

10. Welcoming everyone, of course, does not mean we don't call people towards change that's needed to be faithful to Messiah, whatever that change may be.

11. Although, we shouldn't make the mistake of thinking true nuance doesn't paradoxically include some lack of nuance, or the mistake of thinking non-dualism doesn't include some dualism. If you get rid of all binaries and nuance everything. you're still operating in dualistic and unnuanced thinking and being.

In modernist versions of Protestant Christianity, both what we call "liberal" or "progressive" Christianity and what we call "fundamentalism," we are presented with two options: doubt or certainty, both of which assume German[12] Enlightenment ways of knowing. Having only two options makes sense given that modernist Western culture is extremely dualistic. Having only two options for anything is a distinguishing marker for the modern Western worldview. When I was first departing from fundamentalism, and the certainty I was taught to have, I then gravitated towards doubt, since those were the only two paradigms offered to me. In the same way we lifted certainty up as an idol, we now often do the same with uncertainty.

But today I usually find myself in neither of those categories—neither doubt nor certainty, but some third or fourth option. What I've realized is that there's probably more than just these two categories. I'm not saying I never have doubts of any kind whatsoever, but it's not the central element to my life it once was, or certainty once was. I think it's because I've begun to shed some of the modern Northern European Western cultural assumptions that set this false dichotomy up in the first place. And maybe we recovering fundamentalists need to move away from the either-or paradigm of doubt or certainty into something less dualistic, and more wholistic.

The Euro-Canadian Brad Jersak, himself a recovering fundamentalist, once wrote, "Deconstruction happens. And AFTER? Whether the water turns to wine, Kool-Aid or cyanide is not randomized. It is determined by the hope, cynicism, or fanaticism of the spiritual voices, scripts or herds we follow, mindfully, or with glazed eyes."[13] We who are recovering can and will be either those who helped shaped whatever it is that's around the corner into a beautiful, healthy, loving, kind, welcoming-to-the-other, Indigenizing, Jewifying, peacemaking, unity-loving, just, truth-telling thing that looks like Yeshua as embodied in the great

---

12. Throughout the book, when I use the term "German" I often more generally mean Northern European, a phrase I also use throughout the book and one that of course includes Germany. However, I often use the more specific term "German" rather than the phrase "Northern European" because as a Jew I see the anti-Jewish racism of the Northern European Enlightenment focused, zoomed in, and enhanced in Germany, where it reached its zenith, its peak, and culminated in the holocaust, which of course was an attempt to erase our existence. In other words, whereas the Enlightenment worldview in other parts of Northern Europe is also extremely anti-Semitic and helped contribute to Nazi ideology, it wasn't the Anglo-Saxons, the French, or the Dutch, etc., who initiated and implemented the holocaust, but the Germans.

13. Used with permission from author.

tradition, or we will be a huge part in making it into another extremist movement, one that perpetuates colonization and continues the de-Jewifying of the faith, one characterized by exclusion of the other, hate, disunity, cynicism, elitism, dualism, impatience, injustice, jadedness, lies, and everything that doesn't look like Yeshua embodied in the great tradition. I have hope for what's around the corner, but I also fear for what may come, if I can be honest. It's up to us recovering fundamentalists to take our recovery seriously, to hand over our porn not for sex with prostitutes but for the hand of Yeshua, to find and walk the good and right path of reconstruction, or as I've come to prefer to call it, the path of *reorientation towards the good, true, and beautiful*; the one that leads us to Yeshua. Yet if we are do this, we must, in our free will, admit our powerlessness to do this on our own. We need the church, the seed of Abraham, and God.

1

Prophecy, Pineapples, and Baptists

> If I prayed to God
> that all men should approve of my conduct,
> I should find myself endlessly penitent
> before each man's door.
> I shall not ask this;
> I shall pray instead
> that my heart might be pure toward all.[1]
>
> —Amma Sarra (desert mother)

Hi, I'm Gabe, and I'm a recovering fundamentalist.
Hi Gabe.

In reading a book titled *The Fundamentals of a Recovering Fundamentalist*, you may be wondering if the person writing this book really understands deconstruction. We rightly intuit this sort of book can only legitimately be written by someone who has experienced what they're talking about. I want to start by sharing my own life story of deconstruction out of fundamentalism and its subsequent reorientation. But those

---

1. Amma Sarra, *Apophthegmata Patrum*, 16–17.

experiences, being that they are deeply and intricately connected to my life as a whole, can't be separated into neat little categories. Accordingly, I will share a broad overview of my life to help contextualize where I'm coming from. Hopefully it's entertaining!

I'm not going to pretend I'm objective. The notion of a pure unbiased objectivity is rooted in the Northern European Enlightenment, or as my German-American friend Derek Lofing once called it, the "Endarkenment."[2] This idea inexorably flows from modernity's belief in its racial superiority enabling it to possess and hold a standard universal objective means for assessing reality. One that only they can truly obtain because of their racial superiority and yet in seemingly contradictory fashion must be forced upon the "poor savages" of the world despite their supposed inferior racial status, which prevents them from grasping such objectivity. I reject this colonial ideal and therefore I will own my own bias. In reality, none of us is objective or unbiased.

Like everyone, my life begins not with me, but with my family before me. My maternal grandparents were Pentecostal missionaries who spent time living in Japan and Thailand for several years while my mother and aunt were growing up. When my mom and aunt reached the end of high school, they all moved back home to the Pacific Northwest. Shortly after graduating from high school, my mother began working at a local grocery store in the Seattle area, where she met my father.

After I was born out of wedlock (yep, I'm a bastard, which I'm sure some of you already knew) my parents' relationship quickly deteriorated. My mother almost certainly has some sort of mental illness, although we are unsure of what it may be, and when I was around the age of two she kicked my father out of my life. I would not meet him, or his father, again until I was eighteen. So of course I have daddy issues—every older male in my life gains a certain kind of weird father figure status, which comes out of my wound of growing up without one. When I met my father at the

---

2. Throughout the book I will occasionally use the term "Endarkenment" in lieu of "Enlightenment" in order to subvert and challenge the commonsense assumption that the Enlightenment was overall good a thing.

age of eighteen, I came to learn he was a brown[3] Jewish guy[4] and therefore I was *Jew-ish*, which caused a certain kind of identity crisis. Evidently, they have therapy for that now.

Over the last twelve years I have wrestled with my ethnic identity and I continue to do so. I grew up with my mother's side of the family, which, like many American families, contains a mixture of various Northern European ethnicities: English, Scottish, Welsh, Irish, Swedish, Danish, and Norwegian. I grew up thinking of myself as white, and to some extent I had a certain level of white privilege. However, I have always looked a bit different from my mom's family since my mom is a ginger and I have darker features. In Thailand, the people could tell I was mixed but thought me to be half-Thai. Due to the white supremacy that colonization brought to Southeast Asia, with the accompanying view that the whiter the skin the better, I easily got work modeling, since people lighter skinned or of mixed Thai and white heritage are preferred as models over the darker full-blooded Thais.

Learning I was mixed, that my dad was a brown Jew, wrecked my self-understanding and identity as a white male. Over the years I've struggled with calling myself "brown" or a "person of color" or an "ethnic minority," partially because I don't want to utilize my white privilege (which I grew up with) to co-opt being a person of color, and partially because I think there is a certain level of fear that if I embrace being a person of color, an ethnic minority, a brown Jew, I will lose the power

---

3. I say "brown" here because while Jews are indigenous to the ancient land of Canaan, located on the east coast of the Mediterranean Sea in Southwest Asia, and thus are historically brown, not all diaspora Jews from Europe today are brown. I also say "brown" here because my own father is darker-skinned and doesn't pass as white. Many European Jews could pass as white, although in terms of power dynamics they lack the same kind of privilege that white gentile Europeans do. Jews during Nazi Germany, for instance (whether they were white-passing or not), were coerced into wearing yellow stars of David, segregated into ghettos (well before the Nazis took power), and taken into concentration camps. People who were ethnically Northern European were of course not subjected to the same discrimination. Furthermore, even light-skinned Jews weren't considered white until a few decades ago.

4. Being Jewish is more than simply a religion; it's also an ethnicity. Judaism is the religion of the Jewish people just as many people groups have particular gods and religious traditions associated with their cultural and ethnic heritage. But being Jewish is no more a choice than being Korean, or Nigerian, or Han Chinese, or Lakota. Before modernity religion and culture were not easily separated from ethnicity. A Jew was born a Jew, and because they were a Jew they had a particular kind of culture and religion, which was part and parcel of their identity. For instance, being Jewish without being Torah observant or assuming the existence of God would have been inconceivable before the modernity of Northern Europe.

that I have to a certain extent benefitted from—a fear that I will have to embrace the oppression and marginalization that my fellow brothers and sisters have experienced. Am I willing to identify with my Jewish people? Am I willing to join them in the suffering we as a people have endured for too long? But as a Jew who is also a Christian, will my people be willing to accept me given the oppression they have experienced from those who have claimed to be followers of Yeshua?

Will my gentile Christian brothers and sisters, many of whom have anti-Jewish assumptions and tendencies buried in their cultural and theological DNA, accept me given my brown Jewishness? Given that I'm only part-Jewish, and it's from my father's side, I've struggled with whether I'm even allowed to call myself a Jew and whether I'm committing some sort of transgression by marrying a gentile and further moving myself—and any future children—away from my rich Jewish heritage.[5] While I still struggle with my ethnic identity, I've come to the point, largely thanks to my professor Randy Woodley, where I'm comfortable calling myself a Jew.[6] I'm learning with the help of Yachad BeYeshua to embrace my Jewish heritage in following the Messiah.[7] Going to Israel twice now has also helped me to embrace identifying with my Jewish heritage since each

---

5. While the older Jewish tradition found in the Hebrew Scriptures traces Jewish lineage through the male, rabbinic tradition has more recently traced Jewish heritage through the female, and thus many Rabbinic Jews reject me as a Jew.

6. Cherokee farmer-theologian Randy Woodley writes, "For Native Americans to become Christians has often required us to divest ourselves of most of our cultural distinctives, including language, hairstyle, values and devotional practices. It is assumed that there is nothing in Native American culture worth redeeming. This evangelistic philosophy, brought over to the New World from Europe, made the broad assumption that European culture was 'Christian' and that Indians needed to conform to Euro-American culture in order for God to accept them." Woodley, *Living in Color*, 46. I think something very similar can be said about Jews who become Christians. We are expected to shed our Jewishness since it is seen as an abomination before God, an abomination Yeshua came to liberate us from, namely the bondage of the Jewish culture and religion of Law. Indeed, even more broadly than the topic of Christianity, the European Enlightenment tried to assimilate [colonize] us Jews into being upstanding individual citizens of European nation-states. We were told if we would simply give up our Jewish ways and become like Europeans, we would be accepted. The holocaust proved otherwise. Although because of the trauma caused by the gentile church to Israel, our own people also do not wish to see us Jewish Christians as Jews. We're caught in the middle between colonization and our own trauma, which causes our own people to view us with suspicion.

7. Yachad BeYeshua is a fellowship of Jewish disciples of Yeshua. We are comprised of Jews who follow Yeshua as Messianic Jews, Eastern Orthodox, Roman Catholic, Anglican, Baptist, Presbyterian, Lutheran, etc.

time I've gone I've repeatedly been mistaken by Israeli Jews as one of their own. I feel that if I'm *Jew-ish* enough for them, I'm Jewish enough for myself.[8]

Shortly after my paternal side of the family was out of the picture, my mother and I moved in with my grandparents. I was around the age of three when we all set off for Thailand. From an early age I remember being immersed in the biblical narratives. I particularly remember the story of Noah and the flood, as most children who are raised in a fundamentalist evangelical background do. While I don't remember the actual questions themselves, I do remember asking questions about Noah and the flood, and I've been asking lots of questions since then. Then my mother, whom I would describe as a nominal Christian, decided she wanted to attend some sort of Christian school or Bible college back in the States. She ended up going to Rhema Bible College, which brought us from Thailand into the strange and foreign land of Broken Arrow, Oklahoma.

It was during this period while a part of Rhema, a church steeped in the prosperity gospel, that the pastor's daughter told us about Yeshua. I knew then with the simple trust of a child I wanted to follow Yeshua, although, like many from a fundamentalist and evangelical background, I was unsure of the security of my faith. I was quick to pray the Sinners' Prayer anytime an altar call presented itself. Eventually one of the adults realized what I was doing and subsequently explained to me I didn't need to keep doing it. He told me I only needed to pray the Sinner's Prayer once to be saved, but one wonders why many like me felt the need to say it so many times.

Shortly after the beginning of my journey in following Yeshua, around the age of eight, my mother began to date a man who sexually molested me, and while up to that point in my life she had "only" been emotionally and verbally abusive, she now began to physically abuse me. Later at the age of nine, when Child Protective Services took me away from my mother and handed me into the custody of my grandmother, in court my mother defended her boyfriend. To this day she still denies she ever physically abused me and that her boyfriend ever sexually molested me. As if that wasn't enough, shortly before I went to live with my grandmother, my grandfather, *the missionary*, left her for a Thai prostitute. As you can imagine, this led my grandmother to leave Thailand and move to Oklahoma.

---

8. For more on Jewish people who are followers of Yeshua and the work their doing, see the Jewish-Christian/Messianic Jewish organization Yachad BeYeshua.

Although I don't think God caused the affair, I do think through the grace and sheer goodness of the triune God of Israel some good was squeezed from it—the good being thaht my grandmother was near enough to take me into her home. I've heard horror stories of the foster care system and I'm grateful I ended up with my grandma instead of a stranger. Understandably, I was angry at God for a time and resorted to atheism for a brief period of my life (third-grade atheism is the best, bro). Essentially, my reasoning as a nine-year-old was, "God doesn't have parents, and since all people have parents, God must not exist." I suppose the problem there was assuming God was merely a physical being, part of our own created universe.[9] Yet even in this season of my life, I look back knowing Yeshua never left me.

Due to the incredible instability during this period, I began to fall quickly behind in my education. To this day I have no more than a sixth-grade comprehension of mathematics. I can only sign my name in cursive. I cannot write in it, and I cannot read it with ease. Which explains why in high school, and into college, I seriously—and I'm not even joking—questioned whether I was mentally challenged. The logic went as follows: If I was mentally challenged, how would I know it, since mentally challenged people are unaware of their condition? My initial answer to myself (this all happened in my head) was that since I'm self-aware and asking such critical questions, I must not be mentally challenged. But then I thought, "Wait a minute, how do I know mentally challenged people are unaware of their condition?" Could I, if I was mentally impaired, be self-aware of it? "Well," I thought, "I also seem smart, and everyone acts as if I am. But wait a minute, what if they're just being nice to me, and this is only how it appears to me, but is not the reality of the situation?" Every time I had this argument with myself, I just concluded I didn't know and could never really know for sure. Although I've stopped asking the question (it's really a mystery, so why fret over it), feeling as if I'm stupid is still one of my biggest insecurities.

Because of my childhood trauma, I sought to self-medicate in a way that it turns out runs in the family. As you the intuitive reader may have guessed, my grandfather and his own father were sex addicts. When I was ten or eleven I was exposed to pornography by a neighbor, and given the fact I came of age during the beginning of high-speed internet in a

---

9. I do trust and confess that Yeshua is a physical creature, but also truly and fully God. But God is not merely a physical being, since God is the creator of all physical matter.

highly sexualized culture, one may easily imagine how my addiction took off like a progressive wildfire. From that time on, my addiction has been a constant badgering companion, causing harm to others and myself. Turns out having the freedom to make whatever choices you want doesn't necessarily lead to freedom, but to the enslavement of your will. At least that's what you'll learn in a good recovery group.

When I was thirteen, my grandma lost her job at Albertsons when they went out of business in Oklahoma and Texas, and so we moved from our posh trailer park into government housing in Tulsa. By the time we moved I had only completed the first half of the seventh grade, and I never finished the second half. I started to attend the local middle school in West Tulsa and quickly became isolated due to being bullied by kids at school and in our neighborhood. I dropped out because of this and only completed half of the eighth grade. With the kids who picked on me being African American, my latent viral racism found ample opportunity to blossom into full-blown fever. To this day I'm still in recovery for my addiction to racial bias. Having such racism and finding out about your brown Jewish dad will throw you for a loop. But I'm working one day at a time to become more self-reflective and to surrender this area of my life to be redeemed for the kingdom of God, in which all peoples are seen as God's good creation and image bearers.

During these years in government housing, we lived across the street from a wooded recreational park called Turkey Mountain. To escape from my bullies, I spent much of my time in the woods. It was during this first year in Tulsa while lying in bed that I experienced the first of four identity-shaping events. I heard God audibly call my name, "Gabriel." Having been immersed in Bible stories since my childhood, I was reminded of the story of Samuel and Eli. I ran to my grandmother and told her I heard God calling my name, so she told me to reply, "Your servant is listening." I did so but fell asleep instantly.

My second identity-shaping experience occurred around this same time when I decided to get baptized. The church I was gathering with at the time practiced full immersion. As I stopped at the top of the baptistry, someone pressed the palms of their hands into my back and pushed me into the water. What an arsehole! After I got out of the baptistry, I asked my grandmother who pushed me. In response she said, "No one was behind you." I can't really explain exactly what was going on there, but I have faith this was a divine encounter. So yes, I suspect I just called the Spirit an arsehole, but I'm convinced the triune God has a really great sense of humor and it's kind of what I was thinking at the time.

After about a year in Tulsa we moved to Salem, South Dakota, which at the time sustained a whopping population of 1,400 people. I loved South Dakota. There was something about the northern wide-open plains that God used to stir me. I used to tell people that I left part of my heart there in the prairie. While much of my time as a fourteen- and fifteen-year-old in South Dakota was great, it was also a season in which I chose to be a bit of a prodigal son. I tried, unsuccessfully, to chase girls (really unsuccessfully, painfully so . . .), and to numb the pain of the trauma I got into smoking pot. Now in my old age, weed just makes me paranoid, so I tend to avoid it. A friend was recently shocked, though, when he found out I don't regularly smoke weed. I guess I give off that vibe. I suppose I'm a pretty cool dude.

After a year in Salem, my grandfather asked us to move back to Thailand. At the time both my grandma and I were hungry for adventure and so we happily said yes. The Thai woman had left him, so I secretly hoped my grandparents would get back together. Their divorce had instigated an immense amount of pain in my family. My grandfather was the only man I knew as a father figure, and my grandmother was really the only mother to me. And while it may be a newsflash to Americans, divorce affects a whole lot of people and not just the two signing the divorce papers. Given a number of factors—sex addiction, trauma, patriarchy, depression, normal teenage hormones—in Bangkok I tried to hire a prostitute, but, thank the Lord, I chickened out at the last minute and opted for a foot massage instead. It was the worst foot massage I have ever had in my entire life.

Because of culture shock and the disappointment of realizing my grandparents weren't getting back together, since my grandfather ended up dating and then marrying a Filipino woman, I went into a deep depression. You'd think after the second wife the church would have given him some pushback about getting married a third time. But you have to love those heretical prosperity gospel "churches," which usually don't have much of an ethical standard. I was so depressed I only showered about once a week. The state of my holy aroma was quite the smell to behold except for a short time on Sunday mornings. What a glorious day—shower day. Around this time we started gathering with a Southern Baptist church we had been familiar with because of an Indian family (the Jhangianis) we had known since the 1980s who were part of that church.

Through the influence and friendship of our pastor, Martin, and Carrie, his wife, the youth pastor, Kannon, and the pastor's sons, Caleb and Cody, I began to take my faith more seriously and made it my own. Kannon encouraged me to eat healthier and exercise, since by that time I had reach 109 kilos (around 235 pounds) and I was only 5 foot 5. Through his encouragement I started reading history books and I also started to read through my Bible for the first time on my own. Not that Bible reading is necessary, particularly on your own, since most Christians throughout church history didn't have access to a Bible outside their local church or synagogue. But I think I benefitted from it.

After being back in Thailand for a year, my grandfather informed us he no longer wanted to support us through paying for our rent and food. We returned to Tulsa yet again, and found ourselves in a homeless shelter for single women after trying to live with my mother and her new husband for a short time, which, as you might have guessed, didn't work out. It was about this time when we (my grandmother and I) attended a church in Tulsa that our pastors in Bangkok had recommended: Southern Hills Baptist Church. I didn't go to school while in Bangkok due to the broken promise of my grandfather, but after moving back to Tulsa I started attending high school again. While we were in Thailand the pastor's wife had brought in a specialist to test my educational level. And it turns out at the age of fifteen, when I was supposed to be in the tenth grade, I only had a sixth-grade reading comprehension, which was probably partially due to the reality that I never really read. But after getting back into high school I started to read more. By my junior year of high school when we took our yearly comprehensive reading exams, I ended up scoring as a college freshman. Not too shabby.

I really plugged into our church's youth group and met my best friend there, whom I later roomed with at college for several years. I grew a lot in my faith while a part of Southern Hills Baptist Church. After beginning my senior year of high school and deciding where I was going to college, I remained unsure of the Lord's will for my life. But then the third identity-forming experience occurred. Following a handful of weeks spent in prayer, I had a prophetic dream. In the dream or vision or whatever you want to call it, God the Father came to me sitting on his throne. In it everything was shrouded in deep and mysterious darkness, what I imagine the author of Exodus 20:21 was trying to convey when the author wrote, "Now the people were standing at a distance, but Moses entered into the darkness where God was."[10] I could only see the outline of God the Father and of its[11] throne. In the dream God lifted his left hand from the armrest of his throne and pointed to me. He spoke, and said, "You are a prophet."

I awoke afraid and unsure of what to do next. I discussed the matter with my grandmother, who, coming from a Pentecostal background, believed me but was unsure of what guidance she could offer. I went to college the next year without resolving this conundrum. Spring break rolled around my freshman year and I went on a trip to Russia with probably one of the greatest men I've ever known: my church-planting professor, Dr. Bruce Carlton. There I met a prophet who affirmed my own calling, so I came back to OBU as a super-Pentecostal, speaking in tongues and being slayed in the Spirit. *Good golley-wolley*! My grandmother was so proud. I had up to that point been a Southern Baptist, but from then on I began trying to reclaim my childhood Pentecostal roots. With hindsight I've come to see this as more or less the beginning of my theological reorientation.

A week or so after I got back from my trip to Russia, the fourth identity-forming event in my life occurred. I was sitting on the couch of my residential assistant's dorm room with my head nodding backwards due to the constant exhaustion of being a college student, and probably some jet leg. All of a sudden I felt oil being poured onto my forehead and running down both sides of my nose. I immediately slapped my hand to my forehead and started to feel my nose to investigate why there was oil being poured on me, but to my surprise there was no oil—bone dry. Yet I remembered prophets, kings, and others were anointed like this in ancient Israel. Since then I've understood this event to be God's affirmation and anointing of me for the Spirit's prophetic calling on my life.

---

10. My translation from the Septuagint.

11. I used "its" this time instead of using the pronoun "his," to demonstrate that pronouns, whether *it*, *she*, or *his*, when used to talk about God are metaphorical. The term "Father" in the great Christian tradition is understood metaphorically. No one actually thought God had a physical body with XY chromosomes that constitutes the biological male sex. God does not have biological sex (because God doesn't have a body and therefore doesn't have chromosomes) and God does not have gender (because gender is a more or less a cultural social construct unique to humans), although paradoxically God also *does* have a body, and male chromosomes, because of the incarnation. I have no problem using the term "Father," as again this is metaphorical, and as much as it's metaphorical, I also have no problem saying "Mother," as long as we acknowledge we don't literally mean an actual physical mother or father.

Part of what mellowed out my unhealthy over-exaggerated Charismania, and much of the blatant misunderstanding of what I thought it meant to be a prophet, was the gift of being wrong. During the mission trip to Russia I believed (for some reason I can't remember) that God had revealed to me who I was supposed to marry. Conveniently—maybe too conveniently—it was one of the girls on the trip. I came to find out this apparently happened with other (usually guy) students at small private Christian colleges. I guess there must be something in the water.

Eventually after about a year and a half of all my friends telling me I was an idiot, I finally realized God hadn't revealed to me who my soulmate was and indeed that the idea of a soulmate wasn't really a Christian doctrine anyways. Most importantly, I learned the vital lesson that prophets are not infallible. One of the events that led to this realization was a question the Lord posed to me in the summer after my second year of college: "If you lost everything today—your spiritual gifts, your calling as a prophet, OBU, a roof over your head, the Bible, your brothers and sisters in Messiah—and you didn't get to marry this girl you're so convinced you're going to marry, *would I be enough*?" Damn, God, why you gotta be all salty??

Of course, I was stunned and knew I couldn't answer yes honestly. The Lord exposed everything in my life I had made into an idol. Within a few weeks of having moved into my new campus apartment to start my junior year, I was reading a book about prayer, and in that moment the Spirit asked me to put down the book and ask her what she wanted to say. So, I put down the book and asked. I heard the reply, "*I am enough*." The words both stung and comforted. The question I was asked earlier that summer, the one I was not strong enough to answer myself, God supplied for me, as if God was saying, "I know you don't know if I am enough, but I am telling you 'I am enough' and I want you to trust me." This continues to be something Yeshua has to teach me. Like Texans, I also tend to be really stubborn.

By this year of college my extreme "Charismatic" phase had mellowed out. While there were things that happened I have come to believe weren't authentic, I also continue to trust that some of my experiences during this season of life were in reality genuine. The next two years of college were spent deconstructing my fundamentalist theology and its idolatry of the Bible. Since my fundamentalist faith was based on the Bible, rather than Yeshua as embodied in the great tradition of the church, the deconstruction of my theology was also primarily centered around the nature of Scripture and its role and place in the church. I came to believe, ironically, that we fundamentalists had reached an unbiblical position by placing the Bible as the foundation of our faith rather than Yeshua. So I gave up my idol of the Bible (as the inerrant Word of God) for something better, the Word of God who grew a beard when he hit puberty.[12] I did not give up Scripture; rather I gave up the worship of Scripture—an important distinction to make.

An amazing thing happened. After doing so, the Bible was given back to me, but this time in its rightful place as a submitting sacramental faithful Jewish witness to Messiah! While my faith continued to grow in those last two years, my theology continued to become less fundamentalist, eventually I found myself leaving evangelicalism and even the Protestant tradition. I finally graduated from OBU after four years and moved back to Seattle to do a church-planting internship with a Southern Baptist Church. What's important to highlight is I did this internship because I was beginning to sense God's call to seek unity in the church, which meant working with all churches, including the ones that were Southern Baptist. After a short six months, but which seemed like a lonely lifetime, I was asked to leave because according to the pastor I was unteachable, and I pushed back too much.

How many prophets throughout the ages have heard something similar? While this thought kind of comforted me, it did not altogether soften the sting. Back in college, maybe prophetically, my mentor, friend, and professor Alan Bandy had predicted I would be kicked out of churches.[13] That's right, *churches, plural*. I'm still waiting for the next one to kick me out. One of the other church planters I knew while living in Seattle offered to have me come work alongside him. It was either that or move back to Oklahoma. While I promised myself I would never move back to Oklahoma, I was engaged at the time to my now wife and we decided it was best for me to move back to Shawnee, Oklahoma and push up the date of our wedding. So yeah, I chose my wife over the paradise that is the Pacific Northwest. You're welcome, babe.

Soon after moving back into exile, I was initially attracted to the Episcopal Church because of the German-American Bible scholar Peter Enns, who at the time had been influential in my faith and thinking. It

---

12. This is my own version of a saying from Euro-Canadian Brad Jersak.

13. For any SBC person reading this, and for the sake of Alan Bandy, let me assure you he does not share my views espoused in this book or probably any of my other books. He is a faithful Southern Baptist and you guys are lucky to have him.

also helped that my anthropology professor from my undergrad was a part of the Episcopal church in Shawnee, where my wife and I went to college. This particular Episcopal church identified itself as a sort of Anglican middle way between the Catholic and Protestant traditions, which was also a huge draw. Later I learned about the Eastern Orthodox theologies in the Episcopal Church, and that really tickled my theological fancy. I found the Episcopal Church to be the first place I truly felt at home even if at times I also felt estranged and ostracized by that same Church. I may not agree with everything we say, think, or do. In fact, I'm quite critical of much it, but at least for now I'm comfortably uncomfortable as a Jewish follower of Yeshua within the Episcopal-Anglican tradition.

Part of the ostracization and, frankly, disillusionment I had with my fundamentalist and evangelical brothers and sisters was the smallness of their orthodoxy. It's important to note I didn't reject orthodoxy, only the small supposed orthodoxy of my fundamentalist background. One of the things I came to love and that eventually led me to become confirmed in the Episcopal Church was the minimal doctrinal requirements for persons joining, found in the Apostles Creed. At its best there was room to think and be different while still affirming the apostolic tradition found in the creeds, a sense of triune diversity in triune unity. As I've grown in my faith, particularly while in the Episcopal Church, I've come to resonate more and more deeply with the pleas of the seventeenth-century English Anglican bishops Thomas Ken and John Pearson, who sought to profess the faith of the whole church before the schism between the East and the West and who sought renewal by looking toward the richness of the Tradition.[14] The best of the Episcopal-Anglican tradition is driven by such pleas, and I am honored to be a part of that to the extent that we embody such petitions.

Early on in this season, (particularly while the wound of being kicked out of that SBC church was still fresh), I sought to surround myself with others who were either in the same boat I was or were friendly to our kind.[15] I quickly developed an us-versus-them sort of mentality, or more accurately, I merely kept the us-versus-them attitude I had grown up. Later, after moving back to Oklahoma, my friend Chris and I were

---

14. Ware, *Orthodox Church*, 311.

15. It's important to note both that people seek community and that sometimes, oftentimes, that good drive to belong is also mixed with the bad inclination towards tribalism.

walking through OBU's campus and lamenting the lack of a safe[16] place to doubt, question, and explore our theological quandaries. We decided to form a group to meet such needs and it happened to be the formation of the Misfits Theology Club. On Saturday mornings we met in our apartment, drank coffee, and ate snacks, and I pontificated on why fundamentalists were wrong and I was right. I'm just being honest . . . of course it wasn't all about being a jaded asshole. We did need a place where we could wrestle with some of these things, and we did so on a regular basis. While I loved every Saturday, eventually the group died off, was resurrected as a blog, and now is mainly a conference.

During the development of the blog and recruitment of writers I told myself we would exclude all fundamentalists/evangelicals. The Misfits Theology Club would only include people who thought like us. Man . . . can you see a resemblance between us and our fundie brothers and sisters? *It's like looking in a mirror.* One day I was minding my own business (as we Americans like to say, as if it's the worst sin in the world to butt into somebody else's business. Come on, Americans, stop be so self-centered and selfish.) and God was like, "Hey, bro, remember that one time in Colorado when you were working at that fundamentalist camp your first summer out of college?" Yeah, I did remember. Let me give you some context: right out of college, before I moved to Seattle, I decided to work at this camp out in the Sangre de Cristo Mountains. During the first few days of training one of the head honchos from the headquarters in Texas came up and went through their doctrinal statement. And of course he concluded that their modernist statement of faith was what all Christians believed and had always believed. At the very top of the list was their belief that the Bible is the inerrant Word of God.

By this point in my journey, I had rejected this very modern European notion of what it meant for the Bible to be inspired, and so I had a choice to make. I could be open and share my disagreement and get fired, or I could hide my Messiah-centric and Trinitarian convictions for the whole summer. Obviously, this wasn't an easy choice, so I spent a couple of days talking to Yeshua and literally crying. Then one day in my cabin the Lord spoke to me, not quite audibly, but clear enough, saying, "If they want to get to you, they have to go through me." Oh boyyyyyyy, I was

---

16. While it's important to have "safe" places (which are often seen as places where everyone thinks like you), it's also important to have *brave* places that push us beyond our comfort zones and challenge us.

excited! I thought to myself, "Fuck yeah! God is on my side, and not on the side of these idol-worshipping punks."

Now obviously this was straight up prideful, ungracious, and ignorant of who God actually is, but in the moment that's how I felt. And if I may suggest, it's also how many of us former fundamentalists act. God quickly let me know I was in the wrong: "But . . . if you want to get to them, you also have to go through me." So basically, God wasn't putting up with my jaded former-fundamentalist cage-stage bullshit. God apparently doesn't play sides in the way I do, but loves all his children (even his children who occasionally use the masculine pronoun even when they know it's only metaphorical). I took this to mean I should stay. So, I did, and it was one of the hardest summers I've ever had. But there was something I needed to learn, which I only could be taught while surrounded by fundamentalists: *most fundamentalists love Yeshua and Yeshua loves them too.*[17]

This is what God reminded me in my moment of progressive bigotry, when I was ready to exclude any and all fundamentalist writers from the new Misfits Theology Club. It was just as much of a red-hot slap of rebuke then as it had been in my cabin the previous summer. Then, as any good teacher, God gave me some afterschool homework. "Go and share with Nathan Roach what you're doing and ask him to be one of your first bloggers." My first thoughts were: "Uh . . . you mean my Southern Baptist friend from college . . . ?" While I may be abnormally stubborn—*Texas-level stubborn*[18]—I figured I had best do what needed to be done. I called up Nathan after seeing him in the local coffee shop and did what I was told. Surprisingly he prayed about it and said yes. It was the best decision I could have made; not only because Nathan is a great guy who loves Yeshua and has a heart for the church, but because I needed to do so to begin the long journey out of my former fundamentalist cage stage.

It was around this time I started seminary and begin to really dig into my formal theological training. I was blessed enough to have decided to attend a broadly evangelical seminary, which aided my journey out of the former fundie cage stage. While those four years in seminary

---

17. But please notice, I said "most," not "all." While God loves all, including all fundamentalists, there are fundamentalists I'm sure who don't really desire God. In this case it's not an either-or.

18. My best friend and notorious Texan insisted as a response on the following: "Hey, it's that Texas stubbornness that got us to the moon—remember that." Colt Meyer, used with permission.

were some of the greatest years of my life, far too much has happened to recount everything. Suffice it to say, I had a good group of friends, professors, priests, and mentors who screwed my head on straight when it became loose or crooked.

It was also during this season of life I really got into Eastern Orthodox theology and became more and more convinced many of our modern problems in fundamentalism and the American church in general could be solved, avoided, or properly dealt with if we reclaimed premodern and pre-European Christianity. Throughout the last couple of years I have concluded many former fundamentalists are still *fundamentally* fundamentalists in the way they think and act. My story has been long, painful, and maybe sometimes tedious, but for good or bad it's all gotten me to where I am today. Yeshua has been faithful to continually work with me to reorient my life to the true, good, and beautiful, which is just another way of saying to himself, the true, good, and beautiful.

*Oh Adonai, Rabbi Yeshua, Messiah and King of the universe,
fill my wounds with the gold of your loving kindness,
not that they may disappear, but that they may become
something new and beautiful, life for the world. Amen.*

… 2

Fundamentalism, Evangelicalism, and Historical Christianity

> There are whole chapters of stuff before you ever got here![1]
>
> —Bilbo Baggins (hobbit from the Shire)

Now that we have discussed my own story, we need to define what we mean by the terms "fundamentalism," "evangelicalism," and "historical Christianity." Too often in conversation we assume we mean the same things when we use these terms, or any other terms for that matter. Furthermore, these terms are often used in popular culture in ways that don't adequately account for these traditions as historically understood. To understand the problems often plaguing us former fundamentalists, we need to address some of the inherent issues I think are found within this tradition and the broader modernist outlook. Considering this, we will then look at how some former fundamentalists respond badly to their former tradition, or rather how they never really left it.

---

1. Tolkien, *Fellowship of the Ring*, 243.

What Is Fundamentalism, Evangelicalism, and Historical Christianity?

There seems to be the sentiment in the air these days (it's been here for a while, like for at least a hundred years) that what is evangelical (or more specifically fundamentalist), is what is historically Christian. In other words, fundamentalist and often more broadly evangelical theology is equated with what true Christians have always believed and practiced. While I suspect fundamentalists are more guilty of this than evangelicals, it is nonetheless a sentiment that can also be found among *some* evangelicals.

But what exactly is a fundamentalist or evangelicalism for that matter? The difference between the two is an important distinction to make, because although it can generally be said that all fundamentalists are evangelicals, certainly not all evangelicals are fundamentalists. Rather, the former is a specific kind of evangelical. Historically speaking, Protestant fundamentalism is a hundred to a hundred and fifty years old, having its origins in the late nineteenth and early twentieth centuries, whereas the evangelical tradition goes back about two hundred and fifty years to the First Great Awakening, with such leaders as Jonathan Edwards, John and Charles Wesley, and George Whitfield.[2] So, let's define our terms: What do Protestant fundamentalists believe and what makes someone an evangelical? While the following definitions are not meant to be comprehensive, indeed there is no consensus on how to define these terms, they are nonetheless helpful starting points.

There are generally five central tenets identified with the fundamentalist movement. But let's be clear: being an asshole is not one of them.[3] They are as follows:

1. The inerrancy of Scripture (the idea that the Bible has no errors)
2. Penal substitutionary atonement (the doctrine that Yeshua took our place for God's just punishment for sinners)
3. The virgin birth (the dogma that Yeshua was born of a virgin woman)

---

2. Three of which I would like to point out were Anglicans, my own tradition, and thus lest Evangelicals not forget that you have us to thank for your tradition, and for those in our tradition who tend to disdain Evangelicals, don't you forget that Evangelicalism is largely a homegrown movement.

3. I am indebted to my friend and neighbor Derek for pointing out to me that the terms "Fundamentalist" and "asshole" are often understood as more or less synonymous.

4. The bodily resurrection (the dogma that Yeshua rose physically from the dead)

5. The divinity of Yeshua (meaning Yeshua is fully God)[4]

While I've just listed five tenets that define a fundamentalist, there's a lot more that fundamentalists believe and don't believe. A general rejection of the modern historical-critical method of studying the Bible, for instance, in preference for what they call the "historical-grammatical method," which is essentially just a modification of the historical-critical method. They also *tend*[5] to deny evolution and read the Bible as a completely historical and scientific book. Moreover, they cultivate such a high view of Scripture they end up making the Bible and God synonymous.[6]

Evangelicalism on the other hand has four pillars:

1. Biblicism

2. Crucentrism

3. Conversionism

4. Activism

Now "biblicism" here simply means the Bible is somehow an authority; it does not necessarily mean acceptance of biblical inerrancy, particularly since this doctrine did not exist prior to the fundamentalists. It does mean that Scripture is supreme, commonly known as "Sola Scriptura"; while tradition, reason, and experience have value and may be used in doctrine and the life of faith, Scripture is ultimately the final authority. Yet Sola Scriptura does not, as commonly misunderstood, mean that tradition, reason, and experience must be rejected. Crucentrism means that evangelicals give centrality to the cross. Conversionism expresses that one must experience being born again and have an intentional turning away from one's former way of life to now live a life of following Messiah.

---

4. See González, *Story of Christianity*, 2:257

5. Not all Fundamentalists deny evolution or read the Bible as a science and history book. In fact, some of the fathers of Fundamentalism, such as Benjamin Warfield, affirmed evolution. Charles Hodge, a mentor and predecessor of Warfield, found nothing about Darwin's theory of evolution particularly threatening to his tradition. It wasn't until the mid-twentieth century that evolution become a pillar of the Fundamentalist movement. See Olson, *Story of Christian Theology*.

6. Also helpful for learning about this perspective is MacArthur, *Inerrant Word* and Barrett, *God's Word Alone*. For those who are interested in going into depth about what they believe, check out the four volumes early twentieth-century Fundamentalists produced, Torrey and Dixon, *Fundamentals*.

And lastly, activism means being active in the sharing of one's faith both through preaching and social action. Thus, as seen these elements that constitute evangelicalism make it a much broader tradition within Christianity than most people realize.

However, given the reality that both movements are relatively new, they cannot, by definition, contrary to frequent claims, be representative of what Christians have always believed and practiced. Even classical Protestants didn't come onto the scene until five hundred years ago and so can't claim to be the measure for what all Christians should believe and practice. And indeed, such a claim is a coded way of saying Northern European Christianity is the measure and rule for what the faith should be, since all these traditions have their origins in Northern Europe. While these traditions may contain themes or certain teachings older than the movements themselves, these traditions certainly do not represent what Christians have always looked like. This is one reason why studying historical theology is important, because it gives us a wider perspective on how particular traditions are situated within the breadth of Christianity in their various cultural and geographic locations. It humbles us by allowing us to realize what we believe and practice is oftentimes not what Christians have always believed and practiced. You may disagree with what others historically have believed or done, but one cannot deny such historical reality.

A while back I read an article written by a fundamentalist essentially arguing her tradition, namely fundamentalism, is what constitutes historical Christianity in terms of practices and beliefs.[7] One problematic aspect of her argument was her operating assumption there exists only two kinds of Christianity, namely progressive and fundamentalist. Yet there have to be more than two types, since these only appeared in the last couple hundred years, both being modernist-Enlightenment versions of Protestantism. There were many Christian traditions well before these two modernist iterations were birthed; in reality there were 1,800 years' worth. I think it's presumptuous for a group of Christians the length of whose existence is only 150 years to create and use their own criteria, in this case Northern European criteria, to judge what is and what is not orthodox/historical Christianity. Although to be fair, when you know nothing else and you're taught your entire life fundamentalism is representative of the entire Christian faith, like I was, it's understandable.

---

7. Childers, "5 Signs."

Given the Messiah's vocation for the church to be one (John 17:21), we have a responsibility to use the criteria for orthodox Christianity developed before there were fundamentalists, evangelicals, and Protestants, and even before there were Catholics, Eastern Orthodox, and our most forgotten Oriental Orthodox[8] brothers and sisters and the church of the East; back when the whole church professed as one what we believe, or rather who we worship and embody. Yet what exactly constitutes the criteria by which to judge what is properly Christian in faith and practice?

Living in the fifth century, in the aftermath of the Augustinian-Pelagian controversy, Vincent of Lerins was troubled by what he perceived to be doctrinal innovations, particularly Augustine's novel view of double predestination. In response Vincent sought to develop criteria by which orthodoxy and doctrinal innovations could be identified. In the year 434 he wrote, "Now in the catholic[9] church itself the greatest care is taken that we hold that which has been *believed everywhere, always, and by all people* [all Christians]. This is what is truly and properly catholic [universally Christian]."[10]

In other words, what is properly to be believed by all Christians is based not on what one tradition—whether Roman Catholic, Eastern Orthodox, Oriental Orthodox, evangelical, or fundamentalist—decides but is determined by what all Christians, everywhere, in all times have affirmed; that is, the whole one, holy, catholic, and apostolic church. The church universal determines the key non-negotiable doctrines of its faith. Of course, the church has always disagreed on quite a lot of things, so the list of what we all have always agreed on is bound to be short. But I believe there are two categories that can be broken up into four doctrines that Christians everywhere in all times and in all places have affirmed, and therefore these alone are the measure of orthodoxy. Yet before we dive into those, I would like to suggest that thinking of orthodoxy as merely what we think about God is reductionist. Orthodoxy, while not

---

8. I realize this term to describe our brothers and sisters of the so-called non-Chalcedonians is a pejorative word, namely "Oriental," but for the sake of clarity and distinction from the Eastern Orthodox, I will use this term. I mean no harm or ill will by it. I am fond of the Oriental Orthodox tradition.

9. In the early church whenever the term "catholic" is used it just means universal. It is not a reference to the Roman Catholic tradition, which only really came about with the split between the East and West in the year 1054—although it's a bit more complicated than that. Until then and even now when we read "catholic" in the creeds, it is in reference to the whole church.

10. Vincent, "Vincent of Lerins on the Role of Tradition," 78.

excluding what we think about God, is more than that. It is not propositional statements of belief but a description and confession in allegiance of who God is and what God has done with all that we are in thought, word, and deed.

Orthodoxy in the early church and today has always been tied to the church's worship, and since the church worships God and orthodoxy is tied to the church's worship, orthodoxy consists only of doctrines about God. Anything we don't worship falls outside the measurement of orthodoxy. We don't worship the Bible and therefore our views of the Bible are not determinative of orthodoxy.[11] We worship what we make essential, and since we should only worship God, only our doctrines of God are essential. The moment you add something to the list that is not God, as a matter of orthodoxy you have begun to worship something other than God. Now concerning what all Christians worship, English Eastern Orthodox Metropolitan Kallistos Ware writes, "Non-Chalcedonians and Lutherans, members of the Church of the East and Roman Catholics, Calvinists, Anglicans, and Orthodox: *all alike worship One God in Three Persons and confess Christ as Incarnate Son of God*"[12]; in other words, the dogmas of Trinity and Christology, which can be further divided into four doctrines.[13] These I suggest fit the above criteria presented by St. Vincent:

1. The Trinity
2. The full humanity and full divinity of Yeshua fully united
3. The virgin birth
4. The bodily resurrection

---

11. In reality many do, which is why many consider it a matter of orthodoxy. I would also suggest sexuality is often made an object of worship in both "conservative" and progressive churches.

12. Ware, *Orthodox Church*, 204.

13. For works that touch on various aspects of these four dogmas, see the following: Origen, *On First Principles*; Basil the Great, *On the Holy Spirit* and *On Social Justice*; Gregory of Nyssa, *Life of Moses* and *Catechetical Discourse*; Lossky, *Mystical Theology of the Eastern Church*; Zizioulas, *Being as Communion*; Louth, *Introducing Eastern Orthodox Theology*; Walters, *Eastern Christianity*; Penn et al., *Invitation to Syriac Christianity*; Green et al., *Trinity among the Nations*; Barron, *Light from Light*; Johnson, *Creed*; Sebhat, *Harp of Glory*; Athanasius, *On the Incarnation.*;Jacob of Serug, *On the Mother of God*; Irenaeus of Lyons, *On the Apostolic Preaching*; Gregory of Nazianzus, *On God and On Christ*; White, *Light of Christ*; Ayres, *Nicaea and Its Legacy*; Anatolios, *Retrieving Nicaea*; Kombo, *Theological Models of the Doctrine of the Trinity*.

Now what's interesting is that in the fourth-century debates many of these doctrines were held by even the unorthodox. You may even be surprised, as I certainly was, to learn that all parties involved in the Trinitarian controversies surrounding the Nicaean Council in the fourth century, both the heretics and the orthodox, affirmed a somewhat astonishing number of fundamental commonly held beliefs, and they commonly rejected several beliefs as well. Among the long list[14] of commonly held beliefs was an affirmation of the Trinity; belief in creation out of nothing; the lordship of Messiah; the preexistence of Messiah (that is, that he existed before becoming human); that the preexistent Messiah created the world and in some sense contained in himself the paradigm of creation; that Yeshua was human and divine and that such a combination of each nature was salvific; that Yeshua was the savior of the world; and that Yeshua's work of salvation was conceived within Trinitarian language.

Speaking about these commonalities between the various groups surrounding Nicaea, Indian-born Melkite Greek Catholic historical theologian Khaled Anatolios in his book *Retrieving Nicaea* writes,

> All parties and individuals accepted the Trinity as the object of Christian faith and worship. There were different understandings of the relations between the three, or their relative ontological standing, but reference to the Father, Son, and Spirit were inscribed into the grammar of Christian faith through liturgical formulae, creeds,[15] and, of course, the rite of baptism, so that all took for granted that Christian faith and worship was oriented to Father, Son, and Spirit.[16]

Commenting on the commonly held affirmation of Yeshua's humanity and divinity, Khaled goes on to write,

> All believed that Jesus was both human and divine and that this combination of humanity and divinity was salvific. There may have been different understandings of what "human" and "divine" mean, but all significant participants in the fourth-century debates agreed that Jesus's being human at least ruled out gnostic

---

14. The following is not a full listing of all the commonly held beliefs among all parties involved in the Trinitarian controversies of Nicaea in the fourth century. In addition to the commonly held assumptions, there were also common beliefs rejected by all parties, which I have also not listed here. See Anatolios, *Retrieving Nicaea*, 36–38 for a full listing of all commonly shared beliefs and commonly rejected beliefs.

15. There were creeds before the Nicaean Creed.

16. Anatolios, *Retrieving Nicaea*, 36.

Docetism; his humanity was not mere appearance. On the other hand, everyone could agree that Jesus was not "a mere man", as Paul of Samosata was alleged to have asserted. Everyone had to find a way to call the preexistent Christ "God."[17]

Despite what many believe happened during the Nicaean controversies of the fourth century, the debate was not over whether we should affirm God as Trinity, or Yeshua as human and divine. The questions had more do to with *how* God is Trinity, and *how* Yeshua is both God and human. And in case anyone has seen *The DaVinci Code*, the council also did not address the topic of what books should or should not be included in the Bible, and it certainly wasn't comprised of all white people like the movie depicted; in contrast it was mostly brown people at the council. Indeed Christianity was in places like Indian and China long before it was in parts of Europe. If we misunderstand this, we risk misunderstanding more broadly what historical Christianity is; namely, we risk falsely believing historical Christianity to be the religion of the white man.[18] In my view it's more accurate to say creedal theology is *brown Jewish theology*.[19]

But some will ask: Aren't creedal dogmas like the Trinity and incarnation Greek rather than Jewish and therefore European rather than brown and Southwest Asian[20] (Middle Eastern)? English Anglican Gerald Bray writes about this assumption when he says there are some people who are inclined "to the view that the Trinity developed against a backdrop of ancient Greek philosophy that has fundamentally distorted the faith and ought to be abandoned as a matter of principle."[21] This is the Hellenization of Christianity thesis articulated and popularized by

---

17. Anatolios, *Retrieving Nicaea*, 37.

18. For a historical overview of how Christianity came to be seen as European religion, see Bantu, *Multitude of All Peoples*.

19. It may be true to say creedal theology was wrapped or incarnated into Hellenistic garb, or Persian garb (if we keep in mind the Persian church's version of the Nicene Creed), but the core of it is not Hellenistic but brown and Jewish. I also am not unaware that at the Council of Nicaea Constantine enacted supersessionist and anti-Judaic declarations. This fact, while deeply saddening, nonetheless does not negate the reality that the Creed's essence itself is Jewish. For the Persian version of the Nicene Creed, see Bantu, *Multitude of All Peoples*, 171.

20. Commonly known in Eurocentric fashion as the "Middle East." It is Eurocentric in that the phrase "Middle East" refers to what is east of the European continent but not quite as far east as say China. This phrase makes Europe the center of the globe. The term "Southwest Asia" is more appropriate because it speaks of this region in terms of its own continent.

21. Bray, "One God in Trinity," 20.

Fundamentalism, Evangelicalism, and Historical Christianity

the German Lutheran Adolf von Harnack. Russian Orthodox Alexander Schmemann describes it well, writing, "According to this myth, the organized catholic Church, as we see her from the middle of the second century on, with her doctrine, worship and discipline, was separated by a deep gulf from her Hebrew beginnings, and was the fruit of the Hellenistic metamorphosis which the original teaching of Christ underwent . . ."[22]

There are a number of problematic assumptions behind Harnack's thesis and while the field of biblical studies as a whole has yet to catch on, in historical theology the tide has turned against Harnack's thesis and has largely been discredited.[23] The first problem, clearly articulated in Bray's quote, and one that's an inherently Protestant (and therefore Northern European) impulse, can be summed up thus: *We just need to get back to the Bible and sideline the tradition, which was a distortion of the Bible.*[24] Messianic Jewish theologian Mark Kinzer discusses this perspective when he writes, "Distrust of all extra-biblical tradition does not derive directly from the Bible itself but from a particular stream of Protestant interpretive tradition."[25] In other words, this attitude that disparages tradition is itself a certain tradition and therefore self-defeating.[26]

---

22. Schmemann, *Introduction to Liturgical Theology*, 54.

23. Orthodox scholar Paul Gavrilyuk speaks to this with a bit of a punch: "The Theory of Theology's Fall into Hellenistic Philosophy must be once and for all buried with honours, as one of the most enduring and illuminating mistakes among the interpretations of the development of Christian doctrine." Gavrilyuk, *Suffering of the Impassible God*, 46. English Origen scholar Mark Edwards speaks to this particularly in regards to Origen, who is one of the poster children in the theory of Christianity's Hellenization, when he writes, "we may say that, far from exhibiting the symptoms of contagion, Origen's work contains the antibodies to Platonism as proof that he has suffered and resisted its attacks." Edwards, *Origen Against Plato*, 161. English Catholic Patristic scholar Lewis Ayres also speaks to this when he writes, "Recent scholarship has argued that characterizing the fourth century as the culmination of Christianity's 'Hellenization' is misleading. This is especially so if Hellenization is understood as resulting in a philosophically articulated doctrinal system only distantly related to the words of Scripture." Ayres, *Nicaea and Its Legacy*, 31. See also Wilken, *Spirit of Early Christian Thought*, xvi–xvii. It is noteworthy that all of the above references are from books published almost twenty years ago. For a recent reexamination of Origen that does not assume Harack's thesis, see Therrien, *Cross and Creation*.

24. Martin Luther didn't exactly hold this attitude but I think he laid the ground work for it, although he did believe the tradition, although not entirely without worth, was corrupt and less reliable than Scripture.

25. Kinzer, "Scripture and Tradition," 29.

26. Jewish scholar Jon D. Levenson also speaks about this viewpoint when he says that there is "the tendency of some influential forms of Protestantism to understand scripture in sharp contradistinction to tradition, even the tradition of the Protestant use and interpretation of the Bible. Without attention to postbiblical tradition, scripture

This attitude also assumes an inherently Western false binary, suggesting Scripture and tradition are separate and one must be more valuable than the other. I see this sentiment a lot in open theism, process theology, and in both branches of "conservative" and liberal Protestantism.

The second issue with this thesis is it implies Judaism was quite weak and therefore easily susceptible to being overcome by the stronger Hellenistic culture. It assumes that true power and strength comes from the colonial powers, rather than from the margins. Except God, who is Power itself, chose to be incarnated into the marginalized Jewish people. Why? Not because God was getting rid of God's power in the way the so-called powerful define it,[27] but because God, who is true Power, who knows what true power is, chose the most powerful culture of all. He who is Power chose to wrap himself in that which was like him. Power chose power. In choosing one of the most marginalized cultures in the world God was choosing, in God's definition of power, one of the most powerful cultures in the world since true power comes from the peripheries.[28] Harnack's thesis assumes a false notion and locus of power and thereby denigrates Judaism by suggesting it was weaker than Hellenism. Yet if true power comes from the margins, then Judaism, and the church, which resides in her womb, was much more powerful than Hellenism.

Euro-American Catholic Robert Louis Wilken has also rightly pointed out this thesis is a false one.[29] It is more accurate to say it was the other way around; that Greek culture was Christianized. And I would add that through Christianity, the core of which is Jewish, Greek culture was Jewified. The Jewish doctrine of the bodily resurrection, for instance, was seen by Hellenistic culture as irrational and distasteful, and yet many from Greek backgrounds, having become Christian, accepted this Jewish doctrine and practice.

---

vanishes before our eyes, for the basis of religion in biblical times was not a Bible: the religion *in* the Book is not the religion *of* the Book. The prophets did not preach a book or show any awareness that God had revealed one to Moses on Mount Sinai, and when early Christian documents mention the 'scriptures,' they are referring not to the Gospels and Epistles but only to what Christians would later come to call the 'Old Testament.' That in which the earliest Christian communities put their faith was not a book, but a person." Levenson, *Hebrew Bible*, 107.

27. This would seem to imply God's power is more like the power of the colonizers. It also seems to imply a change in the nature of Divinity.

28. I'm thankful to Dennis R. Edwards for teaching me where true power comes from.

29. See Wilken, *Spirit of Early Christian Thought*, xvi–xvii.

While of course the church developed some anti-Judaic inclinations early on and utilized Hellenistic culture in their theological praxis, I think the picture is more complicated than is often depicted. Messianic Jewish theologian Mark Kinzer talks about it this way:

> Supersessionism and the crumbling of the ecclesiological bridge, i.e., the Jewish ekklesia, damaged the church in a profound way. But we must avoid the temptation to see church history in purely negative terms. The Gentile ekklesia preserved the essential message entrusted to it. It continued to proclaim Israel's risen Messiah. It rejected Marcionism and accepted the Jewish Bible as inspired, authoritative, and canonical. It collected the books of the New Testament and arranged them in a manner that further countered Marcionite anti-Judaism. The most virulent forms of anti-Jewish teaching in the second century did not carry the day but were moderated by Irenaeus and later by Augustine. The church faithfully preserved and carried within it the truths that would allow it eventually to reexamine its history and recognize supersessionism as an error demanding correction.[30]

Though Rabbi Kinzer is spot on, I might say it this way: while the orthodox gentile church developed its supersessionism and anti-Judaism, at the same time it mitigated the more intense forms found among the heretical groups by holding on to the essentials of the Christian faith, which had their origins not in the Hellenistic world but the Jewish one. In contrast to Harnack's thesis that the early church succumbed to Hellenization, in truth, I think it's more accurate to say huge swaths of the Northern European church today have succumbed to distortion and the complete jettisoning of the Jewishness of the faith through acceptance of German Enlightenment theology, which seeks to purge Christianity of any Jewish qualities.

We thus shouldn't be surprised that German Endarkenment theology, i.e., liberal Protestantism, has discarded Jewish dogmas such as the bodily resurrection. While it's true the church has, since very early on, struggled with anti-Judaic tendencies, it has never discarded the essential elements of the faith, which come from its Jewish roots. It has only been heretical groups such as the Gnostics or those of the Northern European Endarkenment that have done so. Closely connected to Harnack's thesis as it's articulated today is the idea that creedal dogma is

---

30. Kinzer, *Postmissionary Messianic Judaism*, 211.

the product of empire and colonialism, as if the theology articulated at Nicaea was mainly if not entirely invented at this council by the Roman Empire. But while orthodoxy is often thought to be a product of empire and colonialism, if the church's dogmas and essence are rooted in Israel, then orthodoxy is not the result of colonial imperial power, but rather has its origins in the marginalized peoples and communities of Israel, who themselves were and continue to be the object of oppression, empire, and colonialism. In other words, in the church's DNA is the theology of the oppressed, not of the empire.[31]

Now regarding the Jewishness of the Trinity and the incarnation, Jewish American biblical scholar Benjamin Sommer, in his book *The Bodies of God and the World of Ancient Israel*, argues that the Trinity and incarnation find their origin in ancient Israelite religion, rather than Greek philosophy as is often thought.[32] Furthermore, the Jewish Talmudic scholar Daniel Boyarin makes an important contribution to this point:

> MOST (IF NOT ALL) OF the ideas and practices of the Jesus movement of the first century and the beginning of the second century—and even later—can be safely understood as part of the ideas and practices that we understand to be the Judaism of this period. The ideas of Trinity and incarnation, or certainly the germs of those ideas, were already present among Jewish believers well before came Jesus on the scene to incarnate in himself, as it were, those theological notions and take up his messianic calling.[33]

The significance of the Jewishness of Christianity I think is still in the process of being realized and needs to be further explored and disseminated into the masses. It is a process I believe is in need of Jewish disciples of Yeshua, whether Jewish Christians or Messianic Jews. Let me suggest we need to consider the possibility more Jewish thoughts, practices, culture, and theology got through into Christianity than we often give credit for. Yet it isn't just the Trinity and incarnation that are Jewish. Speaking of early Christian liturgy, Schmemann writes there is "a genetical link between this cult [Christian liturgy] and the liturgical tradition of Judaism

---

31. This is true even if some empires have accepted, often distorted, and used the church for their own political gain.

32. It should be noted that Sommer, as a Jew who doesn't identify as a follower of Yeshua, isn't arguing that Jews should believe in the Trinity, only that the Trinity is not foreign to the Jewish people. See Sommer, *Bodies of God*, 135–37.

33. Boyarin, *Jewish Gospels*, 102.

as it existed in that period. The study and evaluation of this link has been hindered for a long time by a myth which has been central in liberal theology, the myth of the rebirth of the Church under the influence of the Hellenistic world."[34] In other words, early Christianity's liturgy itself is deeply Jewish and Harnack's poorly conceived thesis only distorts and distracts from this reality.

Messianic Jewish theologian Jennifer Rosner broadens Schmemann's claim beyond *early* Christian liturgy to include contemporary Christian liturgy when she writes, "liturgical worship is the closest thing Christianity has to traditional Judaism. The printed prayers on the pages of bound books, the embodied movements of standing, sitting, and kneeling, the sacralized consumption of certain foods—this was all Judaism stripped of its name and repackaged in Christian garb."[35] I would also add that in the Gnostic work the so-called *Gospel of Philip*, the author(s) and/or editor(s) seem to associate the virgin birth and bodily resurrection with being "Hebrew," a term they use as a slur for immature Christians who lack the saving knowledge that they themselves possess. So, these dogmas, which the Gnostics did not accept, were in some sense seen as being Jewish, rather than as gentile, at least by the editor(s) and/or author(s) of the *Gospel of Philip*.[36]

In addition to recognizing the Jewishness of the Trinity, incarnation, and liturgy, we also need to understand where that confession of God has historically occurred. The Trinity and all other dogmas have always been professed within the context of the worship and life of the church; not just in creeds[37] (as important as those are, and of course the creeds are also always in the context of worship) but also in the ritual of baptism, the liturgy, in letters, in conversations, icons, tombstones, mosaics, and so forth[38]—not in high towers among white men, smoking pipes, wearing tweed jackets with elbow patches, discussing it purely in the abstract, separate from any real-life concerns. As cool as pipes and elbow-patch tweed jackets are, this simply is not the context for Trinitarian theology, the liturgical life of the church is.

---

34. Schmemann, *Introduction to Liturgical Theology*, 53–54.

35. Rosner, *Finding Messiah*, 6.

36. See chapter 5 for my discussion on the *Gospel of Philip's* use of the terms "Hebrews" and "gentiles."

37. Creeds are of course also found not outside the context of the church, but inside the context of the church.

38. See Cohick and Hughes, *Christian Women in the Patristic World*, xix–xxxviii.

Now regarding Christology, it has been popular in "Christian" Northern European circles to discredit the divinity of Yeshua since the time of the Endarkenment. Given that throughout this book I will claim the essential dogmas of the Christian faith are Jewish rather than Greek, I'd like to make a few comments about the divinity of Yeshua. It is often falsely thought that the original gospel message and earlier Gospels like Matthew, Mark, and Luke were more Jewish than, say, John or the later councils, and therefore did not profess belief in the divinity of Yeshua;[39] and only later when Greek thought triumphed did the church come to view Yeshua as divine. In contrast to these false notions, which assume a false distancing between Christian dogma and Judaism, when one reads those Gospels as *Jewish literature*, and recognizes the echoes and allusions to the Scriptures found in those Gospels, it becomes fairly clear the authors are claiming Yeshua to be divine, God himself somehow in the flesh.[40]

Even Matthew's presentation of the angel announcing the virgin birth of Yeshua is declaring something along these lines. Matthew 1:21 reads, "She will give birth to a son, and you will give him the name Jesus, for he will save his people from their sins." Yeshua means "God saves."[41] So, the angel declares that Mary and Joseph are to name him *God Saves*, and the angel further declares this boy *will save his people from their sins*. Who saves? God saves. And who will save his people from their sins? Yeshua will. So, who then is this Yeshua? They were to give him the name *God Saves* because *he is* God, and he will save his people from their sins. This is further confirmed when the gospel writer declares two verses down all of this to be a filling of the prophecy of Isaiah: "'Behold, the virgin will become pregnant and she will give birth to a son, and they will give him the name Immanuel,' which means, '*Our God is with*

---

39. In his book, Daniel Boyarin explains that during the time of Yeshua many Jews, "were expecting a Messiah who would be divine and come to earth in the form of a human." Boyarin, *Jewish Gospels*, 6. He makes the case that a divine Messiah was not a foreign idea to the Judaism of the time, nor was it unJewish for Jews to believe that Yeshua was that divine Messiah in human flesh, and indeed there were Jews who believed this for a long time.

40. It should be noted that in the Old Testament we find the reoccurring theme of God's ultimately exclusive Kingship. Antonio Gonzalez I think rightly argues that this is the reason early Christians had a high Christology of Yeshua. Namely, since Yeshua declared himself King, in light of the exclusive Kingship of God in the Jewish tradition, Yeshua was thus declaring himself to be God, the only rightful King of the world. See Gonzalez, "Trinity as Gospel," 69–85.

41. More specifically it means "the Divine Name saves." As a Jew I do not pronounce the Divine Name, nor do I write it.

us.'"⁴² Somehow, mysteriously the God of Israel is this Jewish man named Yeshua (God Saves) and he is God with us.

In Mark 4:35–41 we find the story in which the disciples and Yeshua are crossing the Sea of Galilee, when suddenly a storm appears that threatens their lives. After being awoken by his disciples, Yeshua miraculously calms the storm. At the end of this miraculous event performed by Yeshua, his disciples in awe ask, "Who is this, that the winds and the sea are obedient to him?"⁴³ Once you realize the Septuagint version of Psalm 107 is in the background of this narrative subtlety being alluded too, particularly verses 23–32, it becomes clear what Mark is claiming about Yeshua's identity. Euro-American Methodist New Testament scholar Richard Hays writes, "For any reader versed in Israel's Scripture, there can be only one possible answer: it is the LORD God of Israel who has the power to command wind and sea and to subdue the chaotic forces of nature."⁴⁴ Psalm 107 reads:

> Some went down to the sea in ships, doing business on the mighty waters; they saw the deeds of the LORD, his wondrous works in the deep. For he commanded and raised the stormy wind, which lifted up the waves of the sea. They mounted up to heaven, they went down to the depths; their courage melted away in their calamity [cf. Mark 4:40]; they reeled and staggered like drunkards, and were at their wits' end. Then they cried to the Lord in their trouble, and he brought them out from their distress; *he made the storm be still, and the waves of the sea were hushed* [cf. Mark 4:39]. Then they were glad because they had quiet, and he brought them to their desired haven. Let them thank the LORD for his steadfast love, for his wonderful works to humankind. Let them extol him in the congregation of the people, and praise him in the assembly of the elders.⁴⁵

As Hays remarks, anyone who knew Israel's Scriptures when hearing Mark read would recall this passage and know the one who calms the storms and waves is God. So when the disciples ask, "Who is this that the seas and the wind are obedient to him," the one engaging Mark's Gospel

---

42. Matthew 1:23. Emphasis added.
43. Mark 4:41.
44. Hays, *Echoes of Scripture in the Gospels*, 66.
45. Hays, *Echoes of Scripture in the Gospels*, 67.

couldn't help but think of this psalm, and therefore know the answer Mark is suggesting; namely, that Yeshua is God.[46]

Mark 10:17–18 reads, "As he traveled on the road, a man ran up, falling on his knees and asking him, 'Good teacher, what should I do to inherit eternal life?' 'Why do you call me good?' Jesus said to him, 'There is none good, except one only—God.'" We often take Yeshua's question to the man as clarification that he is not God. But if that's what Mark is trying to show us, why does he point out before the man asks his question that he fell on his knees? Did the man intuit something he did not yet comprehend? Instead of distancing himself from God, Yeshua is doing the opposite. Like the good teacher he is, Yeshua often does not give the answer to his students but asks questions, so they come to the answer themselves. To the man falling on his knees Yeshua asks, "Why do you call me good? There is none good except one only—God." He does not deny he is good; he only points out that only one, namely God, is good. He wants the man to fully realize what he already intuits: that Yeshua is good because he is God, the only one who is good. The man's declaration that Yeshua is good is right, but Yeshua wants him to realize what he is really declaring when he calls him good. By not denying the man's statement but asking why he said it, he's drawing a connection between the man's statement "Good teacher" and the identity of himself as God. The Jewish authors and audience of the Gospels weren't just claiming Yeshua was the Jewish Messiah; they were also claiming this Jewish Messiah was somehow mysteriously God in the flesh.[47] It's more than a little patronizing when modernists suggest we Jews on our own weren't able to theologize a high Christology, that only later when the Hellenistic philosophers got their hands on Christology could it advance past the "simple" low Jewish Christology.

Moving on from the divinity of Yeshua, I would be careless if I failed to comment on the virgin birth, since I have found this to be the most likely out of the four dogmas to be dismissed first; and yet it is foundational to both Yeshua's humanity and his divinity, as the Cappadocian Gregory of Nazianzus[48] says, "she was a virgin. That it was from a woman makes it human, that she was a virgin makes it divine. On earth he has

---

46. See Hays, *Echoes of Scripture in the Gospels*, 66–69. See his entire book for more of these illuminating echoes of Scripture found in the Gospels.

47. According to Daniel Boyarin, the idea of a divine Messiah was quite at home in Judaism's Second Temple period. See the introduction in Boyarin, *Jewish Gospels*, 1–24.

48. St. Gregory of Nazianzus was from Cappadocia, which is in modern-day Turkey.

no father, but in heaven no mother. All this is part of his Godhead."[49] St. Gregory of Nazianzus writes quite strongly, sharing the majority opinion throughout the church that the virgin birth is not optional to our faith, a confession that outside of heretical groups has been held within the universal church until European modernity began its theological colonialism. Gregory writes,

> Whoever does not accept Holy Mary as the Mother of God has no relation with the Godhead. Whoever says that he was channeled, as it were, through the Virgin but not formed within her divinely and humanly ("divinely" because without a husband, "humanly" because by law of conception) is likewise godless. Whoever says the human being was formed and then God put him on to wear him is condemned: this is not God's birth but the avoidance of birth.[50]

So given the centrality of the virgin birth throughout Christianity (outside of modernist Northern Europe of course), before we move forward we need to look at a few aspects of the virgin birth. St. Ephrem the Syrian,[51] who died in 373, commenting on the virgin birth, wrote, "Adam brought forth travail upon the woman who sprang from him, but today she [Mary], who bore him a Saviour, has redeemed that travail. A man [Adam] who himself knew no birth, bore Eve the mother: how much more should Eve's daughter [Mary] be believed to have given birth without the aid of a man!"[52] Using Ephrem's theology, I would like to suggest the virgin birth is feminist in its orientation, in the sense that a woman is given prominence over a man. It is not Joseph who is the parent of God, but Mary—and without his aid.

Mary did not need a man to give birth to a man, nor did she need a man to mediate between her and God, who enabled her to give birth to a man without the help of a man. By denying the virgin birth, we are subtly assuming that for God's will to be done a man must be involved in the process, that Yeshua must have a human father, that even God, who is Spirit, with no biological sex or gender, needs patriarchal permission and power to enact salvific intention. God's action, cooperated with by Mary in the virgin birth, is God's way of undermining patriarchal power. By

---

49. Gregory of Nazianzus, *On God and On Christ*, 86–87
50. Gregory of Nazianzus, *On God and On Christ*, 156.
51. For an introduction to St. Ephrem, see Brock, *Luminous Eye*.
52. Ephrem the Syrian, "Introduction," 8.

bringing about the salvation of the incarnation through a woman without the sexual intercourse of a male, God was subverting the male power structures of the world. Progressive or German ideology, so far as it fails to confess the virgin birth, is in its own way subtly yet more subversively upholding patriarchal power by unconsciously centering the male, even to the exclusion of God's power.

In the story of Genesis, Sarah, lacking the ability to bear children, requested that Abraham produce an heir through her maid Hagar. In other words, she asked a man to use his own power in place of God's. But this was not God's promise to Abraham and Sarah. In chapter 17 God declares Abraham's heir, who will inherit the blessings and covenant of God, will come through Sarah, not Hagar. Sarah and Abraham believed they could fulfill God's promise to them for God, that by their own power they could produce the son and heir who would carry forth the Abrahamic blessing. They attempted to do this through Hagar, even though God desired and promised to do it through Sarah. And what does God do?

God fulfills his promise to Sarah by his own power, rather than through the power of humans. And God does the same for Hannah many generations later when God through his power opens her womb and gives her a son. All of this is the Jewish background for understanding the virgin birth. In the virgin birth it's not the lack of sex per se where the meaning of this event is found, but in what the lack of sex conveys, or points us too, in what such virginity signifies. In the virgin birth the lack of sex communicates that it is by God's power, not our own, that the promised Son, the Messiah, would be brought into creation. This is what the deeper symbolic meaning of the story of Sarah and Abraham teaches us; that humans have tried to take our salvation into our own hands and sought to displace God's just rule of creation. And in doing so we've only broken the shalom of the world.

The salvation of this world cannot happen through us alone; we lack such *ex nihilo* (creation out of nothing) power to do so. Instead it is in us partnering with God in our free consent that God's power brings about the promise of a finished creation. Just as in Paul Yeshua is noted to be the new Adam who does not sin, so in the virgin birth through Mary Yeshua is shown to be the child of promise, the new Isaac, if you will, given in God's way by God's miraculous power and not by male power. If Yeshua was born of a male and female as normally happens, we would not have been taught our need to rely on the Godhead's creative power; instead our own self-sufficiency and need for control would have been affirmed.

This would be quite out of step with the Abrahamic story and would be quite unJewish,[53] and more in line with Greco-Roman thought.[54] Our sex-obsessed culture blinds us to thinking the virgin birth is primarily about sex in and of itself, or rather the lack of sex. Such a focus misses the point I think of the virgin birth and this orientation is more akin to Greco-Roman ethics than it is to the Jewish ethics the story is steeped in.

As Gregory of Nazianzus noted above, the virgin birth is directly tied to both the full humanity of Yeshua and his full divinity, fully united. If Yeshua, the Word and Son of God, the second person of the Trinity, God itself, did not take the flesh of Mary alone, then he is not all those aforementioned titles. If he was born not of a virgin, but of a male and a female parent, then he is not God. We end up with some sort of adoptionism rather than the Word taking on human flesh. It is precisely through the taking on of Jewish flesh, through only the virgin mother, that he is fully human like his mother, and yet retains his divinity. It is within this partnership between Mary and God, in which the nature of Yeshua Messiah is able to bring both divinity and humanity together into union with one another. This union of God and the world happens only through the virgin birth. This is one reason why in most of Christianity Mary is so highly exalted, because it is through her partnering with God that the salvation of the world occurs through the incarnation of the God of Israel.

If there are two human parents rather than one, and therefore no Word taking on the flesh of one parent, then there is no union between God and humanity. There would simply be a union between two humans, but not God and humanity. "The incarnation equally is a doctrine of sharing or participation. Christ shares to the full in what we are," through the taking of flesh through his virgin mother, "and so he makes it possible for us to share in what he is, in his divine life and glory. He became what we are, so as to make us what he is."[55] Our salvation, and that of the entire material creation, hinges on God, in the second person of the Son ontologically becoming part of that material creation, becoming a creature; and so, by becoming material creation while remaining fully God, he thus brings creation into full union with himself in his own person. Two natures, God and human, fully united as Yeshua Messiah. It's through this

---

53. In the sense that in the Jewish tradition humans must be dependent on God and not merely themselves.

54. In the sense that in the myths from this culture people must usually take things into their own hands since the gods are only self-interested.

55. Ware, *Orthodox Way*, 100.

union, through his incarnation, that the rest of us can be brought into union with God. This was God's plan from the very beginning; to create a material world and, while retaining his Godhood, to become one of his created creatures, and by so doing bring Creator and creation into full union with one another, sharing God's very life with us.

Moreover, in a world where anti-Jewish racism runs deep, often unconsciously so, it is quite understandable that many, especially those shaped theologically from Germany and Luther,[56] would opt for theologies that downplay, devalue, or rid themselves altogether of the humanity of Yeshua Messiah, the Son of God. To not do so runs the risk of having to affirm the God of the universe, of all creation, is an observant Jew. The same goes for those who devalue, deemphasize, or completely reject the full divinity of Yeshua Messiah, the Son of the Jewish virgin Mary. For if Yeshua is fully human and a specific kind of human, a Jew, while also being fully God, then God is Jewish. Or, said beautifully in the words of Jennifer Rosner, "the incarnate God was an observant Jew."[57] Perhaps this is also why the church has often struggled affirming the Jewishness of Yeshua, because to do so would affirm the logic of God becoming a Jew.[58]

Euro-American scholar R. Kendall Soulen writes, "the God of Israel is the firm foundation and inescapable predicament of Christian theology."[59] If I may build on Soulen's statement and make it stronger:

---

56. I am not saying all Germans, Lutherans, or Protestants are anti-Jewish. What I am saying is that such anti-Jewish sentiment runs deep within German, Lutheran, and Protestant culture, and we must be on guard for it. Of course this is also certainly true in various degrees throughout much of the church tradition as a whole, including the Catholic tradition and Orthodoxy.

57. Rosner, *Finding Messiah*, 7.

58. I came to the conclusion on my own that the incarnation means God became a Jew; however, while not as explicit as myself here, I think Jennifer Rosner and Bruce Marshall have essentially come to the same conclusion. "Marshall contends that the incarnation is the final safeguard that this distinction [between Jews and Gentiles] will always remain. Jesus' Jewishness and membership in the people of Israel is irreducibly constitutive of his identity. By virtue of God taking on Jewish flesh in the person of Jesus, "God's ownership of this Jewish flesh is permanent . . . The incarnation of God in Jesus is the concentration and intensification of the indwelling of God in the Jewish people collectively." Rosner, *Healing the* Schism, 6. I also came to find the Swiss Reformed theologian Karl Barth also wrote about this in his *Church Dogmatics*. "The Word did not simply become any "flesh," any man humbled and suffering. It became Jewish flesh. The Church's whole doctrine of the incarnation and the atonement becomes abstract and valueless and meaningless to the extent that this comes to be regarded as something accidental and incidental." Barth, *Church Dogmatics: The Doctrine of Reconciliation of God*, 166.

59. Soulen, *God of Israel and Christian Theology*, ix.

the God of Israel who permanently took on Jewish flesh, who became an observant Jew, "is the firm foundation and inescapable predicament of Christian Theology."[60] God's covenant with Israel is in this way eternally secured. God can never go back on it, not only because his gifts and callings are irrevocable but because he is now physically and eternally part of Israel.[61] This Jewish core of Christian theology, namely the Jewish incarnation, is thus the antidote to our antisemitism and supersessionism. The way to dispel anti-Jewish racism in Christian theology is thus to reclaim orthodoxy in the fullest, most Jewish sense—that of a Jewish God. It is not enough to admit that Yeshua was Jewish. If we only do this, we will simply sidestep and mitigate such a confession by removing the divinity of Yeshua. It was once normative to ignore the Jewishness of Yeshua or outright deny it, but now that this is no longer an option, people are fine with saying he's Jewish, just not that he's God or the Messiah.[62] Anti-Jewish racism makes theologians uncomfortable with professing that God became Jewish.

The full dogma of the incarnation proclaims not that the Word and Son of God, the second person of the Trinity, became a generic human

---

60. Soulen, *God of Israel and Christian Theology*, ix.

61. Paul van Buren, a Euro-American scholar who studied under Karl Barth, declared something similar when he wrote, "Every proper Christological statement will make clear that it is an affirmation of the covenant between God and Israel." God's covenant with Israel and proper Christology is therefore deeply connected. Buren, *Theology of the Jewish-Christian Reality*, xix.

62. Barbara U. Meyer, a German Lutheran, writes, "The presence of Jesus the Jew not only complicates but also intensifies the efforts of Christians today to make Jesus 'one of us'" (Meyer, *Jesus the Jew*, 66)—the "us" often being Northern European Enlightenment thinkers. As long as the Jewishness of Yeshua could be ignored by gentile Christians, there was no competition when it came to making Yeshua "one of us," but now with competition, namely that it is widely acknowledged that he is a Jew, efforts must be ramped up to make him "one of us," namely a Northern European Enlightenment figure. Meyer also makes the observation, which I sense is connected to her above quote, that Jews who do not follow Yeshua are less skeptical of what the Gospels report Yeshua saying and doing than are Gentile Christians. The things Yeshua is reported to have done and said seem most natural for a Jewish man of the first century to be saying and doing. I dare say he is familiar to us Jews even for those of us who don't follow him as our Messiah. I wonder if some of the reason for this skepticism on the part of gentile Christians is that the Yeshua of the Gospels doesn't look like them; namely, he doesn't look like, act like, or sound like white liberal Protestants such as those of the Jesus Seminar, who don't trust the Gospel accounts. To put it bluntly, white liberal Protestants want and expect a Jesus who looks and sounds like them, namely Northern European Enlightenment men, so when the Gospels (as they most often do) present and report a Yeshua who doesn't look like a man of the Northern European Enlightenment, they assume it cannot be an accurate presentation of Yeshua.

being, but rather that *God in the person of the Word took on the flesh of a Jewish human being; God became Jewish.* The full humanity and full deity together are therefore unacceptable for a theologically white Endarkenment culture, whether *liberal* or *conservative*, which holds anti-Jewish racism as precious and invaluable and disdains particularities. Yet if it is theologically correct to say Yeshua is God, God became human, Mary gave birth to him, and therefore she is the *theotokos or* "God-bearer," the mother of God, then it is also equally theologically correct to say, since Yeshua Messiah is God and since he is Jewish, God is a Jew. As a colonizing culture we are deeply uncomfortable with particularities and prefer supposed valueless objective universalities, which despite our cries to the contrary look particularly particular. The universal Yeshua produced from such German Enlightenment thinking defaults to what a white normative culture believes is universal, namely whiteness. In truth it's not particularity we are uncomfortable with, but any particularity that isn't Northern European.

However, the triune Creator isn't the kind of God who is willing or able to bring about salvation through colonial universalities. In contrast, particularity is the medium of creation's salvation; God acts in the particulars for the sake of the world. Or as Messianic Jewish theologian Jennifer Rosner puts it, "God's redemptive purposes are cosmic in scope, and his means for bringing about cosmic redemption are localized in the people of Israel."[63] The tendency of imposing a pure universality upon Yeshua and the disdain towards the particularity of the incarnation is a key facet of the colonial modernist enterprise.[64] The incarnation, because of its particularity, is therefore anti-colonial.[65] But in fact the Word of God

---

63. Rosner, *Healing the Schism*, 187.

64. Think of such notions today as *the universal Christ*, which make the Jewish Messiah an abstract universal, denying his particularity by way of separating the Jewish man Yeshua from the cosmic Christ, and thus advocating for the divorced status of his humanity and divinity. The colonial enterprise needs universals, because if their own Northern European ideology they seek to impose is simply local rather than universal, then logically it follows they have no right to impose their own locality on the world since it's not universal but local. Whatever universals may actually exist, they are universals rooted in particularity. The true Christian faith of Yeshua the Messiah doesn't boast a universal Christ, but a particular one rooted in the particular colonized Galilean and Judean dirt of the first century, who boasts a Jewish male body with a particular height, eye color, hair color, phenotypic expressions, culture, religious tradition and so forth, just like the rest of humanity exists in particulars. And yet this particular Messiah is the King of the universe, and infused in and through all things.

65. This does not mean Christianity has never been in bed with colonization or empire; on the contrary, it is a historical reality that it has been. But what it does mean

could not have done otherwise. In God there is the quality of *universal particularity*. Whether God specifically and intentionally chose to incarnate as a male I know not, but there may have been a level of inherent randomness given the uncontrolling nature of God.[66] Thereby I would suggest the speculative possibility that the incarnation of the Word as a male could just as well have been an incarnation into the female sex. While it is theologically accurate to say the second person of the Trinity, the Word of God, is both a male and a Jew, and therefore because he shares in the divinity of the Godhead it is true to say God is both male and Jewish, in saying this we're not saying that the Father and the Holy Spirit are male or Jewish. Indeed, they are not.[67]

The divine essence of the Trinity from eternity to eternity transcends such biological categories; it is only in the incarnation that a member of the Trinity takes on these biological realities. This tension of God becoming a male is alleviated to some extent when we hold a high view of Mary as the mother of God, who without the Trinity could not have brought about the incarnation of the Word. The incarnation of the Word may be male, but the incarnation on creation's side of things is made possible by a female. Regardless of whether the process of incarnation into the male sex was random or not, this is the reality that has come about, and it is in no way a denigration of the female sex. Neither is the reality of the Word as a Jew denigrating to other ethnic groups.

Even God cannot do some things, and becoming a generic human being with no distinct sex or ethnicity is one of them. In taking on physical matter God was required to do so in particulars since physical matter only exists in particulars. To be human is to be particular; to have an ethnic and cultural heritage and all of the other little concrete particularities that make up what it means to be human. In the hypostatic union between the created human nature and the uncreated divine nature there

---

is that anytime it has been in bed with colonialism it has done so against the grain of its own DNA, and such action has come from outside itself rather than from within.

66. Although my friend John Hatch pointed out to me the biblical prophecies mention a Messiah king and not a Messiah queen, so maybe God did intentionally become a male. I don't claim to understand how prophecy works but I would suggest the possibility that the sex of the Messiah could have been random and still square with biblical prophecy if the prophecy indicted a male, because it took into account what would actually happen, namely that randomly the child would be born as a male. A prophecy can name something without expressing how that thing comes about.

67. For work concerning how God is not male, see Peeler, *Women and the Gender of God*.

is full union as one person, yet without confusion of the two natures; they both remain distinct and fully their own, neither taking over the other. The divine nature the second person of the Trinity shares with the other two members is not male or Jewish; it is the human nature the Word takes on that is both Jewish and male. So, while God becomes a Jewish male in the incarnation of the Word, by taking it on, the divine nature in and of itself is neither Jewish nor male; yet because the Word is both fully divine and now also fully Jewish, God now shares those qualities, but only in God's Jewish human nature. There is a balance to be struck in the mystery of the incarnation: paradoxically so, Yeshua Messiah, the Word, is both God and a Jewish human, fully united, without losing the distinction of the natures or full unity as one person.

When creation is finished, when God is all in all and the mystery of the incarnation is fully realized in and through all of creation, *all—male and female, Jew and Gentile*, animals, trees, rocks; that is, all the material realm—will partake in the incarnation of the Word. In other words, all that is not God will be brought into full union with God without becoming something other than itself. Yet this union to take place between the created and the Creator will not undo or diminish Yeshua as a Jew or male. Creation as incarnation has always been God's plan, yet incarnation of the whole must start with incarnation of the part. God cannot simply bring into union with God's self all of creation all at once, but must start first by becoming part of creation through the incarnation of the Word as a Jewish male. Then by our own free participation we are brought into union with the incarnated Jewish male named Yeshua Messiah, who comes to fully embody us while remaining what he is. Nevertheless, this should not be mistaken for pantheism, where everything is God. This is incarnation, in which creation remains creation; it does not lose itself in God, but while remaining fully what it is it participates fully in God's nature by grace.[68]

Next we should consider Western culture's rationalism and its approach to the affirmation or denial of the virgin birth. A question many of us need to ask ourselves is: Wasn't the hyper-rationalism of our fundamentalist upbringing part of what turned us away from fundamentalism? Yet when it comes to foundational doctrines, or said another way the mysteries of the faith, such as the virgin birth and the bodily resurrection, we have no problem utilizing such hyper rationalism; and yet since

---

68. See Wood, *Whole Mystery of Christ*.

they transcend our rationality, we reject them. How can we at one moment speak of the mystery of God and yet at another moment reject the mysteries of our faith such as the virgin birth? Is this not simply the same rationalism we inherited from fundamentalism? Why does rationalism get such a high pedestal? In contrast, within the early church and the Christian tradition as a whole the category with which to talk about the virgin birth is primarily mystery, not rationalism. The Syriac Jacob of Serug exemplifies this in writing, "From a virgin who would expect birth without martial union? Tell your tale which is baffling and concealed from the intellect."[69] To Jacob, and Christianity outside of modernist Northern Europe, the virgin birth is a mystery beyond the creature's ability to comprehend it.

Modern rationalism is more or less a recent invention from Europe; most of the world even today still does not hold to this Endarkenment rationality.[70] (When it does it's usually because it came through some sort of ideological colonialism.) Is it not because it is white that modern rationalism maintains such a high pedestal over mystery? If rationalism had come out of Western Africa or Southeast Asia, we would have dismissed it without a second thought, but since it's from Germany and Northern Europe it is accepted without question, and thus Westerners find the majority world irrational, pre-scientific, and backwards according to Western values and ways of thinking, which are seen as the canon and standard by which all the non-Western world must be judged and measured. Indeed, modernity thus has the audacity to reject the brown Southwest Asian Jewish mysteries of the faith in favor of modern Northern European ideals, as if Germany gets to decide what is foundational to the Christian faith and what must be thrown out.[71]

Unfortunately, Western culture is complexly racist, whether or not we realize it or we think we realize it. As Americans, when miracles happen we are surprised, but many people in the majority world are surprised

---

69. Jacob, *On the Mother of God*, 45. For an introduction to the early Syriac tradition, see Murray, *Symbols of Church and Kingdom*.

70. Although certainly rationalism has some of its roots in certain aspects of ancient Greece. However, Greek culture wasn't merely rationalist; there were also elements of mysticism.

71. The dogmas of the faith, such as the virgin birth, have only recently been rejected by traditions that have arisen out of modern Northern Europe. Why does modern Northern Europe get to reject what has been faithfully passed on and accepted by Christians everywhere and throughout the history of the church? Because of white normativity.

when miracles don't happen. The reason for our surprise when miracles occur is our Northern European rationalism. Maybe we shouldn't give such a high pedestal to rationalism when dealing with the central mysteries of our faith; maybe instead we should learn something from our majority-world brothers and sisters, who far from being backwards or irrational realize there are some things beyond human comprehension. Most of the Christian tradition has existed before the Enlightenment's hyper-rationality and most of it still exists outside of its realm.

Nonetheless, it is important to note that the Christian tradition has never rejected reason (it is not irrational), but reason has always been subjected to the mysteries of the faith and has been understood to have its limits. In the Gifford Lectures of 1931–1932 Etienne Gilson said, "Now it is a fact that between ourselves and the Greeks the Christian revelation has intervened, and has profoundly modified the conditions under which reason has to work."[72] Given the historical events rooted in and surrounding the incarnation, what and how one thinks must now be measured not against reason alone, but against the Jewish incarnation of Messiah, against the mysteries of the faith. The difference between the Greeks and the first Jewish and gentile Christians was that for Greeks God was the end of an argument, while for Christians God was the beginning or first principle. Christian reasoning thus is "reasoned from Christ to other things, not from other things to Christ."[73]

So, what am I saying here? That those who reject the virgin birth or bodily resurrection are doing so because they are consciously choosing white supremacy? Not necessarily. What I am saying is there is a systemic and cultural worldview, namely white normativity, which the modern Western world created, that many of us were born into without any choice of our own, and it is this worldview that underlies modernity's rejections of the mysteries of the faith such as the virgin birth. Until we recognize this common worldview that all Americans share, whether liberal, conservative, or what have you, we are going to continue to contribute and perpetuate this harmful cultural tradition, with its ways of thinking and being in the world that also prevent us from affirming, embodying, and living out these essential mysteries of the faith. White normativity, I'm suggesting, is getting in the way of our orthodoxy. None of us choose to be born into and enculturated into a white supremacist culture, but we

---

72. Etienne Gilson, quoted in Wilken, *Spirit of Early Christian Thought*, 22–23.
73. Wilken, *Spirit of Early Christian Thought*, 15.

must choose as persons and as a society to participate in the gospel's work to redeem Western culture from its less-than-godly attributes.

Continuing on, there is another angle we need to address to prevent certain misunderstandings regarding the incarnation through the virgin birth. Now allow me to note a couple of additional points. The first point comes from a homily on the Annunciation given by Nicolas Cabasilas in the fourteenth century,

> The incarnation was not only the work of the Father, by His power and by His spirit, but it was also the work of the will and faith of the virgin. *Without the consent of the Immaculate, without the agreement of her faith, the plan was as unrealizable as it would have been without the intervention of the three divine Persons Themselves.* It was only after having instructed her and persuaded her that God took her for His Mother and borrowed from her the flesh, that She so greatly wished to lend Him. Just as He became incarnate voluntarily, so He wished that His Mother should bear Him freely and with her full consent.[74]

What Cabasilas is saying is that without Mary's agreement of faith the incarnation would have been as impossible, as much as if the triune God itself had not acted. For the incarnation to have taken place God both needed to act and needed to receive the free consent of Mary. The mother of God only became the mother of God by her freewill. In other words, there was no *coercion* in the virgin birth. In a related vein, the dogma of the virgin birth does not claim God had sexual intercourse with Mary; if it did, it wouldn't be called the "*virgin* birth."[75]

Lastly, the dogma of the virgin birth has nothing to do with original sin. In confessing the virgin birth as a matter of faith, I don't believe it's necessary to believe that for God to take on human flesh, to become a human, God needed a pure vessel to do so. Sin does not taint God, but, if you will, God taints sin, or rather he cleanses and heals it. It is often thought among liberal Protestants that the virgin birth is a result of the doctrine of original sin and its entailment of original guilt, the thought being the Son of God could only be born in a sinless (or sexless) woman. Yet the virgin birth preceded the doctrine of original sin

---

74. Nicolas Cabasilas, quoted in Lossky, *Mystical Theology of the Eastern Church*, 141. Emphasis added.

75. This is often a misunderstanding found among Muslims, although I once heard a similar misunderstanding by someone who would in some way identify with the Christian faith.

invented by Augustine. In a rather different understanding from Western Christianity, the Eastern Orthodox hold to the older view, what we might call "ancestral sin."[76] In this teaching there was an original sin in the sense someone must have been the first to do it, but humanity is not guilty or culpable for our ancestor's original sin committed. Rather, we suffer the consequences of the sins of our ancestors—something I know from personal experience. Despite our belief as Americans that our individual choices only effects ourselves, the reality is much different; our sin never simply affects only us.

The virgin birth was an acknowledged reality well before Augustine came on the scene and therefore does not require the doctrine of original sin. In this light and with the notion that sin could taint God being easily disproved from reading about Yeshua's interactions among sinners in the Gospels (his holiness is not dampened but spreads) and considering the doctrine of God's omnipresence (God is present everywhere, including where sin is), the idea that God could not stand in the presence of sin is absurd. It is as the English theologian Julian of Norwich once confessed: "I was astounded with wonder and admiration that he who is so holy and awe-inspiring was willing to be so familiar with a sinful being living in wretched flesh."[77] Despite our own inclinations to stay away from sinners, God's holiness is exactly what drives God to be so familiar with sinners. But the reality remains that for the first Christians the virgin birth, chronologically preceding these notions, was predicated on none of them. God needed a virgin not for purity's sake but so the Son of God could become human while remaining God, in order to bring about the union of creation and Creator, and through this act became one of us.

While we haven't exactly looked at all the four doctrines I suggest comprise historical orthodox Christianity (we will come back to some of those later), I want to quickly add that if a doctrine is somehow explicitly tied to these, then it is also part of the orthodox worldview. As an example, the doctrine of the general bodily resurrection (that the bodies of all human beings will be raised from the dead) is tied to Yeshua's own bodily resurrection. Paul makes this connection clear in 1 Corinthians 15. For Paul, Yeshua's resurrection is not separate from the general Jewish doctrine of the bodily resurrection, but the firstfruits of it. All that to say there's a lot more room in historical Christianity than many Christians

---

76. For an Eastern perspective on human beings and sin, see Harrison, *God's Many-Splendored Image*; and Louth, *Introducing Eastern Orthodox Theology*.

77. Julian, *Revelations of Divine Love*, 46.

have allowed for. For more on the content of orthodoxy, see creeds such as the Apostles Creed, the Nicene Creed, and the Persian church's contextualized version of the Nicene Creed.[78] We will explore in chapter 4 the interconnectedness of orthopraxy and orthodoxy.

Fundamentalists and the Desire to Please God

Now that we have defined what historical Christianity, evangelicalism, and fundamentalism are we can move on, but before we move on to criticisms we need to briefly look at the heart behind many of our fellow fundamentalists. Often those of us in the jaded cage stage of former fundamentalism write off current fundamentalists as a bunch of ignorant bigots more interested in abuse, power, and control than they are in the gospel. Let me be the first to say I have been here. I remember a time when I was working at a foster home, shortly after I was kicked out of a Southern Baptist church in Seattle, when some Southern Baptist volunteers came by to spend time with the kids, feed them, and share the gospel. This was really the height of my jaded cage stage and so I wrote them off. In fact I thought, "How dare they show up here to corrupt these kids, who've already been through enough." I didn't see their desire underneath all the bad theology. What really smacked me in the face was the invitation from one of them (an older woman) to eat with them! You know who else invited people to eat with him? Yeshua! It was in that moment I caught a glimpse of Yeshua, and the heart of these fundamentalists.

On the one hand, I see fundamentalist and progressive theologies as non-normative, meaning these theologies conflict with traditional historic orthodoxy,[79] while on the other hand, many fundamentalists and progressives seem like they are attempting to live out the values and love of Yeshua. It seems clear to me fundamentalist theology makes the Bible equal to God and therefore God, and yet it also seems clear to me many who hold this theology do so not because they are trying to be unfaithful to God but because they believe this is the best way to be faithful. Can someone be both faithful and unfaithful at the same time?[80] I think the

---

78. See Bantu, *Multitude of All Peoples*, 171.

79. For instance, to claim the Bible and God are synonymous is inherently anti-Trinitarian, because you have added a member to the Godhead. Rest assured this is not a straw man of Fundamentalist theology; I have found over and over again people literally say Yeshua and the Bible are the same thing—both scholars and lay people.

80. Not if you're a dualist.

Welsh American Trappist monk Thomas Merton can help us answer this. During a difficult time in his life, he wrote this prayer called "Prayer to Do God's Will," which is helpful for thinking about this paradox of idolatry for the sake of faithfulness. I'll italicize the parts I think are helpful for our conversation here.

> O Lord God, I have no idea where I am going. I do not see the road ahead of me. I cannot know for certain where it will end. Nor do I really know myself, and *the fact that I think I am following your will does not mean that I am actually doing so. But I believe that the desire to please you does in fact please you. And I hope I have that desire in all that I am doing.* I hope that I will never do anything apart from that desire. And I know that if I do this you will lead me by the right road, though I may know nothing about it. Therefore I will trust you always though I may seem to be lost and in the shadow of death. I will not fear, for you are ever with me, and you will never leave me to face my perils alone.[81]

Exactly how does this help us better understand the paradox at hand? Well, we all have idols in our lives, even me—*I know that's hard to believe*. Now given this reality, are we actually following Yeshua? I think the answer is no and yes. No because we have replaced God with an idol to follow and give our attention to instead of Yeshua. And yes because we have done so unknowingly, against our conscious will and intention to follow Yeshua. Indeed, most of our idols remain hidden in the shadows, our minds blissfully unaware of their lurking presence. There are certainly times when we think we're following God when we're actually not. (One time I was utterly convinced God told me I was supposed to marry this girl I had codenamed Pineapples. Guess what? I was wrong.) Yet we can take comfort in believing, with Merton, "That the desire to please you does in fact please You."[82]

God is truly followed when we *desire* to follow God; and this is so even when we have idols in our life. So it's possible that those who hold the Bible as synonymous with God *are doing so only because they are convinced this is the most faithful way to follow Yeshua*. While I'm convinced this view of Scripture is heretical, I also believe they're holding to it out of *a genuine desire to please and love God. Thereby they are actually, though*

---

81. Merton, *Thoughts in Solitude*, 79. Emphasis added.
82. Merton, *Thoughts in Solitude*, 79.

very imperfectly, following Yeshua. It's a paradox/mystery, kind of like the central tenets of our faith. But I think it best explains what's going on.

So why even bother removing idols from our lives if we're following God when we truly desire to please God, thereby actually pleasing God? This may not be an easy question to answer, but I think the answer is somewhat along the lines of this: *Those who truly desire to please God also truly desire to find and remove the idols lurking in the shadows of their lives.* If you aren't desiring to become less idolatrous, to become more faithful in your thoughts, words, and deeds, then are you desiring to please God, or are you merely using God as a coverup and excuse for your idols? Although our desire to please God, in reality, pleases God, that same desire also desires to remove those idols that grieve God, thereby pleasing God more.

This paradox is not an excuse to hold on to our idols, to have bad theology, to commit sin against our neighbors or any other various acts of injustice we can think of, all of which are kinds of idols. When discerning or judging the fruits of our brothers and sisters, fundamentalist or not, we must consider that there are different levels of sinning. As the Egyptian Origen wrote: "To act badly out of ignorance is one thing; to do so, as it were, because one is overcome is another; but to want to do badly is something different, namely "'evil,' and, because of this, he [the devil] is called 'the evil one.'"[83] Our level of rebuke, while always needing the seasoning of gentleness, mercy, and boldness, needs to correlate to the level of the action committed.

We should have one response when someone does something badly out of ignorance, another when it's done compulsively (say through an addiction or demonic oppression[84]), and another one entirely when it's done out of a desire to do bad. Of course, it can be hard to know the motivations of people, which is why we should work hard to know the people and situations. Yet with humility we also have the encouragement

---

83. Origen, *Homilies on the Psalms*, 95.

84. Most of the world believes in some kinds of spiritual beings, both good and evil ones. It's the white, modern, Western world with its supposedly superior rational capabilities that has largely given up on recognizing the existence of spiritual beings. The assumption that the white non-belief in spiritual entities is superior to the brown belief in spiritual beings that most humans today and throughout history have held is, lets be frank, rooted in a notion of white superiority. What it does is set up European "rationalism" as the measurement by which brown peoples and their beliefs are judged by modern Europeans to be unscientific, backwards, and irrational. Given that I reject the premise of white superiority, and since most humans today and across time have accepted the existence of spiritual beings, I find more reason to accept this belief than not, especially given my own encounters and those of close friends with demonic beings.

from Yeshua that we will know them by their fruit. So rather than all of this being an excuse, this paradox gives us opportunity to respond with love and thankfulness for who God is. All that to say I think there are some who believe the Bible is equal to God who *actually love Yeshua, and are therefore indeed my brothers and sisters!*

God will honor the desire to know the Eternal One, but those of us who see a bit more clearly, as in a dimly reflecting mirror, must spur our wayward brothers and sisters into deeper faithfulness to God through the disposal of their idols, even as we ourselves seek to have our own idols disestablished from our hearts. It is not as if only some of us possess idols. But each of us sees certain idols that only we can see in those around us. The body, as varied as it is, sees different idols in different parts. To the extent that I see a certain idol in my kindred, I am obliged to point it out as clearly and effectively as I can. Now that we have addressed the paradox of idolatry for the sake of faithfulness, we can offer some critiques of modernist Christians, of both the fundamentalist and progressive varieties.

Criticism of Former Fundamentalists

As humans formed in and by cultures and communities, we're like fish swimming in a great big ocean, and the water around us is an unquestioned reality of life. We don't really think about water, nor are we aware the water exists. Without someone from outside the water pointing out to us that we live in water, and describing the properties of that water for us, we will remain unconscious of both the reality that we live in water and said existence of water. Keetoowah Cherokee Randy Woodley speaks to this well: "Sometimes we don't understand what we are all about, and it takes someone who has developed a different perspective to tell us what we are about."[85] I don't expect the reader to simply get it. And I don't mean that in a patronizing way. Sometimes to see things that might be obvious (once they're obvious, that is) we need to have some help from the outside. In this sense, I see my job here and throughout much of the book as being a sort of outsider, a cultural navigator who for whatever reason is outside the water, and has been called to hop in the water and explain to my fellows that we are surrounded by water. So keep this in mind as we get into these hopefully constructive and helpful criticisms.

85. Woodley, *Indigenous Theology and the Western Worldview*, 24.

In Euro-American Stephen Long's book *Theology and Culture: A Guide to the Discussion*, he makes the observation that right-wing Christians (here we're specifically talking about fundamentalist followers of Yeshua) are a type of liberal Protestant. There he writes,

> The tradition of liberal Protestantism assumes that Christianity and modern culture are compatible, or can be made compatible by updating Christianity. It is pre-occupied with modernity, which is defined by an insistence on "liberation" or liberalism . . . As a tradition, "liberal" Protestantism argues that the church must be free from the past, free from any ancient commitments to ritual, tradition, dogma, or a unifying institutional authority in order always to be flexible in adjusting to new cultural developments . . . The identity of the Church is largely derivative in liberal Protestantism; it gets its identity by its relationship to civil society and the nation state whatever forms they take. Thus this tradition is preoccupied with those relationships. Here movements on the Political right, such as the Moral Majority, and on the left, such as the Rainbow Coalition even though they have very different policy prescriptions, *represent two variations of the tradition of liberal Protestantism.*[86]

Taking his observation, I think we can expand it to include not just the right-wing politics of the Moral Majority, who happen to be fundamentalists, but fundamentalist theology in general. Cuban-American Justo L. González, a brilliant and prolific historical theologian, makes this point poignantly:

> While liberalism and modernism may be seen as the result of the surrender of theologians before modernity, fundamentalism was also a less obvious surrender, *for it was as modern as liberalism* in its quest for objective and universal truths. The difference was mostly that, while liberalism sought those truths in one place, fundamentalism sought them in another.[87]

If liberal Protestantism is an attempt to accommodate and update Christianity according to modernity, that is to say German and Northern European sensibilities, then fundamentalism is certainly a form of liberal Protestantism. Or said in slightly a different way, "both Evangelical [fundamentalist] and liberal movements . . ." are ". . . the twin children

---

86. Long, *Theology and Culture*, 81–82. Emphasis added.
87. González, *History of Theological Education*, 109. Emphasis added.

of modernity."[88] The difference between the fundamentalist strain of liberal Protestantism and the variant that is usually thought of as liberal is that the former believes what they are doing is conserving the tradition. They are unaware they are indeed seeking to modernize Christianity. The latter tradition of liberal Protestantism is thoroughly aware of trying to modernize the faith and even takes pride in it. While these two groups have defined their identities in opposition to each other since the time of the modernist-fundamentalist controversy of the early twentieth century, they are two parts of the same whole. I think the vehemency between these two groups is caused by a hatred rooted in their similarities. You hate what you see in the mirror even if you're unaware it's your reflection in the mirror. The qualities I hate most in my family are the ones I see in myself, whether I'm conscious of that or not.

The main problem I find with liberal Protestantism as a whole, both its "liberal" and "conservative" varieties, is that it carries the many problems that come along with modernism: hyper-rationalism, detachment from the past, an extreme form of anti-Jewish racism, general racism, colonialism, and the ego associated with all of that. Decolonial thinkers and doers have known for some time that colonialism and the European Endarkenment have gone hand in hand. In their book *On Decoloniality* Walter D. Mignolo and Catherine E. Walsh state, "Modernity, of course, is not a decolonial concept, but coloniality is. *Coloniality is constitutive, not derivative, of modernity* [emphasis added]. That is to say, there is no modernity without coloniality, thus the compound expression: *modernity/coloniality*."[89] In other words, colonialism is the foundation of modernity. The two cannot be separated. A theological worldview that is an adoption of modernity is therefore colonial in its foundational bones.

One of the goals of the colonial Endarkenment is to de-Jewify Christianity. Euro-American scholar R. Kendall Soulen in his book *The God of Israel and Christian Theology* writes, "Kant and Schleiermacher epitomize the process whereby the standard model of Christian theology is outfitted for life in the modern era through a process of de-Judaization."[90] In other words, part of the Enlightenment's project of updating

---

88. Jersak, *More Christlike Word*, 57.

89. They go on to say, "Decolonially speaking, modernity/coloniality are intimately, explicitly, and complicitly entwined. The end of modernity would imply the end of coloniality, and, therefore, decoloniality would no longer be an issue. This is the ultimate decolonial horizon." Mignolo and Walsh, *On Decoloniality*, 3–4.

90. Soulen, *God of Israel and Christian Theology*, 78.

Fundamentalism, Evangelicalism, and Historical Christianity

Christianity meant ousting anything Jewish about the faith. The German Enlightenment philosopher Immanuel Kant assumed the Jewishness of Christianity, but this for him was precisely the problem of Christianity that the Enlightenment needed to deal with. In his view it was the Jewish element of Christianity that was to blame for all the ills of church history. According to Kant, writes Soulen,

> The Jewishness of Christianity is the product of "an evil propensity of human nature," and therefore is nothing less than *the historical manifestation of radical evil*. The Jewish dimension of Christianity elevates statutory faith above the claims of moral religion and therefore stands at the source of the church's fanaticism, bloodthirsty hatreds, wars, and ecclesiastical tyranny.[91]

Both Kant and Friedrich Schleiermacher wished to universalize the Christian faith by getting rid of its particular Jewish qualities.[92]

Another key element of modernity is our inclination towards the new and our obsession with youthfulness. This is at least part of the reason why in the West we discard our elderly into retirement homes to die alone, along with all their wisdom and experience. It's why we often hear an expression that goes something like this: "We just need to wait for the older generation to die off. Then everything will be dandy."[93] In stark contrast to this, Lakota author Joseph Marshall III expresses the antithesis of this well when he writes, "Among us the old ones are the best models for how we should live our lives. Every old person is a collection of stories because of all that each one has seen and lived and all that happens in the world around them in a lifetime. I have not met an old person yet who was not a strong exemplar of at least one virtue, and many are outstanding exemplars of more than one."[94] But again, why does Northern European modernism, or post-modernism for that matter, get such a high pedestal? Why is it the arbitrator for everything we believe and practice? Is it not because it's from Europe? Does it not get center stage and normalcy because of white normativity?

For most of world history and in many parts of the world today, it's been the opposite way around; the old wine is better as Yeshua once said. (Anyone who drinks wine or whiskey understands this principle.)

---

91. Soulen, *God of Israel and Christian Theology*, 66–67.
92. For more on this see Soulen, *God of Israel and Christian Theology*, 57–80.
93. By the way, I've often been guilty of this in the past.
94. Marshall, *Lakota Way*, 1.

Modernism or post-modernism isn't the lens for most of the world today and hasn't been for most of world history, even among Europeans. Old Testament scholars Matthews and Benjamin write, "People in modern western industrial cultures expect future research and future discoveries to solve present problems. People in the world of the Bible looked for solutions to their problems in past experience."[95] To reiterate, it's not just people in the world of the Bible who look to the past for solutions to their problems, but most cultures, which either existed before modern Western industrialization or exist today outside of it. For the vast majority of world history, we have looked to the wisdom of our elders and our traditions for guidance.[96]

To be sure, as González pointed out, both forms of liberal Protestantism, including fundamentalism, seek to modernize/whiten Christianity in different ways. But at the end of the day both are operating under white, Western, modernist ways of seeing the world. And I dare say there is *at least* an unconscious assumption that this modernist white way of doing things is better because it's from Europe and not from a majority part of the world, because it's white and not brown. Whenever you hear or express the sentiment that fundamentalism or progressive Christianity is proper Christianity, what your hearing or expressing is essentially a coded way of saying Northern European white Christianity is *proper Christianity*. If we're really interested in decentering white ideologies and theologies, we will have to stop placing modernism and its Christian variants as the final arbitrators of how we see the world and the Christian faith.

Since liberal Protestants and fundamentalists are white modernists,[97] they therefore share the same questions. Both ask, "Is the Bible inerrant?"

95. Matthews and Benjamin, *Social World of Ancient Israel*, 240.

96. So is anything new good, or are we just stuck with tradition? That question itself is probably a modernist question, but I'll try to answer the question this way: In the Roman Catholic tradition, theology that is seen as a natural development and maturation of what came before is an acceptable expansion to the tradition rather than a break away from it. This is what in my mind separates modernist liberalism from say the Catholic tradition. Whereas liberalism finds breaking away from tradition acceptable and even desirable, this tradition sees tradition as ever growing and coming more and more into its fullest self. The seed of a Douglas fir tree might not resemble a fully mature 250-foot-tall version of its self, but the DNA is the same, the difference being the tree over time has developed and matured into what was always the potential housed in its DNA. Liberalism wants to break away from the tradition by cutting down the Douglas fir tree and planting a whole new tree with a different set of DNA. In this way we stick with the old, but it is ever being renewed in its continual growth and development.

97. That's not to say there aren't Jews or other people of color who share and operate in the white modernist worldview. Part of the colonial system involves subjugating

Fundamentalism, Evangelicalism, and Historical Christianity 53

They merely provide different answers; one says yes and the other says no. They both hold to modern, white epistemologies (the study of how we know things), rooting their knowledge in the individual and assuming that intellectual certainty is possible through the Endarkenment epistemology of foundationalism. The so-called progressive strain decides that since miracles cannot be understood "rationally" or be scientifically verified (according to Northern European standards of knowing), they must be impossible. White people are "rational," and those brown ancient people were "irrational" and believed in miracles, but modern white people know better. Fundamentalists share liberals' rationalist assumptions, but they believe that miracles *can* be proved rationally. Those ancient brown people thought miracles couldn't be explained; they weren't smart enough to understand them scientifically, but we, their more "evolved" kin, have the capacity to rationally explain miracles. I once had a conversation with a fundamentalist woman who "explained" the incarnation for me using a rational mathematic formula on a napkin. When she asked how we could understand the incarnation, I said we couldn't because it was a mystery, and she replied, "We can now!" The "conservative" branch locates certainty in an inerrant book, the other branch in an inerrant scientism. One argues the bodily resurrection can be verified with certainty because the inerrant Bible says so, then builds off that, while the other says we can know with certainty in light of science that the idea of a bodily resurrection is absurd and impossible. Both in one way or another think of truth as merely propositional and something that can be grasped.[98]

Both these types of liberal Protestantism hold to a modern historicism that locates truth in the past. This is why both have a big focus on textual criticism. It's also why the Jesus Seminar looked to history to discover the truth about Yeshua, and its why *some* fundamentalists often exclaim that if they did not have the New Testament, they could not know Yeshua, since Yeshua is forever located in the past rather than the here and now. This adoption of modern historicism, which locates truth in the past, is essentially a rejection of the sacramental worldview, in which God

---

people of color by replacing their native worldviews with the white Northern European worldview. It's not enough to physically rule a people; you must make them think and see the world as you do. So in that sense it's quite "natural" we would find people of color who are some kind of liberal Protestant or Fundamentalist.

98. In contrast, Truth (who is Yeshua Messiah) is not something we grasp but something that reaches out and grasps us.

is encountered in the here and now through material things. You end up with a sort of deism that divorces God from the world.[99]

There is certainly a spectrum in how much one believes God can only be encountered in the past, but each of these ultimately see truth as located in history rather than in the present moment. This is seemingly a contradictory perspective to hold given the modernist disdain for the past and it's championing of the future. For them the tradition of the present is what obscures the truth of the past, whereas for the sacramental worldview tradition doesn't necessarily obscure the past but brings the past into the present, where truth resides, and can even be the proper lens that gives us clarity to see the past. While the sacramental worldview values the past, truth nonetheless is available and present in the here and now. For instance, in liturgical services during the Christmas season, Messiah is not proclaimed to have been born two thousand years ago, but today. During Passion Week he is not crucified back then, but today. Neither during Easter is he resurrected yesterday, but today. In the sacramental worldview the past and future break into the now.

Liberal Protestantism[100] as a whole also tends to be dualistic, like Western culture in general. While many on the more "liberal" side take pride in being non-dualists, they tend to be just as dualistic, just as they tend to be racist despite their claims to the contrary. This is generally a trait of white Americans. (For instance, their full rejection of dualism is a dualistic move. True non-dualism includes some dualism.) This is most readily seen when former fundamentalists opting for the more progressive variant of liberal Protestantism throw the baby out with the bath water. As Euro-American Diana Butler Bass phrases it, "When Christians broke with misguided traditions, they succumbed to the 'baby out with the bathwater' syndrome, ridding themselves of the past—a scenario repeated in thousands of mainstream churches."[101] Having been taught that humanity is totally depraved, in reaction they dualistically exclaim that humans must be totally good, rather than allowing for nuance and both-ands.[102] Having been taught that the Bible is the inspired, inerrant

---

99. Not coincidentally, deism also comes from the Enlightenment, i.e., the modern European worldview.

100. I'm including Fundamentalism under this term.

101. Bass, *People's History of Christianity*, 9.

102. The early church didn't believe humans were totally good or totally depraved. Rather, humans were made good by God and again *given by God*, in their creation, the ability to choose good or evil. This view was inherited from Jewish culture, which believes in both a good inclination and an evil inclination within human beings.

Word of God, former fundamentalists have a tendency to outright reject Scripture or its full inspiration.

As we've seen, both forms of liberal Protestantism have a tendency to disdain the past, and to see the future as the location for the solution of all our problems, albeit sometimes in different ways. Anglo-American Wendell Berry, writing to critics of an essay he wrote in which he explained why he wasn't buying a computer, could, with slightly different wording, be speaking just as truly about liberal Protestantism:

> I can only conclude that I have scratched the skin of a technological fundamentalism that, like other fundamentalisms, wishes to monopolize a whole society and, therefore, cannot tolerate the smallest difference of opinion. At the slightest hint of threat to their complacency, they repeat, like a chorus of toads, the notes sounded by their leaders in industry. *The past was gloomy, drudgery-ridden, servile, meaningless, and slow. The present, thanks only to purchasable products, is meaningful, bright, lively, centralized, and fast. The future, thanks only to more purchasable products, is going to be even better.*[103]

While Berry is talking about consumerism, I can't help but think this is also true in a way for both the liberal and conservative fundamentalists. In general what he says here is true for Americans as a whole, and this cultural element has been deeply influential on the shaping of all sorts of American Christianities, no less on the fundamentalist types. We create echo chambers, and when somebody disrupts those we turn on them as if they just insulted our child. We look to the past as anything but true, good, and beautiful. We are consumerists in the worst kind of way, listening to the next hot podcast, course, or book as if it will solve all our problems. And we're willing to pay money to do so. We see the future in a sense as our savior; the new is good and the old is bad.

The issue among many former fundamentalists isn't that they're denying certain tenets of fundamentalism; it's that they're still asking the same questions they once did as fundamentalists. To say it more bluntly, the problem is many former fundamentalists are still fundamentalists in a deeper sense: they're still rooted in a modernist Northern European version of Christianity that has deep connections to white normativity, anti-Jewish racism, colonialism, and general racism. There's also a tendency to practice a progressive form of bigotry in which they exclude

---

103. Berry, "Why I Am Not," 234–41. Emphasis added.

everyone they see as not fitting into their new orthodoxy of progressive Christianity. Tribalism is still there; it's just directed in a different direction. The only way to really escape from fundamentalism (and liberal Protestantism in general) is to go back to the premodern notions and understandings of the Christian faith, to convert to a different worldview than the modern Northern European one.

Going back to the early church, to older forms of Protestantism, Roman Catholicism, and most especially to Eastern and Oriental Orthodoxies will open new horizons and categories for us because we never knew they existed. I wonder if for many the familiarity of modernity is why so many "former fundamentalists" stay within liberal Protestantism. I don't suspect many consciously recognize their comfortability with liberal Protestantism as the reason for their stagnation. I imagine some of the issue is it's often the only "alternative" presented, and it's falsely presented as an alternative. To many their "new ways" of thinking and being in the world are radically different from what they grew up with. But as I've tried to show here briefly, it's really not that different; in reality fundamentalists are progressive Protestants, but again, we don't know what we don't know.

Oh Ancient of Days, the Almighty One, show us your ancient paths, the good way we should walk in, and we will find rest and shalom for our lives in your strong refuge, the rock of the universe.

3

Principles and Practices for Recovering Fundamentalists/ Evangelicals

Snow can never emit flame. Water can never issue fire. A thorn bush can never produce a fig. Just so, your heart can never be free from oppressive thoughts, words, and actions until it has purified itself internally. Be eager to walk this path. Watch your heart always. Constantly say the prayer "Lord Jesus Christ, have mercy on me." Be humble. Set your soul in quietness.[1]

—Hesychios

ONE OF THE BIGGEST issues I have seen within the deconstructionist world, most notably in myself, is the phenomena of the jaded former fundamentalist. In the Southern Baptist world I was trained in, we had a term for people who recently became Neo-Calvinists and were aggressive, angry, and jaded about it. We called this the "Calvinist cage stage." I'm now convinced many former fundamentalists, including myself, went through a sort of cage stage. Maybe not the Neo-Calvinist type, but certainly we had our own kind. For us it was the jaded former-fundamentalist cage stage. Now let me be clear: I'm not saying there isn't a

---

1. Hesychios, "On Watchfulness," 15.

time for being jaded. I'm not sure one can avoid this jaded part of the journey. Maybe some people can, and that's great, but for me and many others it has and will be inevitable. Over the years of my own journey out of the fundamentalist, evangelical, and ultimately Protestant traditions, I have struggled *to not remain jaded*. I have been jaded and sometimes still struggle with it. Over the course of the last few years I have discovered a few principles and practices I think are helpful, if not necessary, to either prevent oneself from becoming jaded or for moving out of a jaded perspective and attitude. Below, I'll unpack these principles I've found to be helpful in overcoming jadedness and cynicism. Then I'll look at time-tested faith practices that can help us move towards genuine embodied spiritual and religious health.

Here are eight principles that can help us avoid getting stuck in the cage stage of our disillusionment with fundamentalism/evangelicalism.

1. Don't cut yourself off from fundamentalists.
2. Read as broadly as possible from the whole of the Christian tradition.
3. Befriend fundamentalists and evangelical Christians who are sincerely seeking Yeshua and his kingdom.
4. Seek new ways to further partner with fundamentalist and evangelical Christians in doing ministry.
5. Withhold judgement about fundamentalist and evangelical Christians you don't know much about.
6. Don't throw the baby out with the bath water.
7. Stay in church.
8. Vent only to close friends .

So let's look at each of these principles in greater depth.

The first principle and maybe the most important is making sure not to cut yourself off from you're Fundamentalist and Evangelical Brothers and Sisters

German Lutheran Pastor and theologian Dietrich Bonhoeffer once wrote, "He who no longer listens to his brother will not listen to God."[2] Dorotheus of Gaza once said to the extent one takes care to be united

---

2. Bonhoeffer, *Life Together*, 98.

Principles and Practices for Recovering Fundamentalists/Evangelicals

with their neighbor is the extent to which they are united with God.³ Or to put it in the inverse we might say: to the extent one does not take care to be at one with their neighbor, one does not take care to be united to God. If you cannot listen to your fundamentalist brothers and sisters, you will not listen to God, and if you are not united to them, you cannot be united to God. And if you will not listen to God and be united with God, how on earth can you become unjaded?

The communities we spend our time in shape us for better or for worse. If we choose to isolate ourselves from our fundamentalist brothers and sisters and merely spend our time with jaded, angry former fundamentalists such as ourselves, do not be surprised if five years from now we are still bitter, angry, and overall more jaded. Euro-Canadian Eastern Orthodox theologian Brad Jersak captures this well: "Deconstruction happens. And AFTER? Whether the water turns to wine, Kool-Aid or cyanide is not randomized. It is determined by the hope, cynicism, or fanaticism of the spiritual voices, scripts or herds we follow, mindfully or with glazed eyes."⁴ But if you engage with multiple communities, including those in your fundamentalist background, don't be surprised if you learn to see people as God sees them, as people dearly loved, sometimes trying to figure out the best ways to be faithful to God and sometimes not, but loved nonetheless. Reading from multiple perspectives and spending your time having coffee, beer, or a meal with someone different from you has a way of softening your heart towards those people. It doesn't mean you'll agree with them, or endorse everything they believe and practice, but it does me you can see them as human beings. We tend to create echo chambers; we did when we were fundamentalists and we do so now.

Too often, when someone becomes a former fundamentalist they completely cut themselves off from their previous tradition. Granted, sometimes a person is asked to leave or is straight up kicked out of their former community and this can create a bitter resentment that can lead them to do everything in their power to distance themselves from that community. The hurt and resentment makes it easy to never want to have another coffee with someone from those traditions, let alone being in a church gathering on Sunday with them; and even the mere thought of doing something like this can cause anxiety and panic attacks. It's somewhat natural to put up walls when you've been hurt. But besides

---

3. Bass, *People's History of Christianity*, 47.
4. Used with permission. And yes, the quote is so good I've used it twice.

maybe for a short season, this is one of the worst things you can do for your own spiritual health as it produces further tribalism, and it won't help with your anxiety levels. I say "further tribalism" because many of us former fundamentalists were already tribalists when we were still in fundamentalism, and we have a hard time shedding such tribalism. Yeshua the Messiah once warned us, "if you do not forgive, neither will your Father in heaven forgive you your offenses."[5] Something we need to think about is if we don't forgive the fundamentalist communities that hurt us, our Abba will not forgive us for our own offenses against others, which we are surely committing.

Find ways to stay connected with your previous traditions. This will give you the opportunity to practice such forgiveness. Of course, this probably doesn't mean making a fundamentalist church your primary community you gather with on a Sunday morning for worship, but it doesn't mean you can't find other ways to still engage and worship with these communities; try getting creative. Before I was a youth minister in my own church, I was a volunteer with my best friend's youth group at a Southern Baptist church, the same denomination as the church I was once kicked out of. In fact, I even went with them to their six-thousand-person-a-week youth SBC summer camp two years in a row, even after I was our Episcopal church's youth minister. I even decided to attend a broadly evangelical seminary, which I loved! Those at my seminary are certainly not fundamentalists, but being around some more broadly conceived evangelicals has been good for my health. There are always ways the Holy Spirit is inviting us to stay in fellowship with fundamentalists and evangelical Christians. You just might need to look for them.

St. Isaac of Nineveh, a native of Beth Katraye, on the Persian Gulf, and a monastic bishop who lived in the seventh century, once wrote advice entirely relevant to our situation thirteen centuries later. It is worth quoting in full:

> When you meet your neighbor force yourself to honor him beyond his measure. Kiss his hand and his foot and piously warm your heart with great love for him. Grasp his hands many times and place them on your eyes, and caress them with great honor. Attribute beautiful things to his person that are not his. And even when he is far away, speak good and beautiful things about him, calling him by special titles of honor. By these things and their like, not only will you constrain him to desire beautiful things,

---

5. Mark 11:26.

because he will be ashamed of receiving renown for what he has not really done, and thereby you will sow in him the seed of virtue; but also by these and similar ways to which you accustom yourself, you will establish in yourself peaceful and humble habits and be freed from many hard struggles, from which others acquire preservation by [ascetical] labors. And not only this, but also if that one who receives these honors from you has some defect or voluntary fault, when you show him it clearly, even with only a gesture, he will easily receive healing from you because he will be ashamed of your honor toward him and because of the demonstration of love that he sees in you constantly. Keep this disposition toward all persons. And if you become indignant with anyone, and you burn with zeal for the sake of the faith or because of his evil works, or you accuse him or blame him, be attentive to your soul. We all have a judge in heaven. But if you have pity and seek to turn him to the truth, certainly you must suffer for his sake. And with tears and with love you must speak a word or two to him, and not be enraged against him; you must even put away from your face any sign of hostility. Love does not know how to be angry; it is not enraged; it does not reprove passionately. Wherever there is a sign of love and knowledge, there is profound humility from within the mind.[6]

Sticking around your fundamentalists brothers and sisters is also necessary for your own Christian formation into the image of Messiah! As Euro-American Brian McLaren said so beautifully,

> You can't learn to love people without being around actual people–including people who infuriate, exasperate, annoy, offend, frustrate, encroach upon, resist, reject, and hurt you, thus tempting you not to love them. You can't learn the patience that love requires without experiencing delay and disappointment. You can't learn the kindness that love requires without rendering yourself vulnerable to unkindness. You can't learn the generosity that love requires outside the presence of heartbreaking and unquenchable need. You can't learn the peaceableness that love requires without being enmeshed in seemingly unresolvable conflict. You can't learn the humility that love requires without moments of acute humiliation. You can't learn the determination that love requires without opposition and frustration. You can't learn the endurance that love requires without experiencing unrelenting seduction to give up.[7]

6. Isaac of Nineveh, *On Ascetical Life*, 98–99.
7. McLaren, *Great Spiritual Migration*, 184–85.

In short, if you surround yourself with people that all look and sound like you, excluding those from your fundamentalist side of the family, you will have nothing left to help you grow. Fundamentalists are part of your formation process into the likeness of Yeshua! You need them. If you have no one to reject you, hurt you, frustrate you, and offend you, then you will wither away like a tree planted next to a dried-up old streambed. Indeed, according to the Jewish author of 1 John,

> Whoever hates his brother or sister is in darkness and walks in darkness, not knowing where he goes because the darkness has blinded his eyes . . . For everyone who hates his brother or sister is a murderer . . . My beloved, let us love one another, because love is from God, and everyone who loves is born from God and knows God, for God is love, and everyone who does not love does not know God . . . If someone should say, "I love God," and yet that person hates a brother or sister, that person is a liar. For whoever does not love their brother or sister, whom they have seen, how could they love God, whom they have not seen? And this is the command that we received from him: everyone who loves God should also love their brother or sister.[8]

John goes so far to say that those who do not love their brothers and sisters are children of the devil. 'Cause guess what? That's what the devil is all about. Now lastly, to end on a more positive note, let me point you to one of the original Jesuit priests, Peter Favre. Back in the sixteenth century, during the beginnings of the Protestant Reformation, Peter Favre often found himself encountering Catholics who said derogative things to their Protestant brothers and sisters as well as Reformers who did the same when speaking to him about his own Catholic tradition. In that heated context, speaking about Protestants, he wrote, "If we [Catholics] want to be of help to them, we must be careful to regard them with love, to love them in deed and in truth, and to banish from our soul any thought that might lessen our love or esteem for them."[9] We know from his journals that Peter prayed every day for those outside of his theological camp.[10] His words are no less potent to us today, especially to those of us who have found ourselves as some sort of recovering fundamentalist. When I read these words, I was struck, because not only have I disregarded love both in my actions and thoughts when it

---

8. 1 John 2:11; 3:15; 4:7–8, 4:20–21.
9. Favre, quoted in Martin, *Jesuit Guide to (Almost) Everything*, 355.
10. Martin, *Jesuit Guide to (Almost) Everything*, 355.

came to my fundamentalists brothers and sisters; but having become disillusioned with the deconstructionist community, I'm also guilty of it on their behalf. If we wish to be helpful, to bring God's good, loving, bold, and gentle kingdom to this world, we need, as Peter encourages us, to love in thought, word, and deed fundamentalists in both their liberal and conservative varieties, as well as all our brothers and sisters who aim at following Yeshua. If we can't do this for one another, how can we expect to do so for the rest of the world?

The second principle is to read as broadly as possible, from authors (scholars, clergy, theologians, missionaries, etc.) who are from the whole Christian tradition: Protestant, Catholic, Eastern Orthodox, Syriac Orthodox, Coptic Orthodox, Ethiopian Orthodox, and the Assyrian Church of the East

It is particularly important for us former fundamentalist/evangelicals to read from the Roman Catholic, Eastern Orthodox, and Oriental Orthodox traditions. While we don't often think about it, given its Northern Europe origins, Protestantism is white theology.[11] If we are to successively decenter and denormalize white theology, we need to decenter and denormalize Protestant theology. This doesn't mean we don't read white/Protestant theologians, or that people are not allowed to be of European heritage or Protestant, but it does mean Protestantism alone is not the norm or measurement for what good theology is. It does mean it needs to be read alongside other theologies rather than simply being the main one that arbitrates what is normative.

More specifically, we need to keep in mind that liberal Protestantism[12] is rooted in Europe, particularly Northern Europe, and has, given its history, deep colonizing tendencies even today. Progressive ideologies, despite their outward concern with justice, we must not forget, are rooted in Endarkenment coloniality, and thus have a long record of being in bed with white normativity and colonization. Progressive theology is not

---

11. While this may be obvious, I will note liberal Protestantism like the rest of Protestantism is from Europe and thus white theology as well. Northern European theology has had a colonizing tendency (not exclusively; the Roman Catholics have had their share of colonialism as well), and thus we should be suspect liberal Protestantism of having this tendency as well.

12. Remember, I include Fundamentalism under the category of liberal Protestantism.

devoid of ethnic and racial qualities as it is often presented but is German Enlightenment theology. It is too easy for these tendencies towards colonization to assume and make its ideologies the norm by which all must ascribe, even those from outside of Europe. These realities, even as they are manifested within the deconstruction movement, should disquiet us, and cause some serious reflection about the kind of theological and ideological systems we want to perpetuate. When we simply keep reading liberal or white theologies, we're not likely to expose and rid ourselves of any hidden colonizing propensities we may have.

Our history, despite what we Americans might think, continues to shape us. Speaking about the period between the Civil War and the first World War, Cuban-American Justo González points out that one element contributing to the unity of the nation at the time was the idea that it had a God-ordained function to play for humankind's progress. This role was understood usually in terms of the superiority of the Protestant faith, the white "race," and a democratic government founded on free enterprise, all of which have their roots in Europe. Existing among both evangelicals and liberal protestants was the notion that white Christianity (Protestantism) was destined by God to displace weaker races and their religions, to absorb and colonize, to Anglo-Saxonize humanity. Euro-American Josiah Strong, the general secretary of the Evangelical Alliance, said as much. Yet such thoughts from the evangelicals were analogous to those in the more liberal wing, who saw Protestantism and self-determination of opinion as the great gift of "the Nordic races against the tranny and Catholicism of Southern European races, and that therefore people of Nordic origin had the responsibility of civilizing the 'backward' races of the rest of the world."[13] Notice here from González's treatment of nineteenth-century Protestantism that part of the disdain for Catholics was their non-Nordic or non–Northern European heritage. To put a fine point on it, because Catholics were from the wrong part of Europe they were of lesser racial stock and thus Protestantism was superior to the Catholic tradition *because* of its "Nordic" origins.

Today white liberals are fine with empowering people of color to do theology, if it is the theology created by white men from Europe. But if people of color begin to do theology that's has its origins outside of Northern Europe, meaning non-Protestant theologies—whatever stripe of Protestantism it may be that is not being theologized in, whether

---

13. González, *Story of Christianity*, 2:254.

fundamentalist, liberal, classical, or what have you—it is found to be unacceptable. That's because at the end of the day modernist Westerners are not really willing to dismantle white normativity; they will happily build a facade presenting themselves as racially just, but in reality they're too interested in keeping power. Keeping white theology as the center and norm is the foundation of their power; people may be willing to paint the room a new color, or take out a wall, but to rip up the foundation of the whole infrastructure would mean death on a cross, like cutting the branch upon which they sit, and they will do anything but take up the cross and follow Yeshua into the death required for resurrection.

We must therefore recognize that just because a person of color is doing theology does not mean their theology is brown (not if it came from Europe); to assume so leaves white theologies centered. It gives us the false reality that we are doing the hard work of decentering white theologies, and it's one more way theological colonialism continues unabated. Until we have such an awareness, we have not made decentering white theology our center. Given the call by many former fundamentalists and progressives towards seeking racial justice, we can often deceive ourselves into thinking we are not part of the problem. But do not mishear me; I'm not saying we should stop reading people of color if they're Protestant. That could also easily dissolve into another kind of veiled racism. Even reading people of color who are contextualizing white theology still have something important to say, and usually such reading does shed valuable light on whatever topic is at hand.

People of color within Protestantism have a sort of paradoxical insider status and knowledge. They live within a tradition grown outside their homeland and yet precisely because they are the other (that is, peoples from outside of Europe), because they are oppressed and marginalized, they have a keen divergent vision. Their marginalization gives them the power to see injustice clearly; and to some extent because of their non-European origins they have a different way of seeing the world, which allows them to point out blind spots. Furthermore, they can often draw from their own people's traditions and cultures, which only helps to enrich the Protestant tradition and expose and undermine its more colonial tendencies. Throughout oppressed people's suffering and experiences from colonization, we have to a certain extent kept alive our own cultured perspectives, and thus live in two worlds simultaneously vying for our identity. Those existing as colonized brown worlds bring a unique perspective, set of questions, and critique to the project and consciousness of Northern European Christianity. This isn't an either-or; *it's a both-and*. We must read both people of color within Euro-rooted traditions[14] and also very importantly people of color from traditions homegrown and rooted outside of Europe. But if we simply assume its brown theology because it's done by brown people, we fool ourselves into thinking we've decentered white theology.

So we need to make sure to look at traditions from outside Northern Europe. The Roman Catholic tradition with its origins in Southern Europe and Roman North Africa, while certainly guilty of its own history of colonization, has a rich diversity of perspectives, which also helps decenter the modernity of Northern Europe. Eastern Orthodox theologies[15] on the other hand were more or less completely born outside of Europe, in places like Turkey, Syria, Israel, Egypt, and so forth; and Oriental Orthodoxy spread early on and took root in Africa and Asia. For instance, Syriac Christianity reached China by the mid-sixth century, and Christianity reached many peoples of color, such as the Ethiopians and Armenians, by the fourth century and even the subcontinent of Indian by the second century.[16] If we want to lift up brown theology, we cannot just read liberal Methodist theologians who happen to be Chinese or black but are still operating within theologies from Europe. Indeed, we don't need to read strictly white (Protestant) theologies to read people of color, and if we want to read *brown theology*, and not simply contextualized

---

14. I.e., the various Protestant traditions.

15. The Eastern Orthodox tradition, although often thought of as Greek (some of which has to do with the ethnic identification of Eastern Orthodoxy with certain ethnic groups, as well as the historical reality of Greece being a primary cultural influence on the tradition; see Ware, *Orthodox Church* for more), has its ancient centers in what is today Turkey, Syria, Israel, and Egypt, i.e., Southwestern Asia, more commonly known as the Middle East. The four ancient patriarchates or centers of the Eastern Orthodox tradition are the cities of Constantinople, Alexandria, Antioch, and Jerusalem, none of which are in Greece. Greece of course has had a very prominent role and place within the Eastern Orthodox tradition, and was certainly an early center for Christianity going back to at least the time of Paul, but Orthodoxy I think is too Southwest Asian in its theological orientation to be considered a kind of European Christianity. Metropolitan Kallistos Ware once made the comment that out of all the Christian traditions, Eastern Orthodoxy is by far closest theologically and liturgically to the Oriental Orthodox (which includes some of today's Syriac Christians, the Coptic Church in Egypt, and the Ethiopian Church, etc.), rather than to the Roman Catholic or Protestant church. This closeness I think cannot be explained if Orthodoxy is primarily a European Christianity. See Ware, *Orthodox Church*, 305.

16. For an introduction to these neglected Christian traditions from African and Asia, see Bantu, *Multitude of All Peoples*, and Walters, *Eastern Christianity*.

white theology, we will have to sometimes put down the brown liberal Methodist to pick up the fifteenth-century Ethiopian.

Another benefit and reason for reading from Oriental Orthodoxy is to see how Christianity lived, moved, and had its being in contexts in which they didn't merge with political power. Syriac manuscript cataloger (God, that's a sexy title) Euro-American Edward Walters in his introduction to Eastern Christianity wrote, "In many ways, the history of Christianity in western and central Asia is the opposite of that in Europe, where, after the fourth century, Christianity became entwined with political leadership."[17] Instead, many lived outside of the Roman Empire, such as those who lived within the borders and political authorities of the Sassanian Persians,[18] and thus were forced to reckon with and negotiate their Christian identities among a political and cultural context that was at best indifferent and at worst openly hostile to them. After the rise of Islam, many Christians came to find themselves living under Islamic rule. One of the main exceptions is the Ethiopian tradition, whose kingdom merged with Christianity in the fourth century; although it's important to note Christianity was freely accepted by them. Thus, reading from the Oriental Orthodox tradition, like reading from pre-Constantinian Christians, gives us an opportunity to see Christianity outside a political marriage and thus reflect on how Christianity might look divorced from our own political marriages. For all these reasons it is therefore tantamount that if we wish to dethrone white normativity, we need to read theologians from these places and cultures outside of Europe.

In addition to reading from the whole broad Christian tradition, it's also vitally important to read a lot of church history, both primary sources and secondary sources, written by Christians from each of these branches of the Christian faith. Often those of us who are former fundamentalists can fall into the trap of only reading books or listening to podcasts from other former fundamentalists or progressive Protestants. While I certainly would encourage reading from the mainline Protestants, and from people of color within those mainline churches (*and for that matter continuing to read from Fundamentalist and Evangelical Protestants*), if that's all we read, our perspective of the Christian faith and its doctrines can remain wildly small, insufficient, and Northern Euro-centric. Too often we find ourselves creating our own echo chambers to prevent any

---

17. Walters, "Introduction," 1–7.
18. Or as I like to say, Sassy Persians.

kind of criticism that may challenge us. I know of a few instances where former fundamentalists on Facebook have requested those who disagree with them to not engage them anymore.

I suspect this lack of reading from outside the Protestant or white world is part of why there is so much unhealthy expression in former fundamentalist circles. Furthermore, the confirmation bias that comes from reading only former fundamentalists and mainliners, or from not allowing dissent on your Facebook posts, only serves to solidify being jaded. It gives you all the justification you think you need to remain jaded. You need to read broad enough, including from authors that you now disagree with from your fundamentalist/evangelical background, (and not merely for the purpose of "knowing your enemy" but for the purpose of learning from them) so that you are confronted with different viewpoints from your own.

Another facet of the problem of only reading mainline Protestants/former fundamentalists is that Protestants, whether progressive or fundamentalist, essentially have the same kind of thinking as I pointed out in chapter 2. Writing about the Russian theologian Alexis Khomiakov, English bishop Kallistos Ware says, "Khomiakov argued that all western Christianity, whether Roman or Protestant, shares the same assumptions and betrays the same fundamental point of view, while Orthodoxy is something entirely distinct."[19] If this is true between Eastern Orthodoxy and its Western relatives, as I believe it is, it is infinitely truer when it comes to Protestants, particularly the modernist varieties. For instance, a more progressive evangelical will often reject a particular theology or doctrine because it's not in line with the Bible, specifically the Bible literally understood.[20] That's still very much Protestant, and modern! Generally, Protestants ask the same questions; they just give different answers, whereas Catholics, to a lesser extent, and particularly the Eastern and Oriental Orthodox are not only providing different answers but are

---

19. Ware, *Orthodox Church*, 119–20.

20. I would suggest Open Theism's rejection of doctrines such as God's impassibility is at least in part based on a literal reading of Scripture, which is upheld as the ultimate rule of faith. This would not necessarily be the case for Open Theists who are Muslim, for instance. From my understanding, there are many Open Theists who are not Protestant, sometimes not even Christian, but my main interaction with my brothers and sisters who are Open Theists has been among those who are more or less Protestant of some sort. And thus my observations are restricted to that group of Open Theists.

asking entirely different questions and have radically different ways of thinking and being in the world.[21]

The third principle is to find and befriend Fundamentalists and Evangelical Christians who are wonderful people sincerely trying to faithfully seek Yeshua and his kingdom

Seek out fundamentalist and evangelical mentors to pour into your life. Nothing gives you a bad taste in your mouth that will leave you feeling more bitter than a nasty fundamentalist. If you just simply cut yourself off from these Christians, you will only ever have those bad tastes in your mouth and thus confirm your own stereotypes that all fundamentalists and evangelicals are the same. Having the blessing of meeting and engaging grace-filled and loving fundamentalists and evangelicals puts a good taste in your mouth that washes out much of the bitterness from former experiences, and helps to facilitate your own healing. Fundamentalist and evangelical mentors, believe it or not, often have good things to say, and so you should listen to them. Balaam was knocked on his ass by his donkey and was greatly scandalized to find he had something to say. Don't be Balaam. God can even speak through a donkey.[22]

I once read a Facebook post by a former fundamentalist, obviously and understandably hurt by his former denomination, that said something to the effect of, "It boggles my mind how Southern Baptists can still be Southern Baptists."[23] While the hurt caused by this person's former church is understandable (I was kicked out of a Southern Baptist church myself), we need to, without dismissing the injustices committed, have more empathy, mercy, and compassion than this. While there may be a place for this kind of venting, Facebook certainly is not the place for it. I still know Southern Baptists, and I would care to wager many of them,

---

21. I would suspect the reason for this is the fact that Protestants (coming from Europe) share a similar European cultural worldview. Being that the roots of these other traditions are in other parts of the world means their cultural worldviews are very different, providing different questions and ways of seeing, thinking, and being in the world.

22. To clarify, I do not personally think Fundamentalists and Evangelicals are donkeys, but I'm writing from what is sometimes the perspective of jaded former Fundamentalists.

23. This is a paraphrase rather than an actual quote.

good-hearted people, are still Southern Baptists because they believe this is the best way to be faithful to God, not because they're stupid and backwards. While you and I might disagree that this is the best way to be faithful to God, chiding them with unconstructive wrath rather than bold gentleness is not likely to convince them otherwise, and it shows little mercy on our part. We should keep in mind it is the gentle who will inherit the Earth. Although—and this is important—gentleness should not be seen as mutually exclusive to righteous anger, as they have a paradoxical relationship with one another. The author of Ephesians assumes one can be angry and at the same time avoid sinning.[24] Anger is not inherently sinful, and indeed as we see in Yeshua and throughout the Scriptures God is angered by injustice.[25] Rebukes against any kind of anger are often from a place of racial privilege that seeks to *tone down* people of color for being angered about their oppressed situation. It is one tactic used to keep us in our place.[26] So let's keep all of this in mind as we continue to discuss wrath.

Preaching on Psalm 36, the Egyptian Origen spoke,

> But this one wretched passion, *wrath, burns up* even those who seem to be thoughtful . . ."*Put a stop*," then, "*to wrath and abandon anger*"; for example, do not implement it or be moved by it, but abandon it. But we, despising what is said, abandon gentleness, but we do not abandon wrath. Let us take charge of ourselves as even prescribed in Deuteronomy, so that, little by little, by being wrathful to a smaller extent, we may come to this: to be moved to wrath to such a small extent that we achieve a state of not being disturbed by it at all.[27] (First emphasis mine)

As Origen notes, wrath or anger burn up those who take part in it. If you choose to be angry and wrathful in thought, word, and deed towards your former fundamentalist's brothers and sisters, while not avoiding sin, not only will you cause them harm and suffering, but you will cause harm to yourself, the church, and even the world; our actions never affect

---

24. Ephesians 4:26–27: "Get angry, but do not sin, and do not let the sun set on your anger; leave no room for the accuser."

25. See the turning over of the money changer's tables by Yeshua in the Gospel of John ch. 2 as but one example.

26. I am thankful to Dennis R. Edwards for this insight. See his chapter "The Power of Anger" in Edwards, *Might from the Margins*.

27. Note this is Psalm 36 in the Septuagint Greek version of the Old Testament, not in the Hebrew Bible, which Protestants use. The Hebrew has a different numbering of the Psalms. Origen, *Homilies on the Psalms*, 94.

us alone but have ripple effects. Of course, making a hard 180-degree shift away from unrighteous anger and wrath towards bold gentleness is probably just not going to happen. Instead, as Origen encourages us, we practice day by day, action by action, bold gentleness towards our brothers and sisters, and restraint of our unrighteous wrath, and slowly over time we will, as he says, hardly be disturbed by it at all. Being friends with fundamentalists and evangelicals can help us to grow in our empathy towards them, and curb some of that wrath we've trained in ourselves and had trained in us.

Indeed, in making fundamentalist and evangelical friends we will become mindful that many stay, despite all the sin, to witness to the best of their ability a better way of following Yeshua. Those who remain on a sinking ship to save as many as they can, and thus die sacrificially, imitate Messiah; indeed they have even become an incarnation of the Son and Word of God. Likewise, those who faithfully remain in a denomination so long as it is up to them are not to be chided, because they are more concerned with the flock of sheep trapped in the cargo hold of the sinking ship than they are for their own lives. This may not be the case for all fundamentalists, but in my experience of remaining around well-intentioned fundamentalist friends, I think this is more often the case than we give credit for. If we wish for others to give us mercy, we must show them mercy. It is much harder to ask "How are you still Southern Baptist?" when you are sitting across from the person you are asking, a person whom you regularly spend time with as a friend. Such a question may be legitimate, but when you are friends with the people such an inquiry concerns, you are likely to show more empathy, compassion, and kindness infused into such questions, and, having more rapport with them, you're more likely to persuade them.

The fourth principle, which again is related to the first principle, is for people actively doing ministry to continue to seek new ways to further partner with Fundamentalist and Evangelical Christians in doing ministry

One of the ways I have striven to do this is by partnering with multiple churches for youth events with fundamentalists youth ministers. In the past I have also sought to join in the work of ministry with fundamentalists and evangelicals by recruiting them to be contributors to the Misfits

Theology Club blog. I have also regularly met with other college ministers from fundamentalist churches and ministries whom I have often looked to partner with. Look for creative ways to join in the work that God is doing among fundamentalists and evangelicals. And if you don't think God is at work in them, you may need to take God out of your box.

The fifth principle is withholding judgement about Fundamentalist and Evangelical Christians and authors that you don't know much about

More often than I'd care to admit, I have made poor judgements regarding fundamentalist and evangelical pastors and scholars that I've know very little about, Euro-American John F. MacArthur being a prime example. At the time of writing this I have read none of his books and maybe at most have watched a five-minute portion of one of his sermons. While I could make a large wager I'd probably disagree with him if I were to really engage his writings and sermons, and probably win that bet, until I do read his books and listen to his sermons, I need to withhold judgment, because I simply don't have enough information to make a good judgement. When I do make such poor judgements, I more firmly root myself in my jaded attitudes. Withholding judgement in such cases is not only a matter of humility, but it also keeps me from becoming more bitter and tribal.

The sixth principle is to avoid throwing the baby out with the bath water. Nothing will make you jaded faster than to automatically reject all the basic doctrines you grew up with

One reason why it's important to read broadly from the Christian tradition and church history is to see all the various ways different Christian doctrines have been understood and practiced throughout history among the church's diverse expressions. For example, if you think the only way to understand the inspiration of Scripture is the doctrine of inerrancy, or you think the doctrine of hell is synonymous with eternal conscious torment, and you've found those particular renditions of those doctrines lacking in veracity, you will have to, for the sake of intellectual honesty, reject the inspiration of Scripture and the existence of hell. On the other hand, knowing that hell and the inspiration of Scripture have been understood in wildly different ways gives you a better opportunity to not reject the doctrines themselves, but to reject only specific versions of those doctrines. From studying church history and what the rest of contemporary Christianity believes and practices, you'll often find that the versions of these doctrines you were taught growing up are exclusively fundamentalist versions of these Christian doctrines rather than how most Christians have understood and embodied them.

To prevent throwing the baby out with the bath water prematurely, withhold judgement or rejection until you have a somewhat broader conception of whatever doctrine is under consideration. If you only know how mainline and evangelical Protestants think about something, you don't have a good reason to outright dismiss the teaching all together. Such a narrow perspective leaves you bitter since from this understanding the truth of the matter was obvious, and therefore you must have been lied to or, worse, they must have been idiots. However, knowing that the church has believed a bunch of different things about many topics allows you to have grace for both yourself and for the fundamentalist and evangelical traditions. But while the church has held diverse opinions on many things, thare are certainly a few teachings and practices they have agreed on. Remember, there's always more to know; there's a lot we're still ignorant of, especially me.

The seventh principle is to stay in church!

We'll have more to say about this in the last chapter, but for now suffice it to say separating yourself from the body of Messiah is not the *answer*. It may be that for a time you need to stay away from a church community to heal. However, the best long-term way to heal is to be a part of a church. Just as some fundamentalists have left a bad taste in your mouth and you need a good taste to wash out the bad, the same goes for churches. Good experiences with church will help heal the bad experiences and therefore will help heal your jadedness and the other hurts caused from previous church engagement.

Moreover, while God's grace and presence certainly extends to those outside the church, it is within God's design for God to be particularly incarnated through Messiah and the Holy Spirit in and through the church. The church is not complete without every member being attached to one another. They need you and your voice as much as you need them. While the church is not always what it is meant to be, leaving it will not aid it in becoming what it should be; in fact, I think we can reasonably suggest it does the opposite. Leaving it helps it remain stagnate and grow worse. The church is meant to be a paradise pointing forward to and enacting God's restoration of the world into God's fully created and finished creation. It may not be like this now, but it is up to us, to me and you, to partner with the Messiah in making it so. God is with us, working; indeed the Divine is the one who invites us into this work God is already doing, but it is our God-given responsibility to participate in the work. If you leave the church you cannot participate in molding it to be the shining gem it is meant to become. With you out of the picture it can only be worse.

The eighth principle is to vent only to close friends

While venting about your former fundamentalist and evangelical life and doctrine or about current fundamentalist and evangelical Christians can be healthy, this should generally only be done with close friends who know your journey and context. To vent to those not close to you, especially those who are fundamentalists or evangelicals, only serves to push fundamentalists and evangelicals away and create a bigger chasm between them and yourself. Again, this is somewhat normal to do to prevent yourself from being hurt once again, but in the long run you'll be worse off for it. Indeed, because people whom you're not close to are lacking your context, they often won't understand why you're bitter, angry, and frustrated. It can come off as an attack and as being offensive, especially if you mean it to be! This creates further division rather than healing between the parts of Messiah's body, which is always the goal.

While leaving one's tradition and former denomination can be hard, remaining bitter and jaded about it is harder. The desire of Yeshua is that his church (and that includes many fundamentalists and evangelicals)—all of it—would be one as he, the Father, and the Holy Spirit are one. All that we do must be towards this end of becoming one body. And that means leaving our jaded season behind and looking forward to the embrace of our fundamentalist and evangelical brothers and sisters. We always have a choice either to become like the people who hurt us, who kicked us out of a church, who excluded us, who abused and traumatized us, but just with a "different" theology, or to become more like Yeshua, who sought to heal and include. Too often we merely change our theological clothing, rather than taking the necessary steps to become less like those who represent everything we hated and to become more like Yeshua. For example, instead of excluding LGBT folks from our communities, we exclude those with traditional views from our communities. Nothing has really changed except for the type of people we seek to hate and keep away from our "holy" communities. Henri Nouwen once wrote that where we find healing, unity, and reconciliation, there we find the work of the Holy Spirit.[28] The opposite of that is also true: where we find division, there we find the spirit of the Anti-Christ.

Being gracious, generous, and kind to those whom we find ourselves in disagreement with, both within the broad generous orthodoxy of normative historical Christianity and with those who depart from such normative standards, is rooted in the triune life of God. God is three persons, three others, in full relational unity with one another to such extent that they are one God. Such unity in diversity is not only the reason we should have such a gracious attitude towards those different from us, but *the reason* such a possibility exists. We may strive to live in such unity amongst our diversity precisely because the very ground of being itself is the total union of a community of others, i.e., the Trinity.

These principles are a lot to chew on, so I'm listing them again:

1. Don't cut yourself off from fundamentalists.
2. Read as broadly as possible from the whole of the Christian tradition.
3. Befriend fundamentalists and evangelical Christians who are sincerely seeking Yeshua and his kingdom.
4. Seek new ways to further partner with fundamentalist and evangelical Christians in doing ministry.
5. Withhold judgement about fundamentalist and evangelical Christians you don't know much about.
6. Don't throw the baby out with the bath water.
7. Stay in church.
8. Vent only to close friends.

Keeping these eight principles in mind can help us move beyond the former-fundamentalist cage stage. However, if we really want to become

---

28. Nouwen, *Life of the Beloved*, 135.

holistically healthy, we need to recover the Christian disciplines that have been handed down to us over millennia through church tradition.

Incidentally, Another Principle Is Christian Disciplines

Due to fundamentalism and liberal Protestantism being two versions of modernist Protestant Christianity, i.e., Northern European theology, each of these two sides of the coin have tended to be disconnected from the broad Christian tradition. There largely hasn't been a desire to be connected, since the new is seen as what's better. Unfortunately for those of us coming from and operating out of such German modernist renditions of Protestantism, we are left dry and unrooted like the Midwest during the Dust Bowl. One way to help us leave our jadedness is to begin to reclaim the great Christian disciplines of the broad Christian tradition. And fortunately, most of Christianity today has kept these practices safe and alive for us, waiting to teach us what we've forgotten, if only we're humble enough to learn. These practices are helpful not only in losing our jaded edges, but in having a holistic Christian life, which roots and grafts us back into the broad Christian tradition. Many of these disciplines are centuries old.

While the term often used to describe what we're discussing here is "spiritual disciplines," I will be using the term "Christian disciplines" instead. I'm avoiding using "spiritual disciplines" because it can easily, and often does, imply a Gnostic understanding of the faith, which separates the material from the spiritual and devalues the former while elevating the latter. Often when using the term "spiritual disciplines" people include things like reading Scripture, praying, gathering with the church, and so forth. But they don't normally include physical exercise, eating local nutritious food, recycling, and so forth.[29] When I use the term "Christian disciplines," I'm referring not only to the supposedly spiritual things we do, but to the physical as well.[30] In all of these various practices we find material means for encountering God: centering prayer, gardening, eating local nutritious food, raising chickens, mindfulness, *lectio divina*, physical exercise, the Jesus Prayer, prayer walking, the daily examen, recycling, devotional reading and study of Scripture, reducing your use of

---

29. I'm thankful to Swedish-American Lutheran Daniel Brunner for this insight.

30. Even all of the disciplines we usually think of as spiritual are done using our physical bodies, so in a sense those too are also physical.

plastic, morning and evening prayer, gathering with the church, partaking of the Eucharist, riding a bicycle instead of driving, reducing your intake of beef, spiritual direction, and alms to the poor and needy.

While all of these are worthwhile, let's look briefly at just a couple of them that I think will be particularly helpful for us broadly as people trying to follow Yeshua, but specifically as recovering fundamentalists: giving alms to the poor and needy, the Jesuit daily examen, and centering prayer.

Giving Alms to the Poor and Needy

One of the dangers of being Episcopalian for me and others, or of being a part of any denomination or tradition comprised of wealthy, powerful white people, is we are easily deceived into thinking we deserve to be comfortable, surrounded by all sorts of luxuries, despite the needs of those around us. Even if you're not a part of one of these traditions, this is the "American dream," and it tempts all of us. That's not to say these churches, traditions, and the members who comprise them don't give to the poor; many of them do. But the amount we do give to the poor is often small in comparison to the amount we spend on our behalf, on things that go beyond filling our needs. Euro-American activist Shane Claiborne once mentioned the Methodist church he grew up in spent one hundred thousand dollars on a staind glass window.[31] Churches readily spend millions of dollars on purchasing church buildings, and the members who comprise those churches often have more material wealth than they need.

I'm guilty of this as well. My closets are filled with extra clothes I don't need and don't even wear, and I spend far more on books than I need too. But what about the poor and the needy? Do we really think we're following in the footsteps of Yeshua, who commanded the rich man to sell all he owned and to give the proceeds to the poor as a prerequisite to come follow him, when there are people sleeping on the street, single mothers who can't afford to pay their rent or feed their children? Is it really following Yeshua to spend one hundred thousand dollars on stained glass windows, or two million dollars on a church building, or to buy two hundred dollars of books at one time with my Christmas bonus, or to go to Honduras this month to sit on the beach? If there is need around us, we have no right to extra comforts that go beyond meeting our basic needs of survival. As Americans, we think we do, but we don't. This is the

---

31. Claiborne, *Irresistible Revolution*, 74.

lie the American gods of wealth and consumerism tell us; that we need to buy more and more to be happy and fulfilled. I write this as much for my own sake as for the reader.

We must, as St. Basil the Cappadocian instructs us, learn to expend our wealth on behalf of the poor and the needy. Saint Basil in his homily entitled *To the Rich* teaches us that "those who love their neighbor as themselves possess nothing more than their neighbor . . . the more you abound in wealth, the more you lack in love. If you had truly loved your neighbor, it would have occurred to you long ago to divest yourself of this wealth."[32] As American Christians we often think to love our neighbor is to give the homeless guy on the street the extra dollar in our pocket, or even to donate thousands of dollars to a charity organization, and if we do such things we are entitled to our expensive cars, big houses, our church buildings, and our generally more-than-comfortable lifestyles. But as St. Basil witnesses to us, as followers of Yeshua, loving our neighbor is much more costly. To truly love your neighbor, he says, is to have nothing more than your neighbor. God give us strength to be this kind of people and to practice this kind of generosity.

In another homily Basil stresses that if we only took what was necessary to fulfill our own needs and gave the rest of our excess income away to those who lacked what they needed, there would be no poor and no rich, and no one would have any need unmet. He continues by asking the following question: Who are truly robbers and who are those truly greedy? His answer: the robbers are those who remain unsatisfied by what suffices their needs, and the greedy are those who take what rightfully belongs to everyone. Basil goes further in his rebuke, asking rhetorically, "Is not the person who strips another of clothing called a thief? And those who do not clothe the naked when they have the power to do so, should they not be called the same?" Answer: those who have excess bread, clothing, and silver but keep it for themselves are stealing what rightfully belongs, in the eyes of God, not to them, but to those who need it.[33] In his homily entitled *In Time of Famine and Drought*, he goes so far as to say, "whoever has the ability to remedy the suffering of others, but chooses rather to withhold aid out of selfish motives, may properly be judged the equivalent of a murderer."[34] I am a thief and murderer, and many who are reading this are too. I cannot count the times I have simply

---

32. Basil the Great, *On Social Justice*, 43.
33. Basil the Great, *On Social Justice*, 69–70.
34. Basil the Great, *On Social Justice*, 85.

walked or driven past someone in need. So again, don't hear me saying I'm perfect at this—far from it. I write this section as much for you as for me. Giving alms to the poor and needy, living simple so others can simply live, is integral to the Christian life as Basil teaches us. It's a Christian practice, so we need to do just that—practice it. So maybe I'll go into my closet and get rid of most of my extra jackets, and maybe I won't pass that person in need next time I see them.

The Daily Examen

Although often associated with Ignatius, the founder of the Jesuits, he didn't create the daily examen, but popularized it, so in reality it's not strictly a Jesuit prayer since forms of it existed before the Jesuits came about. But important to note is the prominence that Ignatius gave to this prayer, so much so that he used to say if Jesuits had not gotten around to any other kind of prayer during their day they should not, at all costs, neglect the daily examen. The term "examen" is a good way to think about what the prayer is: you are examining your day and looking back to see how and where God was present. Usually this prayer is done at the end of the day but it can be done at other times as well. To prepare for this time it's important that you ask for God's grace. Yet I find asking for God's grace can be a triggering point for many former fundamentalists, particularly for those from Reformed or Calvinist traditions, given we were taught that humans are totally depraved. For those unfamiliar, "total depravity" means our whole lives are orientated and inclined towards sin, and if we are to be able to do anything good or pleasing to God, we must ask for God's interceding prevenient grace.

For those of us who have, in my mind, rightly rejected total depravity, we have often reacted to this by shying away from asking for God's grace or admitting that at times we can be powerless. It took me a long time to realize Christians were asking for God's grace and admitting their powerlessness (particularly in their addictions) long before total depravity was conceived of five hundred years ago. The Catholics, even though they believe in original sin, and the Eastern Orthodox, who believe in something called "ancestral sin" (meaning we've inherited the consequences of sin, not necessarily the guilt), have much higher views of humanity. For the Orthodox grace is given, infused, if you will, into our human nature as created by God, and the Catholic Church too sees humanity as being able to do good apart from God's intervening grace; in both these traditions there is already a certain level of grace given in human nature by God. But for both these traditions asking for God's grace is still foundational; regardless of how much grace God has already given and instilled in our created nature, we can always use and need more grace. So be assured, simply asking for God's grace and at times admitting you're powerless and in need of God is not an affirmation of total depravity.[35]

After preparing for your time of prayer by asking for God's grace, you move on to the first step, which is all about gratitude, often called the "time of consolations." You essentially replay your day in your head like a movie, going through it the first time, focusing on the good you did, the good that happened to you, and the good that occurred to those around you. By recalling the good things that happened during your day, where you saw God's grace present and active, you are able to give thanks for those moments. This is an indispensable part of the first step because prayer isn't about yourself alone, but is meant to direct you to God, the focus, therefore, is on God and how you relate to God. This also is an opportunity for us to savor these good moments in our lives, which is especially important given the busyness of modern American life. It's an opportunity to slow down, to be mindful, to stop and smell the roses.

The second step is going back through your day a second time; this is known as "desolations." It is an opportunity to ask for God's illumination, clarity, and grace to see where you have turned from "the deepest part of

---

35. Only Protestants believe in the doctrine of total depravity; it is in this sense a uniquely Northern European doctrine. Catholics do not believe in total depravity, but they do believe in original sin. The Eastern Orthodox do not believe in total depravity or original sin but they do believe in ancestral sin. Judaism also does not in believe in total depravity or original sin, and thus the Eastern Orthodox are in my view closest to the original Jewish view. In Judaism every person has a good inclination and an evil inclination and has the free will to choose which inclination they will follow. For the Jewish perspective on sin and the fall, see Rosner, *Finding Messiah*, 87–101. For a scholarly yet accessible work on the Eastern Orthodox view of humanity, see Harrison, *God's Many-Splendored Image*, and Louth, *Introducing Eastern Orthodox Theology*. See also Lossky, *Mystical Theology of the Eastern Church*m chs. 5–6. Here is an example of the Egyptian Origen in the third century more or less espousing the Jewish view: "The God and Father bestows upon all that they should be; and participation in Christ, in respect of the fact that he is the Word or Reason, renders them as rational beings. From which it follows that they are deserving either of praise or blame, because they are capable of virtue or vice." Origen, *On First Principles*, 41. Similar to Origen, the Samaritan Justin Martyr also espoused the Jewish view of being able to choose virtue or vice and said that if we don't have such power, but are controlled by fate, then there is no such thing as good or evil in this world. See his *First Apologies* as found in Richardson, *Early Christian Fathers*, 225–89.

yourself, the part that calls you to God,"[36] the part of you where, by the virtue of your createdness as a rational creature, you have a share with the Word and Son of God, who is Reason itself. To say it another way, desolations is an opening or unveiling to see where we have sinned against God and our neighbor in thought, word, and deed, and of course by our lack of thought, word, and deed, when we needed to act but did not.

As Americans this might rub us the wrong way, since we often, consciously or not, believe ourselves to be perfect the way we are, and thus not in need of change. This assumption is found in the common but false adage, "You're perfect just the way you are"—something we've been told since we were quite young. But this is part of the mass delusion of our culture, particularly of white colonizing culture, which is blind to the evils we commit both as particular persons and as a society. The reality is we're not perfect, yet we are loved anyway; but love doesn't ignore our imperfections, and it doesn't leave us there. Rather it persuades us to come participate in the divine nature by engaging in virtuous living, by living like God. God wants to transform us into fully developed human beings, not less ourselves but more ourselves, into the image of the one hanging on the cross. An integral part of that is becoming more aware of our sins, our wrongdoings, so that we can work on them. The more we become like God, the more we share in God's holiness, the more light fills our lives and our eyes, the more we will see the darkness hidden deep within us.

After going through your day twice, first by focusing on the consolations and the second time by focusing on your desolations, you spend some time holding both the desolations and consolations, accepting reality, and giving thanks to God for the good and for helping you to recognize the bad. At the very end, you ask God for strength and grace to be more aware of God's presence and to do better the next day. There are of course variations to doing the daily examen, but this is one way you may approach it.

Centering Prayer

Centering prayer has become an essential part of the beginning of my day. I don't always do it, because I'm by nature quite the undisciplined person, but when I miss it, I can feel it, and when I'm consistent doing it day after day, I can feel it. As someone who probably spends too much

---

36. Martin, *Jesuit Guide to (Almost) Everything*, 89.

time thinking (I mean, somebody's gotta do it, right?) and spends a lot of time being distracted by squirrels, centering prayer gives my mind a break. Now, you might be wondering, what is centering prayer? Well it's a kind of contemplative prayer from the Western Christian tradition that's been popularized by people such as the late Euro-American monk Thomas Keating, among others.[37]

So, here's how I do it: I first pray a prayer made from a statement of St. Isaac of Nineveh, then I pray one of St. Patrick's prayer's, then a prayer of St. Francis of Assis, and lastly I pray a poem written by St. Teresa of Avila, all of which you will find below. Then, sitting upright in a chair, I pray the Jesus Prayer (again you'll find it below) and, using the centering prayer app, I spend twenty minutes allowing my mind to empty; each time a thought, word, or image, comes to mind, I gently push it away using the word I've chosen, which for me is *logos*. It doesn't particularly matter what the word is, just something to use as a windshield wiper when those thoughts, words, and imagines inevitably come to mind. Centering prayer is a kind of apophatic prayer as opposed to kataphatic prayer. Apophatic prayer is negative prayer, meaning you don't use words, thoughts, or images. It is simply allowing yourself to rest in the infinite mystery of God, which lies beyond all we could say of God, even the good, true, and beautiful things. Kataphatic prayer is something most of us are familiar with—prayer involving thoughts, words, and images. During my time of centering prayer, I begin with kataphatic prayer and then move into apophatic prayer, and lastly after my twenty-minute timer goes off, I end with the kataphatic prayer, "Lord Jesus Christ Son of God, have mercy on me, a sinner."

The last thing you should probably know about centering prayer is that it's hard, as simple as it is. Many of us in the Western world live in a culture that trains us in distraction—noise everywhere, phones, billboards, Netflix, Google, music, Facebook, and a bunch of other stuff. When you do get distracted during your centering prayer, don't get too discouraged. Keep at it; it will get easier. Recently I asked one of our retired priests about his own practice of centering prayer. This is a man who does it twice a day, in the morning around 2:30 or 3:00 a.m. and in the evening after dinner. He's being doing centering prayer since the 1990s. I was born in the 1990s. While I was lamenting to him how hard it was for

---

37. For a good overview of Centering prayer, see Martin, *Jesuit Guide to (Almost) Everything*.

me, he looked at me and said, "Gabe, it's hard for all of us."[38] Even those who've practiced it since the decade I was born often find it hard. But if you're doing prayer right, it's probably not going to be easy, so keep at it.

Lastly, I would suggest we see limiting our social media usage as a Christian discipline. I have and still am learning this from people much wiser than myself. Too many of us, including us former fundamentalists, are enslaved by social media, and thus deeply influenced by it, in ways that are probably on the whole less than helpful, even given that some help may come from it. Ego, arrogance, unrighteous anger, wrath, creating my own echo chamber (which social media promotes through there algorithms), a false depiction of our lives as something they are not [embracing delusion], vain glory, and so forth are much and most of what I learn and am formed by when I open social media. I would suggest we hop off, and spend that time instead reading the classics within the Christian tradition or doing something else like spiritual direction, prayer walking in the woods, therapy or centering prayer.

Lastly, here I have listed a few prayers, some historical, and some I've made myself, that I have found helpful.

The Jesus Prayer:

> Lord Jesus Christ Son of God, have mercy on me, a sinner.

Saint Patrick:

> Christ with me,
> Christ before me,
> Christ behind me,
> Christ in me,
> Christ beneath me,
> Christ above me,
> Christ on my right,
> Christ on my left,
> Christ when I lie down,
> Christ when I sit down,
> Christ in the heart of everyone who thinks of me,
> Christ in the mouth of everyone who speaks of me,
> Christ in the eye that sees me,
> Christ in the ear that hears me.[39]
> Amen.

---

38. Conversation used with permission.
39. Prayer attributed to St. Patrick, quoted in "Reflection on St. Patrick's Prayer."

Saint Isaac of Nineveh, "The Prayer of a Merciful Heart":

> Lord give us merciful hearts. Give us hearts which burn for all of creation, for all people, for birds, for animals, and even for demons. May we, at the remembrance and sight of them, be people of mercy, whose eyes fill up with tears arising from your great compassion urging our hearts. May our hearts grow tender, unable to endure hearing or seeing any injury or slight sorrow to anything in creation. Through all of this give us strength and encouragement to continually offer tearful prayers, even for irrational animals and for the enemies of truth and for all who harm it, that they may be guarded, forgiven and healed. Amen.[40]

Saint Francis of Assis, "Make Me an Instrument":

> Lord, make me an instrument of your peace. Where there is hatred, let us sow love; where there is injury, pardon; where there is discord, union; where there is doubt, faith; where there is despair, hope; where there is darkness, light; where there is sadness, joy. Grant that we may not so much seek to be consoled as to console [others]; to be understood as to understand [others]; to be loved as to love [others]. For it is in giving that we receive; it is in pardoning that we are pardoned; and it is in dying that we are born to eternal life. Amen.[41]

Saint Teresa of Avila, "Christ Has No Body Now but Yours":

> Christ has no body but yours,
> No hands, no feet on earth but yours,
> Yours are the eyes with which He looks
> Compassion on this world,
> Yours are the feet with which He walks to do good,
> Yours are the hands, with which He blesses all the world.
> Yours are the hands, yours are the feet,
> Yours are the eyes, you are His body.
> Christ has no body now but yours,
> No hands, no feet on earth but yours,
> Yours are the eyes with which he looks
> compassion on this world.
> Christ has no body now on earth but yours.[42]

---

40. This prayer is adapted from a translation of St. Isaac as found in Isaac of Nineveh, *On Ascetical Life*, 12.

41. "Prayer Attributed to St. Francis."

42. Teresa of Avila, "Christ Has No Body but Yours."

Principles and Practices for Recovering Fundamentalists/Evangelicals

A prayer for physical exercise:

Lord Yeshua Messiah, Son of Man, and Son of God, you, being God, became Jewish while remaining God, a creature like us, taking on a sacrament of flesh and blood for the sake of union between your triune nature and creation. As you have brought about this union in yourself, fully God and fully human, may we now use our bodies as sacraments, living flesh prepared for union with you, God of all creation. May we honor you by becoming fully ourselves through the proper movement of our bodies, honoring you as you made us and are still molding us, flesh from your flesh. May this sacrament of physical exercise enable us to better lay down our lives in love for our loved ones, our neighbors, and all of creation. Amen.

A prayer for our fundamentalist brothers and sisters:

Lord, Yeshua Messiah, Son of Man, and Son of God, you alone know the depth of our pain, the hurt, the bitterness, the despair, the deep sense of rejection we have faced; even more than ourselves you know these things. But you, Lord, do not show partiality; you love both us and those who have harmed us. We confess that although you are calling us to union with our brothers and sisters, as you yourself are one God in three persons, we know this is not what we desire. But Lord, we desire to follow you, to please you, to remain and increase in faithfulness to you, and since we know this is your desire for us and the whole world, we pray you would instill your desire of healing and unity in us. Unveil the evil that is within us, that we might see it for what it is. Transform it by your loving, graceful power to be an instrument and vessel of mercy, humility, bold gentleness, truth, justice, and love, towards those we've come to hate. We are not excusing our brothers and sisters for the wrong doing they've committed in thought, word, and deed, but we are asking you to pull the plank out of our eye, so we may properly and soundly be able to see, to pull the speck out of their eye. Let us exercise good judgement, not for our sake, but for theirs and yours, for healing and union. Yeshua Messiah, have mercy on these your servants, and bring all of us into your truth, beauty, and goodness, that on the last day we as one voice may cry out together in the new earth that you alone are God. Amen.

Oh Origen, father of the fathers, who taught us that communion with God is attained through the path of charity and love, intercede on our behalf, requesting for us the grace of God that we too might find ourselves on the path of charity and love towards communion with God. Amen.

4

Orthodoxy and Orthopraxy

What obtains between man and God is not mere submission
to His power or dependence upon His mercy. The plea is
not to obey what He wills but to do what He is.[1]

Abraham Joshua Heschel (Ashkenazi
Jew, twentieth century)

The Creeds are a proclamation, a confession of who God is, Orthodoxy
is the affirmation of who God is, precisely by doing what that God is.

G.N. Roth (Ashkenazi Jew, twentieth century)

Again, rejoice, O Christian, in the Trinity, the Father, the Son, and the Holy
Spirit, because the foundation of Christianity is belief in the Trinity.[2]

Zar'a Ya'eqob (Ethiopian, fifteenth century)

The Creed does not belong to you unless you have lived it.[3]

Metropolitan Philaret of Moscow
(Russian, nineteenth century)

---

1. Heschel, *God in Search of Man*, 290.
2. Ya'eqob, "Book of the Trinity," 402–5.
3. Quoted in Ware, *Orthodox Way*, 8.

It Turns Out That Orthodoxy Is Actually Important

CHRISTIANITY IS NOT THE faith of the autonomous individual. Rather it is a communal Trinitarian faith, to the effect that I as an individual do not get to decide what is and is not Orthodoxy; only the whole church has the right to do so, and only the whole church has done so. I think Anglo Aussie Ben Myers says it well:

> In being a Christian, in being a baptized person, you're not called upon to formulate your own personalized confession. You're not called upon to decide for yourself what the essential content of Christianity is. You can do all that later but the sort of birthing, the first act, is to allow yourself to be inserted into something that is already there before you. The body of Christ who collectively across time and place somehow form one voice and say I believe.[4]

Because our faith is not rooted in the autonomous individual but in the collective body of Messiah, in a community connected across space and time, what I have attempted to do throughout this book is to articulate to the best of my ability what the universal church has declared to be normative theology.

The universal church, in attempting to articulate orthodoxy, has not sought to grasp the mystery of God, to cage the triune Creator in their finite minds; to the contrary; they have sought to guard the mystery and thereby protect us. Theological orthodoxy is not our attempt to control the mystery, the way, the truth, and the life; it is the church's trust fall into the ever-thickening abyss. We do not grasp the mystery, and truth; it grasps us. It is the non-normative theologies that seek to grasp and control that which is meant to bring us into the darkest and deepest parts of the unknown and unchartered seas, where we do not see, where we do not hear, where we do not think. The mystery of Messiah is where God speaks, and it is both the loudest, brightest voice, we have ever received and the quietest, darkest silence we have ever experienced. It is a deep misunderstanding of the Christian tradition to see theological orthodoxy as a box that we have created and must outgrow; rather, theological orthodoxy is a cavernous, ever-deepening canyon that goes on for eternity. We do not outgrow it, for it is eternity and existence itself; we can only ever grow more into it. Discarding it as if it was a box we once put God in and now have outgrown is ironically putting ourselves in a box. Instead

4. Hughes, "Apostle's Creed," 15:01–42.

of falling deeper into the mystery, we have fallen out of it. Instead of getting rid of constraining boundaries, we have built them.

It is another misunderstanding of orthodoxy to see it as something meant to protect certainty[5] and as a justification to burn heretics. Nonetheless, non-normative theology has dangerous practical implications, as we will see when we turn to Gnosticism. If we are to understand normative and non-normative theology as defined by the church, we will have to rid ourselves of our modernist, rationalistic, white categories, assumptions, and ways of thinking and doing. American Japanese artist and theologian Makoto Fujimura writes in his book *Art and Faith* that many "Christians have many presuppositions about what Christianity is that are often based upon an analytical approach to understanding truth as a set of propositional beliefs, such that understanding and explaining take dominance over experiencing and intuiting."[6] This tendency among Western Christians comes out of the European Endarkenment and it clouds our vision when we look to the creedal mysteries of the faith such as the Trinity and the virgin birth.

When some of us former fundamentalists find the analytical approach wanting, we attempt to embrace mystery instead, and, believing we have done so as part of our process of "embracing" mystery, we end up discarding much of dogma. What we don't realize is by discarding such dogmas we are still steeped in the misunderstanding that dogma is by nature propositional and analytical. We are still assuming dogma needs to be understood within an Enlightenment European framework. In contrast to this misunderstanding of dogma, French-born Jewish Catholic Dominic priest Antoine Levy writes, "the great theologians of the past did not go in search of solutions to mysteries; rather they contemplated the mysteries of their faith [dogma] when they were in search of solutions. In the Christian tradition, mystery designates the essence of a reality that does not belong to the order that rules our daily lives. It refers to a reality that is intimately connected to the One who created the world, so that it is not itself encompassed by the created order."[7] In other words, the mystery of the faith, which is dogma, is not merely analytical or propositional by nature, because it's a revealed description of the God who is itself not a part of the created order. Analysis and propositions belong to the realm

---

5. Orthodoxy existed well before the Enlightenment invented intellectual certainty. So theological orthodoxy does not imply intellectual certainty.

6. Fujimura, *Art and Faith*, 4.

7. Levy, *Jewish Church*, 15.

of human inquiry within the order of creation, whereas the content of the mysteries of the faith, being God itself, belongs to the realm of the Creator.

Unknowingly, we continue to falsely believe Trinitarian and Christological dogma to be propositional beliefs set within an analytical framework for understanding the faith, which then need to be assessed by the criteria of reason to determine whether they are true and therefore whether they must be intellectually assented too or not.[8] Yet this is a modernist colonial imposition on Christian theology rather than an understanding of orthodoxy on its own terms. Because we assume Enlightenment categories for understanding the Trinity and Christology, seeing them as analytical propositional beliefs, we reject them for the sake of mystery, falsely believing we are upholding mystery when we've really just redressed our rationalism. By understanding dogma within the Northern European worldview we are still centering the white modernist perspective and unknowingly still assuming it. To say it frankly, we have yet to actually embrace mystery and discard our Northern European rationalism.

We see mystery and dogma as antithetical to one another, rather than as one and the same thing, as the great tradition has for two millennium. Not seeing them as distinct, the tradition has said *dogma is mystery*. The East Syrian Babai the Great gives us an example of this when writing about the incarnation, marveling at how Yeshua the Messiah could be at one and the same time both God and human while being united as one person: "Who knows all this as it really is? How can this miracle that cannot be reasoned out be described as it is, this wonder that is unsearchable, that a human being should be with God the Word, the single, unique Son of God, in one person? For this mystery is ungraspable and impossible to reason out."[9] To Babai the dogma of the incarnation isn't a propositional statement seeking to enclose God, but unfathomable mystery. In his dogmatic treatise Babai can on the one hand declare the impossibility of reasoning out this mystery, while on the other hand describe who this

---

8. See Spong, *Why Christianity Must Change or Die* for an example of someone misunderstanding the creeds to be a set of propositional statements. In referring to the creeds Spong writes, "The God I know can only be pointed to; this God can never be enclosed by propositional statements." Spong, *Why Christianity Must Change or Die*, 4. To Spong and many others the creeds are propositional statements.

9. Babai the Great, "Book of the Union," 100.

God is according to that very mystery.[10] Said another way, he's describing the dogma of the incarnation as a revealed and yet impenetrable mystery.

Some of us have the tendency to think that mystery is the same thing as saying nothing, but this couldn't be farther from the truth. Rather mystery is the embodied proclamation of what has been revealed, which is not something that can be assessed by reason, but instead should inspire awe and wonder if we truly understand that it is beyond our understanding. Given this tendency to see dogmatic theological reflection as an analytical destruction of mystery, we might find Babai's ability to call dogmatic reflection "mystery" *a mystery*. But before the modernity of Northern Europe, dogmatic theology wasn't seen as antithetical to mystery. We need to keep in mind that for much of the church's history Christianity has existed predominantly outside of German modernity, and therefore our categorical assumptions inherited from the Enlightenment were not shared by the communities who wrote the creeds, or theologians like Babai the Great.

Christian dogma, or theological orthodoxy, is not to be found or understood within the cultural matrix of the Enlightenment worldview, or even the European worldview in general, but as part of a general Asian and African worldview or even more specifically the Second Temple Jewish worldview. In the tradition, the Trinity, given its Jewish paradoxical nature, is seen less as a propositional belief and more as a mystery to be lived, less of an disembodied idea and more like God incarnated in and through you, less as an object to be analyzed and explained and more as a community of persons to interact and engage with. We do not set up our friends, families, or spouses as objects to be analyzed as propositional beliefs to be affirmed or denied (or if we do, we have a serious issue) but view them as people to live life with. It should be no less with the God described in the creeds.

The creeds are less like a formula or recipe—"Say this about God and you'll get this kind of outcome"—and more like art, like a song you sing with every bit of marrow in your bones, that resonates with and throughout your body, though you cannot possibly put it into words that you can

---

10. "We have learned and believed and continue to hold that there is a unity of the two natures, that is, of the two hypostases, the image of God and the image of the slave, of the temple and its resident, in a single connection, in a single name, in a single power, in single reverence, with the two properties of the hypostases kept without mixture, that of the divinity of Christ and that of his humanity, in the person of being a Son . . . How this can be is unsearchable and impossible to reason out." Babai, "Book of the Union," 100.

later analyze. It's like staring up at a magnificent mountain or across a field of bison in a bit of prairie or looking up at the clouds and blue sky. It's awe inspiring though you can't explain it. Of course, you can say some things about it—"It's a bison; its brown; its hairy with thick and long fur; it eats grass" and so forth, all true things—but there is something deeper, something you can't put your finger on, something you can't explain. That's the creeds. If you want to explore the dogmas of the Christian faith, you must first accept the creedal *way of living*. These are not propositions to assent too, but a reality to be grasped by, to embody and to live out in concrete actions. To understand orthodoxy as found in the creeds and understood by the tradition, or said differently, to give allegiance to the God described in the sacrament of the creeds, we will need to shed our modern, white, liberal Protestant ways of thinking and seeing. We'll need to stop thinking about the creeds or theological orthodoxy in general as white, and or as the triumph of Hellenistic culture.[11] We will need a paradigm shift, old categories, an old imagination rooted in the seeds of the eternal, and the creativity of the triune Creator.

Seneca wisdom keeper John Mohawk, a professor at State University of New York–Buffalo, writes,

> For the most part, contemporary historians have proceeded from the presumption that modern people are different from and superior to those who came before, especially those designated as primitives. Distortions and incomplete and even dishonest renderings of the past are found in many modern accounts of ancient and 'primitive' peoples. These accounts serve to reinforce the sense of difference and to distance moderns from unflattering legacies of the past.[12]

---

11. I believe it's more helpful to think of theological orthodoxy and the creeds as a triumph of the brown Jewification of the Hellenistic world. Euro-American Robert Louis Wilken writes concerning this, "The notion that the development of early Christian thought represented a Hellenization of Christianity has outlived its usefulness. The time has come to bid a fond farewell to the ideas of Adolf von Harnack, the nineteenth-century historian of dogma whose thinking has influenced the interpretation of early Christian thought for more than a century . . . a more apt expression would be the Christianization of Hellenism, though that phrase does not capture the originality of Christian thought nor the debt owed to Jewish ways of thinking and to the Jewish Bible. Neither does it acknowledge the good and right qualities of Hellenic thinking that Christians recognized as valuable, for example, moral life understood in terms of the virtues." Wilken, *Spirit of Early Christian Thought*, xvi–xvii.

12. Mohawk, *Utopian Legacies*, 260.

Unfortunately, John Mohawk's observation here is not simply true of historians, but of theologians, clergy persons, and modern Western people in general. When many Christians speak of the Old Testament, this is their presumption. When many modern white clergy and theologians speak of the creeds and traditional (brown) theologies, this is their presumption.

In his book *Why Christianity Must Change or Die*, John Shelby Spong summarized these sentiments of modern people quite well, specifically, although not limited to, our attitudes towards the creeds. *People back then were dumb. We know more now; we're rational. How could we possibly ever think they had it figured out? And therefore we should reject their conclusions and update Christianity according to our modern rational superiority.* This sentiment is widespread.[13] But let's think about *who these people* back then are that Spong and others are referring to. Well, most of them are brown people (many of them Jews) who formulated creedal theology and wrote the Bible, who were the first Christians and the first theologians. And who are the people who invented modernity, and its attitude that Spong and countless other Western people are espousing? Well, white Northern Europeans, particularly peoples such as the Germans, French, British, so forth. Lest we not forget, modernism and the Enlightenment—its sentiments, attitudes, categories, and assumptions—are built on and derivative of white racism and colonialism.[14] If we keep

---

13. Bishop Robert Barron, commenting on his interactions with those deeply influenced by the rhetoric, language, and arguments of the New Atheists, such as Sam Harris, Richard Dawkins, and Christopher Hitchens, speaks about this attitude: what has been spoken by such people as the new atheists "is a general sense that religious belief is irrational, a holdover from a primitive age. So time and again, my interlocutors, echoing Harris, Dawkins, and Hitchens, characterize the faith as 'bronze-age mythology' or the musings of prescientific people who did not understand the basics of biology or chemistry." Barron, *Light from Light*, xii. Given that modern science and technology came out of modern Western culture, I find the kind of rhetoric used against Christianity, as Barron relates it, to be racist more generally and specifically anti-Jewish, since the prescientific religious beliefs they're ranting against came out of Judaism. Whether it's the New Atheists, the deconstructionist crowd, liberal Protestants, or Fundamentalists, to a degree this is the standard attitude we've all inherited from the Northern European Enlightenment. I've also heard people dismiss the biblical witness because the authors of the Bible (who were all brown Jews) lived in premodern times, and now we know more and should not take them so seriously; we need to move forward and adapt the faith according to our own knowledge and values, i.e., Northern Europeans knowing's and values.

14. See Mignolo and Walsh, *On Decoloniality*. The Scotsman David Hume, the famous Enlightenment philosopher, wrote the following, which was later picked up by Immanuel Kant: "I am apt to suspect the Negroes and in general all other species of men (for there are four of five different kinds) to be naturally inferior to the whites.

those realities in mind, we might be able to see the modern sentiment, expressed so well by Spong, to be veiled racism, antisemitism, and certainly theological colonialism. His book *Why Christianity Must Change or Die* might be more accurately entitled *Why Christianity Must Become White or Die*. The modernist case for Christianity is an argument to drain the color from Christianity, and by so doing, as in draining the blood from a body, kill it. The Endarkenment project of Northern Europe was and is essentially a white-washing project that desires to remove particularities and anything brown or Jewish from the Christian faith.

What God Do You Worship?

Now, while earlier we briefly talked about orthodox/normative Christianity, defining what it is, throughout the rest of this chapter were going to look more at the connection between orthodoxy and orthopraxy, which will require us to practice seeing from outside of a Western dualistic worldview. In Protestant circles, whether progressive or "conservative," many think orthodoxy is simply *right belief*, but this is only half of its meaning. English Eastern Orthodox Bishop Kallistos Ware[15] has rightly pointed out the term means more than just right belief; it also means "*'right glory' (or 'right worship')*."[16] And worship is an action, so orthodoxy really encompasses right belief and right action. While worship certainly includes what we do gathered around the Eucharist on a Sunday

---

There never was a civilized nation or any other complexion than white, nor even any individual eminent either in action or speculation. No ingenious manufacture amongst them, no arts, no sciences. On the other hand, the most rude and barbarous of the whites, such as the ancient Germans, the present Tartars, have still something eminent about them, in their valour, form of government, or some other particular. Such a uniform and constant difference could not happen, in so many countries and ages, if nature had not made an original distinction betwixt these breeds of men. Not to mention our colonies, there are Negroe slaves dispersed all over Europe, of which none ever discovered any symptom of ingenuity; tho' low people, without education, will start up amongst us, and distinguish themselves in every profession. In Jamaica, indeed, they talk of one negroe as a man of parts and learning; but 'tis likely he is admired for very slender accomplishments like a parrot, who speaks a few words plainly." The theology of liberal Protestantism (remember I include Fundamentalism under this term) came from an adoption of the Enlightenment worldview, the worldview of Hume and Kant, which as we see here was extremely racist.

15. While Kallistos Ware was English, the Christian tradition in which he lived, moved, and had his being is rooted in Southwest Asia, in modern-day Turkey, Syria, Israel, and Egypt.

16. Ware, *Orthodox Church*, 8. Emphasis added.

morning, for the Christian every aspect of life, every thought, word, and deed, should be an act of worship.

While orthodoxy is important, it involves only four embodied doctrines, as we have seen. In other words, what makes you orthodox in right belief and right action is fairly minimal. If you have embodied fidelity to the God described in the following dogmas: the Trinity, the full deity and full Jewish humanity of Messiah fully united, his bodily resurrection, and his virgin birth, then you're, at least in my humble and limited perspective, in line with what all Christians, in all places, and in all times have believed and worshipped.[17] And believing in that God, as I'll explain more fully below, is not mere intellectual assent; it's something you must live in *thought, word, and deed*. It's an allegiance, loyalty, trust, and fidelity *to this God* described in the creeds. It's a calling to worship *this God* in thought, word, and deed. We must, as Heschel implores us, "*Do what He is.*"[18] Just as James instructs us that we must be "doers of the Word," so we must be doers of who God is. Yet to *do what God is*, to be faithful to *this particular God* and not another, we must describe who that God is, thus the need for the creeds. The late Slavic-American Orthodox historian Jaroslav Pelikan explains:

> It has been one function of the creed to specify what the correct object of authentic ritual and worship is, and thus to define Christian confession as the presupposition for Christian love and prayer, lest one mistakenly address prayer and adoration to a false deity and thereby fall into idolatry. The second function has been to affirm the inseparable bond between "deeds" and "creeds," between Christian love and Christian confession, and thus to interpret Christian love as the presupposition for Christian confession and Christian worship.[19]

If we do not describe *who that God is*, then we cannot possibly *know what God is* in order to be able *to do that which God is*. In other words, as Pelikan pointed out, without creed, without description and identification of who God is, we have no basis for our deeds, not knowing the

---

17. While the recognition of the Jewishness of Messiah's full humanity has not always been explicit since the first Jewish Christian communities, it has always been latent and I dare say implicit. Given that those who are fully human tend to have particular ethnic, cultural, and religious identities, there has never been a human devoid of a people group. So to say Yeshua is fully human is to some extent to imply his Jewishness.

18. Heschel, *God in Search of Man*, 290.

19. Pelikan, *Credo*, 300.

kinds of deeds we should practice, because we don't know what kind of God we are supposed to be worshipping through our deeds. Yet within creedal confession, within the lived knowledge of the Trinitarian God, who is Love and who has acted in the world as such, we therefore know love as the presupposition for the worship and confession of this God. This is why for the early Christians the creeds and dogmatic theology were not unimportant or separate from their practices.

Since the creeds are a description of who God is, when we confess the creeds we are saying, "This is who God is; this is what this God is like." When I ask someone if they confess the creeds, what I'm asking is, "What God do you worship—the God of Israel, whom the church, comprised of Jew and gentile, is the body of, or some other God?" We recite *this* description of God and make it central to our worship because it tells us whom we're directing our worship to, whom we are pledging our allegiance and fidelity to, and therefore confessing what kind of behavior we should be practicing. If you remove an aspect of that description, then we're no longer talking about the same God. The two Gods might be similar in some ways, but they're not identical, to the effect we're no longer talking about the God of Israel whom Christians follow. This is why we can't deny the virgin birth or deity of Yeshua and still think we're worshipping the same God. The God many of us worship is not the God of Israel, but the god of Northern Europe and it's Enlightenment; not the God who took on brown Jewish flesh, but the white Germanic god.[20]

The Pendulum Always Swings to the Other Extreme—Dualism

As I've moved away from an extremely narrow definition of orthodoxy, while simultaneously growing in my conviction of the importance of a broad orthodoxy, many others, in reaction to such narrow understandings, have leaned towards rejecting orthodoxy altogether in favor of orthopraxy, as if they were two distinct phenomena. Euro-American historian Diana Butler Bass provides us with a good example of this when she explains in her book *A People's History of Christianity*, "I sidestep issues of orthodoxy and instead focus on the moments when Christian people really acted like Christians, when they took seriously the call of

---

20. I think white Jesus, particularly blond blue-eyed Jesus, is an example of this.

Jesus to love God and love their neighbors as themselves."[21] Bass like many Westerners, understands or rather misunderstands orthodoxy as something divorced from how Christians act and behave. The categorical thinking or dualism of Western culture has blinded us from seeing the subject of orthodoxy and orthopraxy holistically as one and the same thing.[22] Because of our dualism, we first divorce them and then reject one or the other. St. Irenaeus in the second century, who fought against Gnostic dualism, wrote, "For what use is it to know the truth in words, only to defile the body and perform evil deeds? Or what profit indeed can come from holiness of body, if truth is not in the soul? For these rejoice together and join forces to lead man to the presence of God."[23] To separate them is to reject both. The theologian Abraham Joshua Heschel, a member of my own people, an Ashkenazi Jew, writes,

> The dichotomy of faith and works which presented such an important problem in Christian theology was never a problem in Judaism.[24] To us, the basic problem is neither what is the right action nor what is the right intention. The basic problem is: what is right living? *And life is indivisible.* The inner sphere is never isolated from outward activities. *Deed and thought are bound into one.* All a person thinks and feels enters everything he does, and all he does is involved in everything he thinks and feels.[25]

For Heschel "life is indivisible"; what we think is not separated from what we do and vice versa. If your orthodoxy includes belief that God is a moral monster who commands genocide of pagans, your orthopraxy is probably going to include genocide of pagans. And it goes the other way around too: if you believe genocide is acceptable practice and behavior, then it's likely your dogma about God fits with such orthopraxy.

Bass continues by writing, "in many quarters Christian communities are once again embracing the ancient insight that the faith is a spiritual pathway, a life built on transformative practices of love rather than

---

21. Bass, *People's History of Christianity*, 15.

22. See Duane Elmer's book *Cross Cultural Connections* for more on how people living in the West think categorically as opposed to those in the rest of the world, who think holistically.

23. Irenaeus, *On the Apostolic Preaching*, 40.

24. I would note this is more or less a problem among Protestant Christians, not all of Christianity.

25. Heschel, *God in Search of Man*, 296. Emphasis added.

doctrinal belief."[26] Here Bass fundamentally misunderstands the early church. This isn't an ancient insight at all, but a particularly white and modern one. In the early church, doctrine was not seen as unimportant or even separate from these transformative practices of love that Bass refers to. The early seventh-century East Syrian Babai the Great once wrote, "Those who have kept the Lord's commands [praxis] together with the right confession [dogma] are truly alive."[27] Even in much of the church in the last couple hundred years practice and teaching are not forced through the lens of dualism. St. Ignatii Brianchaninov, a nineteenth-century Russian Orthodox, wrote to novices entering a monastery,

> From his first entry into the monastery a monk should devote all possible care and attention to the reading of the Holy Gospel. He should study the Gospel so closely that it is always present in his memory. *At every moral decision he takes, for every act, for every thought, he should always have ready in his memory the teaching of the Gospel.*[28]

To an Eastern Christian like St. Ignatii, it is accepted that moral decisions, actions, thoughts, and teachings are not in competition with one another, as they are often seen to be in the West. The fifteenth-century patriarch of Constantinople, Gennadius II, in response to Islamic criticisms, proclaimed, "the souls and the bodies of those *who believe rightly and live rightly* will depart into Paradise."[29] In referring to the inseparability of truth and love, St. Ephrem the Syrian in his *Hymns on Faith* expresses it this way: "Truth and love are wings undivided. Truth cannot fly without love. Love cannot soar without truth. Their yoke is one of unity."[30] In contrast to much of modern Western theology, Ephrem here beautifully exemplifies the non-competitive unity of love and truth as embodied in the Christian East. Love and truth, praxis and dogma are not at odds, as if we have to choose one and reject the other, but are fully united together as one holistic indivisible way of life.

Jaroslav Pelikan, an expert in the Christian creeds from across time and place, sums this up well when he writes in his monumental work on

---

26. Bass, *People's History of Christianity*, 30. I imagine when she mentions "Christian communities" she probably means progressive Protestants.
27. Babai the Great, "Book of the Union," 100.
28. Brianchaninov, *Arena*, 3. Emphasis added.
29. Gennadius II, quoted in Pelikan, *Credo*, 279. Emphasis added.
30. Ephrem the Syrian, *Hymns on Faith*, 156.

the creeds, "Thus orthodoxy and morality, creeds and deeds, dogmatics and ethics, are affirmed to be inseparable *by Christian confessions of all parties*. One reason for their inseparability is that the true venue for both is not merely the faith and life of the individual but the faith and life of the church catholic."[31] A community such as the church called to live life together operates, as Heschel commented, out of both its practices and its held beliefs since *life is indivisible*. What we think affects how we treat one another as a community, and how we treat one another in community affects how and what we think.

In his *Homilies on the Psalms*, the third-century Egyptian Origen writes that *both justice and truth* are matters of obedience to Messiah:

> The Lord Jesus Christ is justice. No one who acts unjustly is subordinate to Christ, justice. The Lord Christ is truth. No one is subordinate to Christ, the truth, who lies or holds false teaching. The Lord Christ is sanctification. No one is subordinate to Christ, sanctification, when he himself is profane and defiled. The Lord Christ is peace. No one is subordinate to Christ who is hostile or bellicose, unable to say, "I was peaceful with those who hate peace."[32]

To beat a dead horse, what is true here about Origen is what we've seen again and again; that for much of the early and contemporary church, justice, truth, sanctification, and peace are not divorced from one another. This is why justice, for instance, cannot be separated from dogma, for God, who is the subject of dogma, is Justice itself. All these attributes flow out of who Yeshua Messiah is. Yeshua is not simply a moral teacher, but the Creator of the universe; the reason there is such a thing as morality at all is because goodness is what it means for God to be God. Yeshua preached goodness and justice because he was the essence of goodness and justice itself. If we wish to be subordinate and obedient to Yeshua Messiah, if we wish to be his friend, namely being brought into union with him, then we must do the things that he is, thereby becoming like him and sharing in his fully divine and fully human natures. To divide practice from doctrine as Bass and others do is a dualistic and categorical Western move, rather than one rooted in the Christian tradition, which at its core is brown and Jewish.

---

31. Pelikan, *Credo*, 288. Emphasis added.
32. Origen, *Homilies on the Psalms*, 90.

Writing in the seventh century, Maximus the Confessor says,[33]

> The divine Logos of God the Father is mystically present in each of His commandments. God the Father is by nature present entirely and without division in His entire divine Logos. Thus, he who receives a divine commandment and carries it out receives the Logos of God who is in it; and he who receives the Logos through the commandments also receives through Him the Father who is by nature present in Him, and the Spirit who likewise is by nature in Him.[34]

Here for Maximus his Trinitarian doctrine is inseparable from his orthopraxy. It is infused into his views of how we are to live. Doing what God has commanded, the living out of our faith, is a means by which we encounter and come into union with the Trinitarian God who undergirds it all. If you took out the Trinitarian dogma here in Maximus' statement, there would be nothing left. Indeed, this is still the case in the Eastern tradition, as the Russian Orthodox Vladimir Lossky put it so well in his book *The Mystical Theology of the Eastern Church*:

> The eastern tradition has never made a sharp distinction between mysticism and theology; between personal experience of the divine mysteries and the dogma affirmed by the Church . . . To put it another way, *we must live the dogma expressing a revealed truth, which appears to us as an unfathomable mystery*, in such a fashion that instead of assimilating the mystery to our mode of understanding, we should, on the contrary, look for a profound change, and inner transformation of spirit, enabling us to experience it mystically. *Far from being mutually opposed, theology and mysticism support and complete each other. One is impossible without the other.* If the mystical experience is a personal working out of the content of the common faith, theology is an expression, for the profit of all, of that which can be experienced by everyone.[35]

In other words, the way you live out your faith is a way to embody theological dogma understood as the great mysteries of our faith. For Lossky and the Eastern tradition, practice, dogma, and mystery are all

---

33. Maximus was possibly born and raised in Constantinople, or in Galilee to a father who was a Samaritan merchant and a mother of Persian origin who had worked in a Jewish home and may have either been Jewish herself or a convert to Judaism.

34. Maximus, "Two Hundred Texts," 154–55.

35. Lossky, *The Mystical Theology of the Eastern Church*, 8–9. Emphasis added.

inseparably tied together. Dogma not rooted in embodied practices is not dogma. And embodied practices divorced from dogma is rootless.

For a more modern example in our own backyard of the inseparability of orthodoxy and orthopraxy, we have no further to look than to nineteenth-century evangelicalism and the invention of the altar call. Many of us recovering fundamentalists are deeply familiar with the altar call as it exists today but are woefully ignorant of its origins. Euro-American Charles Finney, a Presbyterian evangelist and one of the leading revivalists of his time, is credited with creation of the altar call. For Finney this was him giving people an opportunity to walk to the front and proclaim that they were giving their allegiance to Yeshua by aligning themselves to his kingdom. But if one wanted to gain citizenship in the kingdom of God, they were required to give their allegiance to God's rule and reign above any human political institutions, including the legal, social, and economic reality of slavery.

During his altar calls, both men and women responded with repentance for their personal sins and their own complicity with the sins of the nation. "And when they wiped away their tears and opened their eyes, Finney thrust a pen into their hands and pointed them to sign-up sheets for the abolitionist movement."[36] For nineteenth-century evangelicals like Charles Finney, their belief in who Yeshua was as the risen King informed and led to their orthopraxis. Right beliefs and right actions were, once again, inseparable. Within white evangelicalism the separation we know today between right beliefs and right practices really came with the fundamentalist-liberal controversies in the nineteenth and early twentieth centuries.

The False Western Dichotomy of Body-Soul Dualism

One of the problems in the Western world I think is underlying this false dichotomy between orthodoxy and orthopraxy is we have dichotomized the body from the mind or soul. The Hebraic worldview had no such separation of the body from the mind. Our concept of the human person is found in the Hebrew word *nephesh*. In the West we translate this word as "soul." But that's a bad rendering of the word into English. Even in the Greek translation of the Old Testament the word *psyche*, which we translate as "soul," has more variation in meaning than just soul; it can

---

36. Harper, *Very Good Gospel*, 7.

sometimes be translated as "life." The practice of rendering *nephesh* or *psyche* simply as "soul" every time we translate it is really more from the Greek world Westerners have inherited than it is from the Hebrew world.

In the world of my ancestors, *nephesh* means your whole being, your very life. It does not categorize human beings into two components, a body and a detachable soul. To the Hebrews the human being is more or less just one thing. This is why the bodily resurrection having come from a Jewish context was so important in the early church, as we see in the creeds ("We believe in the [general] resurrection of the dead"), because in the Jewish context that gentile Christians inherited you didn't have a separate immortal soul that would live apart from your body.

But—and this is an important caveat—even among the various gentile Christian traditions that believe the body, soul, and even spirit to be what comprises the human person, such as the Eastern Orthodox, Roman Catholic, and Protestant traditions, there isn't a sharp divide between the body and soul, as there is in more Gnostic systems of thinking.[37] In the Orthodox church, for instance, it is death that *unnaturally* separates the body from the soul, and the resurrection that puts them back together. For all three of these Christian traditions, the body and soul together make up the human person. It is Gnosticism rather than the Christian tradition that asserts the kind of dualism that not only separates the body and soul but claims the soul to be superior to the body, and even immortal. Generally, in the Christian tradition human beings, comprised of both souls and bodies, are mortal, but by our union with God through the Messiah we come to share in God's own immortality. This assumption about the body and soul being separate, of course, is quite natural to Westerners, given that ideologically we are Gnostic, operating as categorical thinkers rather than holistic thinkers. However, just because this is what our culture is like now doesn't mean we shouldn't change towards being more holistic thinkers. In fact, as I will argue later, we must, if we wish to ensure our survival on this planet. If we go back to the more holistic Hebrew and Christian understanding of anthropology (understanding of what it means to be human), I suspect it'll be harder to divorce orthodoxy and orthopraxy.

---

37. The so-called *Gospel of Thomas* represents this dualistic sharp separation between the soul and body. "Jesus said, 'Damn the flesh that depends on the soul. Damn the soul that depends on the flesh." Miller, *Complete Gospels*, 322.

We're All a Little Heretical

Continuing on allow me to make once last ditch effort to convince you why orthodoxy and orthopraxy are not separate. As many of us know, for fundamentalists the Trinity is usually acknowledged as a matter of orthodoxy, but loving your enemies often is not. While for progressive fundamentalists[38] the order is reversed; loving your enemies is a matter of orthodoxy (although they usually wouldn't call it "orthodoxy"), but the Trinity is not. My contention is that God is Love, because God is Trinitarian. Writing about this Trinitarian God of love, Kallistos Ware says,

> There is in God genuine diversity as well as true unity. The Christian God is not just a unit but a union, not just unity but community. There is in God something analogous to "society." He is not a single person, loving himself alone, not a self-contained monad or "The One." He is triunity: three equal persons, each dwelling in the other two by virtue of an unceasing movement of mutual love. *Amo ergo sum*, "I love, therefore I am."[39]

In light of this, we can say that to deny love is to deny the Trinity because the Trinity is Love by virtue of being three others, three persons fully united in self-giving love towards one another. Thus, to not live a life of loving behavior is heretical; it is a rejection of the creeds, which describe and confess this triune God. Those who do not love their enemies are just as heretical as those who do not affirm the doctrine of the Trinity. For truly denying the Trinity is to deny love, because God is Love. Since both twin children of modernity reject the doctrine of the Trinity, one through a rejection of orthodoxy and the other through their rejection of orthopraxy, both worship different gods, just in different ways, one through their body and another through their mind.

Love is a matter of orthodoxy, and orthodoxy is a matter of love. None of us lives a life of love consistently. In that way were all heretical or non-normative at times. But on a good day, when we love our neighbor, and especially our enemy, we live in and according to a life-giving orthodoxy. Your behavior cannot be separated from what you believe intellectually. To consistently live a life of love, to embody Messiah-like behavior, means you believe in the Trinity who is Love. To be rooted in the life of the Trinity means to live like the Trinity. And it means those

---

38. I.e., liberal Protestants.
39. Ware, *Orthodox Way*, 35–36.

who kill their enemies are heretical in a least one sense, and those who love their enemies are orthodox in at least one sense. Which is why enacting violence and killing is unorthodox. Let's explore this a bit through the story of the Frenchman John Calvin.

For a lot of people the name John Calvin is synonymous with orthodoxy. He's seen as a brilliant systematic theologian, biblical scholar, and scourge of heretics. But was he really the upholder of orthodoxy as so often thought? Allow me to propose he was not. My sense is that the underlying assumption of Calvin as a defender of orthodoxy is this false dichotomy between right belief and right action—a reductionistic misunderstanding of orthodoxy. But to see why we must tell a story.

An Unpleasant Day in Geneva

Long ago in a beautifully nestled city in the French Alps called Geneva, there lived one of the Protestant Reformers, John Calvin, a Frenchman himself. He was a staunch defender of what would come to be known as Protestant theology. He was also a brilliant man. His *Institutes of the Christian Religion*, a big chunk of systematic Protestant theology, probably the first of its kind, was started by him at the age of nineteen and finished by the time he was twenty-four.

He came to be one of the key leaders of the city, a city ran as a theocracy. But there also was a man named Michael Servetus, who was a heretic because, in fact, he denied the Trinity. Hunted by both Protestants and Catholics alike, he was a wanted man. Servetus had recently escaped prison in France, where he was being tried for heresy by the Catholic Church. Well, Servetus eventually wandered into their little slice of heaven here on earth, and of course was recognized and caught. The city officiates wanted to have him burned at the stake, but Calvin was "merciful" and suggested they merely cut off his head instead. However, the rest were not swayed, and Servetus was indeed burned at the stake. So just as Saul had stood aside giving his approval, so did Calvin stand aside giving his consent to the execution of Servetus (even if not to the manner of execution). It was a day of victory, for the rotten decay of heresy was cleansed from their city—or so the story goes. Or, from that day on heresy raged on disguised, hiding in plain sight. There among those simple city folk lay still a denier of the Trinity—nay, I should say many deniers.

For there are multiple ways to deny the Trinity. One way, as we have seen, is to do so intellectually as Servetus had, separating the mind from the body. Another, more devious way, one masked in "piety," this time separating the body from the mind, is to relinquish the peace of love and attack the image of God. Since the God who is Trinity is so because he is Love, and he is Love because he is Trinity, to reject love (which does no harm) is a denial of the Trinity. The call to love God and neighbor is tied to the doctrine and reality that God is Love because God is Trinity, an eternal community of mutual self-giving love.

Once again, love and orthodoxy go hand in hand. English Orthodox Bishop Kallistos Ware writes,

> Immediately before reciting the Creed in the Eucharist Liturgy, we say these words: 'Let us love one another, *so that* we may with one mind confess Father, Son and Holy Spirit, the Trinity one in essence and undivided.' Note the words, "so that." A genuine confession of faith in the Triune God can be made only by those who, after the likeness of the Trinity, show love mutually towards each other. *There is an integral connection between our love for one another and our faith in the Trinity: the first is a precondition for the second, and in its turn the second gives full strength and meaning to the first.*[40]

As I have thoroughly reiterated throughout this chapter, since orthodoxy and orthopraxy are not separate, to deny either one is heretical. You cannot separate them without throwing them both out. By killing his fellow image-bearer and thus relinquishing love, Calvin, along with the rest involved, in practice denied that very love, thus rejecting the Trinity. Ironically, by trying to use hate, the absence of love, to purge heresy from this earth, he in fact accepted and embodied that same heresy. Ultimately our behavior is intrinsically tied to our orthodoxy, and how we interact with those who have departed from orthodox doctrine will determine our own orthodoxy. This is as true for the Frenchman John Calvin as it was for the crusaders or anyone else in history who chose hate over love. In a sense we are all John Calvin. We all fluctuate between faithfulness and unfaithfulness to God either in thought, word, or deed. But the point of this story remains; we should not call people who have rejected the Trinity in deed people of orthodoxy. For the Trinity must be confessed in thought, word, and deed.

---

40. Ware, *Orthodox Way*, 54–55. Emphasis added.

Faith and Belief as Allegiance

Before we can conclude this chapter, we must once again briefly attend to the concept of belief since this is so confused and misunderstood in our time. What exactly does it mean to *confess belief* in this God who is Trinity? Is it mere intellectual assent? Is it simply a relic from the ancient church before our so-called superior German rationalism developed in the white Western world? Or is it foundational to who we are as the mystical body of Messiah in all that we think, say, and do? I think the Ethiopian Zar'a Ya'eqob was right when he wrote about this. "Again, rejoice, O Christian, in the Trinity, the Father, the Son, and the Holy Spirit, *because the foundation of Christianity is belief in the Trinity*."[41]

Unfortunately, in the Western world, as we've explored, belief in the Trinity and Messiah is seen as mere intellectual assent to propositional statements of truth, which we must either prove or disprove rationally. As a result of our dualism, this version of "belief," as I have argued above, gets separated from our concerns with our practice, behavior, and how we live our lives. The Northern European Enlightenment has given us a faulty understanding of what it means to believe in the God described by the creeds. We see beliefs as propositional statements that we must assess through analytical rational means. But as Gregory of Nazianzus the Cappadocian once said, "'Believing in' is not the same thing as 'believing a fact about.' The first applies to God, the second to everything."[42] The doctrines that orthodoxy consists of are not facts to be believed about God, but are a description of who the God that we believe in is. That's not to say they're not true or when it comes to the incarnation, that they are not based in historical realities, but it is to say it's a different kind of knowing; it requires a different set of criteria upon which to think about.

Euro-American New Testament scholar Matthew Bates speaks about "faith" as explained in the apostolic writings[43] as allegiance or faithfulness to God.[44] This of course includes a certain kind of belief in the existence of the person or thing to which you have given your allegiance and pledged your faithfulness to. If you don't believe in the existence of your wife, for instance, how could you give your allegiance and

---

41. Ya'eqob, "Book of the Trinity," 402. Emphasis added.
42. Gregory of Nazianzus, *On God and Christ*, 121.
43. I.e., the New Testament.
44. For more on faith as allegiance, see Bates, *Salvation by Allegiance Alone* and *Gospel Allegiance*.

faithfulness to her? But even in this example asking whether or how your spouse exists is kind of a moot question, a missing of the point. Biblical faith or belief assumes the existence of God, but it's not the focus of biblical faith and belief. Faithfulness, trust, and allegiance to God is. "For at its core, the word *faith* and its cognates, in all the various languages with which we have been dealing here, means fidelity and loyalty."[45] So while you may wrestle on an existential level with whether your wife is a figment of your imagination or part of a computer simulation developed by our machine overlords, the real object of your relationship, the one that determines if you're a good husband, is your faithfulness and loyalty to your wife, despite any doubts you may have about her existence.

Of course, Trinitarian belief or faith has always been part of the fabric of the Christian church, even before the creeds, as seen in our baptism formulas of Father, Son, and Holy Spirit for instance. In that way the Trinity is foundational to our DNA as the people of God, because it's what has been the case for two thousand years. It's also foundational since God is Love and we as Messiah's people are called to imitate the Trinity by embodying that Love. Love as understood in Trinitarian terms is about laying down your life for the other. It's not self-centered, and therefore it's not individualistic and requires more than one person. If God was simply one person or even two, God could not be Love. Yet since God is three persons fully united as one God, God is Love.

In each virtuous and loving thought, word, and deed we perform, we not only participate with this God but we also incarnate the Father's Word, who is Messiah, in and through our bodies. And that is what we as the church are; we are an incarnation of Messiah, which is why Paul calls us his "body." The confession of the Trinity every Sunday, as we do in most Christian traditions, isn't complete without embodying the Trinity in our thoughts, words, and deeds. If we simply recite the creed and then go out of the church's building and hate our neighbor in thought, word, and deed, either by ignoring their needs or intentionally going out of our way to hurt them, we do not truly confess or believe in the God of Israel described in the creeds. Harkening back to Vladimir Lossky's quote, "*we must live the dogma* expressing a reveled truth, which appears to us as an unfathomable mystery . . ."[46] Our orthodoxy is not a dusty old irrelevant list of doctrines of mere rational assent, but something foundational to

---

45. Pelikan, *Credo*, 303.
46. Lossky, *Mystical Theology of the Eastern Church*, 8–9.

who we are and how we live our lives as followers of Yeshua Messiah, our one and only true King. We must live in and out of the Trinity, allowing our bodies to be conduits and incarnated flesh for this God who is Love. In summary, we in the West should reclaim the more correct and full definition of orthodoxy as right allegiance and right worship/action.

To whom should we go? To where will we find another Messiah to lead us into the kingdom to come? For you alone are worthy of our sole allegiance. To you we pledge our lives and trust that we may rest in the warm intimate embrace of your strong heart.

5

What Do I Do with the Bible?

Other books you can try to account for, but an attempt to explain the Bible is a supreme opportunity to become ridiculous.[1]

ABRAHAM JOSHUA HESCHEL (ASHKENAZI JEW)

I ONCE FOUND MYSELF in a conversation with a friend from seminary who, like me and many of you reading this, comes from a fundamentalist background. During that conversation she confided to me, "I don't know what to do with the Bible anymore," a line that too many of us have come to find ourselves saying. It's not that the Bible did anything wrong,[2] but the theology around the Bible, namely a theology that amounted to the Bible being our God, has in combination with Northern European biblical scholarship[3] and surrounding perspectives from the rest of modernity left us with a God full of holes, one sinking to the bottom of the ocean like that so-called invincible ship called the Titanic.[4]

1. Heschel, *God in Search of Man*, 241.
2. Some of us may think the Bible did something wrong, but I am convinced that's not the best or most helpful way to think about it, and even might have some anti-Jewish sentient behind it.
3. I understand both the historical-grammatical model advocated for by Fundamentalists and the historical-critical method to be more or less two sides of the same coin, both being Northern European modernist readings of the Bible.
4. I wonder if we should be surprised that the German reading of the Jewish Scriptures has in a very real sense tried to dismantle and destroy those Jewish Scriptures.

In light of all this I'm going to attempt to answer the question, "What do we do with the Bible?" In doing so I risk, as Heschel pointed out, becoming ridiculous. To try to address the question I'll first start by looking at how fundamentalists make the Bible synonymous with God, then lead into a discussion about how different kinds of reading create different Bibles. After this I'll briefly make the case that the allegorical or figural reading of Scripture has been the dominant one throughout the church's history. Then we'll look at what the Bible is and is not, and how that shapes how we read it. Lastly I'll end by giving an example of what reading Scripture in light of everything we've discussed looks like.

The Leather-Bound God

There are many contemporary and past fundamentalists who exemplify this identification of the modernist Bible with God, one of which is the Euro-American Southern Baptist Matthew Barrett: He writes, "It is clear that for Jesus, *God and Scripture can be spoken of synonymously*, demonstrating that Scripture *is* the very Word of God. We should not attempt to drive a wedge between the two."[5] For Barrett and others like him Scripture and God are one and the same, to the point there seems to be an implied fourth member of the Trinity. The Euro-American Steven J. Lawson, one of the twenty-three contributors to *The Inerrant Word*, in his chapter "Inerrancy and the Power of Scripture," seems to gesture in this direction while discussing the nature of truth and its relationship to the Trinity. There he wrote, "Scripture tells us that God is the 'God of truth' (Ps. 31:5). The Son of God is 'the truth' (John 14:6). The Spirit of God is 'the Spirit of truth' (John 14:17). *The Word of God 'the word of truth'* (2 Cor. 6:7). *Everything about God*—his nature, his person, and his Word—is truth. *There is no disjunction between God and truth.*"[6] Notice that Scripture, what Lawson calls "the Word of God," is included with God's person and nature. By speaking of the Trinity while simultaneously adding a fourth object or *person*, understood under the category of "everything about God," he ends up using a quadripartite formula to speak of the Godhead. The logic of his statement leads us to the following

---

Should we have expected anything else? Especially given the fact nineteenth-century German scholarship was extremely racist more generally and more specifically anti-Jewish.

5. Barrett, *God's Word Alone*, 243–44. Emphasis added.
6. Lawson, "Invincible Word," 320. Emphasis added.

conclusion: if God the Father, the Son, the Holy Spirit and the Bible are all truth, and there is no disjunction or disunion between God and truth, Scripture therefore must be God alongside the three persons of the Trinity. Without explicitly stating it, he adds a fourth member to the Trinity.

In addition to Barrett and Lawson, Euro-American pastor John MacArthur himself writes, "God is so closely linked to his Word that, in some passages, the term *Scripture* is even synonymous with the name *God*."[7] This is all reminiscent of *The Fundamentals: A Testimony to the Truth*, the foundational text for the early fundamentalist movement. As we saw with Barrett, Lawson, and Macarthur, so we see in *The Fundamentals*; Scripture is so closely identified with God that there is little to no separation between the two. To speak of one is to speak of the other. The Euro-American Evangelist Munhall, one of the contributors to *The Fundamentals*, writes about this equality of Scripture with God, saying there is an *"identification of God with the 'Scripture,'* ('the Scripture foreseeing,' giving to it eyes, mouth and foreknowledge, *as a living organism equal with God*)."[8] A few pages later he elaborates more on this subject: "Jesus is the life and the light of man. The same is true of the Scriptures. Jesus said: 'The words that I speak unto you, they are spirit, and they are life.' The Psalmist said, 'Thy Word is a lamp unto my feet, and a light unto my path.' *In an inexplicable way Jesus is identified with the Word.* 'The Word was God . . . and the Word became flesh.'"[9] Note in this passage the Bible takes on many of God's own attributes because it is understood to be God's Word and therefore indistinguishable with God's own nature. Indeed, Munhall goes so far as to say Scripture is equal with God, and Yeshua and the Bible are identical. It's no wonder that as my faith in the Northern European modernist Bible (rather than the Bible of the Church) came crashing down around me I struggled with the very real possibility of losing my faith in Yeshua.

This kind of theology we grew up with ties Yeshua to the metaphorical boat. So, when holes appear in the boat and it begins to sink, Yeshua, whom we've chained to the boat, is dragged down with it. But it's not just that Yeshua is tied to the Bible, but as we will see more specifically, he's tied to the Modernist German version of the Bible. The risk from all this

---

7. MacArthur, "Introduction," 16. If anyone has been paying attention in the book you may remember in chapter 3 I wrote I had not read any of John Macarthur, that's now changed as you can see.

8. Munhall, "Inspiration," 50. Emphasis added.

9. Munhall, "Inspiration," 59. Emphasis added.

is to potentially lose our faith, which is so precious to many of us, so life-giving. And even if we don't lose our faith in Messiah, we're still left with a Northern European Enlightenment Bible full of holes at the bottom of the ocean. Growing up with a leather-bound Northern European god and subsequently encountering that less-than-perfect German Bible left me with the very real possibility of losing my Jewish friend, Savior, and King, Yeshua.

Your Reading of Scripture Is Scripture.

After being colonized to read the Bible as the Germans and Northern Europeans would have us read it, rather than as the church would, we subsequently have so identified the Northern European modernist Bible with God that when the imperfections of said Bible and its sheer humanness become clear, we are at risk of losing our faith in God. But over the years I've come to learn, experience, and intuit the reality that God and the Bible, whether the German Bible or the church's Bible, are two very different things, and yet the church's Scripture and God are sacramentally connected even if distinct.[10] To reject the distinction between God and the Bible is tantamount to the heresy of rejecting the Trinity. The imperfection of the Northern European Endarkenment Bible does not equate to the imperfection of God. But the question I've been seriously hinting at and the one we should be asking, but are not because of white normativity and colonial tactics is: When we say the Bible is imperfect, what do we mean by "the Bible"? What reading of the Bible, and therefore what Bible, are we assuming? Are we assuming a literal historical reading, namely an Enlightenment Northern European reading? Is that the reading of Scripture we're talking about when we say the Bible is imperfect? And if so, why is it *that Bible*, when for most of church history and most of contemporary Christianity that has not been the Christian Bible?

To be perfectly clear, what I'm saying is that the Bible we have is not, in a real sense, the same Bible as that of the church. These are two different Bibles. Our Bible is the product of the Northern European Enlightenment. As modernists who believe in "objectivity," and as dualists

---

10. When I use the phrase "the church's Scripture," I do not mean this to imply that the Jewish Scriptures once belonged to Israel but now belong to the gentile church. For the church lives, moves, and has its being in the womb of Israel. If the Scriptures belong to the church, it is because the church belongs to Israel, and is saved through Israel, since Yeshua himself proclaims that salvation is from the Jews.

who need to separate reality into various categories, we see the text of Scripture as categorically divorced from the *reading* of Scripture and its liturgical context,[11] as if the text and its exegesis are two separate things. However, in much of the church, including the Roman Catholic, Eastern Orthodox, and early church, Scripture is not separate from tradition because the reading of Scripture is found in the context of the church; it's tradition and the rule of faith is never set apart from the text.[12] Said differently, the particular Christian way of reading Scripture and the church context in which we read it is not distinct from Christian Scripture, but is in fact Scripture itself. The text, its exegesis, and it's liturgical context are not distinct objects but together are Scripture.

Yet if we are to avoid driving a wedge between tradition and Scripture, we will have to know what we mean when we say "tradition."[13] According to English Eastern Orthodox bishop Kallistos Ware, "It means the books of the Bible; it means the Creed; it means the decrees of the Ecumenical Councils and the writings of the Fathers;[14] it means the Canons, the Service Books, the Holy Icons—in fact, the whole system of doctrine, Church governance, worship, spirituality and art which Orthodoxy has articulated over the ages."[15] As I interpret this, I include all of what Bishop Kallistos says—the Scriptures, church governance, canons, art, and so forth—but all of that as it exists in the one, holy, catholic, and apostolic church; that is, the fullness of the universal church, not just the Eastern Orthodox tradition, but also Protestants, various kinds of Catholics, Syriac Orthodox, Ethiopian Orthodox, Coptic Orthodox, the Church of the East, and so forth.[16] Yet while we should be faithful to

---

11. I realize we're technically in the postmodern age in the West, but I think in many ways we're still modernists.

12. *Dei verbum*, the official statement on Scripture from the Second Vatican Council, says, "Sacred tradition and Sacred Scripture form one sacred deposit of the word of God, committed to the Church. Holding fast to this deposit the entire holy people united with their shepherds remain always steadfast in the teaching of the Apostles . . ." Paul VI, "Dogmatic Constitution on Divine Revelation."

13. Of course, there are lots of different definitions of "tradition" even within, say, just the Roman Catholic Church. This is how I understand tradition.

14. I would add here the church mothers.

15. Ware, *Orthodox Church*, 190.

16. I would not include as part of the universal church groups such as the Church of Jesus Christ of Latter-Day Saints (better known as Mormons, although they usually don't prefer that term), Jehovah Witnesses, Oneness Pentecostals, white Christian nationalists, and any group that denies the central tenets of the Christian way, which I outlined in chapters 2 and 4.

transmit this tradition and inheritance unhindered into the future, and refuse to see Scripture outside of tradition, it's also of utmost importance to realize not all aspects of this received inheritancea are equal in value. There is a unique preeminence that belongs to the rule of faith, the creeds (which are in various forms part of the rule of faith), the doctrinal definitions of the ecumenical councils, and the Scriptures.

Furthermore, Scripture is not independent of tradition because while ". . . Christians are People of the Book, the Bible is the Book of the People; it must not be regarded as something set up *over* the Church, but as something that lives and is understood *within* the Church . . ."[17] The church and Israel ultimately is the one by which the Bible derives its authority (in a secondary sense), since it's the body of Messiah who has over time decided what is Scripture and what is not, and it's the church and Israel alone that has any sort of legitimate ability to have normative or authoritative interpretations of Scripture.

In contrast to the ancient understanding of Scripture carried forward across millennia by multiple church traditions, the modernist Protestant view of the text as its own distinct entity divorced from ecclesial readings is a distinctly modern Northern European way of looking at the Scriptures. During a conversation with Father John Behr, he said to my wife and me, "The Gospel is an allegorical reading of Scripture in the light of the Cross, reading it now to understand and proclaim the eternal Word."[18] In other words, the Christian Scripture and the gospel, if you will, are deeply connected to that particular allegorical reading of the text, which is not independent from the text; it is simply Christian Scripture. So when you have a new reading that departs from that general allegorical reading of the Bible, you have in a sense a new Bible. A wholly different reading produces a different text.[19] The Northern European reading of the Bible, like the Bible of the church and Israel, cannot be dualistically divorced from the text itself and as such is a different Bible entirely.

So why then does Northern Europe get to replace the church and Israel's Bible with its own novel one? To answer that question bluntly

17. Ware, *Orthodox Church*, 193.

18. John Behr in person, used with permission. As suggested by Father Behr, see Behr, "Reading Scripture."

19. This does not mean every single different reading of a particular section of Scripture produces a new Scripture. There may legitimately be various readings or interpretations of the same text, if they all fit within the general contours of the Christian reading through the rule of faith. For a brief background on how different readings of Scripture create different Bibles, see Kugel, *How to Read the Bible*, 672.

if not provocatively, the historical-critical Bible has been the dominate Scripture both in and outside the academy not because it's self-evidently superior but because it's a product of the colonial powers of Northern Europe, who because of their belief in their racial superiority see whatever they produce as being inherently superior and therefore what everyone everywhere must ascribe too. Colonial ideology legitimates the discarding of the traditional way of reading Scripture in favor of a modernist Northern European one. This I think largely explains much of the visceral reaction that comes from questioning the historical-critical Bible, because it decenters the white colonial project, thereby threatening their position of power.

I do suspect that the German way of reading Scripture can in some way be used. It may be that the master's tools can be used to dismantle the house he has built. But given that historical criticism was born out of modernity as a product of coloniality, if we are too use it—not as the primary or Christian way to read Scripture, but as a supplemental method that helps us reclaim premodern ways of reading and being in the world—then hard work must be done to delink it from its colonial parentage.[20] Or rather it would need to be reborn, not from the false self of its German parentage but from the true self of its German parentage. In other words, the Germans would need to give up their false self, embrace their true self, and then rebirth the historical-critical method. When the Germans and other Northern European peoples right the wrongs they've committed over the centuries, seeking to embrace their true selves, they will need to determine whether the historical-critical method of reading Scripture is part of their false self as Northern Europeans or their true self that aids in fulfilling their call from God to express his image uniquely in the way in which God has called them to. But that is a project of repentance they will have to do with the voices of those they've oppressed.

To frankly and succinctly sum up the point of this section: *the Bible of liberal Protestants and fundamentalists is not the Christian Scripture of*

---

20. "Modernity, of course, is not a decolonial concept, but coloniality is. Coloniality is constitutive, not derivative, of modernity. That is to say, there is no modernity without coloniality, thus the compound expression: *modernity/coloniality* . . . Decolonially speaking, modernity/coloniality are intimately, explicitly, and complicitly entwined. The end of modernity would imply the end of coloniality, and, therefore, decoloniality would no longer be an issue. This is the ultimate decolonial horizon." Mignolo and Walsh, *On Decoloniality*, 3–4. Any exegetical method that is born out of modernity is thus built on the structure and matrix of colonialism. In this way, as historical-criticism is a modernist reading, so it is also a colonial reading.

the one, holy, catholic, and apostolic church. In much of the West it is allowed, assumed, and empowered to displace the Bible of the church and Israel because they have the colonial power to do so.

The Allegorical Bible Is the Scripture of the Church

Now, if the historical-critical method produces a different Bible, then what has been Christian Scripture? For that we turn to the third-century Egyptian Origen, who wrote, "There is one mind throughout the entire church about this, that *the* whole *law is* indeed *spiritual.*"[21] What he's saying is that all of the church believes Scripture to have a second meaning, a spiritual, figurative, typological, or allegorical nature or however else scholars try to distinguish and categorize the secondary sacramental meaning of Scripture.[22] But it's not just that it has a spiritual or allegorical sense, but that being allegorical is part of its nature. I have found Origen's statement to be true whether its Augustine were looking at, or Cyprian, or the supposedly literal school of interpreters from Antioch;[23] whether the Syriac Orthodox, the Coptic Orthodox, the Ethiopian Orthodox, or the fourteenth-century Greek Orthodox theologian Gregory of Palamas. Speaking on this topic in the introduction to *The Harp of Glory*, an Ethiopian poem from roughly the fifteenth century, UK Eastern Orthodox patristics scholar John Anthony McGuckin writes,

> A modern reader, used to interpreting the Bible according to its sequential narrative content, and its historical or ethical significances, is singularly ill-equipped to realize that throughout the

---

21. Origen, *On First Principles*, 9.

22. The terms for this secondary meaning of Scripture are often varied and there is argument over whether or not they represent different methods, such as the argument of whether there is a difference between the typological and allegorical method. I think not; I think it's more helpful to simply see the second spiritual meaning as the unveiled meaning, the sacramental meaning if you will.

23. Modern biblical scholars trained in the historical-critical or modern method of reading the Bible, whether liberal Protestants or Fundamentalists, will often, when discussing the methods of interpretation of the early church, try to make the case that there were camps of literalist interpreters of Scripture, distinguishing between the supposedly literalist Antiochians and the Alexandrians, who represented the more allegorical readers. I would suggest the possibility that this exercise, if you will, has more to do with the discomfort that the German exegetical colonial project feels because it cannot be supported historically in real communities of exegesis than it does with any evidence to the contrary. Having no part of the early church involved in the kind of white reading of Scripture we do threatens white supremacy.

> vast majority of Christian history this is *not* how the Bible was generally read ... the Ethiopian Church read its sacred scriptures typologically (and ... most of Christian Antiquity did so too).[24]

McGuckin's point here is that for most of church history and in still much of the world today the Scriptures are read with a spiritual sense residing underneath the literal surface. English scholar Sebastian Brock says much the same thing regarding the Syriac Christians:

> Early Syriac exegesis of the Bible was essentially typological ... Much of this typological exegesis will appear to modern readers as forced, or it may even be described as "wrong," but I think it misleading to speak of this kind of exegesis in absolute terms of "correct" and "incorrect." The very fact that quite often one finds side by side two pieces of typological exegesis which are logically incompatible when taken together, seems to be an indication that what is being offered was never meant to be "the correct exegesis," such as modern biblical scholarship likes to impose, but possible models which are held up, and whose purpose is to make meaningful, and give insight into, some aspects of a mystery that cannot be fully explained.[25]

Until the Northern Europeans of modernity broke from this broad exegetical commitment, this was among the global church more or less unanimous across culture, place, and time, and was even practiced by many of the Northern European Reformers.[26] They may have had various allegorical readings that differed across time, culture, and place with different emphases, but they all shared this basic allegorical-sacramental reading, which assumes there is a deeper Christian meaning residing beneath the surface of the literal text waiting to be unveiled by the glory of Messiah.

How Should We Approach the Bible?

Nevertheless, even if we come to understand that God and the Bible are not synonymous, because of our lack of exposure to ancient and Eastern ways of reading Scripture, we are often left with the question, "What do

24. McGuckin, "Introduction," 14–15.
25. Brock, "Introduction," 6–7.
26. For a survey of allegorical readings of Scripture within the Anglican tradition, see Radner and Ney, *All Thy Lights Combine*, although they use the term "figural" rather than "allegorical."

I do with the Bible?" Within the matrix of this Northern European modernist Bible, *we now know this Bible is but an imperfect human product*, and presupposing as we have that anything, imperfect, material, or human cannot be used by God, we are now left with a useless Bible. However, if only for future exploration, it's important to note the imperfection of the German Bible is not the same kind of imperfection of the Jewish Bible. If a different reading of Scripture produces a different Scripture, then it follows each Bible would carry with it different flaws. That's not to say the Bible of the church and Israel lacks imperfections, but the imperfections we see, namely those of the Northern European Bible, are a different set of imperfections than the Jewish Bible. Thus, when we are usually discussing the flaws of the Bible, we're discussing the wrong Bible and therefore the wrong flaws.[27] Although, I would strongly suggest the question of imperfections or "errors" is, at least as it is usually discussed today, a modern question that is boring, usually falls quickly into anti-Judaism, and misses the point of Scripture.

Yet even assuming the imperfections of the Jewish Bible, what the best of the Christian tradition has said since the beginning is that the imperfect, the material, and the human is exactly the locus of God's incarnational or sacramental activity. We seem to have forgotten the Lord's words to Paul in 2 Corinthians 12:9, "For power, in weakness is made complete."[28] If God's power is made complete in weakness, then why would we think Scripture, or rather the literal reading of Scripture, is anything other than weak? Do we dare say it is because we suppose that Scripture is strong, that God's power is not made complete in Scripture? Or maybe another way to think about this is to remember that true power is from the margins. Though Scripture, namely the faithful witness of Israel, is weak in the eyes of the world, yet in the eyes and power of God our people's witness may be proclaimed as strong. For what is strong

---

27. Before we can actually discuss those flaws we need to know that different Bible first, in order to know what the different set of flaws are. Up to this point many of us are still too unfamiliar with the church's Bible to be able to know its flaws. Yet even now I would still maintain the question of whether the Bible is inerrant is a question of modernity, and the wrong question. The Word of God, namely Yeshua Messiah, is Truth, and that true Word is faithfully witnessed too by Israel (and the church grafted into Israel) in, through, and by participation with that true Word, who in his faithfulness to Israel takes up their words to truthfully witness to himself, *the* true Word. Their witness becomes sacramentally his own body, by which he becomes visible to the gentiles and the whole world. The witness of Israel is faithful, but the question of the imperfection of that witness is a pointless distraction.

28. My translation.

to the world is weakness to God, and what is weakness to the world is power to God.

The world, although broken, is good; the material realm, God's chosen means for salvific presence and healing action. As God became a Jewish human, so we are shown that the material has always been the incarnational vehicle of our God. Or as the church father Irenaeus said, "the vessel of the workings of God, and of all his wisdom and power is the human being."[29] Here also is the imperfect, material, and literal level of the Jewish Christian Scriptures picked up as the incarnational and sacramental instrument out of which we encounter that eternal Word enfleshed as a Jewish body, spoken by the Father and mediated by the Holy Spirit. The Scriptures are a sacrament in which the material, the human, meets with the Divine, and they are intertwined in a joyous and hopeful dance.

The human, imperfect, and material literal level of either the modernist Bible or the church and Israel's Bible need not be the end of our faith, since our faith was always meant to be in the person of Yeshua, not the church's book in and of itself; and it need not be an end to the usefulness of the Jewish Christian Bible. Just as Paul once wrote that every knee shall bow and tongue confess that Yeshua Messiah is Lord to the glory of God the Father, so too does the Bible bend its pages to the lordship of Messiah and confess that Yeshua alone is the Jewish King of all creation. So let us give up our leather-bound German god for the true Jewish Lord and King; and in the end we will find that in so doing we are given the Church's Bible, in its rightful place as the faithful witness of Israel and as a sacrament of our friend and God, Yeshua Messiah.

The Word of God Called; He Wants His Throne Back

I think part of our issue in modern fundamentalism, and the wider culture that believes this small stream of Christianity to be representative of the whole, is our misreading of 2 Timothy 3:16. "All Scripture is God-breathed and useful toward teaching, toward reproof, toward restoration of the good, toward training in righteousness, in order that the person of God may be made complete, toward all good works, as one made fully equipped."[30] In fundamentalism and readings influenced by

---

29. Irenaeus, quoted in Behr, *Mystery of Christ*, 103.
30. My translation.

fundamentalism, the compound word *theopneustos*, translated here as "God-breathed," is often understood to mean "That the Bible is the very Word of God."[31] Yet the text does not say "all scripture is God's Word"; this is an imposition of Northern European fundamentalist theology, often genuine and heartfelt, but an imposition, nonetheless. It does say it's "God-breathed," but we will come back to that.

Moreover, when none of the first Christians understood it this way, we should be suspect of such a reading. The German-Russian, British-raised, Eastern Orthodox priest John Behr, probably one of the best contemporary scholars of early Christianity, once wrote, "for the authors of the New Testament, and those whose work resulted in these writings being collected together [the Church Fathers and Mothers], the expression 'the Word of God' did not refer to scripture, as it is often assumed today, but to Jesus Christ himself and the gospel proclaiming him, the crucified and exalted one, as Lord."[32] In fact, even many modern Christians have not understood this passage to be teaching that the Bible is the Word of God. The German Reformer Martin Luther did not believe the Bible was the Word of God; nor did George Fox, George MacDonald, Karl Barth, or C. S. Lewis. Furthermore, the Eastern Orthodox tradition does not believe this either. All these people believe Yeshua, not the Bible, is the Word of God.[33]

---

31. MacArthur, "Introduction," 16.
32. Behr, *Mystery of Christ*, 50.
33. Justo González writes of Martin Luther's view, "The Bible itself declares that, strictly speaking, the Word of God is none other than God the Son, the Second Person of the Trinity, the Word who was made flesh and dwelt among us . . . Given this biblical understanding of the Word of God, what makes the Bible the word of God is not that it is infallible, nor that it can serve as a source of authority for theological and religious debate. The Bible is the Word of God because in it Jesus, the Word incarnate, comes to us. Any who read the Bible and somehow do not find Jesus in it, have not encountered the Word of God . . . Final authority rests neither in the church nor in the Bible, but in the gospel, in the message of Jesus Christ, who is the incarnate Word of God." González, *Story of Christianity*, 2:30–31. Luther developed his doctrine of *sola Scriptura* not because he believed the Bible was in itself the Word of God, but because he believed that tradition had been corrupted in his day and therefore Scripture was a more trustworthy witness to the Word of God. Eastern Orthodox Stanley Samuel Harakas, responding to the question "Is the Bible the Word of God?" from the perspective of the Orthodox, writes, "So it is essentially wrong, in the final analysis, to ask if the Word of God is a book, or if it is found in a book or within the text of a book. The Bible itself and the Tradition of Faith in the Church respond to another question. That question is: 'WHO is the Word of God?' The Word of God is a person: Jesus Christ! (John 1:1–5)." Harakas, *Orthodox Christian Beliefs*, 3. The German Hildegard also held this view of who the Word is: "for the Word, Who is the Son of God . . ." Hildegard, *Hildegard of Bingen*,

Origen once wrote that there are not two words of God, but one! When speaking about the word of the Lord that came to Isaiah, Ezekiel, and Jeremiah, Origen in his *Homilies of Jeremiah* wrote about who is that word that came to "Ezekiel or anyone except the one 'in the beginning with God?' *I do not know any 'word' of the Lord other than the one concerning whom the Evangelist said, 'The Word was in the beginning, and the Word was with God and the Word was God.'*"[34] The same Word that came to the Jewish prophets was not a book, but a person, namely the second person of the Trinity. The French Roman Catholic Henri de Lubac in his book about Origen writes, "there are not two Words any more than there are two Spirits."[35] For de Lubac, as for Origen before him, there are not two words of God, but one, namely the eternally begotten Son of God, who took on Jewish flesh.[36] When we encounter the Word of God in Scripture, it is this same Word of God who walked around Galilee and Judea two thousand years ago, and now embodies the church.

The Ethiopian theologian King Zar'a Ya'eqob, in his *Book of the Trinity*, writing in response to the heresy that claimed there were three words of God, says, "The Word of the Father and of the Holy Spirit is the Son, and that speaking one speaks from himself where he wants. It is not called two words or three words but one Word, who is the Son."[37] There is a confusion in our culture, namely, that there are either two words of God or three words of God. In the first case there is a spoken word and a written word. In the latter case, the third word is Yeshua, and sometimes Yeshua the Word and Scripture the Word are somehow the same thing. All of these options are insufficient, because they make something other than the second person of the Godhead the Word, synonymous with God. The Word of God is one of the three divine persons of the Trinity, unambiguously the one who took on Jewish flesh through his mother

---

359. British Quaker Caroline Stephen wrote in 1891, "I believe the doctrine of Fox and Barclay (i.e., briefly, that the 'Word of God' is Christ, not the Bible, and that the Scriptures are profitable in proportion as they are read in the same spirit which gave them forth) to have been a most valuable equipoise to the tendency of other Protestant sects to transfer the idea of infallibility from the Church to the Bible." Stephen, *Quaker Strongholds*.

34. Origen, quoted in Blaski, "Fleshing Out Christ," 30. Emphasis added.

35. Lubac, *History and Spirit*, 385.

36. Origen says something similar in his commentary on the Gospel of John: "The complete Word of God which was in the beginning with God is not a multitude of Words, for it is not words. It is a single Word . . ." Origen, *Commentary on John*, 163.

37. Ya'eqob, "Book of the Trinity," 402–5.

the virgin Mary, died on a cross, rose from the dead, and ascended to the Father; he should not be mistaken as anyone or anything else.

But then what does 2 Timothy 3:16 say if not that the Bible is God's Word? The way biblical scholars, literary scholars, or even everyday people determine the meaning of a word is its use. For scholars they look at the use in both the passage in question and the broader literature of the time. So when engaging with the word *theopneustos* (translated as "God-breathed") in 2 Timothy 3:16, scholars look to see if the word is used anywhere else in this epistle, the New Testament corpus, the broader Jewish literature of the time, and the contemporary Greco-Roman literature. The issue we run into after doing all this searching seems to be that the word is found nowhere else. It seems as if the author of 2 Timothy 3:16 invented the word, which at least at first leaves us little course of action to determine its meaning. When pastors, scholars, and whoever else from the fundamentalist tradition declare the meaning of *theopneustos* as abundantly clear, they either do not know what they're talking about or they are ignoring the evidence to uphold their heartfelt worship of the Bible.

The first place outside of the Jewish New Testament where we find this word used is among the church fathers of the second through fifth centuries and so on, with a possible exception found in Clement of Rome, writing in the late first century, roughly contemporary to the writing of the Gospel according to John. This means that if we want to understand what this word means, we need to take seriously how the church fathers used this term and concept. And as we briefly saw above, they did not use it as a term synonymous with the Word of God. Instead it was used to refer to Greek philosophers such as Plato; by bishops like Clement of Rome, who used it to speak of his own writings; in the writings of church fathers, such as when Gregory of Nyssa claimed his brother's commentary on Genesis was inspired; and in reference to the decisions of councils, anchorites, and so on.

Yet when we ignore the historical-critical method and go back to the ancient understanding of the Scriptures, we can also find the meaning of *theopneustos* illuminated in the Scriptures. Within the framework of ancient Christian interpretation it was understood and assumed that because the Word of God, namely the Messiah, was present in the text, all of its words and concepts, no matter how seemingly disconnected, were in reality united together through a web of connected meaning rooted in that risen Word of God present and saturated in and throughout the text. So a word that was used in multiple books or passages of the Bible signified to the reader through that web of interconnected meaning that one passage could be understood in light of the other passage in which that same word occurred. This is the rule known as "Scripture interprets Scripture."

Taking our cue from our fathers and mothers and using the principle of Scripture interpretating Scripture, we can look to the following passages as interconnected and therefore shedding light on the meaning of one another: 2 Timothy 3:16, the creation of Adam in Genesis 2, and the Wisdom of Solomon, all of which speak about God's breath, and although Matthew 5:17 doesn't refer to the breath of God, it does refer to the filling of the Messiah, which is what the breathe of God does, and thus all of these passages can be seen as interconnected and shining light on what it means for the Bible to be inspired. The author of 2 Timothy seems to be pointing us back to the creation of Adam, where God creates Adam in two parts. Genesis 2:7 in the Septuagint reads, "And God formed the human being from the soil of the earth and he breathed into his face the breath of life, and the human being became a living life."[38] The first part of God's creation of Adam is the formation of the man from the dust of the earth. Notice in this part Adam is still not a living being. Only from the second part of his creation, when God *breathes into his face a breath of life*, does he become animated as a living creature.

The author of 2 Timothy 3:16 does not say Scripture is "God-formed"; the author says it is "God-breathed." If we take this to be a connection that either the author of 2 Timothy is making or that the present divine Word wishes us to make, we can understand the Scriptures as created not by God but by humans, and yet when read rightly it is also breathed on by God and as a result is brought to life. This view does not denigrate the Scriptures simply because they were made by humans. Remember, God declared creation, including humans, to be good, and in creating us in the image of God tasked us with the vocation to create.[39] So simply because humans, specifically Jewish humans, formed the Scriptures does not mean the Scriptures are bad or unvaluable.[40]

Now keep in mind that the Gospel according to John says in 14:6 that Messiah is the way, the truth, *and the life*. So, when God breathes the breath *of Life* into Adam and subsequently into the Scriptures, it is Yeshua who is breathed into Adam and the Scriptures by the Holy Spirit. Human

---

38. My translation.

39. In the Genesis story Adam is given the creative task of naming the animals.

40. To believe the Scriptures are not valuable or that they are bad because they are made by humans is more Gnostic than Christian.

beings and the Scriptures are both incomplete until Yeshua is breathed into them, but unlike our initial creation, God partners with us in the completion of creating the Scriptures. We the Jewish people formed them and God breathed into them, thus bringing them to life. The Wisdom of Solomon, a writing the early church considered to be Scripture, and which is still considered Scripture outside of Protestantism, in speaking about the figure of Wisdom, whom the church identifies as the Word and Son, says,

> For wisdom moves more freely than any movement; she pervades and penetrates all things because of her pureness. *For she is a breath of the power of God* and an emanation of the pure glory of the Almighty . . . For she is a reflection of eternal light and a spotless mirror of the activity of God and an image of his goodness.[41]

Now if Scripture is God-breathed, who is the breath of God? According to the *Wisdom of Solomon* the answer is Wisdom, otherwise known to the early church as Yeshua. Yeshua, the Word, Son, and Wisdom of God, is the *breath of the power of God*.

Next we need to look at Yeshua's statement in Matthew 5:17, particularly considering Origen's commentary on the passage. In Matthew's version of the Sermon on the Mount, Yeshua declares, "Do not suppose that I came to destroy the Torah or the Prophets; I came not to destroy but to fill."[42] In the Syriac-English New Testament and the NRSV of this passage, the word *plerosai* is rendered as "fulfill." Many translations in fact translate it as such. Origen, however, appears to think this word should be understood differently, or if not differently at least that it has a double meaning. And this shines a whole *old* light on how we should understand 2 Timothy 3:16, specifically in conversation with Genesis 2:7—an interpretation that takes Yeshua at his word, namely, that he didn't come to destroy the Jewish tradition. In Origen's commentary on Matthew, speaking metaphorically about Scripture as a net, he writes, "And before our Saviour Jesus Christ *this net* was not *wholly filled*; for the net of the law and the prophets had to be completed by Him who says, *'Think not that I came to destroy the law and the prophets, I came not to destroy but to fulfil.'"*[43] The lexical form of the word behind "fulfill" in Matthew 5:17

---

41. Wisdom of Solomon 7:24–26 (NETS). Emphasis added.
42. My translation.
43. Origen, *Commentary on Matthew*.

can also mean "to make full of" or "to fill," which seems to be how Origen is taking its meaning here in his commentary, since he says before the coming of Messiah, "this net [Scripture] was not wholly *filled*," by which he proceeds to cite Matthew 5:17.[44]

If we take Origen's direction on this, we can translate this passage from the sermon on the mount as such: "Do not suppose that I came to abolish the Torah or the Prophets; I did not come to abolish *but to fill*."[45] Notice from this perspective, given what we said above, Yeshua as God is coming alongside the Jewish authors of Scripture, not negating their creation, but partnering with them to complete their creative project by filling it with himself. Translating this passage to say he didn't come to abolish but to "fulfill" can imply that Yeshua came to finish the task begun by the Torah and Prophets and therefore they can now be set aside as something that was good but has fulfilled its role and is no longer relevant. However, our translation above, influenced by Origen, implies a continued role and use of the Scriptures, rather than being something that can now be discarded because it's job is done. In light of our conversation on Genesis 2:7, we see Yeshua has come to fill Scripture sacramentally or incarnationally with his own presence. He honors what they have made by filling it with his own sacramental presence. Or to borrow language from Origen, he is the honey for which the honeycomb (the Torah and Prophets) was made to be filled with. In Origen's *Homily on Leviticus* he gives further credence to this sacramental filling when he writes,

> As "in the Last Days," the Word of God, which was clothed with the flesh of Mary, proceeded into this world. What was seen in him was one thing; what was understood was something else. For the sight of his flesh was open for all to see, but the knowledge of his divinity was given to the few, even the elect. *So also, when the Word of God was brought to humans through the Prophets and the Lawgiver, it was not brought without proper clothing. For just as there it was covered with the veil of flesh, so here with the veil of the letter*, so that indeed the letter is seen as flesh but the spiritual sense hiding within is perceived as divinity.[46]

---

44. Origen may have both meanings in mind, but at the very least he seems to understand "to fill" as one of the meanings.

45. My translation.

46. Origen, *Homilies on Leviticus*, 29. Emphasis added.

In other words, Messiah fills the Scripture, in its fullest sense, by being the one who takes on "the veil of the letter" as a kind of body.[47] The letter of Scripture created by the Jewish prophets is not dishonored or discarded by Yeshua's coming; rather it is honored by his taking it on as his own garment. In Judaism we have the concept of Heavenly Torah and Earthly Torah, and maybe the natural question arising from this is one the rabbis debated, namely to what extent does the Earthly Torah resemble the Heavenly Torah? As a Jewish Christian I understand the Heavenly Torah to be Yeshua the Messiah, the Son and Word of God.[48] While in gentile Christianity the figure of Wisdom becomes identified with Yeshua, in Judaism Wisdom became identified with the Torah. In addition, Judaism also understands the Heavenly Torah as the blueprint by which creation was made and even that which made and continues to sustain creation. In gentile Christianity it is Yeshua the Word who fulfills those roles as Wisdom and blueprint for creation. As a Jewish Christian I think we are speaking about the same thing. Rabbi Simeon once wrote, "Wine cannot be kept save in a jar; so the Torah needs an outer garment. These [the garments] are the stories and narratives, but it behooves us to penetrate beneath them."[49] Both Origen and Rabbi Simeon see this *thing, the Word, or the Heavenly Torah*, as taking on the stories, narratives, what is the letter of Torah or more generally the letter of Scripture, as a body,

---

47. In Origen's homilies on Isaiah, he uses the analogy of a honeycomb and the honey within it to describe Scripture. "'Go,' he says, 'to the bee, and learn how productive she is.' And the prophets are found to be bees, since indeed they fashion artfully the wax cells of the hives and make honey and, if, being bold, it is useful for me to say, their honeycombs are the Scriptures, which they have left behind . . . And perhaps the more simple letters are the honeycombs; but indeed he [Christ] is the honey, who in these [honeycombs] is understood." In other words, for Origen the honeycomb is symbolic for the literal meaning of Scripture, while the honey symbolically refers to Yeshua within the text, who serves as its allegorical meaning. Notice how he does not denigrate the work of the prophets, the honeycomb, or the literal level, but honors them in and of themselves, while also honoring them further by showing how they are adorned with the honey of Messiah. Origen, *Homilies on Isaiah*, 55–56.

48. It has been suggested to me, notably by non-Jews, that this notion of recognizing Yeshua as Heavenly Torah is supersessionist. As a Jewish Christian I wholeheartedly disagree. In reality, I think it's the other way around. If I as a Jew am not allowed to utilize my own Jewish theological heritage to understand my Jewish Messiah and therefore, being barred from my own Jewish heritage, must adopt gentile theological constructs to understand our Messiah, how is that not supersessionist!? Seeing Yeshua as Heavenly Torah is the opposite of supersessionism; it's seeing Yeshua in continuity with the Jewish tradition both before and after he walked around in Israel.

49. *Zohar*, quoted in Heschel, *God in Search of Man*, 267–68.

garment or clothing to encounter his people; in other words, they see it as an incarnation.[50]

Considering all this, we can understand *theopneustos* or "God-breathed" to mean that Messiah, who is the Life of God,[51] who is Heavenly Torah, the Word, Son, and Wisdom of God, God's very breathe, is breathed, or carried by the Holy Spirit, into the Scriptures. For Scripture to be inspired or God-breathed thus means Messiah, who alone is the Word of God, is spiritually and really incarnationally present throughout the Scriptures. St. Athanasius, speaking of this mystery, writes, "For no one else is found in the scriptures except the Savior common to all, the God Word, our Lord Jesus Christ."[52] He is their spiritual meaning; indeed, he is their true Christian meaning.[53] Without reference to him sacramentally present in the text, we are not reading Christian Scripture.

This brings us to an important distinction between where modernists locate inspiration and where the ancient Christians located it.[54] As John Behr put it so succinctly,

> For early Christians, this inspiration was not thought to reside solely within the text of scripture or in the mind of the inspired prophet as he uttered or wrote his words. If it were this, our task would then be to discern the "original meaning" of the text or the "mind of the author," ideas which are distinctively modern and which have been abandoned by recent literary theory.[55]

---

50. Origen elsewhere explicitly calls the narratival or literal meaning of Scripture the "body" of Scripture. What we see from his *Homilies on Leviticus* is that for Origen this body of Scripture, "the veil of the letter," serves as a garment for the Word himself. "[I]f I may speak thus, the very body of Scripture (for such do we term that common and narratival sense)." Origen, *On First Principles*, 252. In addition to Rabbi Simeon and Origen, such garment language is also found in St. Maximus and St. Ephrem. Speaking about the literal meaning of Scripture, Maximus writes, "For the Logos eludes the intellect which supposes that it has grasped the incorporeal Logos by means of His outer garments, like the Egyptian woman who seized hold of Joseph's garments instead of Joseph himself . . ." Maximus the Confessor, "Two Hundred Texts," 155. For a brief commentary on this concept in Ephrem, see Brock, *Luminous Eye*, 60–66.

51. John 14:6, "I am the way, and the truth, and the life." My translation.

52. Athanasius, *On the Incarnation*, 88.

53. Yet the Holy Spirit isn't just the one who breathes Yeshua into Scripture; she is the one who breathes Yeshua into us every day.

54. The ancient Christian locus of inspiration is still largely adhered to outside of the Protestant purview, although it is being reclaimed by many Protestants. Among Protestants it's often called the "theological interpretation of Scripture."

55. Behr, *The Mystery of Christ*, 64.

Instead, for the first Christians inspiration was found in its interpretation, an interpretation that turned upon the crucified and risen Messiah.[56] As Origen has said it, Messiah as sacramentally present in the Scriptures is their spiritual meaning enfleshed in the literal text. "The testimony of every Scripture concerning Messiah is a witness of Messiah."[57] And how can Scripture's testimony of Messiah be a witness of Messiah? Because as Origen writes, "The wisdom of God is in the Torah and the Prophets,"[58] and the wisdom of God *is Messiah*. Messiah himself, as himself, is present in Scripture, giving testimony of himself, as the spiritual sense of Scripture. Lordship indeed determines how we read or interpret the Scriptures, or anything for that matter. If our Lord is Messiah then we will read Scripture according to him, and if our Lord is history then we will read Scripture according to the rules and methods of history. When history is our Lord, we are in danger of being captured by the literal historical words, and we become in danger of missing the divine encounter with the Word, which is the sacramental point of Scripture.

Yet if the Bible is human as I said above, why not read it primarily historically? To answer this let's look at what the Swiss theologian Karl Barth says about the Bible: "even where it appeals expressly to divine commissionings and promptings, in its actual composition it is everywhere a human word, and this human word is obviously intended to be taken seriously and read and understood and expounded as such."[59] According to Barth, when we do take the reality seriously that the Bible is human, we also must attend to the reality "that as a human word it points away from itself, that as a word it points towards a fact, an object."[60] To linger too long on this human word is to risk missing that which the word is pointing us too. Only when we take the Bible seriously as a human word can we then accept the reality it is trying to tell us something. When

---

56. We in the West, particularly the post-enlightenment West, think of inspiration as happening to the text and its author in a historical moment in the past. But if we took the author of Timothy's metaphor seriously we see that breathing never stops, and it's always in the present moment. The Spirit of God, God's breathe, is continually breathing through the text, and doing so as the giver of Life, giving us Messiah in the text. If God merely breathed into Scripture once in the past, then the text is dead, for that which does not breath does not live. The text is only made alive when and if the Spirit is continuing to breath Messiah into the text here in the present moment as we seek Messiah in the text while the Spirit is breathing Messiah into us.

57. My translation. Origen, "Commentary on 1 Corinthians," 233.

58. My translation. Origen, "Commentary on 1 Corinthians," 237.

59. Barth, *Church Dogmatics: The Word of God Volume II*, 464.

60. Barth, *Church Dogmatics: The Word of God*, 464.

humans speak, it isn't simply for the sake of speaking but for the purpose of indicating something outside the words themselves.

Let's take an example: If I were crossing the street, and you, being the good person you are, saw a vehicle was soon to make roadkill out of me, but were too far for me to hear you, you might find yourself waving your arms and pointing towards the oncoming vehicle. If I were to mistakenly locate the meaning of your frantic arm waving in the form of the communication in and of itself, namely your waving arms, divorced from any external point of reference and meaning that the movement of your arms were trying to communicate, I would surely find myself quickly hit by the oncoming vehicle. While a historical-cultural contextual analysis of your method of communication, namely the waving of your arms, might be interesting and shed light on how your people in this time communicate and pass on meaning, if I got stuck there, I would actually miss the deeper, more important meaning. Your persistent communication through arm waving and pointing are meant to signify and indicate the truck that is going to hit me. The meaning in this case is not in the form of communication, the waving arms, but in the thing you are intending to witness too. Studying the form of communication from a historical-cultural method might eventually lead me to that, but not before I'm hit by the truck. Barth says it this way:

> If I were to . . . concern myself only with the word as such and the one who speaks it, how I should deceive myself! As far as I am concerned, he would have spoken in vain. We can speak meaningfully of hearing a human utterance only when it is clear to us in its function of indicating something that is described or intended by the word, and also when this function has become an event confronting us, when therefore by means of the human word we ourselves in some degree perceive the thing described or intended.[61]

That word is successful only to the extent that I've come to that which the word was intending me to see and encounter. And this is why in the case of our playful scenario above I died; because I failed to "perceive the thing described or intended." Getting caught up in the surface level without regard to the actual meaning below the surface is what got me killed. Of course, this doesn't negate the importance of the surface level, the waving arms as it were; those also are needed to embody the inner

---

61. Barth, *Church Dogmatics: The Word of God*, 464–65.

message that is intended for me to receive. Without the outer surface, the letter or body, there is nothing to contain the inner meaning. We need wine skin to hold the wine as it were. The very function of human words is to convey something outside of the words themselves, or said differently, they are meant to convey something external that is expressed internally to direct our attention externally.

Indeed, the *telos* of our speech as intended by God has a sacramental character to it. Ibn Ezra, a Jewish commentator, once wrote, "Know that the words are like bodies, and meanings like souls; and the body is a vessel for the soul."[62] Meaning is not found in the word itself but in the object to which the word is signaling us, an object that finds and makes its home in the word as body. Euro-American Catholic patristics scholar Jordan Daniel Wood gets at this when he writes, "Theology seeks revealed truth. And divine truth, who is the frolicsome Word playing in ten thousand places . . . *can surface in words whose original intent was not the fullness of that infinite Word—for all true words remain preeminently the Word's before any author's.*"[63] Meaning that words, speech, communication, indeed all material reality has been created with the intended function, goal, and end to be embodied and expressive of *the Word*, regardless of what its literal-authorial meaning may be. Similar to Barth, Origen understood Scripture as human in order to contrast it with a distinct object, the divine treasure, Messiah, found embodied within the text. In his work *On First Principles* he writes,

> . . . so neither is the divinity of Scripture, which extends to it all, annulled because our weakness cannot in every expression approach the hidden splendour of the teachings concealed in poor and humble language, *For we have a treasure in earthen vessels so that the transcendent power of God might shine forth and not be thought to be from us human beings.* For if it had been the hackneyed methods of demonstration used by human beings, laid up in books, that had prevailed over human beings, our *faith* might reasonably be supposed to rest *upon the wisdom of human beings* and not *upon the power of God* . . .[64]

"The hidden splendor" of the teachings Origen is referring to is the Messiah, who is "concealed in poor and humble" language for the purpose of

---

62. Ibn Ezra, quoted in Heschel, *God in Search of Man*, 277.
63. Wood, *Whole Mystery of Christ*, xvi. Emphasis added.
64. Origen, *On First Principles*, 243–44. Emphasis added.

shining forth God's power. But there is a second reason that the Scriptures are human:

> ... the Word of God has arranged that *stumbling blocks*, as it were, and *obstacles and impossibilities* be inserted into the midst of the Law and the narrative, in order that we may not be drawn away completely by the sheer attractiveness of the language and so we either completely reject the teachings, learning nothing worthy of God, or, not moving away from the letter, we learn nothing more divine.[65]

In other words, they are human, with all there "stumbling blocks," "obstacles and impossibilities" precisely so that we will not linger too long on the surface of the text, where the literal meaning is, but instead find ourselves going within the text to find Yeshua, the spiritual meaning, sacramentally present within the Scriptures. Not because human words are necessarily and always bad, but because all creations of human beings, especially Jewish humans, are meant to ultimately connect us with our Creator. After all, the incarnation was, through the womb of Mary, on her side of the deal, a Jewish creation intended for the purpose of connecting the world with our Creator. Maximus the Confessor writes, "a person who seeks God with true devotion should not be dominated by the literal text, lest he unwittingly receives not God but things appertaining to God; that is, lest he feel a dangerous affection for the words of Scripture instead of for the Logos [Word]."[66] These stumbling blocks, this use of human words, of earthen vessels to store the treasure of Messiah, is preciously for the purpose of creating a barrier to prevent us from falling into the idolatry of worshipping our own creation rather than the Creator.

Yet that's not to say all literal readings need to be thrown out. This is often the mistake made by self-identified progressive Christians. Again as we've seen throughout this book, the answer is often not either-or but both-and. But how do we determine whether to embrace the literal sense of the text or not? Origen shows us criteria for whether we can accept and read a particular passage of Scripture according to its literal level or if we need to dive deeper into the spiritual meaning. His criteria was a question: Is this worthy of God? Particularly, is this worthy of the God we worship that's described in the rule of faith? So what comprises this rule of faith? There were various renditions of the canon or rule of faith,

---

65. Origen, *On First Principles*, 261. Emphasis added
66. Maximus the Confessor, "Two Hundred Texts," 155.

but they all shared some overlapping elements. Each affirmed, in contrast with the Gnostics or with Marcion's theology that there is one God, who is good and just, who created all things good, both the spiritual realm and the material realm; that this one God was the same God worshipped by the Jews; that this God existed eternally as three persons, Father, Son, and Holy Spirit; that the second person of this triune God, the Son of God, who existed eternally as part of this divine community, entered into time and the material realm through the virgin Mary by becoming a Jewish human while remaining the divine Word, whom we call Yeshua the Messiah; and that he lived, suffered death on a cross, and three days later rose again and ascended into God's space. In other words, to the orthodox followers of Rabbi Yeshua, *who God was*, he determined what was to be read literally and which literal readings should be disregarded. The early church and contemporary allegorists *do not* reject all literal readings, and even those literal readings worthy of God still have a deeper allegorical meaning.

It is primarily *strictly* literal readings that avoid the deeper meaning of Scripture that are problematic. Origen in the third century, living a few decades after the literalist Marcion, understood this all too well when he wrote, "The reason, for the false beliefs and impious or ignorant assertions about God appears to be nothing else than Scripture not being understood according to its spiritual sense, but taken as regarding the bare letter."[67] In other words, the literal readings of Scripture read without reference to the canon of faith or the deeper meaning within are why people have false beliefs and ignorant assertions about God. For people like Marcion these literal readings that rejected any deeper spiritual meaning depicted the God of the Old Testament as a moral monster, but for orthodox Christians these mere literal readings were not and are not determinative for who God is.[68]

---

67. Origen, *On First Principles*, 248. Moses Maimonides, a Sephardic Jew born in twelfth-century Spain, said something eerily similar in his book *The Guide for the Perplexed*: "The adherence to the literal sense of the text of Holy Writ is the source of all this error." Maimonides, *Guide for the Perplexed*, 129.

68. The late seventh-century East Syrian Isaac of Nineveh also gives us an example of this: "Just because [the terms] wrath, anger, hatred, and the rest are used of the creator, we should not imagine that he [actually] does anything in anger or hatred or zeal. Many figurative terms are employed in the scriptures of God, terms that are far removed from his [true] nature. And just as [our] rational nature has [already] become gradually more illumined and wise in a holy understanding of the mysteries that are hidden in [scripture's] discourse about God—that we should not understand everything [literally] as it is written, but rather that we should see, [concealed] inside the bodily exterior of the narratives, the hidden providence and eternal knowledge that guides all." Isaac of

Rather, who God has been revealed to be in Yeshua within the faithful witness of Israel as described in the canon of faith is determinative for what we may truthfully say of God. In the absence of the rule of faith and a sacramental reading of Scripture in accord with the rule of faith, we, basing our depictions of God off a literal reading, come up with false notions of God that remain unworthy of the Creator. Modern liberal Protestants in both their conservative and liberal branchs[69] unwittingly make some of the same errors that Marcion did. They do so not necessarily because they throw out the Scriptures (what we call the Old Testament), as Marcion did, although some of them certainly do so; rather the mistake of Marcion they are repeating is found in the way in which they read Scripture, namely according to a strictly literal reading void of the rule of faith.[70]

Now, if the inspiration of Scripture isn't located in the text or authorial intention, then where is the meaning of the text to be found? In contrast to the strictly literal reading of Marcion, which identifies meaning in the text, Philip's encounter with the eunuch reveals to us where the meaning of Scripture really is found. Looking to the eunuch's encounter with Philip, we find his question

> was not the one that we would ask today—"What is the meaning of this passage?"—as if the "meaning" were located in the text itself, and so in the past, and our task is simply to uncover it, what the text "meant," and then perhaps try to find "meaning" for ourselves in the present by some kind of analogy. Instead, the eunuch asked, "About whom does the prophet say this, about himself or about someone else?" (Acts 8.34). *"Meaning" resides in the person*

Nineveh, "On Gehenna," 185–88. Although I think this needs to be balanced with the reality that a good and just God is truly angered by injustice; otherwise that God is not good. God is not, in light of such injustices like slavery, theft of land, colonialism, and the holocaust, simply smiling and singing "All you need is love" as if love and anger are always antithetical to one another. Love and anger are somehow paradoxically in need of one another. While God is not the wrathful god of penal substitutionary atonement, neither is she the god who ignores the injustices committed by oppressors with a smile on his face. For a positive view of anger when used for the sake of righteousness and justice, see Origen, *Homilies on Genesis and Exodus*, 69–70.

69. If you remember from earlier in the book, I define Fundamentalists as the so-called conservative branch of liberal Protestantism.

70. Whether literal in the sense that the text is always history, as it is for Fundamentalists, or literal in the sense of what the text meant in its historical cultural context according to its authorial intention.

of whom the text speaks, and our task is to come to know this person by understanding how the text speaks of him.[71]

To read the Bible historically is to see the location of meaning as residing in the text, which is not the purpose, goal, or function of the text. And it's not where the early Christians or most Christians for most of the church's history have seen the locus of meaning.[72] Meaning is always to be found in the Jewish Messiah crucified and resurrected as the Word of God. He is the Jew who opens the Scriptures to us and shows us that he is incarnationally present in them as their meaning. To look to the historical context for Christian meaning is often to miss Messiah, for he is not always in the literal historical meaning, as if frozen in the past; rather he is the treasure buried beneath the text, whom you can only find when you look through him as your interpretative lens here in the present moment.

We understand the human word meant to mediate and signify that divine Word only retroactively in light of that divine Word. We cannot truly understand what was initially spoken to us by that human word of Scripture until we are grasped by that which the initial word was signifying to us, by the inside occupier of that human word. We understand the human word backwards in light of that divine Word that the human word of Scripture was pointing us too. Or as Barth wrote, "We have to understand it as a human word in the light of what it says."[73] And what it says, what it signifies and points to, is the divine Word. Certainly the one truly speaking is the divine Word himself. We understand this Jewish human word in light of the divine Jewish Word it carries.

The reader who only sees the human word of Scripture and fails to see the divine Word it signifies fails to read the Bible. They fail to see the sacramental presence of Messiah within because they are so enamored by the perceived *beauty* or *ugliness* of the text. This all is why a strictly historical literal reading of the Bible is not a Christian reading. Because reading the Bible historically is not rooted in the Jewish kingship of Messiah but in history, and because it is not rooted in the one, holy, catholic, and apostolic church but in the modernity of Northern Europe, such reading misses the meaning intended by the words of Scripture as they

---

71. Behr, *Mystery of Christ*, 49–50. Emphasis added.

72. It's the Europeans, the Germans, and their Enlightenment that has departed from such a global and historical consensus and consequently colonized biblical studies and theology, imposing their worldview as normative, when in reality their worldview is not normative, but the minority.

73. Barth, *Church Dogmatics: The Word of God*, 466.

point to Messiah outside themselves. But while the human words are by nature distinct from the divine Word and take us outside of the text, Messiah pulls us back into the text beneath the mere historical letter of the Scriptures, for he lifts the veils and we enter into him, thus finding ourselves in our own personal encounter with the Word of God through the opening of the Scriptures by the Word of God.

How to Read Scripture Properly (Messiah Centrically)

In light of everything we've discussed, we should end with an example of how to actually read Scripture in this way. But when reading the Scriptures, or even before being mature enough to read the Bible, we need to be people of character who daily practice the virtues that form us into the image and likeness of Messiah. It is not enough to read Scripture according to the rule of faith; we must be people of the rule of faith who embody it in their thoughts, words, and deeds. Now of course some process of formation can be done through the reading of Scripture; after all this is one of the purposes and functions of Scripture, to form our character. But too often we come to the text at the exclusion of such character formation. Those coming to the text, especially those who reject the canon of faith, who are angry, hateful people will read Scripture as angry, hateful people and will see God as angry and hateful (even if they claim otherwise), which in turn will only encourage them to remain so, and even to grow in such vices. In contrast, those who remain in prayer, silence, solitude, meditation, who practice giving alms to the poor, acts of mercy, and compassion, who in short are laying down their lives in love for their neighbors, becoming fully human like Yeshua, will be enabled to see him throughout the Scriptures, and will be formed by such Messiah-centric readings into more Messiah-like followers.

Moreover, Scripture is primarily meant to be read in community, and I don't merely mean your local church community, although I don't mean less than that. But when I say we need to read the Bible in community I also mean we should read it alongside our brothers and sisters from the whole contemporary church, comprised of Protestants, Catholics, the church of the East, Eastern and Oriental Orthodox, as well as my people, the Jews, both those who follow Yeshua and those who do not. We can and should do this in person with actual people from these traditions, yet we can also do this through reading their commentaries and books, and watching their sermon/homilies, YouTube videos, and so forth. To read the Bible in community also means to do so with people of color, traditions of color (don't simply read Protestants), and other marginalized groups, such as the female sex, who help us to see a more holistic picture and shine light on the ways in which our societies have read in un-Messiah-like ways in order to subjugate and control those very people.

Lastly, to read the Scriptures in community is to do so alongside the numerous dead, or rather alive members of the church of the past, since as Yeshua said, God is not the God of the dead but of the living. Whether you're reading with the Swiss Karl Barth, the Irish-Welsh C. S. Lewis, the Englishman John Wesley, the German Hildegard of Bingen, Thomas Aquinas the Italian, Origen the Egyptian, the Cappadocian Macrina the Younger, Ephrem the Syrian, or Zar'a Ya'eqob the Ethiopian, it is important that you read with Christians from the past, especially ones who lived in the first few centuries of the church . C. S. Lewis once commented on the benefit of reading old books, namely that modern people in reality, despite their protests to the contrary, all see the world in the same way, and that reading old books allows us to see the errors of our own time and culture in a way that reading other modern people doesn't.[74] All of these are helpful if not necessary to becoming the kind of people who can read Scripture well and responsibly.

Now that we have finally reached the end of this chapter, we can look at an example of an allegorical reading from Christian antiquity. We need look no farther than the North African Augustine of Hippo and his reading of the conquest narrative in Joshua. In keeping with the rest of the early church, and as we've seen much of the church today, Augustine read Scripture according to the rule of faith, so that when the literal meaning was not worthy of God, a search for the deeper sacramental meaning was sought. As we learned from Origen, the stumbling block, in this case the Canaanite conquest, was Augustine's signal to go beyond the literal meaning. Yet connected to this signal by the stumbling block to go deeper, Augustine's reading of this text was also spurred on by his close reading. Augustine knew Yeshua's name was the same name as Joshua, which was yet another signal to the reader that this Joshua was on the deeper reading really a symbol for Yeshua. The seven nations of Canaan stood for the seven deadly sins, and thus God's command to Yeshua is to wipe out the seven deadly sins from within each person's soul. Here the figural or allegorical reading of this text

---

74. Lewis, "Preface," 10–11.

leads us not to a God who commands us to remove our enemies through violence but a God who is concerned for our formation as a people being more fully molded into the image of God.

Now, let's consider a few things. Given the Northern European assumptions you are probably bringing to the text, this reading of it is probably a bit at odds with what you're expecting from the text. Or maybe said more accurately, given the German Bible that you carry with you in your mind, encountering the church's Scripture may feel foreign. That's okay; learning to decolonize our reading of Scripture and worldview to jettison the German Bible and reembrace the church's Scripture is a process that takes years. I'm still going through that process myself. So as you read this story the question of what literally or historically happened or even the question of the implications of such a literal reading might be pressing upon you. But this is exactly why the allegorical reading is important in the first place. While on the surface we might find it easy to say, "Sure, Joshua conquers Canaan, and Yeshua conquers sin, but this isn't exactly a one-to-one comparison. Messiah conquering sin and healing us is a holy and good thing, but in the slaughter of men, women, and children who have our sympathy, Canaan's conquest understood historically is a hard thing to grapple with."

But as we ponder that, don't we also notice that even some of our own people's sin seems malicious enough that's it's difficult to swallow that Yeshua would conquer and heal that sin too? Many Americans, even if they did not personally take part in slavery, genocide, and land theft, are still perpetuating and benefitting from those evils and therefore are partaking in the sin themselves. If we look closely we might even come to discover we hold our sin preciously and thus the idea of Messiah trampling it down might be scandalous and threatening to the false kinds of powers we hold on to. We now might find reading the text as Messiah's victory as something that might appear dangerous too us. Great! We should understand Yeshua's victory as both a source of joy and troubling trepidation to the part of ourselves that doesn't want our sin vanquished.

Furthermore, the question of whether or not this was a literal historical event is often the wrong question because it distracts the reader from their own sin, namely the sin of white normativity and anti-Jewish racism. By focusing on their own supposed superior goodness, they continue the "white man's burden" of serving as the ethical arbitrator and judge of "less-civilized" peoples, in this case the "sinful" Jewish people of the text, and thus the reader, insidiously blinding themselves, averts an encounter of reconciling judgement through the text with the true judge, Yeshua.[75] In other words, the literal-historical question is often a way for white people to maintain their "racially superior" ethical status by creating a German strawman of the Jews in the text, in order to denigrate them by attempting to show their supposed inferior ethical status, thus maintaining their own superiority over the Jew and avoiding any responsibility for their own sin.

From the allegorical reading we can see how the entire narrative of Scripture itself is considerably more synthesized. The criticism of the harsh "God of the Old Testament" as opposed to the loving "God of the New Testament" is a criticism that can only arise, as it did when the Gnostics read Scripture, when we fail to see how all of Scripture works together to exude Messiah by focusing exclusively on the literal meaning. While there certainly have been Christians who have used the church's reading of Scripture to justify supersessionist and anti-Judaic theologies, the common kind of literal-historical reading that produces a supposedly Christian New Testament, on the one hand, that supports liberation and love and a Jewish Old Testament, on the other hand, that promotes oppression and hate is in reality the more inherently anti-Jewish reading of Scripture.

The assumption built into this characterization of the bad Old Testament and the good New Testament is that Yeshua was a progressive teacher who broke away from the common restrictive Jewish Old Testament understanding of God to forge, let's be frank, a more white, progressive, non-Jewish construction of God. This is the spirit of anti-Judaism lying in the background of many of our "Christocentric" readings of the Bible. Let's not forget it was anti-Jewish Gnostics rather than the Jewish Christians, gentile Christians, or non-Christian Jews who employed these kinds of literal readings that led to such a disunity between the Old and New Testaments. Yeshua never saw himself as forging a new understanding of God that differed from the Jewish understanding of God found in the Jewish tradition of the Old Testament. Rather, he saw his presentation of the God of Israel in deep continuity with his Jewish tradition. A "Christocentric" reading that assumes we need to read the Bible "Christocentrically" because, precisely in this view, the Jews missed the mark in their understanding of God and as a result Yeshua had to

---

75. We Jews have historically been a foil for the purpose of making others seem righteous, the logic being if the Jews of the text or outside of the text are evil, then gentile Christians can more clearly see how good they are in comparison—or at least how good and moral they think they are.

spend most of his time correcting their ignorance and evil is one that falls flat in its anti-Judaic muck since Yeshua himself always emphasized his continuity with what came before. In contrast, the allegorical reading at its core is a non-supersessionist reading that maintains the unity of the Scriptures rooted in a continuous understanding of the God of Israel and therefore maintains the story of God's unbroken continued covenant with the people of Israel. Pitting Yeshua against the Old Testament and our people's understanding of our God is not what the allegorical Scripture is ultimately about.

What we see with our eyes is not all there is to see. Look, for he who comes in the name of the Lord is before you, the Rabbi, the ancient way, is inviting you to come and follow him. If you do not find new eyes to see, you will miss all that there is to see.

6

The Gnostic Heresy

> God is a lover of humanity and intends to cleanse and educate the adherents of heresies. How many do we have here who have been pulled down from the heresies, caught in Christ's nets![1]
>
> Origen of Alexandria (Egyptian, third century)

> Where is the presence, where is the glory of God to be found? It is found in the world ("the whole earth is full of His glory"), in the Bible, and in a sacred deed.[2]
>
> Abraham Joshua Heschel (Ashkenazi Jew, twentieth century)

IN THIS CHAPTER I want to bring up three points about why I don't think former fundamentalists should adopt a Gnostic theology. The first is that it's the theology we grew up with and, as you know by now, I don't think we should hold to fundamentalist theology. If we wish to leave fundamentalism, we will have to leave behind our Gnostic theology as well. The second point I'll argue is that Gnosticism is to blame for our current climate and ecological disaster. Therefore if we really believe stewarding

---

1. Origen, *Homilies on the Psalms*, 312.
2. Heschel, *God in Search of Man*, 311.

creation well is something we should do, then we can't hold a Gnostic worldview. And lastly the third point I want to make is that Gnosticism is an inherently anti-Jewish worldview, and since God has now permanently taken on Jewish flesh, anti-Semitism is therefore anti-theism. It is, as the Swiss theology Karl Barth once said, a particular kind of godlessness compared to which atheism is quite innocuous.[3]

We've Been Gnostics Without Knowing It

While many fundamentalists may not be familiar with the so-called Gnostic gospels or the term "Gnosticism," I would argue they are nonetheless deeply familiar with the ideas, concepts, doctrines, and practices of Gnosticism. For when we look beneath the surface, what they teach in their Bible studies, proclaim from the pulpit, preach at funerals, and live out in their relationship to their bodies and the rest of creation frequently has a Gnostic thread.[4] In fact, some would argue Gnosticism is their theology.[5] I remember as a boy my grandma teaching me what human beings were really made of. She taught this to me through a creative metaphor that caught my attention as a child. People, she said, were like astronauts with space suits on. The space suit was our body, and the man or woman inside was our soul, which was who we really were. Our bodies were not actually what we were; they were more like husks that we would depart from when we left the physical earth and entered the spiritual realm of heaven. Our bodies would rot in the ground while our real selves, our souls, would depart and go to heaven. Indeed, creation was ultimately seen as lacking intrinsic value, because in the end God was going to burn it all up. The earth was not our home; heaven was.

Years later, in the summer after I graduated from college, I went to work at a fundamentalist Protestant summer camp in Colorado. Throughout that summer many of my coworkers were getting sick. This didn't seem to bother anyone except for maybe me and a few others. No one seemed to question why so many of us were becoming sick throughout those few months, but once you put together that we weren't getting

---

3. Barth, *Dogmatics in Outline*, 77.

4. I recently attended a funeral held by a Fundamentalist Baptist church where Gnosticism was preached.

5. Joe E. Morris makes this argument in his book *Revival of the Gnostic Heresy: Fundamentalism*. Namely, he argues that the Fundamentalist movement of the late nineteenth and early twentieth centuries was a revival of Gnosticism.

nearly enough sleep, our main meals were terribly unhealthy, we ate desert every day, and we were at an altitude most of us were not adjusted too, it seemed somewhat obvious. This combination of factors is as you may realize not great for our immune systems—especially sugar, which again we ate all the time. I began to wonder why so many fundamentalists simply did not seem to think taking care of our bodies was important.[6] I knew there was something wrong with it, and there had to be some reason behind it, but I couldn't put my finger on it until a couple years later.

About a year after working at the camp, I became a part of my first Episcopalian church, which, compared to my previous denominations, had more of an emphasis on the importance of church history. In college the only church history class I took was on Baptist history, which is only about four hundred years' worth of time and is more or less limited to English history, with a bit of mainland Europe and the stolen land of Turtle Island (North America)[7] thrown in the mix.[8] I was missing about 1,600 years' worth of church history, most of which happened in the rest of the world![9] Growing more interested in church history during this season of my life, I spent a lot of time catching up on this subject as I was preparing for seminary, and I still am to this day!

---

6. I remember a conversation with my boss in which she relayed the fact that the leaders of the camp thought saving money was more important than buying salad that had any sort of real nutritional value, and therefore they purchased iceberg lettuce. Given the Gnostic theology, it sort of makes sense. Money is a kind of an abstract thing that only has value because we assigned value to it, and the nutritional value or lack thereof inherent to the salad is something embodied. Choosing the abstract and ethereal over the embodied makes sense within a Gnostic framework.

7. Turtle Island is what some Indigenous people called this land before the European colonists renamed it "North America" in an effort to erase the memory of its Indigenous inhabitants. The Romans did a similar thing when, after banning us Jews from our holy city of Jerusalem, they renamed Galilee and Judea "Syria Palestine" in an effort to erase our memory from the land. When modern scholars use the term "Palestinian" to describe Yeshua or any other first-century Judean/Galilean Jew, they are at best being anachronistic since Rome had yet to rename the land, and at worst are perpetuating the intentional colonial action of the Romans to erase our memory from the land. If we are actually interested in decolonization, then we should stop using the terms and names colonizers have given in their effort to solidify such colonization. At the very least you would think historians would use the first-century names of the land of Israel, namely Galilee and Judea, when describing this land in the context of the first century, but the absence of such an action shows how deeply anti-Jewish colonialism is embedded in scholarship even by well-meaning scholars.

8. Although Baptists through their missionary work are now all over the world, and have been for some time.

9. I have heard they have since ramped up their history courses.

The Gnostic Heresy

One day I was reading a book by Euro-American church historian Rebecca Lyman[10] in which she was describing Gnosticism,[11] one of the oldest heresies, and it dawned on me: *she was describing the theology of my childhood and much of fundamentalist Christianity!*[12] I thought to myself, "The problem is we're all a bunch of heretics!" That's why so many fundamentalists couldn't care less about taking care of their bodies or our fellow creatures, or the rest of the earth. Writing about this Gnostic view of the body, Euro-American Elaine Pagels says, "For the gnostics stood close to the Greek philosophic tradition . . . that regards the human spirit as residing 'in' a body—as if the actual person were some sort of disembodied being who uses the body as an instrument but does not identify with it."[13] I didn't need a scholar of Gnosticism to teach this to me, and I didn't need to read the so-called Gnostic gospels to learn this, because this is what my fundamentalist grandma and our fundamentalists churches taught us.

10. She's also an Episcopal priest.

11. A note on the terms "Gnostic" and "Gnosticism": I am aware the term "Gnostic" was only recently (in the last few hundred years) used to describe the people we're talking about in the second and third centuries. But for the sake of simplicity I continue to use this term, and also because it is perfectly reasonable to use new terms to describe an existing phenomenon, ideological system, or practice of some sort. But so the reader won't fret too much, it's important to note that Christians like Origen called the groups that we today call "Gnostics" by something like "those who purport the knowledge falsely so-called." The term *gnosis* in the early church wasn't necessarily used exclusively with reference to the Gnostics. Sometimes the orthodox would use it in their own writings, although they meant something different by it. It was simply the common word for knowledge used by anyone that spoke or wrote in Greek. The orthodox when using the term *gnosis* to specifically refer to the groups we today call "Gnostics" would often add a further descriptor to show how they misused knowledge or *gnosis*. I am also aware that scholarship has pushed against using the terms "Gnostic" and "Gnosticism" as opposed to "Gnostics" or "Gnosticisms," given that the group we're referring to is more so a set of groups than any sort of singular thing, and that their existed among them a plurality that was diverse to the point of making it hard to categorize and define what Gnosticism is. While some of this is legitimate, I can't help but suspect that some of it is a way to get away with researching and or adopting heretical teaching, and that some of it is a way for academics to keep a job. (They won't fire you if you keep putting out material.) But I find the arguments (as briefly as I may have heard them) uncompelling given that Christianity today is also extremely diverse and many of us, whether we identify with it or not, still use the term for such a large group of people; but we like the Gnostics have some core tenets that tie us together, so I think it's fair in most instances to use broad terms like "Gnostics" or Christians" as long as we nuance and clarify with further descriptors when warranted, such as when we're speaking of specific groups within the overall umbrella term.

12. See Morris, *Revival of the Gnostic Heresy*, and Wright, *Surprised by Hope*.

13. Pagels, *Gnostic Gospels*, 27.

Now, I realize associating fundamentalism with an ancient heresy will sound like a big stretch to many readers, and most fundamentalists are sincerely trying to stay in line with the true faith as they understand it. However, good intentions do not guarantee good theology, whether those of self-identifying progressives or of fundamentalists. So please bear with me and hear out my explanation for why I believe much of the theology in American Christianity, particularly in fundamentalist traditions, is a rendition of the old Gnostic heresy. Cuban American church historian Justo González describes Gnosticism this way:[14]

> Drawing from several sources, the Gnostics came to the conclusion that all matter is evil, or at best unreal. A human being is in reality an eternal Spirit (or part of an eternal spirit) that somehow has been imprisoned in a body. Therefore, the Gnostic's final goal is to escape from the body and the material world in which we are exiled. This image of exile is crucial for Gnosticism. The world is not our true home, but rather an obstacle to the salvation of the spirit—a view which, although officially rejected by orthodox Christianity, has frequently been part of it.[15]

Essentially Gnostics taught a conflict dualism in which the material-physical realm and our bodies were evil, whereas the spiritual realm was seen as good and holy. Since they taught the world was evil, salvation was therefore understood as an escape from the world to a spiritual realm, and this salvation was achieved through a secret knowledge or belief. *Sound familiar?*

This is more or less the "gospel message" in many fundamentalist churches: The world is evil and is going to be destroyed, so we need to hear the gospel (this secret information that only Christians know) and believe it (defined as intellectually assenting to propositional truths with our minds), and then our soul will be saved and when we die we can leave the physical world behind and go to the spiritual realm of heaven. In the meantime, we need to retreat from the world as much as possible. We will do this by making our own "Christian" coffee shops, bookstores, homeschool co-ops, our own music and radio stations to play it on, and our own movies, most of which will be B-rated at best. And because our bodies don't matter, since really our souls and the spirit are what's important and what will live on, we

---

14. He's also United Methodist, and the youngest person to have received a PhD in historical theology from Yale.

15. González, *Story of Christianity*, 1:70–71.

can eat junk food, never exercise, drive our fellow creatures to extinction, ignore climate change, and destroy our rainforests!

Writing about Gnosticism in the Western church, English Anglican bishop N. T. Wright says in his book *Surprised by Hope*,

> I have heard it seriously argued in North America that since God intends to destroy the present space-time universe, and moreover since he intends to do so quite soon now, it really doesn't matter whether we emit twice as many greenhouse gases as we do now, whether we destroy the rain forests and the artic tundra, whether we fill our skies with acid rain.[16]

The sad reality is this is all too common in fundamentalist theological thinking (as well as broader Western culture in general) and the communities in which this thinking and practice takes place. In his book *Revival of the Gnostic Heresy*, Euro-American Joe Morris argues that the core tenets of fundamentalism are the core tenants of ancient Gnosticism. Although Morris's understanding of the historical realities, development of orthodoxy, and the details of early church controversies is unfortunately questionable, his basic thesis is, in my humble opinion, spot on. Speaking about Gnosticism, he writes, "The center of gravity of this system is individual salvation. For the Gnostics, personal knowledge, rather than behavior, is the focus of salvation."[17] If you replaced the word "Gnostics" in this quote with "fundamentalists," it would often be just as true. For Morris this is demonstrated in the *Gospel of Thomas* saying 3, where poverty is viewed as a lack of knowledge of oneself, and thus poverty is seen as an abstract quality rather than as a physical concrete reality. The true poverty that must be eliminated is poverty of self-knowledge, not the real-life conditions of so many people in this world.[18]

In fundamentalism's version of Gnosticism this immaterial definition of poverty is played out in the way many of us define and practice evangelism. It's more important to give someone the personal knowledge of the gospel, explaining to them, "who they were, how they came to be here, where they came from,"[19] and how they can return. This quote is from Euro-American Bruce Metzger's description of the Gnostic message of salvation, and yet it maps fairly well onto how many fundamentalists

---

16. Wright, *Surprised by Hope*, 90.
17. Morris, *Revival of the Gnostic Heresy*, 17.
18. See "Coptic Gospel of Thomas," 20.
19. Metzger, *New Testament*, 190.

proclaim the gospel. First they explain the pre-fall time, then they describe how the fall happened, and lastly they claim this world isn't our home. If we believe this message with our minds, then our souls will consequently be saved and when we die we will go to heaven. The spreading of this special knowledge is viewed as more important than alleviating the poverty of the ones we're sharing this saving knowledge with. Of course, there are people who identify themselves as fundamentalists of whom this wouldn't entirely be true—there can be and is sometimes a spectrum—but the point remains this is common enough within fundamentalism because of the dominate Gnostic theology therein.

In the so-called *Gospel of Philip* (a Gnostic text), the author in regards to the material world writes, "The world came into being through an error,"[20] and then has this to say about bodies: "Flesh [and blood can] not inherit the Kingdom [of God]."[21] Since Gnosticism views our bodies and more generally the world as evil, the secret knowledge that is necessary for salvation from this world cannot be found in the world. In other words, flesh and blood, materiality, cannot be saved or be the medium for salvation. This denigration of the body that exhorts that it has no value is repeated by the author of the *Gospel of Philip* when they write, "No one will hide an extremely valuable thing in something of equal value. However, people often put things worth countless thousands into a thing worth a penny. It is this way with the soul. *It is a precious thing which came into a worthless body.*"[22] Also speaking about the body, the author of the Coptic *Gospel of Thomas* in saying 29 writes in this same vein, "I am amazed at how this great wealth [the soul] has made its home in this poverty [the body]."[23]

In contrast, within the very *Jewish* Christian message, the location of salvation or union with God is found precisely in the material world, within the embodied flesh of the incarnate Jewish Word. For the church, which only exists within the womb of Israel, salvation is sacramentally embodied; it is found in creation rather than outside of it. God's presence is with us, not separate from us. The view of the material world as separate and distant from God is more part of the worldview of Enlightenment deism and Gnosticism than part of Christianity, where in contrast God is seen as present in and through all the material universe even as

20. "Gospel of Philip," 43.
21. "Gospel of Philip," 40.
22. "Gospel of Philip," 40. Emphasis added.
23. "Coptic Gospel of Thomas," 20.

God is by nature distinct from creation; God's space and the material world overlap.

Thus our bodies are not damned, and do not prevent us from inheriting salvation, but as the Egyptian Origen says, "But what is more marvelous than all of these is that the body has been divinized [brought into union or salvation with God]."[24] Unlike in the *Gospel of Philip*, where we must "peel off the flesh" in order to "be found in repose,"[25] our bodies are not an obstacle to salvation but participate in it. In saying 37 from the Coptic *Gospel of Thomas*, when talking about leaving the body, the writer places into the mouth of Yeshua the following words: "When you disrobe without being ashamed and take up your garments and place them under your feet like little children and tread on them, then [will you see] the son of the living one."[26] For the author of the Coptic *Gospel of Thomas*, in order to see the "son of the living one," Yeshua's disciples must take off their fleshly bodies and trample on them.

This is reminiscent of what Celsus, the second-century opponent of Christianity, wrote when in citing Plato he claimed the material world and the flesh were obstacles that one must turn away from to see God with the eyes of the soul.[27] According to this view, salvation can only happen through turning away from the material world and our bodies. Similarly, fundamentalism says: *if you wish to inherit salvation, you must reject this world and turn towards heaven.* For the ancient Gnostics, because of "their own dualistic premise (spirit is good, matter is evil), anything material is alien to a supreme God. Thus, by default, Gnostics automatically dismiss any concept of incarnation."[28] According to the ancient Gnostics, this is why Messiah didn't come in the flesh but only *appeared* to be in the flesh to the uninitiated. To them Messiah was simply a spirit, and unlike human beings was not trapped in a fleshly body. I can see why this might be attractive to an anti-Jewish culture, being yet another way to avert God becoming Jewish flesh.

This view of an immaterial Yeshua has similar renditions in fundamentalism, where his humanity is also downplayed or totally ignored and he is seen as more of a superman figure than as a real human being. This is because in the Gnostic view the body is not part of one's real self and

24. Origen, *Homilies on the Psalms*, 442.
25. "Gospel of Philip," 42.
26. "Coptic Gospel of Thomas," 20.
27. Wilken, *Spirit of Early Christian Thought*, 9.
28. Morris, *Revival of the Gnostic Heresy*, 22.

is evil. If Yeshua is good, he cannot have a body, and thus his humanity must be ignored or done away with. In all of these examples from the two Gnostic gospels we've just looked at, the body is understood to be in the way of our salvation and must be shed rather than saved, and it is certainly not the locus of salvation alongside the soul as it is understood among the orthodox.

In contrast to the Gnostic denial of fleshy incarnation, for the church not only is flesh good, but it is through Messiah's body we are saved. To the chagrin of the Gnostics, I would add it is not only through flesh that we are saved but more specifically Jewish flesh. The two things Gnostics are most uncomfortable with, Jews and materiality, are ironically the two things through which our salvation occurs.[29] Origen in *On First Principles* writes, "The Son of God, therefore, *for the sake of the salvation of the human race*, wanting to appear to human beings and to sojourn among them, *assumed not only a human body*, as some suppose, but also a soul."[30] In his *Homilies on the Psalms*, he writes, "he had a body just like ours, so that he might save us."[31] Whereas in the *Gospel of Philip* Messiah only appeared to be human like us, but in reality was not.[32] For the church not only is the body not an obstacle to our salvation, and not only are our bodies part of our salvation, but it was necessary for the Word of God to take on a body (a Jewish one at that) to obtain for us our salvation. The body it seems is necessary for salvation. This is because for the orthodox a human being is a body as well as a soul, and therefore for Messiah to save us he needed to become all of what we are, soul and body, to heal all of what we are. This Christian perspective is explained in the East Syrian text *Discourse on the One God*: "If a person has no body, he is not complete, nor is he complete without soul; nor is he complete without spirit."[33] For orthodox gentile Christians a human being is a soul

---

29. "for salvation [life] is from the Jews." John 4:22. Also see John 14:6 in which Yeshua declares that it is only through him as the way, and the truth, and the life that anyone comes to the Father. Meaning since Yeshua is Jewish that it is only through a Jew anyone can come to the Father.

30. Origen, *On First Principles*, 288. Emphasis added.

31. Origen, *Homilies on the Psalms*, 309.

32. "Jesus secretly stole them all. *For he showed himself not to be as he really was, but he appeared in a way that they could see him.* [He appeared] to the angels as an angel and to humans as a human." "Gospel of Philip," 41. Emphasis added.

33. "Discourse on the One God," 368. It is a composition probably from the early seventh century, which was likely composed in Chinese but was possibly translated into Chinese from Syriac.

(sometimes a spirit as well) and a body fully united.[34] If being human means being embodied, then for Yeshua to save us he had to become all of what we are, including a body.

Another area in which fundamentalism, and the broader American culture, displays its Gnosticism is in its tendency for conspiracy theories.[35] Not surprisingly, my own family, many of them fundamentalist Gnostics, are hard-core conspiracy theorists and were so before it was mainstream. Preferring untested conspiracy theories over well-established realities amounts to choosing unreality (a false narrative about the world). As Morris writes, "The Gnostic way to the Light was escape from the world. *Salvation thus constituted a form of escape from reality*, a phenomenon evidenced today in Fundamental theology."[36] *Salvation was a kind of escape from reality*. What are conspiracy theories if not escapes from reality? Think about it: We have all these people, many of them fundamentalists, running around believing they have, in whatever way, the true reality of things, which has been revealed to them and a small group of people. This secret knowledge is unknown to the masses and it is their group who alone knows what's really going on. We saw this on a mass scale with the election deniers and the various ways in which people saw conspiracy theories as underlying the COVID pandemic.

In addition, much of Gnosticism within fundamentalism is also found in its music. Norman Greenbaum's song "Spirit in the Sky," along with Building 429's "Where I Belong" and the song "I'll Fly Away," represent Gnostic rather than Christian theology. Within fundamentalism often our hymns and "Christian" music radio stations are filled with Gnostic theology. Many of these songs assume the physical world is antithetical to Yeshua and gets in the way of our salvation, teaching that if we love Yeshua, we must abandon this world and *fly away* to a spiritual home. Another place we see this kind of theology is in the Left Behind series, in which people are taken away from this world and carried off to heaven while this world burns. As we will see in the next chapter, this is completely antithetical to the gospel. Yeshua said, "Your Kingdom come!," not, "Take my followers out of this world." Indeed, in John 17:15 he prays specifically that his followers *would not* be taken out of the world, but be

---

34. Which is true of Messiah in that he is fully human.

35. Irish American bishop Robert Barron points this out in his own discussion of Gnosticism. It's well worth a listen. See Barron and Vogt, "Gnosticism, the Enduring Heresy."

36. Morris, *Revival of the Gnostic Heresy*, 21. Emphasis added.

protected from Satan. Regarding the Christian understanding of salvation, Indian-American New Testament scholar Nijay Gupta writes,

> The biblical writers and the people of God did not associate "salvation" with heaven, inner peace, or spiritual enlightenment per se. They saw the redemption vision of the gospel in the Old and New Testaments as a world restored to righteousness. Not souls and spirits rescued and reclaimed, but bodies and communities, trees and forests, sky and earth restored to health and vitality. All things made right from the utter wrongness of sin and wickedness.[37]

This genuine gospel message in contrast to the Gnostic fundamentalism of our upbringings does much for promoting and embodying a theological praxis that stewards creation and maintains its well-being, while the Gnostic-fundamentalist "gospel" has promoted the raping and pillaging of the earth.

Gnosticism the Culprit of Climate and Ecological Disaster

Admittedly this is to some extent, although not entirely, a conclusion I've come to through intuition. There are scholars like Cherokee Randy Woodley, and English N. T. Wright who have essentially come to this same conclusion in their own scholarship. Even so, intuition is not a mode of knowing without merit. Back in college I had the intuition the Bible was not the Word of God, and after years of prayerful historical, theological, and biblical study I found this intuition confirmed within the Christian tradition. Intuition may not be the modern German way of knowing things (epistemology), which we've inherited from the Enlightenment, but the German ways of knowing are not the only ways of knowing and should not be treated as such. Scholars and theologians who are dominated by these German Enlightenment epistemologies need to learn this and open up the way for scholarship that assumes other ways of knowing from outside of Europe. Otherwise we are continuing epistemological colonization in our theologies and scholarship.

Now, while Gnosticism is seemingly gaining popularity outside of fundamentalist circles, among both former fundamentalists who were already Gnostic and those in progressive Protestant circles, as I've tried to show above, for fundamentalists it was always there. Gnosticism has

---

37. Gupta, *15 New Testament Words of Life*, 2.

been a constant companion to Western Christians, Western theology, and the broader culture for hundreds of years. And while many of those in deconstructionist circles find the term and idea of heresy outdated and barbaric, allow me to be so bold to declare, *this heresy* is responsible for our current ecological and climate crisis. I should clarify that heresy is not simply an idea that is out of favor or disliked by the majority, for this or that reason; that may be how people on both sides of various argument think of it, but that's a rather insufficient understanding of it; rather true heresy is what distorts who God is, and as a result is harmful. If I believe God is like Molech, I will sacrifice my children to this god in fire; and if I believe in the Gnostic god who is at best indifferent to the material realm and at worst is utterly opposed to it, then I will act accordingly by either ignoring the material realm or, worse, destroying it.

You simply cannot be a Gnostic and care about creation; it's not in its DNA. So yes, heresy can be very dangerous. If you don't believe me, just remember that in the summer of 2021 Portland reached the record-breaking tempt of 109 degrees and there were people without air-conditioning who literally died.[38] When my grandma was growing up in Oregon, it never reached the 80s even at the hottest part of the summer. But now thanks to Gnosticism the Western world has brought us to the brink of climate disaster. I find it deeply ironic that the Coptic (Egyptian) word for the land of the dead, or hell, *Amente,* literally means "the western place."[39] Gnosticism, which has been at the root of so much of Western culture, is producing hell on earth. The land effected by the West has been prepared for death by its death-dealing Western Gnostic dualism and has created it into a sort of hell. If we get our Gnostic way, the whole world be a land of the dead.

Keetoowah Cherokee Randy Woodley has made a similar argument. He says Platonic dualism is at the root of white supremacy and our current climate and ecological crisis. I agree, since Platonic dualism is the root from which Gnosticism sprang. We can sort of think of Gnosticism as radical Platonism. So I believe Randy and I are talking about the same thing. The hierarchy that comes from dualism/Gnosticism places some ethnic groups as superior to others (as we will see in regards to the Gnostic's anti-Jewish racism), spiritual things as superior to material (as we saw in the Gnostic view of the material realm, and

---

38. In the past people living in the Pacific Northwest lived without air conditioning because the summers weren't hot enough for it.

39. Shenoute, "I Have Been Reading," 341.

the location of salvation), male over female (which we see in the Coptic *Gospel of Thomas* for instance),[40] humans as superior to animals, thought over practice (as we saw in the Gnostic view of poverty and their view of knowledge as being salvific), and souls as superior to bodies (which we also saw above). Speaking about Western culture, which has held to the Platonic worldview, or as I would put it, radical Platonism, Randy writes,

> These systems also relate to White people's relationship to nature. Consider the state of Western Europe 500 years ago. Most of the hardwood forest had been cut down to build fortresses, cathedrals, and castles, to heat iron for making tools and to shape weapons of war. Western European urban centers were filthy from pollution, the rivers and creeks polluted from human refuse, discarded animal remains; the fisheries, including bays and rivers, becoming depleted, crime was rampant, large mammals were going extinct, and justice was mainly for the wealthiest 1 percent. I can understand why White Europeans wanted the unspoiled Indigenous lands that were being kept in harmony and balance with nature but, unfortunately, they did not adopt the necessary Indigenous worldview to maintain it. As a result, we are now experiencing an ecological crisis similar to, and more serious than, the Western European crisis in the mid-late Middle Ages.[41]

Randy is describing what I believe are the effects of Gnosticism, a worldview that has been part of Western culture for hundreds of years and what fundamentalists and many in the West were and are still taught explicitly and implicitly. The Gnostic teacher Monoimus, as if he were writing in twenty-first-century America, exhorts, "Abandon the search for God and the creation and the other matters of a similar sort. *Look for him by taking yourself as a starting point.*"[42] In other words, (particularly for us modern Americans) individualism and the Gnostic worldview that denigrates creation are connected. If you take yourself as the starting point, you are probably not going to care much about the environment. This connection

---

40. In saying 114, "Simon Peter said to them, "Let Mary leave us, for women are not worthy of life.' Jesus said, 'I myself shall lead her in order to make her male, so that she too may become a living spirit resembling you males. For every woman who will make herself male will enter the kingdom of heaven." "Coptic Gospel of Thomas," 28. Although to be fair the so-called *Gospel of Mary* seems to be have a different picture of women.

41. Woodley, "White Supremacy." Used permission from author.

42. Pagels, *Gnostic Gospels*, xix. Emphasis added.

between individualism and Gnostic theology drives much of what Westerners in general think and do, and even much of what Christians in America believe and practice. As I'll talk more about in the last chapter, our hyper-individualism in America, both within the church and outside of it, effectively makes ourselves God and thus we have abandoned our search for God and God's creation in favor of ourselves as the starting point for everything.

One of the reasons Origen saw the Gnostics as problematic—whom he often referred to by way of three known Gnostic figures in his time, Valentinus, Basilides, and Marcion—was because what they taught was from themselves, not the Lord. The church, like most human peoples throughout history, has seen the community and tradition as the source of truth and normative authority, a sight that can only be given through humility. In his *Homilies on the Psalms*, referring to the Parable of the Talents, Origen expresses that we are not allowed to lend our own silver, but are only allowed to lend the Lord's silver. This is his way of saying we aren't allowed to impart our own teaching, but are only permitted to teach what comes from the Lord.

He then asks who is it that "lends what is his own? Who lends what is the Lord's?"[43] His answer to the first question is Valentinus, Basilides, and Marcion, i.e., the Gnostics. Isn't this self-orientation as the criteria for truth and the certainty it's based on similar to what fundamentalists struggle with? I've been in many conversations with fundamentalists (sometimes I was the fundamentalist) in which they themselves really served as the measurement for what truth was, and no matter what you presented them with externally from themselves, they could not be convinced otherwise. It was *their* Bible and Yeshua, and *their hyper-individualized* interpretation of that Bible and Yeshua, that was normative for truth and thus determined truth.

Euro-American Gnostics scholar Elaine Pagels confirms this self-orientation when writing about Valentinus and his followers: "They argued that only one's own experience offers the ultimate criterion of truth, taking precedence over all secondhand testimony and all tradition—even

---

43. "If you should see Valentinus fashioning *logoi* and teaching what is his own, say, 'That man is lending what is his own and falls under a curse.' The same applies if you see Basilides, if you see Marcion. But if you see someone speaking, not what is his own, but what is God's, and daring to say truly, 'Or do you seek proof of Christ speaking in me?' know that such a person lends, not what belongs to him, but what is the Lord's." Origen, *Homilies on the Psalms*, 117.

Gnostic tradition!"[44] This self-orientation is not foreign to us as Americans, or Westerners in general. We take it as more or less a fact that the world revolves around us as individuals and thus of course we are our own starting points. It wasn't us Americans who first came up with the selfish and delusion concept of "my truth"; Trump and the liberals inherited this from the Gnostics. No wonder Congress or any of our denominations can't get anything done; they're all guided by their individual selves as their own criteria for truth. This runs against the grain of how most cultures throughout human history have viewed tradition and the community. How arrogant is this? I'm confident enough, particularly as an addict, to know that when I become my own criteria for truth I'm in a bad place. When I can't look to the tradition and my community to correct me, I'm swimming in the filth of my own pride. Making ourselves our own criteria for truth is not helpful; it's selfish.

In contrast, the worldview of the Indigenous people of Turtle Island is antithetical to the Gnostic worldview from the West that colonized this land. Theirs, like my own Jewish culture, is one that views the land, the material, our bodies, the animals, and all of creation as sacred, infused with the Spirit. It's probably a good idea if we look to the people God has called to steward this land and ask them to take their surgical materials and perform a life-saving operation on Western culture—which is one of the points Randy Woodley makes in his article "White Supremacy and the Fate of the Earth": namely, we need to look to Indigenous peoples to get us out of the ecological mess that Western culture has gotten us into. Randy, writing again about the Western worlview, says,

> To carry forth a Platonic Western worldview is to invest in the ethereal or spiritual or metaphysical or abstract realm to a higher degree than the physical. In the West, our thoughts and our theologies become too easily disembodied through silly notions such as the separation of the secular and the sacred, and believing God is at work in the church more than in the world. The physical sphere, such as land or good works or our bodies, all become suspect, leading to false hierarchies and binary thinking.[45]

We have to ask: What are the consequences of the Gnostic worldview? What effects does this radical Platonism produce? When we view the

---

44. Pagels, *Gnostic Gospels*, 25.
45. Woodley, *Indigenous Theology and the Western Worldview*, 99.

spiritual as more important, as what's real, and see the body and material things as not only less valuable than the former but as evil and therefore an obstacle to our salvation, how do we think we're going to behave? If Gnosticism is our orthodoxy, what will be our orthopraxy? What did Westerners do to Turtle Island with this kind of orthodoxy? And what have Westerners been doing to the rest of the world with this orthodoxy? What happens when we make individual selves rather than the community our source of authority? Should we be surprised that social justice doesn't matter to many, that we're on the brink of a climate and ecological disaster with many animals rapidly approaching extinction? Should I be surprised like I was that we don't care about taking care of our bodies? Should we be surprised given our ethereal abstract thinking when we divorce our orthodoxy from our orthopraxy? No, I think not.

The problem with Gnosticism is a failure to recognize that all created materiality is a sacrament. Gnostics think they need secret spiritual knowledge because for them the material world is evil, and therefore cannot mediate the Divine presence. This makes creation not only unnecessary for salvation, for encountering God, but an obstruction to it. And if it is an obstruction, it is something that must be destroyed, something that must be escaped. In contrast, the ancient church rooted in the people of Israel recognized that God created the material world as good and, having become a material creature himself in the incarnation of the Word made flesh, has sanctified it, and has brought it into union with the triune community and is continuing to do so. As a result, the world is sacrament, and through the Jewish flesh of Messiah we come to know God. We exist in a reality where it is through physical things that the Jewish Logos[46] is mediated. One worldview denigrates creation; another holds it as sacred. One is destroying our world; another is healing it.

Now, speaking of the Gnostics in the third century, the Egyptian Origen writes,

> But even now the heterodox, with a pretense of knowledge, are rising up against the holy Church of Christ and are bringing compositions in many books,[47] announcing an interpretation of

---

46. Since the Logos has taken on Jewish flesh permanently, and the incarnated Logos here and now is all we know, I do not find it helpful to divorce the pre-incarnate Logos from the incarnated Logos. Even the pre-incarnate Logos was hanging out with Jews, preparing for his becoming one of them. He has taken this Jewish flesh on permanently and we best get used to it.

47. Likely referring to the Gnostic gospels.

the texts both of the Gospels and of the apostles. If we are silent and do not set the true and sound teachings down in opposition to them, they will prevail over inquisitive souls which, in the lack of saving nourishment, hasten to foods that are forbidden and are truly unclean and abominable. For this reason it seems necessary to me that one who is able intercede in a genuine manner on behalf of the teaching of the Church and reprove those who pursue the knowledge falsely so-called [Gnosticism]. He must take a stand against the heretical fabrications by adducing in opposition the sublimity of the gospel message, which has been fulfilled in the agreements[48] of the common doctrines in what is called the Old Testament with that which is named the New.[49]

While Origen wrote this in the third century, eerily I find it could have been written yesterday as it seems to me to speak vividly to our current condition. Many being unaware, to no fault of their own, of the Gnosticism in which they were reared have continued to hold on to Gnostic theology while also now having discovered the so-called Gnostic gospels. These "inquisitive souls," namely former fundamentalists, in the lack of nourishing theology from their fundamentalist background, have unknowingly ran straight back to the fundamentalist-Gnostic theology of their childhood. They have therefore grasped on to these unclean foods that have diminished our planet, looking for something to feed their faith. We therefore need faithful people who are able to intercede on behalf of the church and by the immensely more beautiful gospel show these maggot-filled foods to be wanting, truly lacking the truth, beauty, and goodness they are so faithfully seeking to the best of their ability. Of course, as I have tried to show in the chapter, this isn't simply an issue needing to be dwelt with among those who call upon the name of Yeshua, but if I am right, as I have tried to show however briefly, that Gnosticism is to blame for our current ecological and climate crisis, then this is an issue that affects everyone who lives on this planet—all of humanity, dogs, cats, cattle, lions, snakes, reptiles, frogs, insects, soil, trees, mountains, the rivers and oceans.

---

48. By "fulfilled in the agreements" Origen is not necessarily referring to agreements according to the literal sense alone, but when the letter falls short of being worthy of God and therefore of Christian teaching, he means agreements according to the spiritual sense of Scripture.

49. Origen, *Commentary on John*, 166.

The Anti-Theism of Gnosticism

Yet particularly for former fundamentalists in the deconstructionist world, what is the appeal of Gnosticism? Does it have a certain comfortable familiarity to it due to the fact this is what many of us were reared with, like busting out Grandma's old cookie recipe after a break up? Is it again an unconscious uncomfortability with the Jewishness of the gospel and the Christian faith? A looking to establish a more European version of Christianity? Euro-America Christian historian Robert Louis Wilken writes, the "Gnostics, believed that the Old Testament was a book about a lesser God who created the world of matter, a jealous and vengeful deity, the votary of a single people, the Israelites."[50] This could more or less summarize what many in deconstructionist circles believe today. In the Gnostic version of things the God of the Jews is an evil demigod who created the material realm, and from their perspective only an evil god would create the material realm since matter is inherently evil. The Greco-Roman world that colonized the Jewish people saw them, and almost everyone else for that matter, as barbarians. Is there not an inherent anti-Jewish quality to the Gnostic system of belief? Absolutely. No wonder it's so appealing to a culture founded on anti-Semitism.[51]

Bart Ehrman in his introduction to the Gnostic *Gospel of Peter* states, without claiming it's a problem, that this piece of literature has an "anti-Judaic slant"; indeed he even writes, "One of this Gospel's principle concerns is to incriminate Jews for the death of Jesus."[52] This is an anti-Judaic slant that in contrast the church's Gospels aren't guilty of. The persective of the New Testament as anti-Jewish was more so from anti-Jewish readings of the Gospels and the rest of the New Testament than it was from faithful Jewish readings.[53] Certainly the majority of the New

---

50. Wilken, *Spirit of Early Christian Thought*, 62.

51. David Nirenberg makes the argument that anti-Judaism is deeply foundational for Western culture; see Nirenberg, *Anti-Judaism*.

52. Ehrman, *Lost Scriptures*, 32. According to Roman law, only the Romans had authority to enact the death penalty, which is why the Judean religious leaders had to take Yeshua to Pilate. So in the end it was the Romans who crucified Yeshua, not the Jewish people, nor even the Judean religious leaders, who themselves had no authority to do so. Furthermore, only the Judean religious leaders handed Yeshua over to Pilate, not all of the Jewish people, many of whom were following or ready to follow Yeshua as the Messiah. "Take him yourselves and judge him according to your law [Torah]," Pilate told them. "We are not allowed to kill someone," the Jews [Judean leaders] said to him" (John 18:31).

53. Euro-American New Testament scholar Craig Keener in *The IVP Bible*

Testament is a kind of Jewish literature produced by Jewish Christians. But what is true of the *Gospel of Peter* in this regard is also true of the *Gospel of Philip*. Describing a key facet of the Gnostic system, namely the distinguishment between the elect, who have the *gnosis* (knowledge), and the non-elect, who don't, Ehrman writes,

> One of the clearest emphases is the contrast between those who can understand and those who cannot, between knowledge that is exoteric (available to all) and that which is esoteric (available only to insiders), *between the immature outsiders (regular Christians, called "Hebrews") and the mature insiders (Gnostics, called "Gentiles")*.[54]

It is interesting that those called "Hebrews" in the *Gospel of Philip* are accused of erring because of their confession of the virgin birth and the bodily resurrection of Yeshua as events that actually occurred bodily, rather than being mere symbolic expressions of spiritual truths.[55] So

---

Background Commentary: New Testament writes about the term often translated as "Jew" in the Gospel of John, "Although Jesus and the disciples are clearly Jewish, John usually uses the term "Jews" in a negative sense for the Judean authorities in Jerusalem, whom he identifies . . . with "the Pharisees."" In other words, the term *Ioudaioi*, which is often rendered as "Jew," would be better rendered as "the Judeans" or even "Judean religious leaders," because the author of John's Gospel isn't always using it to refer to the whole of the Jewish people but to a specific group within the Jewish people. Keener, *IVP Bible Background Commentary*, 262. See also Euro-American New Testament scholar Marianne Meye Thompson, *John: A Commentary*. Indeed, John's author is a Jew himself, and this shows in his writing style. In Hebrew you will often find redundancy such as "and he *answered* and *said* to him." You find this Hebrew redundancy often in the Greek of the Gospel of John, indicating that its author was Jewish. See also Euro-American, Quaker, and New Testament scholar Paul Anderson's *Riddles of the Fourth Gospel*, 37–38 for a brief discussion on the supposed anti-Judaism of the Gospel of John. Jewish scholar Daniel Boyarin writes that it is virtually universally accepted that Yeshua "was a Jew who followed ancient Jewish ways. There is also growing recognition that the Gospels themselves and even the letters of Paul are part and parcel of the religion of the People of Israel in the first century A.D. *What is less recognized is to what extent the ideas surrounding what we call Christology, the story of Jesus as the divine-human Messiah, were also part [if not parcel] of Jewish diversity at this time.* The Gospels themselves, when read in the context of other Jewish texts of their times, reveal this very complex diversity and attachment to other variants of 'Judaism' at the time. There are traits that bind the Gospel of Matthew to one strain of first-century 'Judaism' while other traits bind the Gospel of John to other strains. The same goes for Mark, and even for Luke, which is generally considered the 'least Jewish' of the Gospels." Boyarin, *Jewish Gospels*, 22. Emphasis added.

54. Ehrman, *Lost Scriptures*, 38. Emphasis added.

55. To be clear, the early church (in which I do not include the Gnostics when I speak of the early church) did not have a problem with spiritual or allegorical readings of these events, but they also didn't have a problem with literal readings of these events,

these dogmas were in some sense, it seems, seen as Jewish, rather than as gentile, at least by the editor(s) and or author(s) of the *Gospel of Philip*.[56] The term "Hebrews" in the *Gospel of Philip* is used as a foil for those considered in the eyes of the author to be immature outsiders, i.e., the "regular Christians," in contrast to "the mature insiders,"[57] the Gnostics themselves, who are self-described as "gentiles."[58]

What we learn from this is that the *Gospel of Philip* is showing its anti-Jewish hand by using the term "Hebrews" as a sort of slur for Christians who are not part of the elite, namely the Gnostics, who possess the secret knowledge, and who in contrast to those Gnostics hold doctrines that are seemingly Hebrew rather than gentile. There is a clear hierarchy here between the gentiles and the Hebrews, the gentiles representing those in the know who are saved, and the Hebrews representing the ones not in the know, who lack any kind of credible understanding that could possibly display a saved status. According to St. Irenaeus, Saturninus, a Gnostic, taught as with all the Gnostics that the true God was not the god of Israel and was not the creator of this material world. Instead there were seven angels who made the world, one of which was the god of the Jews. Moreover, Saturninus taught that the Messiah was from the true God, whom he called his father, rather than from the god of Israel, and was sent to destroy the Jewish god. Writing about Saturninus's teaching, Irenaeus says, "he maintained that the God of the Jews was one of the angels; and, on this account, because all the powers wished to annihilate

---

since they understood them to be events that actually happened.

56. I believe this gives at least some credence to my argument throughout this book, but particularly later on, that the dogmas of Christianity are inherently Jewish.

57. Ehrman, *Lost Scriptures*, 38.

58. It is interesting to note that Origen's use of the term "gentile," in contrast to the use of the term in the *Gospel of Philip,* is for denoting non-Christians. This is the exact opposite of how the *Gospel of Philip* uses this term. In the *Gospel of Philip* the term "gentile" is used to denote those who are saved, thereby using the term "Hebrew" in a negative connotation for those who are not saved. In Origen's language, "gentile" means non-Christian. In his *Homilies on the Psalms* Origen preaches, "It is not possible to be just without participating in Christ, and if someone supposes that he is someone just outside the faith, one of two possibilities applies: either the gentile participates in Christ, or, if he does not participate in Christ, he is not just. Which do you want to demonstrate, that a gentile participates in Christ? But this is incongruous." By Origen using "gentile" to refer to non-Christians he thereby rhetorically identifies the Christians not with the gentiles but with the Hebrews and thus Christianity is seen as Hebrew rather than gentile and the term "Hebrews" becomes a positive rather than a negative term as it is in the *Gospel of Philip*. Origen, *Homilies on the Psalms*, 156.

his father, Christ came to destroy the God of the Jews."[59] Overall I find Gnosticism, particularly as a Jewish person, deeply anti-Jewish and horribly offensive and dangerous. If we Jews worship an evil god, then it's not hard to believe we must be evil and therefore need to be "dwelt" with. It's deeply troubling that many in the deconstructionist communities are dabbling with such an anti-Jewish worldview.

For the Gnostics, the Logos taking on flesh, let alone the flesh of a people they viewed as inferior, a people who worshipped in their eyes an inferior god, was and is completely unacceptable. Euro-American Benjamin P. Blosser writes about this saying, "At the core of the Christian kerygma, of course, was the belief that the divine *Logos* had taken on human flesh, a belief that was repugnant to the Gnostic and a non sequitur to the Greek philosopher."[60] In the various forms of Gnosticism, Yeshua the Messiah is not human, let alone someone with the particular quality of being Jewish.[61] The affirmation of the material order, this Christian embrace of matter found embodied in the church's teaching on creation and the incarnation, is rooted and comes from the Jewish origins of Christianity, which are completely antithetical to the Gnostic worldview.[62] You can't read the Scriptures or the words of Yeshua without getting the distinct impression that land matters, plants matter, animal's matter, matter matters—that it was created good and has been given for blessing, stewardship, and enjoyment for all of God's creation. *The Gnostic rejection of matter is a rejection of the fundamentally Jewish quality of the Christian faith, and therefore should be rejected.*

In this chapter I have tried to show 1) that fundamentalism is fundamentally Gnostic, and therefore in embracing Gnosticism in the deconstructionist movement we are simply reaffirming something we have always believed and practiced; 2) that Gnosticism is at the root of our current climate and ecological crisis; and 3) that Gnosticism has a strong anti-Jewish inclination and is thus hostile to and radically opposed to the Jewish people and the Jewishness of the Christian faith. Given these three reasons, I hope it is clear why Gnosticism is not only an unacceptable worldview to hold but a dangerous one.

---

59. Irenaeus, *Against Heresies*, 69.
60. Blosser, *Become Like the Angels*, 44.
61. We can't go having the Messiah be a Jew, now can we.
62. As I discussed in chapter 2.

*Flesh of flesh and bone of bones, goodness itself enfleshed,
breathe the earthy air that it was your good pleasure
to create. And make us as you are, true flesh of flesh
and bone of bones, goodness itself enfleshed.*

7

The Gospel

> ...for salvation [life] is from the Jews.[1]
>
> YESHUA (GALILEAN AND JUDEAN JEW)

> The glory to which man is called is that he should grow
> more godlike by growing ever more human.[2]
>
> FR. DUMITRU STANILOAE (ROMANIAN ORTHODOX)

But of all the marvellous and magnificent things about him, this altogether surpasses the astonishment of the human intellect, and the frailty of mortal intelligence does not discover in what way it can think or understand how that mighty Power of divine majesty, that very Word of the Father and that very Wisdom of God, in whom were created all things visible and invisible, can be believed to have been within the compass of that man who appeared in Judea; and indeed that the Wisdom of God entered into the womb of a woman, to be born an infant and to utter cries like the wailing of infants; then, afterwards, that he was also reported to be troubled by death, as even he himself acknowledges, saying, My soul is sorrowful even unto death, and that, at the end, he was brought to that death which is accounted by human

---

1. The Syriac term "salvation" can also mean "life," as noted in the Syriac-English New Testament version of John 4:22.
2. Staniloae quoted in Ware, *Orthodox Way*, 90.

beings the most shameful, although he rose again on the third day. When, then, we see in him some things so human that they appear to differ in no respect from the common frailty of mortals, and some things so divine, that they are appropriate to nothing else but that primal and ineffable nature of divinity, the narrowness of human understanding is bewildered and, struck with amazement at so great a wonder, it knows not which way to turn, what to hold to, or whither to take itself. If it thinks of God, it sees a mortal being; if it thinks of a human being, it perceives him returning from the dead with spoils after conquering the kingdom of death.[3]

ORIGEN (EGYPTIAN)

GIVEN THAT MANY OF us were presented with Gnosticism rather than the gospel, it seems vitally important, now that we've discussed what the gospel is not, to say what it is, namely in thought, word, and deed. Although since I will not meet most of you, here we will have to settle with merely the thought and word of the gospel, which is of course inherently problematic and reductionistic of a much more holistic gospel. If the gospel I speak of here is not lived out, in not only thought and word but also deed, then it is not the gospel. With this caveat and warning we must proceed. Roman Catholic Irish-American bishop Robert Barron has provided a helpful breakdown of the gospel into three aspects. The following exposition of the gospel is both based on his threefold breakdown and builds on it. The three parts are as follows: Yeshua is King, which I call *the way of faith*; the cross and resurrection, which I call *the way of hope*; and finally theosis and the vocation of becoming fully human, which I call *the way of love*.

Yeshua Is King—the Way of Faith

If the gospel isn't just Gnosticism as many of us were taught, then what is it? The Gospel according to Mark tells us in 1:14, "After John had been handed over, Jesus went to Galilee and preached the good news of the kingdom of God, saying 'The time is fulfilled and the kingdom of God has arrived. Repent and believe in the good news." *The good news or gospel is that the kingdom of God is near*! But what does that mean?

3. Origen, *On First Principles*, 103.

Many of us are familiar with the prayer Yeshua taught his disciples to pray but are not familiar with what it means. African-American theologian Lisa Sharon Harper writes, "To our ears it is nowhere near as explosive and dangerous as it would have been to Jesus followers in the first century. The Lord's Prayer is a prayer of subversion."[4] When Yeshua taught his disciples to pray "Your kingdom come," it was a direct affront to the Roman imperial powers who were colonizing ancient Israel.[5] Caesar claimed he was the rightful ruler of the world. In direct disputation of that claim, "your kingdom come" is a call to God for the nonviolent dismantling of the current powers, of the imperial and colonial institutions who have rebelled against God's compassionate and just rule and allied themselves with the demonic; and thus it's a call for their replacement by God's kingdom. It's a call for God's rule to be established instead of Caesar's, or in our case instead of the president's, whether Republican or Democrat. In fact, when we look at Paul's statement in 1 Corinthians 15:20–26, we find him riffing, if you will, on this call and theme from Yeshua's prayer"

> but as it is, the Messiah has risen from the dead and has become the first-fruits of those who have passed away, and life after death is coming through a human being, in just the same way that death came through a human being. Also, everyone is coming to life in the Messiah in just the same way that everyone was dying in Adam. This will happen for each in their turn; the Messiah is the first-fruits, and after that, when he comes, those that are in the Messiah. Then it will be the end, when he delivers the kingdom to God the Father, *once he has brought to and end every ruler, authority, and power.* He will rule until he has placed all his enemies beneath his feet, and the final enemy to be destroyed will be death. (Emphasis added.)

In his argument for the resurrection of the Messiah and our bodily resurrection, Paul teaches that after the dead rise then the end will come, when Yeshua, having brought to an end all the current governmental and political institutions, will hand over the kingdom of God to the Father. He will remove the current empires and established his own. "Messiah is

---

4. Harper, *Very Good Gospel*, 173.

5. I intentionally do not use the name Palestine, not because I am trying to offend my Arab brothers and sisters, but because it was the name Rome gave to the land after having colonized it and forcefully removed the Jews from Jerusalem. It is therefore a colonialized term.

King" is not a nice phrase for your car's bumper sticker, but a subversive call that probably got Paul killed, and it's certainly what got Yeshua killed. When Yeshua was nailed on the cross by the Romans, the Gospel according to Mark reports, "The reason for his death was inscribed in writing. 'This is the king of the Jews.'"[6]

The writers of the Gospels knew why the Romans executed him, and the anonymous Arabic-speaking Eastern Orthodox writer of *Homilies on the Gospel Readings for Holy Week* also knew why. In the homily on Luke 23:32–49, given around 1191 CE, the author states that Satan taught the priests and elders to envy and hate Messiah as he himself did, and by this he blinded them, convincing them to kill him lest their nation be destroyed (John 11:50):

> *The priests and elders said to themselves*: As is clear to all, we are subject to the Romans and under their authority. *Our people have proclaimed that this man is the Christ.* The Romans, our masters, have heard us say and know well that we regard the *Christ as a king who will make us rulers of the world and who will destroy our masters.* When they hear us saying that this Christ is our king, and we flock to him, praising him and describing his great power, *even as the rest of the nation now does*, the Romans will quickly attack us and destroy us, because they see us behaving subversively against them with this new king from among us. If we do not make haste to destroy him, the Romans will destroy the whole nation because of him. We have but one option: we must seize him and hand him over to the Romans, telling them: "This man claims to be our king and he wants us to behave subversively against you. We do not concur with him in this, but see, we have handed him over to you." When we hand him over to them, we shall urge them to kill him, persisting in this until they kill him.[7]

When I was in my first year of college, one of the guys who lived in my dorm would often greet me with the refrain, "Hey Jew, you killed Jesus." Given this historical anti-Semitic interpretation of Yeshua's death, namely *the false idea* that we Jews killed him, I want you to notice here, just as its also reported in the Gospels themselves, that it was only the priests and elders who refused to proclaim Yeshua as King and who wanted him

---

6. Mark 15:26.
7. "Homilies on the Gospel Readings for Holy Week," 289. Emphasis added.

dead; *the people* were in fact proclaiming him as King and following him.[8] As seen in our above text, it was specifically the priests and elders, the Judean religious leaders, whom Satan was teaching to hate Yeshua. It was certainly not all the Jews who hated Yeshua, who *is* himself a Jew, but a specific group of religious elites from Judea who handed him over to the Roman colonizers to be executed. But even not all of the religious leaders were opposed to Yeshua, for there were among them people such as Nicodemus who followed him. Lastly, as the Gospels and the text above reports, it was the Romans who put Yeshua to death, not the Jews.

As important as that caveat is given our historical situation, for us here the additional point of this text is to highlight the central aspect of the Gospel preached by Yeshua and his first followers, namely that he alone was the only rightful ruler and king of the world, because it was made through him, by him, and for him, and he is the only one good, true, and beautiful enough to rule it in such a way as to bring it to its final intended completion as the new Eden—a world ruled by his just laws, such as we see in the Sermon on the Mount or the Parable of the Sheep and Goats. Moreover, as we also saw in the text above, this was a subversive claim to the reigning powers! I suspect the reason why many Christians in America today aren't subversive in the way we're supposed to be is because we've forgotten this key aspect of the gospel and have aligned ourselves with the Roman powers (in our case the American powers) rather than with King Yeshua.

After Yeshua' bodily resurrection, but before his ascension, he entrusted the following to his disciples: ""All authority in heaven and on earth has been given to me," he told them. "As my Father sent me, I am sending you. Therefore go and make disciples of all nations, and baptize them in the name of the Father and the Son and the Holy Spirit, and teach them to obey everything I have commanded you. And behold, I am with you always, until the end of the age. Amen.""[9] When Yeshua declares all authority has been given to him, he's saying he has been made King. Yeshua, who spent his three-year ministry proclaiming himself as the King of Israel, the true King of the whole world, is now seen passing this vocation of proclamation on to his followers. They now have the vocation to go into the world and declare Yeshua, the King of Israel, is King of all peoples. We need to understand this was quite a radical thing for his

---

8. For instance, in John's Gospel after one of the mass feeding miracles the people attempted to make him King by force. See John 6:15.

9. Matthew 28:18–20.

followers to do. Can you imagine Paul saying to the Romans, "Hey, you Romans, Caesar, senators, and all the rest of you colonizers who think you rule the world, this colonized Jew named Yeshua is not only the King of Israel, but the only rightful ruler and King of the world; he is the actual emperor, the true Caesar, and he's coming back to establish his rule over Israel and the whole world, and end yours. And we his followers will live according to his rule and laws now instead of yours, and he alone has our allegiance!"? I can't imagine Paul was popular among the Romans.

Yet exactly what does this kingdom of God look like? When we hear the phrase "kingdom of God," we often think of a dictator ruling with an iron fist. I suppose some of this imagery is rooted in our nation's history of rebellion against England and thus such hate of monarchy is built into our DNA as Americans, but I imagine some of it comes from seeing how absolute rule among leaders has devasted the world. One only needs to think of Caesar, Hitler, Stalin, and so forth to see the danger we worry about. Authoritarian dictators and their mustaches filled our last century, and the kings of the past were often not much better. So in a sense we have good reason to worry about such "kingdom of God" language. Yet one thing we need to discuss to clear some of this up and to describe the kind of kingdom Yeshua and his followers were proclaiming is to ask: What does God's power look like? Is it the kind of power we fear from dictators and the kings of old?

The short answer is no. God's power is Yeshua Messiah crucified on the cross. Indeed, his death on the cross is described in the Gospel of John as his enthronement to kingship, his coronation; contrary to all human expectation, it is his glorification. "It was by death—that most human of actions, and the only thing that we have in common from the beginning of the world onwards, and an action which expresses all the weakness and the impotence of our created nature—by this, and nothing less, has Christ shown himself to be God."[10] I might add it was by his death and resurrection, by this and nothing less, that Messiah showed himself to be King. God's power is not manifested in Caesar's colonial oppression over peoples and lands, but is most fully expressed and visible in the marginalized and colonialized brown Galilean Jew nailed to a Roman cross. Once again true power, as Dennis R. Edwards says, is from the margins.[11]

---

10. Behr, *Becoming Human*, 47.
11. Edwards, *Might from the Margins*. See also Thurman, *Jesus and the Disinherited*.

What the kingdom of God looks like is determined by what kind of King rules that kingdom. In describing what this King is like the East Syrian Isaac of Nineveh says it this way: "Among all his actions there is none that is not entirely a matter of mercy, love, and compassion: this constitutes the beginning and the end of his dealings with us."[12] It is precisely on the cross that Messiah culminates his display to us of what kind of King he is, and therefore what the kingdom of God does and will look like. One of the words used by early Christians to describe God's power was "almighty." In our modern colonial context such language conveys understandings of power that stand in sharp contrast to how the early Christians thought about God's power using this same language. Many of us humans generally have broken ideas of power, so that when we hear terms like "power" and "almighty," they convey to us themes like domination, colonization and coercion. But as Euro-Aussie Ben Myers so elegantly puts it,

> But that is not how "might" or "power" is understood in Christian teaching. The early Christians often compared God to a breastfeeding mother: it is a favorite image in numerous sermons and writings from the ancient church. We relate to God not like loyal subjects submitting to a powerful ruler, but like infants drawing nourishment from a mother. God's power is not only above us but also alongside us, beneath us, and within us. It is not the power of subjection and control but a power that frees and enables.[13]

This God and power doesn't resemble the evils of colonial empires, or the Greek and Roman gods who cared not for humanity but only for their own pleasures. Julian of Norwich, a fourteenth-century English theologian and mystic, writes of Yeshua as our mother, saying, "The mother can lay the child tenderly to her breast, but our tender mother Jesus, he can familiarly lead us into his blessed breast through his sweet open side [the

12. Isaac of Nineveh, "On Gehenna," 185–88.

13. Myers, *Apostles' Creed*, 17. To Ben's point, we find an example of this in the Syriac poetry of the *Odes of Solomon*, written sometime in the early second to early third century, specifically in Ode 19: "A cup of milk was offered to me, And I drank it in the sweetness of the Lord's kindness. The Son is the cup, And he who was milked, the Father, And [the one] who milked him, the Spirit of holiness. Because his breasts were full And it was not desirable that his milk should be poured out uselessly, The Spirit of holiness opened [the Father's] bosom And mixed the milk of the two breasts of the Father. And she gave the mixture to the world, while they did not know." *Odes of Solomon*, 53. Also note here God is being described as Trinity, Father, Son, and Holy Spirit, or "the Spirit of holiness" as the author writes.

side which was pierced by a spear and of which blood flowed out]."[14] To Julian, reminiscent of early church imagery, Yeshua is a kind mother who through his own blood and body nourishes us, sustaining and giving us life. To the Cappadocian Gregory of Nyssa, the perfection of life itself is being God's friend.[15] So, when we talk about God being King and the kingdom of God as God's rule and reign, we're not talking about a tyrant who wields the sword, but a friend and mother who takes up the cross for the sake of her child. We're talking about someone who can be compared to a loving mother who breast feeds us, a friend whom we aspire to trust and to lay open our hearts to, who seeks our good above their own.

In addition to looking at Messiah crucified to get a good picture of what God's power and rule looks like, we can also look to the Sermon on the Mount, which can be described as a kind of blueprint of the laws that will govern God's kingdom. It is Yeshua, if you will, casting his vision in his presidential election for how things will be run when he's in charge.[16] When Yeshua is in charge, so goes his presidential campaign speech, the humble and the poor rather than the rich and arrogant will blessed. The ones who mourn rather than the ones who rejoiced will be comforted. The humble and gentle will be the ones who will inherit the world, and the ones who hunger for things to be set right as they should be will be satisfied. Mercy is the way rather than cruelty, and those who show it will receive it, and those who are pure are the ones who will see God rather than the powerful. Yeshua goes so far as to say those who are peacemakers will be called "children of God."

The reign of shalom that Yeshua depicts is one that seeks to put the world into harmony, to make relationships right between humans and other humans, and between humans and the rest of their fellow creatures and the world, and to set right the relationship between creation and God. It is a world where divorce, which tears families and friends apart, doesn't happen, where you can trust those who give you their word, where instead of violent retaliation there is nonviolent, loving,

---

14. Julian of Norwich, *Revelations of Divine Love*, 141.

15. See Gregory, *Life of Moses*, 132.

16. Just to be clear, Yeshua's Sermon on the Mount is not a new law to supersede the old law or Torah, but is his authoritative interpretation of the Torah, as the one who himself gave the Torah to Moses. Severus of Antioch tells us that Yeshua was the "lawgiver and healer, who knew better than they his own (law) which he established and laid down." Severus of Antioch, "Homily XVIII," 119.

justice-filled resistance—a kingdom and people that loves its enemies because the God of Israel is like this.

A kingdom of and for the least of these does not have people who worry about where their next meal is going to come from, or how they're going to clothe their children, because these necessities of life, of which this material creation provides abundantly, are so graciously shared among the community of the King. "All those who believed [followed the King] were together, and everything that they had was held in common. Those who had some possession sold it and distributed it to each person according to what he needed."[17] Yeshua's way of ruling as the only rightful ruler, the only one truly good, true, and beautiful enough to rule, is upside down to how we think nations should be run; it's counterintuitive to our "commonsense" notions of what makes for good governance. Thus, far from his rule being that of an authoritative dictator, it will be that of a merciful parent who seeks what's best for their children. This of course doesn't mean everything is permissible, as a good parent knows there are things not good for the child to think, say, or do.

Now, how is Yeshua as King the way of faith? Well in the gospel, while faith is tied to this central aspect of Yeshua's kingship, as we discussed in chapter 4 it's not a propositional belief that needs to be rationally assessed and either affirmed or denied. Faith is allegiance to this King, faithfulness, fidelity, and trust in this King. If we are to take seriously the claim of universal kingship made by the Jewish Messiah, i.e., the gospel, then to me we must gain the vision to see our own governments and political institutions ultimately as illegitimate rivals and usurpers to the throne of the God of Israel, who is the Creator of heaven and earth. Just as in 1 Samuel 8:4–7 we see that Israel's King was originally God until the people requested a human king (something that grieved God for it was a rejection of his kingship), so the God of Israel was also once the King of the whole world, and in the Messiah's death and resurrection he's taking back his rightful rule over the whole world. Our allegiance therefore must be put and found in Messiah alone. In this sense, we must be subversive agents, living not according to our cultural and political false selves and the norms and laws of those false selves (for we answer to a higher law tied to our true selves rooted in God's image), but according to the rule and reign of the God of Israel in Yeshua Messiah.

---

17. Acts 2:44–45.

In this way we seek to participate in God's bringing of the kingdom, when one day the current governmental institutions will be overthrown not by us, but by God, and not through violence, but by the self-decay and self-destruction of the governments themselves. Mercy, justice, truth, and love, all things that God is, will outlast and outlive what does not have life in itself. Evil and sin are inherently self-destructive and self-corrosive since they are not self-existent but parasitic. Mercy, truth, justice, and love are like the yeast slowing being kneaded through the bread of the world by the hands of Messiah, his body, the church. Given time, these nations will fall by their own hands and the yeast will have spread and filled the risen bread of the world. Overthrowing the current political systems of the world thus does not take place through violence but through the love of neighbor. It's the yeast being kneaded throughout the world as we actively bring and wait for the consummation of the kingdom here and now. The bringing of the kingdom is the reconfiguration of the world as it is now to what it should be in the *telos* (the end goal) of God. As my friend Adam D'Achille once said, "The kingdom of God is the theosis of the world,"[18] meaning the kingdom of God is God's partnered act of divinized union of God's self as the Creator with the created. As long as the current political institutions stand, God's will cannot be fully realized; God will not be all in all.

Once again, as we saw in chapter 2, Mary is central to God's salvific plan. Hensa Krestos, an Ethiopian scholar-monk, in his devotional hymns to the virgin Mary entitled the *Harp of Glory*, writes concerning the bearer of God (Mary),

> Justly *are you the beginning of the creation of this world*,
> For you are at once the foundation and the gateway of the whole endeavor.
> O Dawn which knows no eventide,
> It was on your account that God created the heaven and the earth,
> The sea and its depths, the sun, the moon and stars,
> The times and the season, the winter and summer,
> Days and sabbaths, festivals and jubilations,
> All the worlds, whether visible or hidden.[19]

---

18. Adam D'Achille. Used with permission from author.

19. Krestos, *Harp of Glory*, 83. Emphasis added. Granted that what Hensa Krestos says is true, and I believe it is as I explain below, it is once again significant that it is through a Jew, in this case Mary, that God's plan of salvation unfurls. The centrality of Israel, of Jewish flesh, for the creation of the world and the world's consummation is ever present.

While this poem is quite striking, how does this relate to the kingdom of God as the world's theosis, and how can Hensa say the virgin Mary is "the beginning of the creation of this world" if the world was fully created long ago when God spoke it into being out of nothing? How can this scholar-monk say that Mary is even "the foundation and the gateway of the whole endeavor"? Hensa can say it firstly because the world has not yet been created in the full sense of the word "creation," not in the sense found when Paul says, "God will be all in all." Sure, the material universe came into existence fourteen billion years ago by the will and power of God, but that isn't creation in its fullness; it must first reach its *telos* before it becomes *creation* proper. The goal of the world, the thing that must happen before it is fully created, is incarnation. Like yeast kneaded through bread, this starts at a particular point and works its way through each particularity until the whole of the bread is filled with the yeast.

To this point Messianic Jewish theologian Jen Rosner writes, "the holiness of God that dwells within Israel will *expand outward* into the ordinary world beyond. Ultimately, God's holiness in the midst of Israel, the Sabbath and the tabernacle/temple points forward to the final consummation of creation—God's unrestricted presence and the definitive removal of the secular/holy barrier."[20] This consummation of creation, where God is all in all, happens through the particularity of Israel and even more so through one of Israel's own, Yeshua, God incarnate as an observant Jew. This particularity rubs our colonial universalizing DNA the wrong way. The particularity of the incarnation isn't a scandal because it's not inclusive, but perhaps because we don't understand that it is intended to prepare for the including of everyone in God's salvation, or perhaps we dislike the idea of *a specific people* being chosen as the vehicle for the whole world's salvation.

What's more, those of us who were raised Protestant have inherited the legacy of Luther's blasphemous anti-Semitism, amplified by the Endarkenment's distaste for cultural particularity and Jewishness—a distaste that culminated in the holocaust. A quote from Luther illustrates the problem: "Therefore, dear Christian be advised and do not doubt that next to the devil, you have no more bitter, venomous and vehement foe than a real Jew who earnestly seeks to be a Jew."[21] With this kind of German liberal anti-Jewish DNA, some of us cannot stand the reality that

---

20. Rosner, *Finding Messiah*, 51.
21. Luther, *Essential Luther*, 284–303.

God in the second person of the Trinity became "a real Jew who earnestly seeks to be a Jew." Yet this is the particular access point into the dough of creation that God has chosen to inject the Jewish yeast to work out the whole world's salvation.

God's plan to create a people for himself in the people of Israel was the beginning of God's mysterious plan for incarnation, working its way in and through the particularity of the people of Israel, which grew in its concentration until finally the Word of God physically became a Jewish human being two thousand years ago. The mystery of God's particular and full incarnation as an observant Jew will spill over and consummate in the *telos* of creation, when all things will be brought into union with God and filled with God to their fullness. The Son becoming human, intensifying the incarnation of the people Israel, is if you will the yeast being added to the bread, which is still being kneaded. Maximus the Confessor wrote, "*The Word of God, very God*, wills that the mystery of his Incarnation [what happened two thousand years ago] be actualized always and *in all things*."[22] Indeed, for Maximus, as Euro-American theologian Jordan Daniel Wood argues, *true creation is the world's incarnation by and through and in the Word*.[23] God must be all in all by the world finding its union in and with God, God fully God, creation fully creation, but fully united together, in two natures, one union.

So, as Hensa so poetically put it, the virgin Mary, and I might add the *Jewish* virgin Mary, indeed is "the beginning of the creation of this world" and is "the foundation and the gateway of the whole endeavor," because in her both the beginning of the world as it now stands and the end as it will be when God is all in all meet in her Jewish womb, in the incarnation of the Word made Jewish flesh. In her the Creator and creation meet and unite in bliss; in her, creation proper, namely incarnation, is begun. Now Mary's Jewish womb, the gateway, is the foundation and beginning of the world's beginning and its true end into complete and proper creation, and so it is here in her Jewish womb that the *telos* of true creation finds its way into reality through the big bang of incarnation.

In the book of Revelation we see a glimpse of the new heaven and new earth, of the world's theosis, of God's kingdom fully inaugurated and consummated, of creation fully finished.

---

22. Maximus, quoted in Wood, *Whole Mystery of Christ*, 17.
23. See Wood, *Whole Mystery of Christ*.

> Then I saw new heavens and a new earth. For the first heaven and the first earth departed, and the sea was no more. And I saw the holy city, the new Jerusalem, descending from heaven, from with God, prepared like an adorned bride for her husband. And I heard a loud voice from heaven which said: "Behold the dwelling of God is with men, and he will dwell with them, and they shall be his people, and God is with them, and he shall be to them God." And he shall wipe away all tears from their eyes, and death shall be no more, nor mourning nor clamor nor pain shall be on her face. And I departed, and the one sitting on the throne said to me: "Behold I am making all new." Moreover he said to me: "Write these words—they are faithful and true."[24]

This new earth, this kingdom of God, which is the theosis of the world, or as a former professor of mine has called it the "Community of Creation,"[25] will not look like the Gnostic depictions of the afterlife, where we are floating off in some sort of spiritual oasis far removed from the physical world. Instead, the writers of the Bible and the tradition of the church had a fuller meaning embodied when they talked about salvation.[26] The late metropolitan Kallistos Ware describes this fullness.

> "A new heaven and a new earth": man is not saved *from* his body but *in* it; not saved *from* the material world but *with* it. Because man is microcosm and mediator of the creation, his own salvation involves also the reconciliation and transfiguration of the whole animate and inanimate creation around him—its deliverance "from the bondage of corruption" and entry "into the glorious liberty of the children of God" (Rom 8.21). In the "new earth" of the Age to come there is surely a place not only for man but for the animals: in and through man, they too will share in immortality, and so will rocks, trees and plants, fire and water.[27]

---

24. Revelation 21:1–5.

25. Woodley, *Shalom and the Community of Creation*, 39.

26. For more on an embodied view of the afterlife, see Middleton, *New Heaven and a New Earth*. Although I suspect he misunderstands Origen. See also Wright, *Surprised by Hope*.

27. Ware, *Orthodox Way*, 186. Irenaeus and Origen also advocate that the material world will not be destroyed or abandoned, as the Gnostics do, both old and new (i.e., the Fundamentalists), but in contrast will be made new. See Irenaeus, *Against Heresies*, 509–10; and Origen, *On First Principles*, 57–58.

The Cross and Resurrection—the Way of Hope

The Cross

Throughout the early church, the cross and resurrection were central aspects of the preached gospel. Unfortunately, when many of us former fundamentalists think of the cross, we imagine a purely angry God who requires Yeshua to be killed in our place as a sacrifice to satiate his wrath towards us. Yeshua's death is indeed a sacrifice, but not in the sense that moderns think of sacrifice. We tend to see sacrifice as the act of violently killing an animal to appease an angry God, but this is more of a pagan notion of sacrifice than it is a Jewish-Christian one. As Euro-American Episcopalian scholar and priest Matthew S. C. Olver writes, "A sacrifice is the offering to God of what the creature understands to be a gift from God."[28] In other words, sacrifice from a Jewish point of view is understood to be more a gift from what has already been given by God, presented in gratitude towards the Creator for God's abundant provision in creation, than it is understood as an act of violence to appease a self-absorbed wrathful God.

Given these pagan assumptions of sacrifice as an appeasement of God, we often fail to see the therapeutic aspect to the cross alluded to by Yeshua's reading of Numbers 21. In the story of Numbers 21, while the Israelites were wandering around in the desert, they were, because of their sin, bitten by serpents. As they cried out, God commanded Moses to build a bronze serpent and raise it up in the air for the Israelites to look upon, and if they merely looked at it they would be healed and live. In Yeshua's allegorical reading of this text, he himself is the bronze serpent who must be raised into the air—a reference to the cross—so that all who look upon him may be healed from the sickness of sin (John 3:14–15), a sickness that like the venom of those serpents will kill. In contrast to some of the Reformation notions of the Messiah on the cross, in the early church the problem solved on the cross was not God's need to punish humanity through his outpouring of wrath but God's defeat of sin as a sickness, Satan, and death.[29] St. Irenaeus wrote about the problem Yeshua was solving in this way:

---

28. Olver, "Missed and Misunderstood Jewish Roots," 85.

29. See Aulén, *Christus* Victor. See also Wright, *Day the Revolution Began*, and Jersak, *More Christlike God*.

> . . . for, in accomplishing and recapitulating these things in Himself, in order to obtain life for us, "The Word of God became flesh" by the economy of the Virgin, *in order to undo death and vivify man, for we were in the prison of sin*, we who have become sinners and fallen under [the power of] death. Rich in mercy was God the Father: He sent the creative Word, who, coming to save us, was in the same place and situation in which we were when we lost life, *breaking the bonds of the prison*; and His light appeared and dispelled the darkness of the prison, and sanctified our birth *and abolished death*, loosening the same bonds by which we were trapped.[30]

To St. Irenaeus, we had become captured by death, stuck in the prison of sin, and were thus subject to death; but Messiah, by becoming a human being like us through the virgin and by dying on the cross, he who is Life defeated death from the inside out. Indeed, this reality of the Messiah protecting us from death, found in both the Renewed Jewish Testament[31] and the early church, *is rooted in the context* of the Passover feast, in which Yeshua was crucified.[32] Passover is the commemoration of our time in Egypt, when God to protect us from death instructed us to eat the sacrificed Passover lamb and smear it's blood on our doorposts, so that when death came upon the land of Egypt it would *pass over* us. The blood of the Passover protected us from death, and the quick meal of the unleavened bread and lamb gave us the energy to flee Egypt over the next couple of days.

When Yeshua during the Last Supper (a Passover meal) broke the bread and said, "Take and eat; this is my body," and gave thanks for the cup of wine, saying, "Take and drink of this, all of you. This is my blood,"[33] being himself the Passover lamb, the Jewish disciples recalled and understood all of this to be reminiscent of the exodus Passover. In other words, Yeshua is the Passover lamb who's Jewish blood protects us from death, who causes death to *pass over* us, a reality we're mysteriously connected to every week when we drink from the eucharistic cup. And his body, the Jewish bread, is the sustenance we feed on every Sunday to nourish us for our flight out of Egypt. Yeshua's death, understood in its Jewish context, is what liberates us from the Egyptians, the forces of death, chaos, and

---

30. Irenaeus of Lyon, *On the Apostolic Preaching*, 64. Emphasis added.
31. See Paul in 1 Corinthians 15 for instance—"oh death, where is your sting?"
32. See Exodus 12.
33. This is my own paraphrase.

the demonic rulers of this world. His Jewish blood is what gives us life, by conquering death while at the same time freeing us so we can live in his new kingdom and rule in freedom, not bondage. Having maintained the Jewishness of the gospel, the problem according to Irenaeus is not a wrathful God who needs to punish sin with death, but death itself, to which we freely gave ourselves and by which we have become trapped. St. Athanasius describes the work of Messiah in this way:

> *Christ came that he might overthrow the devil* . . . this must have been by death, and by what other death would these things have happened except that which takes place in the air, I mean the cross? For only he that completes his life on the cross dies in the air. Therefore it was right that the Lord endured it. For being thus lifted up, he purified the air from the diabolical plots of all demons, saying *"I saw Satan falling as lightening"* . . . *That death has been dissolved, and the cross has become victory over it*, and it is no longer strong but is itself truly dead, no mean proof but an evident surety is that it is despised by all Christ's disciples, and everyone tramples on it, and no longer fears it, but with the sign of the cross and faith in Christ tread it under foot as something dead.[34]

For St. Athanasius, when we turned from God, who is Life itself, our only source of life, we thus cut ourselves off from life. In turning away from the source of life, God, there is only one alternative, death. Therefore sin, which is this turning away from the source of life, has death as its natural consequence. Yet because there was no sin in Messiah, because he never turned away from the source of life, and he was Life itself, death was not a natural consequence due him. If the natural consequence of touching fire is being burned and yet, being burned, you never touched any fire, such burning really has no claim over you. In the same way, although Messiah experienced death, the consequence of sin, since he never experienced sin, death therefore had no claim on him. It is because of this voluntary choosing of death that Messiah has transformed death into the beginning of new life.

The Arab Chalcedonian bishop of Haran Theodore Abu Qurrah,[35] in his treatise *That God Is Not Weak*, explains that Messiah died on the

---

34. Athanasius, *On the Incarnation*, 76–78. Emphasis added.

35. Bishop Theodore Abu Qurrah lived in the second half of the eight century and the early part of the ninth century. He was one of the first Christians to write original works in Arabic, rather than in Greek, Coptic, or Syriac.

cross because it was the only way God could save humanity out of slavery from Satan in a way that was not inconsistent with his characteristics of justice, generosity, might, and wisdom.[36] This short treatise is worth reading in full, but for our purposes here it is important to simply point out a few of Abu Qurrah's reasonings for Yeshua's death on the cross. Abu Qurrah states that God gave humanity free will, and in that free will they gave themselves over to slavery under Satan. Realizing their newfound predicament, they could do nothing about it except cry out to God. But because God is just, the ways in which God could set humanity free from Satan were limited.

Before Adam had freely given himself over to Satan, God had "showed him the path of wickedness and carefully warned him against it, promising him death should he take that path."[37] After Iblis (Satan in Arabic) used deceit rather than strength to deprive him of the favor and paradise God gave him, something Iblis envied and wished to take from him, Adam, having turned from God, fell to the consequences of death, and now, being weak, found himself captured by Iblis. Being merciful, God wished to save him, but since God had warned Adam in advance, he could not simply snatch him back from Iblis. "If he [God] were to go ahead and save him from Satan by force, however, he would transgress the limits of justice and only increase Iblis's just claim."[38] Iblis would then be able to boast that God cannot save humanity from him except by not being just. Since God is just, he would never act against Iblis in force to save humanity. God's justice is so intrinsic to God's nature that even God cannot transgress God's own justice even to save humanity from Satan.

This, however, leaves God with a dilemma, namely how could God rescue humanity without violating God's justice. Abu Qurrah provides an analogy for God's clever plan to save humanity without the use of force, starting first by explaining how humanity became enslaved in the first place: A mighty and just king sent some of his soldiers (representing both angels and humans), with liberty, into a field, but with established boundaries they weren't supposed to cross for their own safety. Indeed,

---

36. The liberation from slavery under Satan, to which all humanity had been subjugated, is something that, according to Narsai the Syrian, happens through the Jewish people. From the narrative of Narsai's commentary on the Canaanite woman speaking to Yeshua, she says, "for you are from that seed in which the freedom of humanity is inscribed." Narsai, "On the Canaanite Woman," 76. In other words, the freedom of humanity from Satan happens through the people of Israel, "Abraham's seed."

37. Qurrah, "That God Is Not Weak," 293–94.

38. Qurrah, "That God Is Not Weak," 294.

he warned them that whoever crossed the boundary would become the slave of the one who deceived him into crossing. One of the angels, Iblis, however, being weak, was deceived by and became a slave to his own desire. Being unable to restrain himself, he became like a wild animal. Thus, Iblis repudiated fidelity to the king and himself became "the leader of error and obduracy."[39] He then proceeded to deceive the king's free soldiers in the field, leading them to become slaves of their own desire. In due time he captured and enslaved all of them.

The king, not wanting to use force against his own soldiers, instead sent his son, who was like him in all ways. He disguised himself as one of the soldiers and entered the field. When Iblis saw him, he sought to lead him astray as he had done all the others, but although using all his strength he failed to do so. When he saw he wouldn't be able to enslave him too, he became enraged, so "he attacks him and kills him without cause, committing an outrage against him, in that the king's son had not pledged himself to him as his companions had pledged themselves."[40] The son willingly allowed himself to be killed so that his father might have reason to justly reclaim his soldiers, and because he lacked a just claim on the king's son, Iblis thus forfeited his claim on all those he had enslaved. The king then spoke to the unjust one, saying, "'Did you not lead astray and enslave all whom I set at liberty in this field? And yet, did I use force against you with respect to any of them?" He said, "No." The king then said, "What of this man who stuck by me and remained in my domain? On what grounds did you kill him? It is thus that the just claims of that weak and depraved man are annulled."[41] Since the king's son was greater than all the other men that he had captured, Satan forfeited any claim he might have.

After explaining all of this, Abu Qurrah ends by summarizing the reason why Messiah died on the cross:

> It is in a similar manner that we speak of Christ's crucifixion and everything else that befell him. That is, he is the Son of God, and he disguised himself from Satan. He clothed himself from the Virgin Mary in a body like our bodies, with a soul like our souls and a mind not different from our minds. He then went forth from her and walked about in the world. Satan thought him to be like one of us, and so he yearned to possess him and

---

39. Qurrah, "That God Is Not Weak," 295.
40. Qurrah, "That God Is Not Weak," 295.
41. Qurrah, "That God Is Not Weak," 295.

he desired to overcome him, even as he had overcome us. He was unable to do this, however. When Christ had thwarted his efforts, Satan flew into a rage and made bold to kill him. Because Satan had killed his Son, God was justly entitled to save us from slavery to him, as well as from its consequences, such as death and the like.[42]

Interestingly enough, C. S. Lewis gives us an analogy similar to Abu Qurrah's in *The Lion, the Witch, and the Wardrobe*. When Edmund freely gives himself over to the service of the witch out of his own selfish desires, Aslan out of his love for Edmund gives himself to the witch in Edmund's place in order that Edmund might go free. The white witch then proceeds to kill Aslan, yet because Aslan is innocent, he comes back to life, defeating death and the witch. Similarly, for Athanasius Yeshua came to overthrow the devil, and he does so by his defeat of death. As proof of Messiah's triumph over death on the cross, Athanasius offers up the reality of the martyrs who freely choose death rather than denying their allegiance to Yeshua. They have no fear of death, so Athanasius argues, because the Messiah has defeated it.

With all of these figures and their works, we see the issue that God needed to deal with was not his own wrath and the need to satiate it, or the need to punish us for our sins, but our slavery to Satan through our sin, and the death that came as a consequence of our sin. What's more, Messiah's death not only defeated death but transformed it into the pathway for our resurrection; and because death itself has gone through its own process of theosis, through its own adoption into the family of God, the Italian mystic Francis of Assisi would be able to call it "sister death."

Now if this is why Yeshua died on the cross two thousand years ago, how does it shape and inform what our following of him should look like today? It means we too, like Yeshua, must have a cross-shaped life. In Luke 14:27, Yeshua says, "Whoever does not carry *the cross* themselves and come after me, is not able to be my disciple."[43] We are told whoever does not pick up *the cross* and come after him is not able to be his disciple. This is curious wording, both in some English translations and in the Greek. It does not say take up *a cross*, or even *our cross*, but it says take up *the cross*.[44] But how are we to take up the cross of the Messiah, which surely by now has decomposed? Since it is a command from Yeshua the

42. Qurrah, "That God is Not Weak," 295.
43. My translation. Emphasis added.
44. The NRSV translates it as I do, although some English translations do not.

Messiah, we must follow it if we wish to be his disciples. But how shall we bridge the two-thousand-year-old gap between us and Messiah crucified? And how, when we do so, will we be able to provoke the Roman colonialists to let us carry this same cross that the God-man Yeshua of Nazareth the Messiah himself carried and was nailed to?

Our first obstacle seems physically impossible to overcome, so are we doomed to never have this opportunity to carry *the cross*? Is not this cross trapped in the past and we in the present? The answer to this odd dilemma is found in carrying *the cross* mystically through union with and in Yeshua. When the Messiah is born in us, when we through our practicing of the virtues come to share, in those instances, in the nature of Yeshua, we find him enfleshing himself in us, and thus like Paul we find ourselves saying, "Not I, but Messiah in me." Then, mystically united to Messiah, with the eternal Word collapsing time, we too find ourselves in Jerusalem two thousand years ago identified and present with Yeshua carrying the cross. This happens through dying to ourselves, living not for our ego but for God and our neighbor, and in doing so we find ourselves through the power of the Holy Spirit in the process of theosis, coming to share in the divine nature.

Furthermore, the way of the cross is the way of discipleship. Christianity is not about being comfortable. Hunayn Ibn Ishaq, an Arab Christian living in the ninth century, even claims the suffering of Christians as one of the reasons Christianity, rather than Islam or Judaism, is true.[45] In his theological treatise *How to Discern the True Religion*, he argues one can determine whether a religion is true or false by looking at the reasons people initially accepted it. He says there are several reasons for why the first Christians accepted Christianity that we can use to determine the truth of it. It is interesting to note that most of these reasons fly in the face of our cultural values as Americans. They are extremely counterintuitive to those with the white Enlightenment worldview. The first is that Christianity was not accepted by its first adherents because the governmental authorities, kings and princes, coerced them to do so against their will; rather the kings and princes were hostile to the faith and sought to eradicate it through torture and all sorts of dreadful deaths. Despite this, Ibn Ishaq says, it prevailed, not only surviving but thriving.

---

45. Although the distinction between Judaism and Christianity would have been a foreign concept to the first Christians, who were all Jewish, by the time of Hunayn Ibn Ishaq, as in ours, this has errantly become the norm.

Secondly, he says, Christianity did not beckon its members to abandon conditions of hardship and constraint for conditions of ease, comfort, and abundance. To the contrary, it called them from ease, comfort, and abundance to hardship and constraint, a state that was most undesirable. But despite this people still accepted it. The next reason he gives seems related to the previous one: Christianity did not invite people from lowliness, commonness, and self-abasement to might, power, renown, and fame; rather, it called them from power and might to humility and self-abasement. But despite this, "it was so readily accepted that its followers used to prefer death to life for its sake."[46] For the first Christians, as the Egyptian Origen and African-American scholar Dennis R. Edwards argue, true power is from the margins.[47]

Ibn Ishaq's fourth and fifth reasons are again related. Christianity wasn't accepted by people who were cunning and crafty in their way of speaking. Instead, those who received it were ignorant, uneducated men, fishermen by trade, who were unable to express themselves well; in an idiom of the day he says they were "indeed, men who were more mute and more incapable of expressing themselves than are fish (as the saying holds)."[48] At the same time, these were not the only people to accept Christianity; rather some of them were among the best philosophers and logicians in all the world, gifted with scholarly arts, and discernment, wiser than all other people. In summary, all sorts of people accepted Christianity.

The sixth reason Ibn Ishaq gives is that those who became followers of Yeshua did not join up because all their friends and family were joining; rather, having accepted Yeshua as their King, they would become severed from all those they were at one time tied to through connections of affinity, both friends and family, and yet they still chose to follow Yeshua. Lastly, the seventh reason he gives is that the apostle's preaching about Christianity was more demanding than anything else in regard to its "outward observances."[49] In other words, their behavioral and ethical standards were quite demanding. Nobody wanting a religion that

---

46. Ishaq, "How to Discern the True Religion," 307.

47. Origen writes, "if you want to hasten, taking the road toward the good, do not shrink from flourishing in weaknesses and from being such a person as to say, 'When I am weak, then I am powerful.'" Origen, *Homilies on the Psalms*, 50. Dennis Edwards says it this way: "I believe that those who have been marginalized have power that is not only unnoticed, but often underutilized." Edwards, *Might from the Margins*, 26.

48. Ishaq, "How to Discern the True Religion," 307.

49. Ishaq, "How to Discern the True Religion," 308.

advocated and licensed them to do whatever was pleasing to them would accept Christianity.

The point I want to make here is Christianity is a cross-shaped religion, and despite this people have accepted it, and understood it to be so, for a long time. Despite the bastardization of Christianity in America, particularly by the prosperity gospel, which seems to have something particularly American about it, the faith delivered once and for all, carried along in and by the church, *is not* a faith of comfort and prosperity, something meant to make us feel good on any given Sunday morning.

Yes, it's an allegiance that hopes in God's kingdom being brought to the earth, a kingdom in which the King wipes away our tears, a kingdom where there is harmony, peace, and justice; but the work that it takes to participate with God to bring that kingdom to the earth is one that takes the path of the cross. We will only arrive, or rather the kingdom will only arrive, through blood, sweat, tears, and fire. With Hunayn Ibn Ishaq, I say Christianity is true because despite the suffering, discomfort, and all the other terrible things that might come our way while serving Yeshua, our friend and King is worth it, and his vision and rule are something worth fighting for.

Christianity is first and foremost a religion of death, of laying down your life in love for your neighbor, so that resurrection may occur. It is not merely a religion of death, but it is nothing less, and it is through death that we enter into life, where we find hope. The way of the cross is the way of hope, because we know in an embodied way that on the cross Yeshua defeated sin, death, and Satan, and God has redeemed and transformed suffering and death to become our means of bringing the kingdom of God, the theosis of the world. While today in the West we tend to think of Messiah's resurrection as his defeat of death, in reality his resurrection is only made possible by his defeat of death on the cross; he only resurrected because he had already defeated death on the cross. The resurrection shows us that the cross was his victory rather than his defeat. We are not just left to an empty void ceasing to exist when we die, but like him we will be raised. In this way his death on the cross gives us hope.

Resurrection

This then begs the question of how the resurrection fits into the way of hope. Examining 1 Corinthians 15, people often think Paul's primary argument is about the Messiah's resurrection, and it is, but more specifically it is about Messiah's own resurrection as the first fruits of everyone's bodily resurrection to come in the new age. As we saw above, it's his defeat of death on the cross that makes possible not only his resurrection but ours as well. For Paul and the early church, the Jewish doctrine of the resurrection of the dead and Yeshua's resurrection on Passover/Easter are deeply connected. To deny one is to deny the other. He writes, "So then, if what was proclaimed was that the Messiah rose from the dead, how can it be that there are some of you that are saying that there is no life after death? And if there is no life after death then the Messiah has also not risen."[50] Paul goes on to say if Messiah wasn't raised from the dead, then the proclamation of Christians is in vain, our faith is in vain, and we are to be pitied above all peoples.

We are to be pitied because if there is no resurrection of the body, we are going to rot in the ground and cease to exist into oblivion. This is because for Jews if there is a soul, it's not detachable. For us we are not souls that have bodies, but bodies that have souls. When you die, your soul and body die too. If Messiah is not risen, then death and nothingness is all that awaits us, and all has no meaning. Without the resurrection it's a pretty bleak picture. It makes sense this doctrine has been prevalent among us Jews since we have long experienced persecution and murder under the boot of empire after empire. Given their privilege of whiteness, wealth, and colonialism, it also makes sense why white progressive thinkers, i.e., the Northern Europeans, who often were the persecutors, think they have no need for resurrection.

Colonial powers that wield the forces of death have been demonically deluded into believing that because of their station of so-called power, they are exempt from death and therefore have no need for resurrection. But those who are poor, brown, persecuted, and generally marginalized know they need resurrection, because they lack the blindness of privilege and so see clearly enough their true need for it. For those who have eyes to see, the resurrection is needed as a matter of hope. In a letter from a Soviet concentration camp, we see that despite the utter meaninglessness of their forced horrendous condition, the Christians there found joy in the pit of despair because of their hope in the resurrection. "Death is conquered, fear no more, an eternal Easter is given to us! Full of this marvelous Easter, we send you from our prison camp the victorious and

---

50. 1 Corinthians 15:12–13.

joyful tidings: Christ is risen!"[51] Imagine a white liberal Protestant telling them the resurrection doesn't matter. It certainly matters to them!

On June 24 of 2020 our dog Allie died. She had heartworms, and like many dogs with heartworms she didn't make it. Allie came to us from my best friend's family. I had known her since they first got her as a puppy, back when Colt (my best friend) and I were still in the youth group. The day she died, Colt and I had just had a wonderful moment with her.[52] We had placed my T-shirt on her and she seemed quite content. Something about a dog wearing a T-shirt was comically comforting. Within the hour she died before our eyes. Over the next week I cried my eyes out; I didn't know what life would be like without her.[53] Shortly after her death my wife and I were laying on our Japanese mattress getting ready for bed when I had a vision. I saw a bright tan grassy field on top on of a hill, the grass swaying in the breeze with a big deciduous tree behind the meadow.[54] And in the pasture in front of the tree was Allie, sitting in the grass with Yeshua squatting next to her with his hand gently upon her. He told her to go see me, that it was alright to go leave his side to say hi. She ran over, and suddenly she was siting once again beside me on the floor next to our Japanese mattress. And I had an opportunity to pet her like I used to. I believe Yeshua was reassuring me that Allie would be in the resurrection and I would one day see her in the new earth.

Moreover, I believe Yeshua was giving me a glimpse of the future resurrection, allowing Allie to reach out from the new earth, if you will, to say goodbye. Now of course I don't expect you to give up on your doubt of the resurrection merely because I had a vision. My point in telling this story is that the resurrection is a better story, one that gives and inspires hope. Who really wants to live in a world that will simply end, in which their life will fall into oblivion, into nothingness, in which everything they do has no meaning and doesn't matter, and will end with the destructive decay of our universe? Is that really a world worth living in? Why does our German doubt get the final say?[55] Doubt your doubt.

51. Letter from a Soviet concentration camp, quoted in Ware, *Orthodox Way*, 119.
52. Colt lived with my wife, my grandma, and myself at the time.
53. I cried while I wrote this.
54. The tree I believe was real, but it was also a symbol of the cross. The cross, a dead piece of wood, lives on in the resurrected world where it grows anew, and where it came back to life.
55. I say "German doubt" because our doubt is rooted in a German or Enlightenment epistemology (way of knowing). I'm not saying all doubt is bad, or even German, but specifically that our doubt is rooted in Northern European ways of thinking and

Question your questioning. The resurrection isn't true because it can be rationally verified using the scientific method. The resurrection is true because it's a better story; because its more mysterious, more true, more beautiful, and more good; because it's the hope we need, the hope that fulfills and satiates our greatest and deepest true desires.

The spiritualization of the Christian faith that often happens among wealthy, white liberal Protestants can at least in part occur because they aren't worrying about where their next meal is going to come from, or whether their child will die from malaria, or if they are going to be arrested or shot simply because they are black. When you're comfortable and living on the nice side of town, away from all the horrors of the world, when you're part of the oppressor people group rather than the oppressed, denying the resurrection works for you. Comfort and privilege has a way of blinding us. When your people weren't enslaved working in the cotton fields, colonized and forced onto reservations and into boarding schools, or slaughtered in the holocaust like swine, you don't need resurrection. And when your cultural way of thinking and existing in the world, i.e. European modernist Endarkenment rationalism, rules the world through its colonization of the mind, you think you don't need resurrection.

By saying the resurrection doesn't matter or it didn't happen, you're saying that the colonizers, the oppressors, won. This Northern European theology proclaims that Rome, the empire, colonizer, and oppressor of a huge swath of the world, the dragon, has beaten the Jewish King and Messiah, has triumphed against the marginalized, has doused the last flicker of hope. This kind of modernist theology is wonderful for colonizers who desire to maintain their power, because it says to all those they continue to oppress and whose land they continue to occupy, "Your situation, your oppression, cannot change; you will never beat us." So it's no surprise this theology came out of colonial Northern Europe. They wish to maintain their power and they need a corroborating theology to back it up. The resurrection of a marginalized Jewish Messiah is threatening to an empire built on the backs of the marginalized that seeks to maintain the status quo of marginalization.

Yet as I have constantly brought up in this book, why does German modernist rationalism from Europe get to have such deciding power when it comes to the faith, particularly in this case the Jewish

---

being that come from the racist, colonial, and anti-Jewish worldview of modernist Germany and the surrounding area. It's Enlightenment epistemology that leads us to our specific kind of doubt, and that epistemology is rooted in a racist worldview.

bodily resurrection? Applying rationalism as the primary and final criteria to determine the validity of the resurrection is a modern Northern European thing to do; it's an imposition of European categories and assumptions. Its applying a European, German ideological framework and epistemology to theologies that are ultimately rooted in a brown first-century Jewish context. Is this not an epistemological holocaust?—the ghost of Germany coming to finish any remaining vestiges of Jewish thought and culture, or maybe even the predecessor of the holocaust.[56] The proclamation of the resurrection, a central aspect of the gospel, came out of a brown Jewish Judean and Galilean context and mainly first took root in the gentile world outside of Northern Europe, throughout Syria, Egypt, North Africa, Ethiopia, India, Persia, and Asia Minor.

I don't believe it's a coincidence that Enlightenment rationalism is discarding the Jewish teaching of resurrection. Writing about the Endarkenment's project of de-Jewifying Christianity, Euro-American theologian George Lindbeck says,

> Under the influence of Enlightenment rationalism . . . everything within Christianity that was deemed to be specifically Jewish came increasingly under attack . . . Old Testament (i.e., Jewish) religion was rejected root and branch as primitive, legalistic, and intolerant. Whatever was good about it, such as the moral duties inculcated in the Ten Commandments, was simply part of the natural law or general revelation available to all human beings. There was nothing specific to Israelite religion that enlightened Christians wanted to appropriate or expropriate. In a move somewhat like Marcion's, they displaced a supersessionist by a rejectionist understanding of the relation of Christianity to Judaism . . . Thus anti-Judaism, in the sense of contempt for the religion of the Jews, became more virulent under Enlightenment influence even while Jews as individuals became more acceptable.[57]

---

56. German Enlightenment theology first sought to get rid of anything ideologically and culturally Jewish from Christianity and the broader culture. But once that was completed, once there were Jews stripped of their Jewishness, the natural next step was murdering the Jews. We kid ourselves to think that the anti-Jewish theology that was rampant throughout German culture and scholarship just a couple of generations before the holocaust did nothing to contribute to the holocaust.

57. Lindbeck, "Church as Israel," 90. I would note Jews only became more accepted as individuals if they adopted the Enlightenment ideals of Northern Europe, though even having do to so as an *individual* was already an act of having to give up their Jewish ways of living in exchange for Northern European ones. It was ideological colonization.

Euro-American R. Kendall Soulen testifies to this growing de-Jewifying position during the Enlightenment when he writes that for Kant, "Purifying Christian doctrine of its residual Jewishness is therefore no distortion of the Christian faith but the necessary expression of its basic genius."[58] It is no coincidence that Enlightenment rationalism is discarding the foundational Jewish proclamation of Christianity because such was the project of Endarkenment rationalism. Having been steeped in the same German Endarkenment tea that gave rise to the Nazis, liberal Protestantism seems to me to be inherently problematic. We thus should not be surprised when we discover racism, colonialism, and white normativity of various types in liberal Protestantism, such as anti-Jewish assumptions and categories. It is part and parcel of the modernist Enlightenment project to de-Jewify the Christian faith. An Enlightenment Christianity is a de-Jewified Christianity.

We need to be more reflective on where these attitudes for rejecting Jewish Christian dogmas like the resurrection are coming from. So again, why does German epistemology and theology get to have such decision power over what we believe and confess? When Enlightenment versions of Protestantism proclaim the ridiculousness, backwardness, and irrationality of the bodily resurrection, really what they're doing is decreeing brown and ultimately Jewish thinking as inferior to their own. By asserting and imposing white European epistemology and general modernist thinking upon the central mysteries of the faith, such as the Jewish resurrection, they are attempting to continue to colonize the minds and bodies of brown peoples, cultures, and religions.

Christianity, having been born in and through the Jewish people, having such prominence in the world, giving hope to broken and oppressed peoples, manifested through such teachings as the resurrection, stands in the way of the supposed superiority and normativity of Northern European ways of thinking and being in the world. It is unacceptable that such a brown Jewish faith has captivated the hearts of billions; therefore the demonic consciousness of white supremacy must seek to "adapt," "update," and cleanse Christianity of its Jewish brown characteristics; it must be "progressed" and have imposed upon it our loftier German Enlightenment categories and assumptions. Until we unveil the colonialism and anti-Jewish sentiment embedded in modernism, and so long as we continue to "adapt" or "accommodate" Christianity according to these

---

58. Soulen, *God of Israel and Christian Theology*, 68.

modern white sensibilities, forcibly applying foreign categories and assumptions onto the brown resurrection, we will continue to uphold white supremacy and colonize the minds and hearts of the world.

We must realize there is a deep, permanent connection between Christianity and Judaism and the Jewish people. Speaking of this connection, Messianic Jewish theologian Jennifer Rosner writes,

> From a Christian perspective, if this permanent and throughgoing connection between Jews and Christians is real, it must work its way through every doctrine of Christian theology. If Judaism is somehow intrinsic to Christianity, then Christianity's self-understanding is necessarily distorted to the extent that it excludes consideration of Judaism and the Jewish people.[59]

The bedrock of Christianity is Jewish, because our foundation is a brown Jew named Yeshua. Said another way, since the foundation of Christian identity lies in Messiah, and Messiah is a Jew, the foundation of our Christian identity lies in the Jewish people. The core of Christian faith is also Jewish because all the first Christian theological work was birthed out of a Jewish context. Any development of theology within our faith that departs from this Jewish bedrock is not legitimately Christian. Indeed, to reject the core of the Christian faith (which is Jewish) is to practice anti-Semitism; it is a removing of that Jewish core. A Jewish or generally brown follower of Yeshua is therefore never truly welcomed in a liberal theological environment that rejects any or all aspects of that brown Jewish core which are the central tenants of the faith.

Yet in order to overcome anti-Jewish systemic sentiments, we don't have to jettison the things that make Christianity distinct, but rather we must remember (remember because the first Christians were Jews who already knew this) and come to recognize (recognize because most Christians today are gentiles and have never known this) that those distinctives of our Christian faith *are Jewish*. And because those distinctives of the Christian faith are Jewish, to jettison such distinctives is in the end an anti-Jewish move that only serves to solidify anti-Judaism. If we wish to dispose of anti-Jewish belief and practice we must remember, recognize, and embrace the Jewish bedrock of Christianity.[60]

---

59. Rosner, *Healing the Schism*, 35.

60. Now, there may be theologies that are also non-negotiables to the Christian faith that are not a part of what constitutes the Jewish bedrock but do not negate, undermine, remove or contradict the core Jewishness of the faith, although I imagine these are few and far between. Of course, these core Jewish tenets of the faith will be expressed

If we indeed question and jettison the Endarkenment's rationalism, which is at the root of modernist Christianity's rejection of the Jewish resurrection, we can like oppressed and marginalized peoples around the world once again rest in the hope of the resurrection. The truth is we are not immortal souls that will shed our bodies when we attain our salvation as Gnosticism teaches. If God truly is ultimate beauty, truth, and goodness, then not being able to spend the ages with the triune God of Israel, but instead ceasing to exist, is a travesty worth mourning about. For Paul and the early Christians, the resurrection is the proof in the pudding that Messiah's death on the cross was indeed his triumph and defeat of death. According to this logic, if Yeshua didn't come back to life in bodily form, then he didn't defeat death on the cross, and if he didn't defeat death and transform it into our means of resurrection, then when we die death wins, we stay in the ground, and everything we worked for in this life is meaningless.[61]

Fortunately, our faith insists otherwise. As the Irishman C. S. Lewis writes, "Christianity is almost the only one of the great religions which thoroughly approves of the body—which believes that matter is good, that God Himself once took on a human body, that some kind of body is going to be given to us even in Heaven [Heaven come to earth] and is going to be an essential part of our happiness, our beauty, and our energy."[62] If we are to have life after death, it will be a bodily life. God created the body as good, and the Creator will not allow his craftmanship to rot in the ground. English bishop N. T. Wright sums up beautifully why:

---

differently and legitimately within all cultures, languages, and peoples, but the core, while being expressed diversely, will always have the particularity of the Jewish DNA of a Jewish Messiah. When that is lost it's no longer Christian; unless somehow "God's ownership of this Jewish flesh," which "is permanent," can be revoked, which I confess it cannot. I would suggest the following are the core Jewish doctrines of the faith: the Trinity; the reality of Yeshua the Messiah's full Jewish humanity and full deity, fully united; the bodily resurrection; and the virgin birth. The virgin birth is certainly a part of this Jewish bedrock; it is a part of our bedrock, and is Jewish in at least the sense it was a Jewish event involving Jewish people and proclaimed and theologized by Jewish Christians. As to whether there is any aspect of it that goes back into the pre-Christian (this does not mean non-Jewish) Jewish tradition, I know not, although I would not be surprised if it did. I lastly would add that at least some, for instance the author(s) and or editor(s) of the so-called *Gospel of Philip*, thought of the virgin birth as Hebrew rather than as gentile as we saw above in chapter 5.

61. Irenaeus said it this way: "if He was not born, neither did He die; and if He did not die, neither was he raised from the dead; *and if He was not raised from the dead, death is not conquered, how are we to ascend to life, having fallen under death from the beginning?*" Irenaeus, *On the Apostolic Preaching*, 65. Emphasis added.

62. Lewis, *Mere Christianity*, 98.

> ... what you do in the Lord *is not in vain*. You are not oiling the wheels of a machine that's about to roll over a cliff. You are not restoring a great painting that's shortly going to be thrown on the fire. You are not planting roses in a garden that's about to be dug up for a building site. You are—strange though it may seem, almost as hard to believe as the resurrection itself—accomplishing something that will become in due course part of God's new world. Every act of love, gratitude, and kindness; every work of art or music inspired by the love of God and delight in the beauty of his creation; every minute spent teaching a severely handicapped child to read or to walk; every act of care and nurture, of comfort and support, for one's fellow human beings and for that matter one's fellow nonhuman creatures; and of course every prayer, all Spirit-led teaching, every deed that spreads the gospel, builds up the church, embraces and embodies holiness rather than corruption, and makes the name of Jesus honored in the world—all of this will find its way, through the resurrecting power of God, into the new creation that God will one day make.[63]

Resurrection, first Messiah's and then ours, is the reason for our hope that what we do now for the sake of the kingdom of God will not be in vain, that we are indeed God's coworkers building the kingdom here on earth now, which will last under the true, good, and beautiful reign of God forever and ever, and we will remain with God and our fellow creatures into eternity. The reality and mystery of the resurrection is rooted in the hope, as fourteenth-century English mystic Julian of Norwich puts it, that "his love never allows our time to be lost."[64] Our time now matters because there will come a day when we will be raised from the dead, and God will put all things to rights. In the Creator's kindness and goodness God will not let our time be for naught.

Theosis and the Human Vocation of Becoming Human— the Way of Love

When I first started the Misfits Theology Club as a deconstructionist group that met in our apartment, one of the retired ladies from our Episcopal church came one Saturday. In the midst of the conversation she mentioned her belief in the sinfulness of Yeshua. This shocked both my

---

63. Wright, *Surprised by Hope*, 208.
64. Julian of Norwich, *Revelations of Divine Love*, 145.

priest and me. She elaborated by saying if Yeshua was truly fully *human like us,* then *like us* he must have been sinful. While it's always refreshing to hear a fellow Episcopalian confess the existence of sin, her statement assumed a lot about humanity that I find to be misguided, even if it isn't unusual. Indeed, it is a common refrain to hear one say something to the effect of, "To be human is to be sinful." But this is more Gnostic than it is Jewish.

The problem with this woman's statement of Yeshua's sinfulness is twofold. First, it starts with defining humanity based upon us, rather than Yeshua, the only one who reveals both what it is to be God and what it is to be human. The second, which is tied to the first, is the misconception that to be human is to be sinful. Now don't misunderstand me. I'm not saying humans are not sinful. I quite believe in sin; it's often been the point of discussion throughout this book even if I haven't used that language. What I am saying is we are not yet *fully human.* To be sinful, in reality, is to fall short of full humanity.

If we accept the common notion that being human, by definition, includes being sinful, then what Hitler did to six million of us Jews was in fact a very human act. Do we really want to say that being the mastermind behind genocide can fit within our definition of what it means to be human? God, I hope not. Do we want to say that hating one's neighbor, lying, cheating, adultery, violence, and so forth are really part of our full humanity? What are the ethical implications of assuming and teaching this kind of low view of humanity to our kids?

In his book *Pedagogy of the Oppressed,* Brazilian educator Paulo Freire writes, "Dehumanization, which marks not only those whose humanity has been stolen, but also (though in a different way) those who have stolen it, is a *distortion* of the vocation of becoming more fully human."[65] Rather than being human in those collected moments, Hitler through his dehumanization of others was ironically dehumanizing himself. To sin, to commit evil in the myriad creative ways we can come up with, is to be deeply un-human. In short, many of us have a terrible definition of humanity. As Christians, we need to relearn how the early church viewed human nature.

In about 107 CE, the bishop of Antioch, St. Ignatius, was being escorted by the authorities to his martyrdom in Rome. On his way, he wrote several letters to various churches. In his letter to the Roman Christians,

---

65. Freire, *Pedagogy of the Oppressed,* 44.

whom he would likely encounter when he got to Rome, he wrote something very interesting in an attempt to prevent them from trying to help him escape his coming death: "The pangs of birth are upon me; have patience with me, my brothers, and do not shut me out from life, do not wish me to be stillborn . . . Suffer me to attain to light, light pure and undefiled; for only when I am come thither shall I be truly a man [human being]. Leave me to imitate the Passion of my God."[66] According to this quote, not only does Ignatius *not want to live*, which is enough to strike us in a death-fearing culture as odd, he goes so far as to say he's not yet been born and he's not yet a human being! It is precisely through martyrdom as an imitation of Messiah's passion that Ignatius believes he will become a truly finished human being.

To understand Ignatius's theology of humanity more fully, we need to see how the author of John's Gospel is echoing the creation narrative in Genesis. In the Greek translation of Genesis, the story recounts God creating through commandments. God says "let there be" a sun, moon, and stars, and it is so. For each of the first five days of creation, the verbal form of a command known as an "injunctive" is used to describe how God creates the material world. Only when God gets to the creation of a human being does the Creator do something different. In Greek grammar there is also a verb form called the "subjunctive," which conveys an act as a possibility. Up to that point in the narrative the command form is used to describe God's creation, in which God speaks something into existence and it then exists as God has ordered it, God says "let it be" and it becomes so; but when the author of Genesis gets to the creation of humanity, the Jewish translator switches the verbal form from an injunctive to a subjunctive. Instead of God saying "let it be" and it becomes so, God says "let us make" a human being. In other words, God begins the project of creating a human being but does not complete it.

Now go forward to John's Gospel when he describes the passion of Yeshua. In 19:5 Pilate brings Yeshua out to the crowd after having him flogged and shamed, and somewhat ironically and unwittingly states, "Behold the human being." A few verses later in verse 30 Yeshua speaks his last words, "It is finished." But what is finished? We often think it's his suffering that is being referenced by his line "It is finished." But considering John's Genesis orientation (that is, John was meant to be read with

---

66. Ignatius, "Early Christian Writings," 87. The translation I'm using renders the Greek word *anthropos* as "man," but here I think a more accurate translation is "human being."

Genesis in mind), this statement following Pilate's is, according to the British-born Orthodox scholar John Behr, about God's completion of his project of creating a human being.[67] Messiah on the cross becomes the first completed, fully developed human being. By taking on Jewish flesh and dying on a Roman cross, the second person of the Trinity becomes fully human. But how does the Jewish Messiah of the world become fully human? As Behr says, he does so by laying down his life in love for his neighbor. So here it is on the cross that Messiah shows us what it is to be fully human and fully divine, fully united.

Furthermore, there is a second project finished on the cross as Yeshua utters the words "It is finished." It is not insignificant that it is through *Jewish flesh* that the God of Israel finishes her project of creating a human being. Genesis recounts two projects that God began but did not finish: the project of creating a human being and the project of creating a people for himself. The latter project starts with God's calling of Abraham. In the same breathe used to expel the words "It is finished," God also finishes the project of creating a people for God's self, of creating Israel. In other words, the project of creating a Jew is also completed by and in the person of Yeshua on the cross. Not only on the cross in Messiah did humanity reach its *telos*, its intended goal, but so did the Jew. Thus we see to become fully human is to simultaneously become ethnically particular, fully the people group God created you to be. Additionally, we should not ignore that it was within the marginalized and oppressed people of Israel that humanity as a whole was completed; not in the Northern Europeans of the Enlightenment did humanity reach its *telos*, but in the glorious dusty backwater land and people of Israel.

In light of all this we can say in the Creator's design to be human is to love. To the extent we fail to love, we have not yet reached our full humanity and full ethnic particularity. In Messiah we are shown not only what it means to be fully God, which is Love, but also what it is to be fully human in all of our ethnic particularity, which is also love. It is not human to ignore your neighbor in need, whether the orphan, widow, refugee, or those who find themselves houseless. Such acts of ignoring the need of your neighbor are profoundly lacking in humanity. It is clear to me we are not yet fully finished human beings. A true completed human being could not orchestrate and execute the extermination of eleven million people. To say this action was in the scope of what it means to be

---

67. For more see Behr, *Becoming Human*.

human is to have a low view of what it means to be human. Murdering men, women, and children, for any reason, let alone the so-called reason of the Nazis, is simply not a human action. It is the antithesis of what it means to be human. Thus, we are still in the process of becoming human, learning to lay down our lives in love for our neighbors, to place their needs and interests above our own.[68]

The apostle Paul writes that Messiah is the Image of God, and we are made in that image. Since Messiah is fully God and fully human, fully united, as we take on this vocation of loving God and our fellow creatures in each thought, word, and deed, we become more human and, like the uniting of Divinity and flesh in the incarnation, we who are flesh become more united with the Divine. To be fully human, one who loves selflessly, is to participate in and become united with the one in whose image we are made, the one who is love for the other itself, the very ground of reality, who has eternally existed as a community of Love. In becoming human we come to share in the Divine's essence, because love attracts love. And this brings us to theosis, the early church's view of salvation.

In 2 Peter 1:4 the author writes about becoming participants of the divine nature. Ephrem the Syrian in the fourth century speaks about it this way: "Today the Deity imprinted itself on humanity, so that humanity might also be cut into the seal of Deity."[69] Said differently, God became one of us that we humans might become divine. The technical term for this process is "theosis"; and it is not to be mistaken for the LDS idea that human beings become their own gods.[70] Rather it is rooted in the incarnation of the Jewish Messiah. Just as in Yeshua the full nature of the Godhead is fully united with the full nature of humanity without minimizing or confusing the distinction between the two natures, so we as fully finished humans will be brought into participation with the triune God in all its divinity. We come to share in God's nature by grace, not by nature. We will remain what we are without actually becoming God, but we will be one with God, akin to the union that occurs in marriage, with wife and husband each maintaining their unique personhood while also being fully united as one.

Like most if not all Christians in the early church, Origen understood salvation as this union of creation with the Godhead. In his homily

---

68. Don't forget this definition of humanity comes out of the Jewish people.

69. Ephrem, *Hymns on the Nativity*, 74.

70. Church of Jesus Christ of Latter-Day Saints, more commonly known as Mormons, although I think they prefer to be called Latter-Day Saints.

on Psalm 81, he discusses the process of theosis at length, also called "deification" or "divinization." Since he understands this psalm to be addressed towards the topic of deification, he opens his homily with Yeshua's injunction for his disciples to be like him. Origen explains:

> the teacher aims for this, that he may, to the extent that he can, make disciples like him; and the lord has visited, not so as to keep the slaves, but so that the lord might make the slaves to be as he is. But our teacher, Christ Jesus, is a god, and if it is sufficient for the disciple that he become like the teacher, the ideal of the disciple is to become a christ from Christ and a god from a god...[71]

He goes on to say that if we avoid vices and therefore by extension participate in the virtues by imitating Messiah, then we are not gathered by God as mere human beings, but as "gods." In imitating Messiah, we participate in God's very nature, and by so doing we become like him and share in the divine nature itself. For Origen it is not just our spirit and soul that is divinized, or partakes in a share of the divine nature, but also the body itself. As Maximus explains, "the body is deified along with the soul through its own corresponding participation in the process of deification."[72]

All of this is made possible by the work of the Son of God, in his virgin birth, life, death, resurrection, and ascension. By the Son of God taking on Jewish flesh he has brought the divine triune nature into union with creation in himself. The doctrine of Yeshua as fully human, fully God, fully united is not mere abstract intellectual rubbish but is the center of our own salvation, our healing, our ability to become human, to reach the *telos* for which God created us. Yeshua Messiah therefore not only shows us what it means to be fully human, and fully God, but also what it means and looks like for creation and God to be fully united. He shows us in himself what the final goal of creation is. In our becoming fully human we become like the Divine; we come to share in its likeness. Full humanity having been made in the image of God not coincidentally looks like God.

But lest anyone think this reality of divinization would lead us to be unconcerned with the world around us, we need to look further at Origen's homily on Psalm 81, which he understands to be a reflection

---

71. Origen, *Homilies on the Psalms*, 439.
72. Maximus the Confessor, "Two Hundred Texts," 160.

on deification. Commenting on the verse that reads, "How long will you judge unjustly and receive the personae of sinners," he says,

> When, in fact, there are two people being judged, a rich sinner and a poor just man, you, taking the persona of the sinner because of his wealth, prefer the sinner to the one who is just, but poor. And this sin is frequent among us wretched human beings. It has become our custom to give preference to those who are exceptional, not according to God, but according to the cosmos, and to exclude and despise those who are exceptional according to God.[73]

To Origen our deification is not otherworldly; rather it is deeply tied to our avoidance of vice and our pursuit of virtue here in this world. How we treat our neighbor is how we put on Messiah, who came to proclaim good news to the destitute and poor. To Origen, we take on the persona of Messiah, we receive him in ourselves, becoming incarnations of him, when we, like him, stand up for the poor and destitute. "If you ever see a poor person being harmed, do something about it. When that person is harmed, stand by him. He is despised because of poverty; the just person is at his side."[74] As we have thoroughly discussed up to this point in the book, the early church does not divorce practice from theology. Rather, Christian practice is an embodiment of theology, and Christian theological vision gives depth, foundation, and refinement to our practice. Standing by the helpless is a path towards becoming like God, for this is what God is like, shining his sun/Son on the good and the wicked. "The Lord Jesus Christ is justice. No one who acts unjustly is subordinate to Christ, justice."[75] Because Messiah is Justice itself, one who acts unjustly does not imitate him and certainly is not becoming like him. Justice for Origen is thus not divorced from theosis but is the path into theosis. Loving our neighbor is thus part of the process of becoming, in the word used by the early church, "gods."

All of this prepares us as tabernacles for the presence of the Jewish Messiah; he takes us on as his flesh when we love our neighbor. In doing so we find that we, like Yeshua's flesh in the incarnation, take on the divinity of God, sharing in his likeness and nature; we thus become an image of the fully human and fully divine Yeshua Messiah found on the

---

73. Origen, *Homilies on the Psalms*, 443.
74. Origen, *Homilies on the Psalms*, 445.
75. Origen, *Homilies on the Psalms*, 90.

cross, the one who in himself brings both natures into union as one. As we become more fully human by doing the things he does and is, following him as the way, we become like God, and in becoming like God we become more human. We thus act as instruments of God, with Yeshua incarnated in and through us, and like Paul we cry out, "do you seek proof of Christ speaking in me."[76] By thus receiving Messiah in us, we bring forth the kingdom of God here on earth as it is heaven. This theosis of union between God and God's creation, started in Messiah in his full Jewish humanity and full divinity, is finished in us, by Messiah, who is in us as the way of love.

> *No more tears, no more anguish; we have seen with our eyes your kingdom, the world truly created, a new heaven and a new earth. All the children we have become dance before your throne, praising you, the King, our true mother, for you have nourished us with your flesh and blood; as infants you have fed us. Grown now inside of us you are, and the world you made has given birth to you.*

---

76. Origen, *Homilies on the Psalms*, 445.

8

The Church

Let us honor the Catholic Church, our true Mother, the true Bride of her Husband, because she is the wife of so great a Lord. And what shall I say? How great is that Husband and of singular rank, that he discovered a prostitute and made her a virgin. Because she should not deny that she was a prostitute, lest she forget the mercy of her liberator. How can it be said that she was not a prostitute when she fornicated with demons and idols?[1]

SAINT AUGUSTINE (NORTH AFRICAN, PUNIC FROM CARTHAGE)

Our greatest strength as the Body of Christ lies in the fact that though we are different individuals, we are one in Him. We must regain what Natives have never lost: the understanding that our togetherness is more important than our individuality, that we are members one with another.[2]

RICHARD TWISS (LAKOTA)

There is one head, one source, one mother boundlessly fruitful. Of her womb are we born, by her milk we are nourished, by her breath we are quickened . . . The Church should exhibit their innocence and practice their affection. We should be like doves in brotherly love, like lambs and sheep in kindness and gentleness. What room is there in

---

1. Augustine, "Sermon 213 on the Creed," quoted in D. Bates, "Church Is a Whore?"
2. Twiss, *One Church, Many Tribes*, 101.

a Christian's breast for the fierceness of wolves, for the madness of dogs, the deadly poison of snakes, the bloody savagery of beasts?[3]

SAINT CYPRIAN (NORTH AFRICAN)

I SUSPECT BECAUSE OF our Gnosticism we find the reality of an impure and imperfect church abhorrent. "God could not possibly work in and through such a foul creature," so the sentiment goes. Yet the incarnation of the Jewish Word in and as the church shows clearly God does not agree with such an attitude. Paul wrote that we are the body of Messiah, a theological reality that has continued to be echoed throughout church history. Another way of saying this is we are an incarnation of Yeshua. The church is the community of those people, first Jews and also gentiles, who, having entered into fellowship with God through the Jewish flesh of the Messiah, "are drawn into the inner dynamics of the Trinitarian life . . . taken up into an altogether new manner of existence."[4] We the church, Jew and gentile, are a sacrament, and thus we in a very real, yet mysterious way participate in the divinity of Yeshua. As Messiah did not shy away from taking up what we consider to be a weak, imperfect body to become the first fully finished Jewish human, so the Word did not, and does not, shy away from taking up this disfigured church as his body, his hands and feet. The Phoenician North African bishop Augustine[5] is attributed as saying, "The Church is a whore, but she's also my mother."[6] We are paradoxically the body and womb of Messiah, from which we are truly born into life, and at the same time we are not yet fully realized humans, and often we are more sinner than saint.

The fact that we are impure and far from perfect does not stop the Creator-Son from working through and in us. Despite the common sentiment of organized religion being inherently corrupt, and therefore necessary for us to leave (which is incoherent since all things human

---

3. Cyprian, "Unity of the Catholic Church," 127–30.

4. Barron, *Light from Light*, 165. Bishop Barron is an Irish-American Roman Catholic.

5. Augustine was half Phoenician. These were the Punics of North Africa who had settled the North African coast from the ancient land of Phoenicia in South West Asia. Interestingly enough, the Phoenicians as a Northwest Semitic people were ethnically, linguistically, and culturally related to Israel. This means Augustine was part of a people group deeply related to the Jews.

6. Possibly a paraphrase of Augustine, "Sermon 213 on the Creed."

are organized; are we going to leave every other human organization we are a part of?), the reality is that nothing in creation is perfect.[7] "Israel's prophets never abandoned Israel in search of a more pure people of God, for it was understood that it was this people that God promised to both bless and chasten."[8] The God of Israel's calling of the church, first to the Jews and then to the gentiles through their adoption into Israel's covenant, is irrevocable. God will not abandon Israel and will not abandon the Jewish-gentile church. It's the Gnostic heresy that teaches the divine Word cannot be mediated through that which is in error, in contradiction, in imperfection, that which is material and human. "Due to its ethereal nature, ultimate truth for Gnostics could not come from any earthly institution."[9] If this was true as the Gnostics teach, God would have abandoned creation long ago, yet this is not what the Jewish Christian faith confesses. So while parts—although certainly not all—of the church committed the evil of marrying empire, that grim reality does not prevent the action and work of God. The Holy Spirit did not suddenly cease from

---

7. Simply because it is organized we believe organized religion is evil, and yet every aspect of humanity is organized, even our own DNA. Organization runs at the deepest levels of the universe, of reality, and thus we cannot escape organization. It is absurd to demonize organized religion simply based off of the fact its organized, because it's an easy way to demonize religion. It's also problematic to demonize all of organized religion when most of the people that are making such claims have not experienced all of the world's many organized religions, let alone their own religious tradition to the fullest extent. Who are you to accuse Buddhism, Hinduism, Islam, Judaism, and so forth of being evil simply because they are organized? Have you experienced, embodied, studied, and visited every one of those traditions? I'm certainly not such an expert as to be able to make that claim. Christianity alone is so big that if you were to spend the rest of your life exploring every part of it in order to be able to substantiate the claim that the organized religion of Christianity (and all of it is organized, even the house churches, as there are many kinds of organization) is inherently evil because its organized, you would die before being able to finish your task. This attitude is tied in to the false Western dualistic dichotomy made between the concepts of spiritual and religious; often those who claim that organized religion is bad will say, "but I'm spiritual." However, is there really a difference between spiritual and religious, or are we just playing with semantics? I'm spiritual in the sense that I worship and follow the triune Creator, who is Spirit, but there's nothing about that that is antithetical to being religious, that is, to be a part of a worshipping community that is doing that following together. In fact, one implies the other. I suspect at the core of this demonization of *organized* religion is the rejection of collectivism in favor of modern European individualism. In other words, because of white dualism, Westerners see religion and spirituality as two separate categories and then reject religion because they don't want to be defined or told what to do by anyone other than themselves. It's the white way—"Do whatever you want to do"—and it's very American.

8. Rosner, *Healing the Schism*, 186.

9. Morris, *Revival of the Gnostic Heresy*, 24.

being at work in the year 312 amongst Christians in the Roman Empire when Constantine stopped persecution and legalized Christianity, and only now is getting back to work at the end and death of Christendom.

This seems like modernist prejudice more than anything. And besides, the church was not perfect before 312; it has always, to varying degrees, been imperfect and incomplete from its very beginning. Yet it is also important to note not all of the church was married to the Roman Empire. The Coptic Orthodox, Syriac Orthodox, and others (sometimes the Eastern Orthodox) lived outside of the political prestige and protection of the Roman Empire and any other empire for that matter. In reality, many of those Christian communities continued to be persecuted after 312 since they lived outside the Roman Empire, and some, such as the Coptic Church, fell into persecution by the Romans well after the Edict of Milan in 312, which legalized Christianity.[10]

The reoriented life (one that has gone there and back from deconstruction) is not, and cannot be, a mere withdrawal, a pure negation, a rejection of the church with its suffering, its crises, its failures, confusion, and errors. No follower of Yeshua can withdraw completely from the body of Messiah, for they are mystically connected to Messiah, the head, and thereby to all those who are connected to Messiah, whether they desire to be or not. To entertain the delusion of not truly and mystically being connected to the church will only bring pain to oneself and the rest of the body. Those who have chosen to leave the church in a visible manner are deeply implicated for better or for worse in all of the church's follies. When one part of the body suffers, we all do. The individualistic perception that we are only guilty of personal wrongdoing does not negate the reality we are all interconnected and therefore share the collective responsibility for wrongdoing.[11] Those who flee the city filled with plague instead of staying to bring healing will have to live with that. Simply because you have left the visible church does not absolve you from the guilt and shame of the church. For the master will ask, "Where were you when your brother and sister fell? Where were you, who have refused to remove the log lodged in their own eye, when your sister or brother needed your guidance to remove the speck out of their eye?"

This is a difficult word, but it is one to which the church fathers and mothers, and Scripture itself, attest: *you cannot truly walk away from the*

---

10. The Edict of Milan didn't make Christianity the official state religion (that happened a few decades later); it only legalized it.

11. Here I'm specifically talking about those who follow Yeshua.

church and at the same time follow Yeshua.[12] The North African Cyprian wrote it this way: "You cannot have God for your father unless you have the Church for your mother."[13] Truly walking away from the church is walking away from Yeshua, because the church is an incarnation of Yeshua. When the French saint Joan of Arc was being interrogated about her views of the relationship between the church and Yeshua, she said, "About Jesus Christ and the Church, I simply know they're just one thing, and we shouldn't complicate the matter."[14] As to how Joan of Arc could make such an audacious statement, we must look to the Judean Jew Paul. When he encounters the risen Messiah on the road to Damascus, we get a glimpse of a vastly important exchange between him and Messiah:

> When he was on the verge of reaching Damascus, suddenly a light from heaven flashed about him. He fell down upon the ground and heard a voice speaking to him, "Saul, Saul, why do you persecute me? Is it hard for you to kick against the goads?" He answered, "Who are you, my Lord?" And our Lord said, "I am Jesus of Nazareth, whom you are persecuting."[15]

When Saul—who, mind you, was on his way to persecute followers of the Way—encounters Yeshua in all his shining glory and asks him who he is, Yeshua identifies himself with the church. "I am Yeshua, whom you are persecuting." If Yeshua was keen on making a Western dichotomy between himself and his followers, he wouldn't have asked Saul why he was persecuting *himself*; instead he would have said, "why are you persecuting *my followers?*" But he doesn't; he says, "why do you persecute *me?*" We see this same identification between Yeshua and his church in the Parables of the Sheep and Goats. In this story as told by Yeshua, those who do not care for their Christian brothers or sisters in need do not care about Messiah.[16] Yeshua says those who feed, clothe, visit, or give

---

12. I do not affirm the Protestant doctrine of *the perseverance of the saints*, sometimes described as "once saved, always saved." I think if we take free will seriously we have to say you can reject God after initially beginning to follow the Messiah. If you truly break fellowship and friendship with the church, his body, you truly break fellowship and relationship with Yeshua the Messiah. You cannot separate the two, although not all those who think they've broke fellowship and shalom with Yeshua or the church have actually done so.

13. Cyprian, "Unity of the Catholic Church," 127–28.

14. Joan of Arc, quoted in Barron, *Light from Light*, 151.

15. Acts 9:3–5.

16. The parable goes to show that how we relate to our Christian brothers and sisters shapes our own identity. Those who take care of their brothers and sisters and

something to drink to the least of these really do so to him.[17] And those who don't feed, clothe, give something to drink, or visit their Christian brothers and sisters don't do so to him.

The Egyptian Origen believed the Word of God, the second person of the Trinity, had three or four incarnations, the most unique being the incarnation of the Word into and as a Jewish body. The second, and the one that preceded his taking on of Jewish flesh, was his incarnation into the Scriptures. And the third/fourth is the incarnation of the Word into personal human souls or the church.

While he speaks of this incarnation as happening into personal souls, we need to keep in mind that Origen, unlike most of us reading this, was not a modern Western individualist. He, like most of humans throughout history and even the world today, was a collectivist. In other words, he believed that "I am because we are," rather than the individualist sentiment of "We are because I am."[18] He understood identity as constructed within and by the community, and not according to a self-referential building of identity. In such a collectivistic mindset his thoughts on the incarnation of the Word into personal souls must be understood as personal identity within corporate belonging. Hans Boersma, a Dutch patristics scholar, says it this way: "So close, in fact, is the link between the church and the individual that it may be more appropriate to speak of the Word's incarnation in the church than of the Word's incarnation in the individual soul."[19]

St. Teresa of Avila, a sixteenth-century Spanish Catholic mystic, reminiscent of Paul's language in 1 Corinthians 12, once wrote the following poem about Messiah's incarnation into the church:

> Christ has no body but yours,
> No hands, no feet on earth but yours,
> Yours are the eyes with which He looks
> Compassion on this world,
> Yours are the feet with which He walks to do good,
> Yours are the hands, with which He blesses all the world.
> Yours are the hands, yours are the feet,

---

therefore love them are truly disciples of Yeshua, and thus their identity is shown to be in Messiah.

17. While I think this parable can be expanded to discuss Yeshua's care for all the needy, marginalized, and oppressed, I think the primary people Yeshua is referring to in this story is the church, his followers.

18. Woodley, *Indigenous Theology and the Western Worldview*, 83.

19. Boersma, "Joshua as Sacrament," 29.

Yours are the eyes, you are His body.
Christ has no body now but yours,
No hands, no feet on earth but yours,
Yours are the eyes with which he looks
compassion on this world.
Christ has no body now on earth but yours.[20]

Afro-Latino American Emilio Alvarez, in his book *Pentecostal Orthodoxy*, retells a vision he had during a prayer that was akin to some of the mystical visons of St. Symeon the New Theologian.[21] During this vision the room was filled with a bright light and he experienced a warm sensation that covered his whole body. Suddenly a picture of a friend popped into his mind and he thought God might want him to pray for him. As he began to pray for his friend amid this ecstatic mystical experience, he heard a voice in his heart asking, "Do you know him?" As the picture remained in his mind, he answered. "Yes, Lord, he's my friend. I know him." After a few minutes of silence, the voice asked, "What's his wife's name?" He was taken aback, and after spending some time trying to think about it, he realized he probably didn't know his friend's wife. After some more silence the voice again spoke, asking how he could say he knew his friend if he didn't know the very person he loved. He was confused by this interaction during the vision, and wasn't sure what it had to do with his desire to recover early Christian spirituality (which was something important to him at the time), when the voice then asked, "Son, do you know me?" Knowing that whatever he answered would be wrong, he replied by saying he always tried to know God, even though he knew no one could know him completely. Lastly the voice asked, "Do you know my bride, the church? How can you say you love me if you don't know what I love?"[22]

This sentiment is no less true of us having come out of fundamentalist Protestantism. We often have a low view of church and don't think we need it, and because of our Western individualism, we believe our faith is simply a personal relationship with Yeshua, not his wife. Anyone who's been married for any significant amount of time knows that when you get

20. It's important to note Teresa is not denying that Messiah still has a body, but simply affirming that his physical body is not among us, and that now we are his body here on earth. Quoted from https://catholic-link.org/quotes/st-teresa-of-avila-quote-christ-has-no-body-butyours/page/2/?et_blog&gad_source=1.

21. St. Symeon was born in the tenth century in what is now modern-day Turkey.

22. Alvarez, *Pentecostal Orthodoxy*, 3.

married you're not simply marrying your spouse, but their entire family, whether you like it or not. In the same way, when you marry Yeshua (i.e., decide to follow him), you're beginning a relationship and new season of life not just with him, but with the rest of his family, the church and his people Israel. There is no marriage contract that includes marrying Yeshua but excludes marrying the church and Israel, in whose womb the church dwells. It's a package deal.

In a real but mysterious way, Messiah has made the church his body. If you truly follow Yeshua, then you are de facto part of his body, dwelling in the womb of Israel, and thus it is impossible to follow him without being a part of his body. Because the church is the body of Yeshua, to hate the church is to hate Yeshua, and to hate Israel is to hate the God of Israel, who saw fit to take on Jewish flesh permanently and eternally become part of Israel. Origen writes,

> . . . if we do anything to the body of Christ, the Church, and to the constituent parts of Christ, our brothers [and sisters], we do them to Christ. In fact, we either behave badly to a believer in Christ—we violate Christ, we insult Christ, we disdain Christ—or we act well, we treat Christ well: we feed the hungry, we give drink to the thirsty. Therefore, do not think that you are liable only to a human being for what you do when you treat your neighbor well or poorly; you are actually liable to Christ himself. When you sin against a Christian, you sin against Christ.[23]

None of this is an excuse to avoid healthy prophetic criticism of the church. Yet too often criticism of the church is rooted in the trifecta of an unhealed, jaded hatred of the church, a low view of church inherited from fundamentalist Protestantism, and the modern Northern European ideal of individualism. That's not healthy prophetic rebuke. It's usually a self-righteous egocentric tearing down of the other to build yourself up. Criticism of the church must be rooted in, and motivated by, love of the church. You cannot really provide prophetic rebuke to something you do not love. African-American prophet Martin Luther King Jr. exemplified this beautifully in his letter from the Birmingham jail, which addressed white ministers' resistance towards racial justice and integration efforts: "In deep disappointment I have wept over the laxity of the church. But be assured that my tears have been tears of love. There can be no deep disappointment where there is not deep love. Yes, I love the church. How

---

23. Origen, *Homilies on the Psalms*, 42–43.

could I do otherwise?"[24] Above all, Messiah is the prime example of this attitude. He loves the whole world, and out of such love and concern for the world he rebukes it in order that it may be set right. In white dualistic culture, many have wrongly divorced justice from love, and the church and Israel from Messiah.

How Are We Defining Church?

Yet what do we mean when we say "church"? It is not a building as we often refer to it. It is kingdom communities of shalom made up of followers of Yeshua, living together in community, in some way, shape, or form gathered by and around the Eucharist. Churches might meet in the park for Eucharist on Sundays, or in pubs, coffeeshops, bookstores, apartments, or houses as they did for the first two hundred years of the church's existence; or they may meet in buildings that they own, what we traditionally call a "church building." Simply because you don't meet in a church building doesn't mean you're not part of a church. The place where you meet isn't necessarily important; it's the commitment to intentionally, eucharistically gather as his body, a commitment to be faithful to one another, admonishing one another in love, to live in eucharistic community together; as the book of Acts describes the early Jewish Yeshua communities, "They persisted in the teaching of the apostles and shared in prayer and in the breaking of the bread in the Eucharist."[25]

Given the church building is not the church, let me make a seemingly radical proposal to white traditions who came over to this land through colonialism, such as my own tradition, the Episcopal Church: let's give all our church buildings and property back to the Native Americans, whose land it rightfully is. Of course, this would be complicated and probably messy, but it is simply reality that our church buildings, and the rest of our property for that matter, are on perpetually stolen land. Even if our churches or denominations bought the property, it was stolen property that they acquired. In the eyes of God, it's not truly ours. Most of us are guests on Turtle Island. If we continue to keep this stolen land, we are living in sin; we are not living in the justice of God, but are perpetuating an injustice that's been going on for five hundred years. It's not ours to keep anyway. If we really cannot imagine church without a

---

24. King, "Letter from the Birmingham Jail."
25. Acts 2:42.

church building, then while giving the property back to the local tribes, make a deal with them to rent the property and continue to use their land and church building for your church gatherings. But lest we do so irresponsibly, if we are to do such a thing as giving back the land, which is one way to do reparations, we need to do so in conversation, partnership, and relationship with the tribes whose land it is. Indeed, we should let them take the lead in such efforts. In trying to make things right, in trying to learn to share the land, we might make things worse. Since property is taxed, it could be a burden to the tribe depending on their financial situation and so forth. But if we can and are willing to live in the shalom and justice of God by giving back the land, then I say let's do it, knowing we will make mistakes, but moving forward by the mercy of the tribes, the land, and God.

After giving the land back to its rightful stewards, let's meet in houses, coffeeshops, pubs, parks, and whatever other place where community is already happening. One of my professors pointed out to our class that by the year 2025 one hundred thousand church buildings will be closed. We often hear in America the church is dying, but this isn't exactly accurate. Since we identify the church as white and the white church is dying, we think the church is dying. As Korean-born Soong-Chan Rah has written, "The church is not dying in America; it is alive and well, but it is alive and well among the immigrant and ethnic minority communities and not among the majority white churches in the United States."[26] The church is alive and well among brown people; it is among the privileged white people in which the church is dying. Since the white church is dying anyways, why not actually be like Yeshua in your death? Sacrificial and selfless.

Or are we only really into racial justice and reconciliation in small easy ways that don't cost us anything? Do we really think we can get rid of our defects without making right the wrongs we have caused? Our defect, in many of our traditions, rooted as they are in Europe, is our colonizing impulses. Without making right our wrongs, we cannot unroot our defects. As non-Native Americans, one way of doing this is giving back some of the land. I say "giving back some of the land" because in all reality white people and a host of other ethnic groups from around the world are here now too, and there's no going back, but that means Euro-Americans are going to have

---

26. Rah, *Next Evangelicalism*, 16.

to learn to share the land that they stole. And the church is called to be a witness in this to the broader culture; indeed it is called to be the driving force in this act of kingdom reconciliation and bringing of shalom.

Recently I was with my wife (whose is a nurse) in Honduras, touring a clinic that sees so many patients they are needing to build a new building next to the existing one to increase their capacity to take in the influx of patients. The nurse explaining the why behind the need for a new clinic said it was going to cost at least a million dollars. And I thought instead of doing million-dollar campaigns for church buildings so we can be "real churches,"[27] let's do million-dollar campaigns for clinics. People need healthcare; they don't need church buildings. Instead of wasting our money on church buildings that are being abandoned and emptied, let's do million-dollar campaigns for wildlife restoration and conservation, clean drinking water, and orphans and widows. While in Honduras we drove by the local trash dump, where people are actually living. In the eyes of Yeshua, a marginalized oppressed Jew,[28] what right do we have to spend a million dollars on a church building when people are living in literal trash dumps? None.

Euro-American Frank Viola in his book *Reimagining Church* claims the church in the United States owns 230 billion dollars in real estate. If that's true, that means the church is harboring 230 billion dollars' worth of stolen real estate.[29] Some might say, "Well, the land might be stolen but we built the real estate, so that's ours." But where did the wealth and material come from to build the real estate on the stolen land in the first place? The wealth and material used to build said real estate comes from, in some form or another, this stolen land, the pillaging of its people, and the enslavement and kidnapping of West African peoples. The real estate is no more that of the colonizers than is the land upon which it is built, land that was violently stolen through rape, genocide, false peace treaties,

27. There is an unhealthy idea among American churches that in order to really be a church you have to have your own church building.

28. We kid ourselves if we think Yeshua is no longer a marginalized oppressed Jew. Every time he's whitened, every time his Jewishness is ignored or oppressed or his people experience these things, he is being marginalized and oppressed as a Jew.

29. "In addition, the overhead costs of a religious building cost God's people enormous financial loss. As George Barna and I point out in our book, *Pagan Christianity*, institutional churches in the United States alone own over $230 billion worth of real estate. And much of that money is borrowed (debt). Christians give between $9 and $11 billion a year on church buildings. How much freer would their hands be to support the poor and needy as well as to spread the gospel if they didn't have to bear such a heavy burden?" Viola, *Reimagining Church*, 89.

and so forth. Land which in the eyes of God was given in stewardship to the Indigenous peoples of this land.

Keetoowah Cherokee Randy Woodley writes, "Imbalance like genocide or enslavement or mass land theft, left unreconciled, ensures that no shalom in the land is possible."[30] If the white church continues to hold on to billions of dollars' worth of stolen real estate, there cannot be shalom in the land, because we still have unrepentant sin against God and our neighbor. Until we make it right, we aren't truly loving our neighbor or God. Until my own tradition, the Episcopal Church, or any other tradition for that matter, gives the real estate and land back, we aren't really concerned with justice, we're not really concerned with following Yeshua. *We just want people to think we are.* And that brings tears to Messiah, and it should bring us to tears. Let's see the dying of the white church in America as an opportunity to pick up the cross and follow Yeshua, an opportunity to make right wrongs committed and perpetuated, and to shift the priorities from comfort, selfishness, greed, and prestige to taking care of the least of those among us—to doing the things we're actually commanded to do, like caring for the orphans and widows and stewarding creation—rather than spending exorbitant amounts of money on our buildings, something we've never been asked to do.

How We Construct Identity and Freedom

Many of us as fundamentalists, and now as "former" fundamentalists, have been taught, believed, and preached that being a Christian is really about your individual relationship with Yeshua, so that while church may be a nice thing to do, it's really supplemental rather than essential to our faith. In case it's not obvious at this point, allow me to point it out: individualism is not brown; it's a modern white cultural value, and our denigration and disdain of collectivism is another way we operate in white normativity and colonization. This brings us to the heart of the problem of American Christianity, namely that it's American. American culture, it's history, and particularly its hyper-individualism, is often completely antithetical to the Christian faith. Within a Trinitarian theological framework, individualism is not only impossible but absurd. Yet America is the most individualistic culture in the world,[31] and for that reason maybe

---

30. Woodley, *Indigenous Theology and the Western Worldview*, 70.
31. Hofstede, Hofstede, and Minkov, *Cultures and Organizations*.

the most absurd culture in the world. Whether conversative or liberal, Americans, particularly Euro-Americans, all assume an individualistic worldview, although Euro-Americans have often colonized brown peoples who've grown up in and as Americans to be individualists. Arguably this is a prime example of syncretism between the church's faith in Yeshua Messiah and our American culture.

Not only is individualism a turning away from one's neighbor, but it's also a turning away from God, always towards the self. Even collectivistic cultures that "turn away" from God towards themselves have in a real and abiding sense not completely turned away from God *so long as they love their neighbor*, since according to Messiah love of neighbor inherently entails love of God. That's not to say all collectivistic cultures are completely operating in their true selves and are totally perfect, only that I think a kind of collectivism rooted in the triune God's nature is part of the true selves of all peoples.[32] This individualistic turn from the external world (God and neighbor) towards the internal world of the self thus makes the self become a god, and consequently the self becomes the creator of our identities. We as individuals become the creators of *our own reality*. For the pro-choice movement, individualism is key and summed up in their mantra, "*My* body, *my* choice." Yet this is just as true for the anti-maskers and anti-vaxxers we've seen throughout the COVID pandemic. During these last couple of years amidst the pandemic, the pro-choice mantra "*My* body, *my choice*" has fit just as well for the underlying ideology of why "*I* don't have to wear a mask or get vaccinated, because it's *my body*."

Despite being on opposite sides of the American ideological spectrum, these two groups ironically share a construction of identity and therefore of freedom that is rooted in individualism.[33] It gets manifested

---

32. While I believe individualism is never part of the true self of people groups, I do think there is a false self, if you will, of collectivism and a true self of it.

33. This is a view of freedom that disregards and abandons the consistent life ethic of the Jewish people. Rabbi Jonathan Sacks says this much when he writes, "with the legalization of abortion for reasons other than saving the mother's life, and the campaign—already successful in a number of countries—for voluntary euthanasia and assisted dying, the West has largely lost the concept of the sanctity of life. Instead it has adopted the principle of autonomy. In this view, my life belongs to me and I can dispose of it as I wish. This is a return to the ethics of pre-Christian Greece and Rome, cultures that had no qualms about abortion, even infanticide, and euthanasia." Sacks, *Essays on Ethics*, xxxiii. The American individualistic view of freedom, which is dispelling itself of such sanctity of life, is another example of the de-Jewifying of Christianity and the broader culture, which is a key facet of the Enlightenment project.

differently in these two groups, but ultimately they are both grounded in the same worldview. Both groups may be different flavors of ice cream, but they're still both ice cream. Even for the pro-life group, once the baby is born any talk of societal (non-individualistic) help such as childcare allowances, food stamps, or universal healthcare is quickly dismissed by the individualistic refrain, "Why should *I* give *my* resources to help *them*?" All of this, namely our construction of identity and freedom in the individual, effects how we understand and see the church, and why many former fundamentalists see no need for the church. The very concept of church, particularly as the body of Messiah, presumes a collectivistic (and therefore Trinitarian) rather than individualistic worldview, a brown rather than a white worldview. Thus, we need to explore a bit more of how we construct our identities here in America in order to understand why many of us don't think we need church.

Anglo-American Wendell Berry, talking about what he calls "rugged individualism," identifies how it manifests itself on both the right and the left.

> The tragic version of rugged individualism is in the presumptive "right" of individuals to do as they please, as if there were no God, no legitimate government, no community, no neighbors, and no posterity. This is most frequently understood as the right to do whatever one pleases with one's property. One's property, according to this formulation, is one's own absolutely . . . The rugged individualism of the left believes that an individual's body is a property belonging to that individual absolutely: the owners of bodies may, by right, use them as they please, as if there were no God, no legitimate government, no community, no neighbors, and no posterity. This supposed right is manifested in the democratizing of "sexual liberation"; in the popular assumption that marriage has been "privatized" and so made subordinate to the wishes of individuals; in the proposition that the individual is "autonomous"; in the legitimation of abortion as birth control—in the denial, that is to say, that the community, the family, one's spouse, or even one's own soul might exercise a legitimate proprietary interest in the use one makes of one's body.[34]

According to Berry, both conservatives and liberals are individualists who share the belief that "freedom" is the pinnacle of all desire and therefore they should be able to exercise this "freedom" to get whatever they

34. Berry, "Rugged Individualism," 265–67.

want, whenever they want, and how much of it as they want. The main difference between the two groups (they're not really all that different) is that sometimes they want different things. This is all rooted in a Western worldview. "My body and my things are my personal property; it is therefore my right to do whatever I want with them, regardless of how it may effect, my neighbor, family, friends, community, the world, the future, or even myself." The sad reality is most Americans are unable to see this for what it really is: pure selfishness, simply unrestrained ego.

There is a reason much of the world sees us Americans as selfish, namely because it's true. And it's rooted in our Western individualistic worldview, one that is not shared by most of the world and is relatively new to the world, having come along with the industrialization of the West and of course the Endarkenment.[35] This view of the body as the personal property of the individual is also deeply un-Jewish. The apostle Paul, the Hebrews of Hebrews, declares first that our bodies belong to God, and thus function collectively as a temple for the Holy Spirit, and second that the body of the husband belongs to his wife, and the body of the wife belongs to her husband.[36] A functioning society cannot sustain itself within the cultural framework of individualism. Every man or woman for him- or herself does not work if you wish to have a functioning society. If I had to guess, this will have something to do with America's downfall.

An entailment of this American construction of identity in the ego is our delusional belief we can construct reality according to our own self-interests and desires, summed up in the American mantra *"my* truth." Honest to God, I really thought this would have died after four years of Trump, since, while he didn't use those exact words, he nonetheless reworded the sentiment and lived according to it. I thought after four years of this from him surely Americans would have seen how dangerous this attitude is. Hitler's "truth" was that there was a superior race, and people who weren't up to snuff according to his "truth" of the perfection of the German race needed to be snuffed out. Jews and countless others needed to be cleansed from the gene pool and the earth. If we really follow the logic of "my truth," then we have no ground to stand on to criticize Hitler or the Nazis, or anyone else, ever. So, as you can imagine,

---

35. For an albeit brief description of the industrialization's effects on individualism, see the beginning of chapter 28 in González, *Story of Christianity*, 2:282–83. While individualism is a recent innovation, it may have roots in the Gnostics.

36. 1 Corinthians 6:19–20 and 7:4.

I was unexpectedly let down while watching *WandaVision* when one of the protagonists proclaimed, "my truth." The ironic bit was the whole plot revolved around Wanda living *her truth* by literally constructing her own reality, which ultimately collapsed upon itself and deeply hurt a lot of people. It was amidst all of it collapsing upon itself that this "my truth" bomb was dropped.[37]

This "my truth" orientation, while being new in terms of world history, isn't completely new; it's been in our culture for a few decades.[38] We've been familiar with it in phrases like "In America if you work hard enough, you can be anything you want" and "You can be anyone or anything you want to be, as long as you just believe it!" I was in the Denver airport not too long ago when I saw a sign with Kermit the Frog on it. Referring to him, it read, "Eats flies. Dates a pig. Hollywood star. LIVE YOUR DREAMS."[39] Many of our movies have propagated these ideas for a long time. It shouldn't surprise us the prosperity gospel came out of America, as it was simply one symptom exposing this broader kind of thinking underlying our culture. The whole prosperity gospel movement is predicated on this American belief we can create our own realities. *To be an American is to be able to construct your own reality.*[40]

COVID has been a perfect example of this. Because we did not like the reality developing before our eyes, those on the right constructed their own reality in which COVID either wasn't as bad as the experts were telling us or didn't exist at all,[41] while those on the left constructed their own reality in which COVID was worse than the medical experts had been telling us and indeed we were still in a pandemic. Certainly the whole death of the expert, in which we've become our own authorities able to discern reality as we see fit, is yet another example of this ideology coming to fruition. Even the Enlightenment phrase "I think, therefore I am"[42] implies that our own existence is self-made; we exist because we think. There's an implied self-existence here that I think has permeated

---

37. Did the writers do this on purpose? Were they trying to point out the absurdity of constructing our own realities, of living "my truth"? I don't know.

38. Which, in terms of human history, let alone the history of the fourteen-billion-year-old universe, is very new.

39. "New Student."

40. While the roots of this go back to the Enlightenment, I'm fairly convinced Americans have "perfected" it.

41. Or any of the other number of conspiracy theories (non-reality constructions) floating around.

42. Descartes, "Discourse on Method," 426.

our Western culture for a long time, has continued to develop and be "perfected" in the Western worldview. In "becoming" self-existent, we come to view ourselves as gods who can invent our own creations. Reality doesn't matter as long as it's not our individual reality.

In contrast to this American idea of self-existence and the ability to create our own realities is the Jewish creation narrative. Looking at the story of Adam and Eve's creation, we see the Creator not simply stopping once Adam is created—what we might expect if God was a Western individualist. In a very real sense, until Eve is created, Adam is incomplete. He is not yet a person, yet to be, without an identity, and has no way of perpetuating (through procreation) an identity.[43] Genesis 2:18 says, "And Adonai God said, it is not beautiful for man to be alone; let us make for him a helper accordingly."[44] Not only is it not beautiful to be alone, but to be alone is to not exist. God does not exist as an autonomous individual but as a community, and neither can we simply exist as autonomous individuals. Think about it: you as a person are a complex organization of things that have come together to form you as you are—forces often, but not always, out of your control. The culture, nation, your ethnicity, time, and family you were born into were not choices made by you, and those forces form and shape you into a particular kind of person. Your existence is not self-existence, but it is given from without, externally to yourself, with no choice of your own.

The people you listen to, books you read, shows you watch, friends you have, and relationships you have and don't have all effect and shape you into you, and of course to a limited but genuine extent you have agency in that. But if somehow you were the only person alive, self-existent as a human being, with no other people (or for that matter any other kind of thing around you—animals, rocks, water, trees), would you really be a person? How would you even determine whether you were a person or what kind of person you were if there wasn't anything other than yourself to compare yourself with? "I am this thing, not that thing." That's how we identify ourselves and others. The other is thus determinative for ourselves, the reason why we can recognize a self. "It is not beautiful that a human should be alone" is in this sense an ontological statement. It is beautiful to be in existence. You have no existence in yourself, no personhood in yourself alone, but have it only in the community of

---

43. That's not to say everyone needs to be married to be a person, but everyone needs community to be so.

44. My translation from the Septuagint.

creation, sustained and created by the eternal triune Creator itself, who is community and consequently the reason all things exist in community.

At the ground of reality there is no basis for the autonomous individual, no source for "I think, therefore I am." Rooted in the source and ground of all existence, i.e., the Trinity, there is only the basis for persons-as-community, or nature-as-communion. The three persons of God, in communion with one another, constitutes God's substance and nature. As the Greek patristics scholar John Zizioulas put it, "Outside the Trinity there is no God."[45] Said differently, the three persons *in union and communion* with one another *is the divine substance*, what it means to exist as God, and outside of that there is no God. God's divine nature, that which constitutes his unity as one God, is three persons in communion. What this all means is that within a Trinitarian framework we humans also only exist as persons in communion with one another, and yet because our nature or substance as humans is rooted in personhood, we don't lose our personhood in the other, but find it there. We become most uniquely and fully ourselves *as persons* when we are in communion with others.

While reality is rooted in the Trinity, who is the foundation of reality, it's also true that free creatures help to shape that which has been created for good or bad. But all that is truly good, true, and beautiful, that is to say all that is really real, finds its existence and it's reality in God, who is the source for all real and true things. All things are interconnected, and since the source of existence itself is not individuality, there is in reality no possibility for the existence of an individual as divorced from the community. Individuals don't exist, but persons do. Communion constitutes not only God's nature but our own. The English Orthodox metropolitan Kallistos Ware writes about the difference between the person and the individual in this way: " a 'person' is not at all the same as an 'individual.' Isolated, self-dependent, none of us is an authentic person but merely an individual, a bare unit as recorded in the census. Egocentricity is the death of true personhood. Each becomes a real person only through entering into relation with other persons, through living for them and in them."[46] In other words, as persons we only exist, live, move, and have our being in communion with one another. By contrast, the concept of the individual is one who exists purely and solely in themselves.

---

45. Zizioulas, *Being as Communion*, 41.
46. Ware, *Orthodox Way*, 36–37.

In light of all this it is not "I think, therefore I am," but *"we are loved, therefore we are,"* and love requires a community. The construction and identity derived from the phrase "I think, therefore I am" depends only upon oneself. But the phrase *"we are loved, therefore we are"* acknowledges the reality that our own existence isn't rooted in ourselves, but in the community around us, and ultimately the triune community of God, who, being existence itself, shares its life with us, so that we too may exist and share in the divine nature, which is love. This kind of identity construction is much more at home in Eastern and African cultures. One example of this comes from the South African Anglican archbishop Desmond Tutu. Speaking about his understanding of the word *ubuntu* and the understanding of identity it represents, he writes, "It is to say, 'My humanity is caught up, inextricably bound up, in yours.' We belong to a bundle of life. *We say, 'A person is a person through other persons.' It is not, 'I think therefore I am.' It says rather: 'I am human because I belong. I participate. I share.'"*[47]

If we exist as persons in communion, because God's nature is constituted by communion, then so does freedom exist within communion. Egocentricity, the rooting of one's identity in oneself, is the death of true freedom, because it fails to be rooted in personhood as constituted by communion. God is free to love but is not free to do otherwise. We come to participate in God's nature freely and come to share and participate in this higher freedom, which is by nature God's alone. We freely exchange our choice to do otherwise, an ability given to us by God so as not to be robots, for the freedom to choose self-sacrificial love for the other. And over time, through our practice and sharing of the divine nature we become freer to do so, having trained our relational muscles for so long it becomes second nature, becomes "muscle memory."

To sum up: Our freedom is not rooted in our own self-existence as individualism would tell us; this ignores a key reality, namely that we had no choice in the birth of our own existence and we only exist in communion with others. Therefore, true freedom is not solely found in ourselves divorced from the community, but in the external realities that brought us into existence, i.e., community—the community of creation and ultimately the triune community, which is God. Otherwise, if freedom is rooted in our own self-existence, then the other, the

---

47. I am grateful to my friend and communications scholar John Hatch, who during a Brewery Theology session brought this quote to my attention. Tutu, *No Future without Forgiveness*, 31. Emphasis added.

community external to ourselves, is always a threat to our freedom. But if freedom is rooted in the reality of our existence being birthed through the external other, a freedom that finds its source constituted in communion, then the other is not only not a threat to our freedom but the locus of our freedom. For us to be truly free, the other is a necessary component in our freedom as the other is also necessary for our personhood. We become truly free when we live for the well-being and life of those around us, the rest of creation (of which we are a part of) and God. So too then is freedom in its truest and highest sense also defined by Yeshua on the cross; true freedom is Messiah crucified on the cross. Voluntarily laying down your life in self-sacrificial love for your neighbor is freedom par excellence. This is why slavery, or the concentration camps of the Nazis, or the Chinese government is not freedom, because it is not love laying down its life for one's neighbor. And it's why the *choice* of not wearing a mask or getting vaccinated is not true *freedom*, nor is the *choice* to kill a perfectly healthy unborn child truly an act of *freedom*.

The key distinction between the person and the fictional individual is the different location for the origin of their existence. The *individual* finds their existence in themselves, particularly in their thinking—"I think, therefore I am." In contrast, the *person* finds their existence in God and in the rest of creation, i.e., in community external to themselves. The distinction of the person is not erased by the community of creation and God; it is maintained, but it is a distinction rooted in the reality that it was brought into existence by the community, not itself. True being or existence is an act of communion, for both God and the rest of creation.[48] God exists as a communion of three persons (not three individuals) each joyfully existing in relationship to the other persons. If we construct our identify and therefore our freedom not in individualistic Western categories and assumptions, but in a collectivistic one rooted in the communal triune God, and if we reclaim Yeshua's own incarnational identification with his body the church, then we will find the church is not a supplemental thing we do, but a fundamental aspect of reality, an essential aspect of who we are in Messiah, a reality of the Christian life.

---

48. See Zizioulas, *Being as Communion*.

The Imperative of Unity

Throughout the New Testament and early church, church unity is not seen as a secondary matter, but as an imperative of first importance. In John's Gospel, Yeshua prays for the unity of his followers, i.e., the church, and roots such a plea for unity in the relationship between the Father and the Son. "In order that they would all be one just as you, father, are in me and I in you, so that they also might be in us, in order that the earth may believe that you sent me."[49] Our unity is rooted in the unity of the three persons of the Trinity as one God. Since there is one God, there is one holy, catholic, and apostolic church. Since God is a community of others, three persons, the church is diverse and is comprised of a community of others fully united. Indeed, as we saw above, our very nature is constituted in and as communion with one another. Not only is this desire of unity from Yeshua rooted in the unity shared between the Father and the Son, the Father in the Son, and Son in the Father, and of course Yeshua' desire for us to be in God, but it also has an evangelistic function, namely that the earth would know the Father has sent Yeshua into the world!

Earlier in John's Gospel, Yeshua had said to his disciples, "a new command I give to you, namely, that you love one another, just as I have loved you all, so also you all should love one another. In this, all will know that you are my disciples, *if you have love among one another.*"[50] Meaning if we don't have love for one another, people won't know we are his disciples, or as Yeshua had implied above, the world won't know he is from God. The North African St. Cyprian wrote, "It is our duty to stand upon his words, to learn and do all that he taught and did. How can anyone profess faith in Christ without doing what Christ commanded?"[51] Cyprian's point is that Messiah commanded us to love one another, not to schism, and those who do not follow Messiah's command cannot profess to have faith in Messiah. Our best, brightest, and truest witness as the church is found in our unity, our hard love for one another.

As important, vital, foundational, and non-negotiable as evangelism and social justice are, *without being rooted in our embodied unity expressed in love for one another*, they fail to comprise the church's witness in all its fullness. When justice and evangelism are divorced from one another and cut off from a united church, they fall short of fully expressing the

---

49. John 17:21, my translation.
50. John 13:34–35, my translation. Emphasis added.
51. Cyprian, "Unity of the Catholic Church," 125.

missional desire of God's justice in the coming rule and reign of Messiah. If you don't have love for one another, you can't properly and fully exercise evangelism or justice, both of which are rooted in our love and unity with one another as the body of Messiah. We've chosen time and time again to live less according to Yeshua's own commands and more as if he had said to us, "If you hate one another, divide, split, and separate from one another over both little and big things, then the world will know you are my disciples."[52]

If we are going to be faithful to Messiah by living in and among the church, our mother and his body, abiding in the warm womb of Israel, then we also will have to be faithful to Messiah by striving to love one another, and by putting a stop to our tearing apart of his body through our schisms, whether over senseless things like the color of the carpet or matters of importance like our sexual ethics. Julian of Norwich, the fourteenth-century English theologian, once wrote, "whenever a man feels kind compassion with love for his fellow Christian, it is Christ within him."[53] The inverse is also true: whenever a person feels cruel indifference with hate for his fellow Christian, it is not Messiah within him or her but some other dark entity, whether the dark side of the person themselves or an external being. Without love in our hearts for our fellow Christians, we lose room in ourselves for Messiah, when we fill our hearts with hate we have less room for him. We must learn in a sense to put up with one another. Doing so gives us time to learn to love one another even if at first we lack such love. The North African Punic bishop Augustine once said,

> He who loves his brother *tolerates everything* for the sake of unity, because brotherly love exists in the unity of charity . . . Listen to the psalm (119:165), "There is great peace for those who love your law and no scandal for them." And why won't there be scandal? Because they put up with each other. As Paul says, "Putting up with one another in love, striving to maintain the unity of the Spirit in the bond of peace" (Eph 4:2–3).[54]

Are we willing to put up with one another? I'll be the first to admit it's a struggle; hardly a day goes by in which I do not wrestle with this. In one sense, it's so much easier to simply not put up with one another, to simply cease fellowship, to leave a church or denomination for another one, to

---

52. My translation, from the book of Church Schism.
53. Julian, *Revelations of Divine Love*, 81.
54. Augustine, "Homilies on I John," 34.

create a whole new denomination, or to the leave the church altogether. I constantly think to myself, often while in tears, "Am I really willing to put up with my liberal Protestant brothers and sisters, my friends in my deconstructionist circles, the fundamentalist apologetics groups on campus where I do college ministry, or the shenanigans of my Roman Catholic or Eastern Orthodox brothers and sisters?" Randy Woodley was once asked if he was hopeful that Western culture would ever change. His response is rather indicative of how I feel about staying in the church and working towards unity.

> Somebody once told me that sometimes you come up against a brick wall and you have to bang your head against the brick wall and you know that the wall is not going to move and you know your head is going to bleed—but it's the right thing to do, so you do it anyway. I think that's probably more descriptive of how I feel than anything, but there's still some hope.[55]

This describes almost perfectly how I usually feel about many of my fellow followers of the Way—the church as a whole, but particularly the Western American church. However, *Yeshua puts up with me*, and his Spirit is teaching me to put up with myself and others. And yes, staying together in unity often starts with *putting up with one another* before it involves warm cuddly feelings.

A couple of days after I graduated from college, I drove up to start a summer job working at a fundamentalist youth and family camp. By this time in my life I had departed from my Protestant roots, let alone my fundamentalism, and yet I decided to work at a fundamentalist summer camp. During training that first week one of the executives of the camp went through their statement of belief, stating that if we couldn't sign off on it, we would essentially be fired.[56] The next couple of days I really struggled with what I was going to do: Would I be honest with my disagreements and be fired, or hide and stay? While in my cabin, God spoke to me: "If they want to get to you, they will have to go through me." "Oh great," I thought, "God is on my side." But then God spoke again: "But if you want to get to them, you will have to go through me."

Essentially God was saying, "While I'm with you, you need to learn to live in unity with all those who call on my name to the best of your ability." In other words, God was teaching me, "If you feed the poor, if

---

55. Woodley, *Indigenous Theology and the Western Worldview*, 79–80.
56. I have no problem with doctrinal confessions if they are from the creeds.

you have faith enough to move mountains, even if you die for the name of Messiah, and yet you don't have love for your brothers and sisters, the whole church, you're not actually being a Christian; you're not following me." So I stayed that summer. At the end of the day, my greatest desire is to follow Yeshua, to be faithful to my King, and that means learning to live in unity with the church in all its crazy diversity and absurdities, especially with the American church. Church unity is the harder way, the narrower way; it is the way of faith, hope, and love. In short, it summarizes the whole of the gospel.

Church unity is also good for the church as a whole, and for the persons who make up the church. In 1784 in a sermon titled "On Schism," the English Anglican John Wesley asserts that schism "brings forth evil fruit; it is naturally productive of the most mischievous consequences . . . [e.g.] severe and uncharitable judging of each other's offence . . . anger, and resentment . . . [and] may issue in bitterness, malice, and settled hatred . . . a prelude to hell eternal."[57] To refuse to live as one striving for church unity, namely to live in and with and for disunity, is actually damaging to not only you as a person, but the entire church. Progressives and so-called conservatives often think the only way to maintain purity is to schism, but I think we have ample examples to show that far from maintaining purity and holiness, schism diminishes it. People are not washed and cleansed by schism; "they are dirtied; theirs sins are piled up, not purged."[58] Schism, as Wesley points out, breeds vice, not virtue. Maybe this is a big reason behind why there is so much vice in the church, so many scandals, because we've been breeding such vice through our constant schisms.

Maybe in striving for unity rather than schism we would simultaneously find ourselves cultivating virtues like patience, humility, gentleness, peace, righteous anger, faithfulness and fidelity, hope, love, joy, kindness, and self-control, all things necessary for unity. Placing ourselves in contexts of unity where we must learn to bear with one another in love rather than simply cut off the relationship is a workshop for becoming people who look like Yeshua and who bear the fruits of the Holy Spirit. In seeking unity, we might find ourselves practicing these virtues and thereby find ourselves steeped in the virtues rather than in the vices and the scandals produced from schism.

---

57. Wesley, "On Schism," quoted in Smith, "Once Again into the Breach."
58. Cyprian, "Unity of the Catholic Church," 131.

One virtue often missing throughout the history of the church has been the art of listening. The Jewish apostle James exhorts us, "my dear brothers and sisters, each and every one of you ought to be eager to listen, take your time before speaking or becoming angry, because human anger does not bring about God's justice."[59] What happens when James's advice is not listened to is heartbreakingly seen in a piece of literature written by Coptic Christians recounting the aftermath of the ecumenical council of Chalcedon in 451.[60] For most of church history this group of Christians has been viewed as heretical, and it is not often we hear from their side of the story.[61] From this so-called non-Chalcedonian recounting of the days after the council we see just what kind of vices are birthed from schism and the lack of listening that leads to it.[62] After the council, the pro-Chalcedonian bishop of Jerusalem returned to find the other clergy and lay people utterly troubled and betrayed by his vote for the Chalcedonian definition of Yeshua as two natures and one person. They even refused to allow him into the church building where his bishop's seat was.

Having no ability to persuade or enforce them to let him in, he left and came back with a company of soldiers from the empire. They returned as the church was gathered for the Eucharist and forced themselves in and began to slaughter the people, while the priests were still serving Communion. By the time the bishop and his soldiers took a break from all the murdering, he complained and asked why the priests did not ask him to serve Communion as was his right given his position as the bishop. Talk about audacity!

One of the main priests then rebuked the bishop, declaring him to be the heretic, and like a bully responding to someone standing up to him, the bishop commanded his soldiers to string him up by his feet upside down, with each foot tied to the two pillars in front of the altar; and once they had done this they were instructed to cut him in half from the genitals to his head. They then preceded to do so. After this, the soldiers and bishop left for a time, at which point the women came to take away their dead husbands. When the bishop heard this, he ordered

---

59. James 1:19–20.

60. History is, as they often say, written by the victors. Here is an instance where it is written by those who lost.

61. I.e., Miaphysites, those who formulate that Yeshua is fully God, fully human, and fully united in a different way than the Chalcedonians do.

62. I say "so-called non-Chalcedonian" because it's now readily acknowledged that they did not actually disagree with the content of the council, but only with the semantics.

his soldiers to rape them, but suddenly some angels came to save some of the women. Now of course, as I argued in chapter 4, anyone who fails to embody the Trinity who is Love fails in their orthodoxy. Regardless of whether these people actually fell into heresy, a true orthodox response called for love, not murder and rape. But there's more to why this story is so sad and pointless, one to do with our lack of listening skills, which led to the schism.[63]

There was a series of meetings in Denmark in 1964, England in 1967, Geneva in 1970, and Addis Ababa in 1971 between the Eastern Orthodox and the Oriental Orthodox, or the so-called non-Chalcedonian churches (such as the Coptic Orthodox, Syriac Orthodox, and Ethiopian Orthodox), in which both sides determined there was not true disagreement between the so-called non-Chalcedonians and the Chalcedonians. The non-Chalcedonians, it seems, are not truly non-Chalcedonians. In the words of the late English metropolitan Kallistos Ware, "It became clear that on the basic question which had led historically to the division—the doctrine of the person of Christ—there is in fact no real disagreement. The divergence, it was stated in Aarhus [Denmark], lies only on the level of phraseology."[64] In other words, they were arguing semantics and simply talking past one another. They had significant language barriers and did not take the time to work through those barriers together.

European scholar A. C. Bouquet once wrote, "It is not impossible that we shall find less disagreement when we come better to understand one another's use of terms."[65] In context he was speaking of non-Christians, but I think this is a rather apt description of the situation among Christians. The deep tragedy of this story is the fact that once we actually started listening to one another 1,500 years later and took time to better understand one another's terms despite the language barriers, we discovered we didn't disagree, and the blood we shed in unrighteous anger and injustice was in a sense for no real reason. There was no actual theological disagreement behind the violence, just a lack of genuine and charitable listening. It should serve as a cautionary tale for us. Of course, sometimes there are real disagreements, but in those instances we need to seriously ask if it's something worth disagreeing about, and keep in mind that it is never Christian to use violence to solve our disputes.

63. Pseudo-Dioscorus, "Encomium of Macarius of Tkoou," 344–51.
64. Ware, *Orthodox Church*, 305.
65. Bouquet, "Revelation and the Divine Logos," 193.

In the song "You Can't Hurry Love," the African-American band the Supremes remind us that love isn't easy, and it often produces heartache. Love produced in us through unity making, both as persons and as the church, can't be hurried; it takes dialogue and give and take, and it often bears frustration and sorrow. Love requires the virtues of patience and listening amidst the suffering that comes from following Yeshua on the narrow path. If we wish to enact God's kingdom, and follow Yeshua in doing so, we can't place church unity as a side issue, as something of less importance than our disagreements. As Cyprian rhetorically asked, "What peace can the enemies of their own brothers [and sisters] promise themselves?"[66]

What About Those Who Haven't Heard the Name of Yeshua?

I would be remiss if I ended this chapter without discussing what I think are acceptable Christian teachings about those who've never heard the name of Yeshua. Since I made a strong case that, as Cyprian once said, "No one can have God as their Father who doesn't have the Church as their Mother," the reader might very well wonder what I have to say about people outside the sphere of Christian influence. Are they barred from knowing Yeshua and his kingdom, simply because they were born in the wrong time and place? I believe the answer is no, and that much of the church has answered no to that question. There are roughly four answers to this question: universalism, inclusivism, pluralism, and exclusivism.[67]

The first option, universalism, teaches that all will be saved through the Messiah and will freely consent to be. In contrast, inclusivism argues while all may choose to follow Yeshua, not all will necessarily do so given the reality of free will. The third option, pluralism, holds all religions are true and all lead to whatever God is. Finally, according to exclusivism, those who have not heard the gospel message are doomed to an eternity without God. I believe the first two of these positions are acceptable to hold as Christian doctrines, while the latter two fall short of being worthy of God and are therefore unacceptable as Christian doctrine. Below I will unpack what I believe to be the strongest of the two Christian options.

---

66. Cyprian, "Unity of the Catholic Church," 133.

67. There might be more, but I'm not aware of any and I find these four sufficient to discuss the topic at hand.

While I think universalism is a Christian doctrine proper, meaning it's not heretical and one can hold to it and still be faithful to Messiah, I nonetheless reject it and have briefly argued elsewhere why I do not find it appealing. Of course, people sometimes more faithful and smarter than I have argued for it and against it, so I will leave it to them to convince you of its value or lack of thereof. Instead, I'm going to outline what I think is the best option, namely inclusivism. This is a doctrine that has been believed and continues to be affirmed by lots of Christians throughout the history of the church. It's the official view of the Roman Catholic Church; figures such as Justin Martyr, C. S. Lewis, and Billy Graham have held to it; and it was likely held by John Wesley.

The first thing I want to say about inclusivism is that it doesn't deny the existence of some sort of hell. I find the automatic denial of hell unsatisfying and dualistic. It often assumes there are only two views: there is hell as eternal conscious torment where God sends us to punish us for eternity, or there simply is no hell. Can there be more than just these two options? I think so, and the Christian tradition certainly testifies to this. While I'm not a fan of the work Euro-American Richard Rohr has put out in the last few years,[68] I find his view of hell in his book *Falling Upward* helpful:

> *God excludes no one* from union but must allow us to exclude ourselves in order for us to maintain our freedom. Our word for that exclusion is hell, and it must be maintained as a logical possibility. There must be the logical possibility of excluding oneself from union and to choose separation or superiority over community and love. No one is in hell unless that individual himself or herself chooses a final aloneness and separation.[69]

In other words, God doesn't send us to hell as a punishment out of God's righteous anger; *we choose hell*, or as C. S. Lewis once put it, "The gates of Hell are locked from the inside."[70] Origen wrote, "For God deals with souls not with reference, let me say, to the fifty years of the present life, but with reference to the limitless age, for he made the intellectual being incorruptible and akin to himself, and the rational soul is not excluded from healing, as [it might seem] in this present life."[71] In other words, someone might not find salvation in this present life, but may do so in

---

68. In fact, I find his separation of Messiah from Yeshua heretical, and I suspect it of being anti-Jewish. We can't have a Jewish Christ, now can we?
69. Rohr, *Falling Upward*, 102.
70. Lewis, "Problem of Pain," 420.
71. Origen, *On First Principles*, 167–68.

reference to the limitless age. Salvation or divine healing may take longer for some than others. But even so, God doesn't create hell; we create hell. Yet that doesn't make it unreal, or only something we experience in this life; it will last as long as we choose for it too. And whatever hell is, it's not physical separation, since God is present in and through, and to all things; it's relational brokenness and separation on our part. Yet even in the reality of hell, "the wicked are not deprived of the love of God, but by their own choice they experience as suffering what the saints experience as joy."[72] A good illustration of this comes from my personal experience: when I'm angry with my wife, for whatever stupid reason I've chosen this time, and she extends kindness, love, and grace to me, in my own stubbornness I experience her compassion not as joy but as torment, and think, "How dare she show me love!"

People might ask—and they have—if God is the ultimate source of goodness, because God is Goodness itself, why on earth would we choose to reject God forever? Because sometimes, as in the example with my wife, we're stubborn and prideful, and we choose to remain in broken relationships all the while knowing it hurts us, and even though it might not be ultimately what we desire. Humans are complicated, but it's also important to note inclusivism doesn't teach that we *will* reject God forever, just that it's a real possibility. It is possible that everyone eventually will choose God out of their own free will and thus choose the higher freedom that is God's freedom, the freedom to choose the good, but if this does occur, it wasn't predetermined; we weren't pre-programmed to do so; it wasn't necessary for it to happen.

From the standpoint of inclusivism, people, not God, choose and create hell,[73] and it's not eternal conscious torment where God punishes us into the ages. But even still, how does inclusivism answer the question, "What about those who have never heard the name of Yeshua?" Well, the short answer is that everyone has access to Yeshua. When certain missionaries have gone overseas and tell of their adventures, stating that "these people were unreached until we brought Christ to them," they are espousing a less-than-adequate Christian theology. God is the first and primary evangelist on the scene, in every culture and people group, long before Westerners showed up.

---

72. Ware, *Orthodox Church*, 255.

73. Bishop Robert Barron, an Irish-American Roman Catholic, as well as bishop Kallistos Ware, an English Eastern Orthodox, and Euro-American Timothy Mackie, an Evangelical, all have to one extent or another said that we create and choose hell.

The Samaritan Justin Martyr, born in about 100 CE in the Roman city of Flavia Neapolis, located in the ancient territory of Samaria,[74] writes about this beautifully in his *First Apologies*: "We have been taught that Christ is the first-born of God, and *we have declared above that He is the Word of whom every race of men [people] were partakers; and those who lived reasonably are Christians . . .*"[75] Justin goes on to say as an example that many of the Greeks philosophers and people of Israel before the Word came in the flesh were Christians, because they were partakers in the Word of God, who is both Word and Reason.[76] The Egyptian Origen, in the next century, essentially says the same thing, writing: "That the working of the Father and the Son is both in saints and sinners is clear from this, that all who are rational beings are partakers of the Word of God, that is, Reason, and in this way, as it were, bear certain seeds, implanted within them, of Wisdom and Justice, which is Christ."[77] What Origen is saying is that all people, simply by being rational beings, have a participation in the Word of God, who, being Reason, made them and, having made them, has a connection with them as the source of their rational natures.

The Cappadocian Gregory of Nyssa writes, "whoever pursues true virtue participates in nothing other than God, because he is himself absolute virtue."[78] C. S. Lewis expresses this theme in his last book of the Chronicles of Narnia series, *The Last Battle*. When the character Emeth,

---

74. By his own account Justin is a Samaritan, "For I was not afraid either of any one of my people, I mean the Samaritans, when I wrote an address to Caesar, and affirmed that they were mistaken in trusting Simon . . ." Justin Martyr, *Dialogue with Trypho*, 181.

75. Justin Martyr, *First and Second Apologies*, 37.

76. Yeshua Messiah who is the Word or Logos of God was also understood to be the Reason of God. This is why the incarnation of the Word or Reason is the rule for our reason and why it must be understood within the light of his salvific incarnational events. Euro-American Robert Louis Wilken writes, "What one thinks is now to be measured by reference to a series of contingent events that happened in Palestine [Galilee and Judea] in the first century. Reason can no longer be exercised independently of what had happened in Christ and, it must be added, came to because of Christ." Wilken, *Spirit of Early Christian Thought*, 23.

77. Origen, *On First Principles*, 38. Similarly in his *Homilies on the Psalms* Origen preached, "It is not possible to be just without participating in Christ, and if someone supposes that he is someone just outside the faith, one of two possibilities applies: either the gentile participates in Christ, or, if he does not participate in Christ, he is not just. Which do you want to demonstrate, that a gentile participates in Christ? But this is incongruous." Origen, *Homilies on the Psalms*, 156.

78. Gregory, *Life of Moses*, 5.

who has served Tash throughout his life and fought against the servants of Aslan, finds himself in the new creation standing before Aslan, he expects to be killed by him, but the lion instead touches his forehead with his tongue and welcomes him. Astonished, Emeth asks Aslan if it was true what he had heard, namely that Aslan and Tash were one in the same.[79] Aslan responds that this was false, and not the reason he welcomed him into his kingdom.

Instead, Aslan explains: "no service which is vile can be done to me, and none which is not vile can be done to him [Tash]." If an act of cruelty is committed in the name of Aslan, in truth it is done not to Aslan but to Tash, and Tash alone accepts it. Conversely, the one who swears an oath to Tash for the sake of the oath swears it not by Tash but by Aslan, and Aslan is the one who will reward him. Still somewhat confused by all this, Emeth brings up again the fact it was Tash he was seeking all his life. To this Aslan replies, "Beloved . . . unless thy desire had been for me thou wouldst not have sought so long and so truly. For all find what they truly seek."[80] In other words, all people have a connection to the Word, as Justin and Origen said, and because God is Goodness and Virtue, the extent to which we find ourselves participating in the good and the virtuous is the extent to which we find ourselves in relational participation with God. Indeed, those who truly desire the true, good, and beautiful really desire God, who is Truth, Goodness, and Beauty.

Those who truly want to know God and participate in God's nature certainly have access to it in whatever time, culture, and religious context they may find themselves, even if they are unaware of the name Yeshua. In the Syriac text the *Doctrina Addai*, likely composed in the fifth century, and reminiscent of Paul's statement in Acts about an altar to an unknown God,[81] the author writes, "For he [Yeshua Messiah] is the God of the Jews, who crucified him,[82] and also the erring pagans—*they also worship him even without knowing it*."[83] This does not mean anything goes, or that the Christian doctrine embodied in the church, the body of Messiah,

---

79. This is the pluralism option.

80. Lewis, *Last Battle*, 154–55.

81. Acts 17:22–28.

82. Let's not forget, it was not all the Jews who handed Yeshua over to the Romans to crucify him, but the Judean religious and political leaders who did so. Under Roman colonialism Jews had no power to execute. It was the Romans who hung Yeshua up on the Cross.

83. *Doctrina Addai*, 33. Emphasis added.

does not matter. Instead, it means that Messiah is, by reality of his being the Word and Reason, present in and through all the universe, world, peoples, times, places, and cultures; even in the religious teachers outside of Christianity, he is "dimly present in the *good* side of the inferior teachers they follow."[84] To the extent that things were spoken and lived truly among all peoples, regardless of religious tradition, ethnic group, or culture, they were said and lived from that true source of our creation and true source of our continuing existence, namely Yeshua, the Word of God. Not everything in other religious traditions or cultures is false or opposed to Yeshua Messiah. In reality, sometimes Eastern cultures are more faithful to Christian teaching than Western "Christian" cultures, more in resonance with Yeshua, who is the blueprint of reality.

But on the other hand not everything in other religious traditions is properly Christian, as Justin wrote, "I confess that I both boast[85] and with all my strength strive to be found a Christian; *not because the teachings of Plato are different from those of Christ, but because they are not in all respects similar*, neither are those of the others, Stoics, and poets, and historians."[86] The position of inclusivism, and indeed of universalism, affirms Yeshua as the Way, the Truth, and the Life, and that nobody comes to the Father but through him. Yeshua is unique, and we are called to be followers of *the Way*, which is both shown to us by Yeshua through creation and is Yeshua himself. Those who follow this Way, even without realizing it, or who may not even know Yeshua's name but are nonetheless participating in God, are full members of the church, his body, by virtue of the reality that they, like all the members of the visible church, are connected to the one head, who is Messiah.

Inclusivism also states because Messiah is present in and through all things, there are true things that accord with his own nature found in all cultures and even in other religious traditions. It rejects both exclusivism, which teaches that you must consciously know and profess the name of Yeshua in order to be a Christian and live in God's coming kingdom, and Pluralism, which teaches Yeshua is simply one way rather than *the Way* to union with God. In this sense, it rejects both heretical extremes, rather

---

84. Lewis, "Letter to Mrs. Johnson," 245–46.

85. When we see Justin "boasting" about being a Christian, it must be kept at the forefront of our mind that he is speaking as part of a persecuted minority to a hostile political and religious culture at the hands of which he would later be murdered.

86. Justin Martyr, *First and Second Apologies*, 72. Emphasis added.

opting for a more mediating and nuanced position that is more properly Christian in its sensibilities.

A Word about Indigenizing Theology

Since this book has made the case that abandoning the brown Jewish DNA of the faith is tantamount to abandoning Yeshua the Messiah, the reader may be curious what it looks like for them (particularly if they're not Jewish) to follow Yeshua in their own ethnic and cultural heritage.[87] In other words, can we culturally contextualize this Jewish gospel in ways that maintain the integrity of its brown Jewish DNA while at the same time remain faithful to the specific cultural mediums of all people groups that each contribute to expressing the image of God? Can non-Jews be faithful followers of the Jewish Messiah?[88]

Since two seemingly opposing things can be true at the same time—for instance, God is both three persons and yet one God—it's possible and necessary both to decolonize and decenter white normativity, which entails upholding the specific covenants God has made with each ethnic group, *and* at the same time to maintain the Jewish DNA of the gospel. This affirmation of both the gospel's Jewish particularity and all people's particularities at one and the same time means people can and should follow this Jewish Yeshua within their own people's sense of covenantal faithfulness, and are able to do so without destroying what's Jewish about the faith.[89] Paul argues along these lines in his Letter to the Galatians, indicating that Jews can be faithful to the Jewish Messiah by being Jews, and gentiles can be faithful to the Jewish Messiah by being gentiles. If Yeshua really is particular in his salvific encounter with creation as I have discussed, it means our own theological praxis of following Yeshua

---

87. Jennifer Rosner phrases the theological situation this way: "approaching Christology through the lens of Israel issues a reminder that Jesus' context matters. He cannot be abstracted from the Jewish people, and his salvific work cannot be unhitched from Israel's mission. While the gospel message can and should be endlessly translated and appropriated into diverse historical and geographical contexts, we cannot allow the significance of Jesus' concrete particularities to be obscured." Rosner, *Healing the Schism*, 190.

88. This is the same question the first Jewish Christians were asking, and I suggest is one that we need to revisit.

89. The prophet Amos speaks of every people group as having a particular covenant with God. I believe that each people has their own unique way of upholding their own covenantal faithfulness to God. The Jews, including myself, do so by observing and upholding Torah.

and embodying the triune God can be done within whatever specific ethnicity and culture we are from, even the Germans, although it may seem at times I have argued differently.[90]

I have done so not because I think the Germans or Northern Europeans are inherently evil but because I think they have lost their way, and have turned away from the seeds of the Jewish Logos inherent in their cultural and ethnic DNA. African-American historical theologian Vince Bantu writes, "As each group works out our cultural sanctification with fear and trembling, the purpose of crosscultural partnership is not for us to become part of a different people group but to become better versions of ourselves."[91] The Germans, or Northern European people, have lost themselves so far as they have entered into an Enlightenment colonial worldview. This modernism I have constantly critiqued in this book isn't the true self of the Northern European people and their culture; it is their false self. And by centering and interacting with the traditions I have referenced throughout this book, they can reclaim their God-given selfhood and become the version of themselves God desires and has gifted them to be. Only can the Germans and Northern Europeans represent the particular aspect of God's image that God has specifically entrusted them to manifest.

We are all going through our own cultural theosis (even us Jews) in which we come to manifest God's image in a unique way that God has called and entrusted us to represent. All peoples as they move towards their true selves take up this vocation of humanity by doing their particular part in cooperation with all peoples to fully express God's image—an image that according to Colossians 1:15 is Yeshua; he is God's image and therefore since he's Jewish, *God's image is Jewish*. All peoples are called to manifest the Jewish image of God in a way that is true to who and what God has called them to be as a people, not as anyone other than themselves, but as truly and fully themselves. Paradoxically non-Jews can only truly manifest this Jewish image in themselves when they have fully

---

90. For those who have read my book and thought I was either too hard on the Germans/Northern Europeans or not nuanced enough, I have the following response: Nuance upon nuance upon nuance is no longer nuance, and in my experience is a tactic of white colonial power to justify their atrocities committed; infinite nuance loses its sense of nuance, blurring the lines between good and evil making everything gray and indistinguishable. True nuance paradoxically includes some lack of nuance. We must maintain the kind of nuance that allows us to call out evil and injustice without getting so bogged down with nuance that we fail to call a thing evil and unjust.

91. Bantu, *Multitude of All Peoples*, 230.

come into their own as gentiles. As we saw in the previous chapter, God's completion of a fully developed human is intricately and mysteriously tied to God's completion of the first fully developed Jew. The completion of all humans, including us Jews, is therefore tied up with the completion of the Jewish people of Israel.

To be fully German is therefore somehow connected to what it means to be fully Jewish, and by expressing the full Jewishness of God's image they do not lose themselves and become Jewish, but they become fully German. Salvation is entered into through Jewish flesh, and so also is full humanity entered into through Jewish flesh, and this becoming fully human is part and parcel of our salvation. Only when all people and indeed all creation paradoxically express God's Jewish image, as fully finished gentiles, will God's image be fully represented.

The salvific intent and potential effectiveness of the Jewish Messiah is universal, but it is universal by way of particularity, through the seeds of the Jewish Logos spread, sown, and grown throughout the fabric of every piece of creation. Given these seeds belong to the Logos, who has taken on Jewish flesh permanently, each seed possesses an inherent non-negotiable quality of this Jewish particularity, a Jewish DNA, but it's also paradoxically true that the seeds grown outside this Jewish particularity take on the qualities of the culture and people they are implanted in; indeed it's the inspiration and source for the good, beautiful, and true found in their culture. Certainly these cultures, to the extent they express the true, the good, and the beautiful, do so by, in, and through their connection to the Logos. Thus, a true indigenized theology is not in conflict with the particularity of the Jewish gospel. All cultures and peoples can express this Jewish gospel in their own culturally appropriate expressions. Indeed the Jewish gospel only becomes fully Jewish when all peoples, precisely by being themselves, manifest God's Jewish image.

Truly, it is because of the particularity of the Jewish incarnation of God that all peoples, cultures, and languages can indigenize their following of Yeshua within their own cultural contexts. This particularity is itself fundamental to the Jewish incarnation and therefore to all of humanity and the rest of creation's particularity. The particularity of God's image prompts, gives permission, and even births the particularity, in all its fullness, of people groups. Just as God's taking on of materiality, becoming part of God's own creation, is an affirmation of physical matter, so is God's taking on of ethnic particularity an affirmation of ethnic particularity. If the incarnation was of a universal human being as we often like to suggest, then all peoples would in reality be barred from particularizing their faith in Yeshua in their own people's ways. We would all have to give up our own unique expressions of following Yeshua for something universal and standard since such a universal incarnation would be an affirmation of universality.

If the Messiah is our model to imitate and that Messiah is universal, then the imitation must be universal; if that Messiah is particular, so must our imitation be. The former is the premise of theological colonialism that we've seen in too much of the efforts of Western missions. Once again it is the particularity of God that affirms the particularity of all his peoples.[92] Indigenizing the faith within particular cultures and peoples is a particularity rooted in the particularity of the Jewish incarnation and therefore in the particular second person of the Trinity, who finds his personhood and existence in relationship to the other two persons of the Trinity, who in turn all find themselves fully united as one God. The triune nature of God allows, commands, and makes possible particulars because this triunity is always three particulars in communion, a communion that constitutes a particular oneness fully united. This particularity in the nature of God is why the gospel and God incarnate can be Jewish while at the same time it's possible for all peoples to follow Yeshua in ways that are internal to their own culture and language.[93]

Theologian Jennifer Rosner, a Messianic Jew, writing about Barth's theology, says, "Because God is only known and knowable in the person of Jesus Christ, to talk about God is necessarily to talk about humanity as well."[94] In the context of our topic here, we can modify it this way: because God is only known and knowable in a Jewish man named Yeshua, to talk about God therefore is necessarily to talk also about the Jewish people, whom this God saw fit to bind himself with in the Jewish incarnation, this being the way God entered into humanity and creation. Something of this sort is gestured towards by the Egyptian Origen when in his homily on Psalm 75 he comments on the phrase "God is known in

---

92. The triune God of Israel is particular in at least two ways. First, God is not a universal God, but the God of Israel who created the universe. God is *this* God, not *that* God, meaning God is a particular God whom we can distinguish. Second, God is particular in that God is three particular persons in communion, which itself constitutes the oneness of God, meaning this one particular God is particularly three persons in one particular God.

93. It is both an affirmation of Jewish particularity and particularity in and of itself.

94. Rosner, *Healing the Schism*, 56.

Judaea." He begins by asking how it can be that God is known in Judaea. Was God not known in Egypt in the exodus, or in Babylon in the exile?

> Why, then, when God is "known" in so many places, is it written, "*God is known in Judaea*"? Could it be, even if they were unwilling, that they were compelled to admit that these things were prophesied in regard to the Savior's time, because Christ Jesus visited [incarnated] in Judaea, being a god and the Son of God, so that it came about that "*God is known in Judaea*"? Of this God—I actually speak of our Lord Jesus Christ—the name is "*great in Israel.*"[95]

In other words, God is known in Judaea as opposed to Egypt or Babylon because God was incarnated as a Judean. If we want to know this God of the creeds, we can only know him in a Jew and therefore in the people of Israel. Yeshua, God in Jewish flesh, so proclaimed to the Samaritan woman, whom he loved, that "salvation [life] *is* from the Jews."[96] What is important to highlight here is that Yeshua said life *is* from the Jews rather than *was*. Meaning Israel's role of meditating salvation/life to the world is an ongoing role. It is a salvation first to the Jews and then to the gentiles,[97] particularly planting itself in all particularities by way of this Jewish particularity. The Jewish philosopher Franz Rosenzweig once wrote, "Christianity, by radiating outwards, is in danger of evaporating into isolated rays far away from the divine core of truth."[98] Since the divine core of truth is Yeshua himself, who is a Jew, that core is thus found within the Jewish people.

---

95. Origen, *Homilies on the Psalms*, 228. It should be noted that while this is an incredibly powerful statement by an early patristic writer about the Jewish incarnation, it is mitigated by Origen's use of Paul's statement that not all of Israel is true Israel, and not all gentiles are true Gentiles. By blurring the lines and distinctions between Israel and the gentiles (something I don't think Paul does) Origen's statement of God being known in Judaea by way of the incarnation is softened. Whether this reading accurately describes the meaning behind Paul's statement, or even if this initial surface reading of Origen's use of Paul's statement is accurate, needs to be explored further. Eastern Orthodox scholar Michael Azar makes the case the term "supersessionism" doesn't adequately describe what patristic writers such as Origen are doing when they write about Jews. Azar, "Origen, Scripture, and the Imprecision of 'Supersessionism,'" 157–72. There may be other ways to read passages like this one from patristic writers like Origen that are less dismissing of God's covenant with Israel and the Jewishness of the gospel and Yeshua.

96. John 4:22. Emphasis added.

97. Romans 1:16.

98. Rosenzweig, *Star of Redemption*, 429–30.

Christians' relationship to the Father is mediated through Israel by way of the Jewishness of Yeshua. "No one comes to my Father except by me."[99] No one comes to the Father except through a Jew, and therefore through the Jewish people. "To be a Jew means to meet God and receive his grace in and through Israel; to be a Christian means to meet God and receive his grace in and through Christ,"[100] yet such meeting of the Messiah happens in the womb of Israel. The salvation of all creation is in the most real way possible through the Jewish people. To discount the Jewish people, by discounting either the Jewishness of the Word of God or the Jewish people, is to discount the world's salvation. To separate Yeshua from his Jewishness, or our faith from the Jewish people and their faith, is to divorce ourselves from salvation. The Jews' ongoing election is secured by God's never-changing nature and by the permanent Jewish flesh God has taken on. Israel's role in the salvation of humanity through the church, Messiah's body, is therefore ongoing; without the Jewish people, there is no salvation for any part of creation.[101]

If we reject that reality, we will, I believe, continue to struggle with supersessionism and its natural byproduct of anti-Judaism. Taking away the particularities of this gospel, this salvation, this Yeshua, who is God in *Jewish flesh*, under the guise of making the Christian faith more inclusive or universal is really only colonialism, because when it loses the particularities due to it, then it absorbs not a salvation for all, but one determined by white normativity (which is exactly what we've seen; anything universal is simply whiteness understood as the universal norm). I wonder if this is one reason the universal Christ is gaining so much popularity among Euro-Americans. Is it a white-normative hegemonic reaction against the emphasis of Yeshua as Jewish that has been happening in the last few decades? I'm not sure I have the answer to that, but I think we need to seriously ask it. It's at least cultural appropriation in that it is taking the Jewish understanding of the Messiah, which gentile Christianity inherited, and remolding it according to cultural categories foreign to it.

---

99. John 14:6. Furthermore, since Yeshua is Jewish, and he is the Way, the Truth, and the Life, so also is the Way, Truth, and Life Jewish.

100. Herberg, "Judaism and Christianity," 247.

101. Although I would certainly not limit Israel's role to Messiah's body, the church, since the church itself resides in the womb of Israel, where it lives, moves, and has its being.

As long as white normativity is still in existence, any tendencies towards universalizing, at least in the West, will by default mean a universalizing towards whiteness. As African-American theologian James Cone once wrote, "I contend that there is no universalism that is not particular... As long as they can be sure that the gospel is *for everybody*, ignoring that God liberated a *particular* people from Egypt, came in a particular man called Jesus, and for the particular purpose of liberating the oppressed, then they can continue to talk in theological abstractions."[102] Because universality only happens in particularities, and one of those particulars must be defaulted too as what gets defined as universal, anything "universal" is really just the particularity of whiteness since white normativity rules our culture. A universal gospel for everybody that ignores the particularities of the gospel is not truly a gospel for everybody; it usually ends up being a gospel for Northern European colonizers. Rather, a particular gospel, as Cone gestures towards, is paradoxically a gospel for everyone. True universality happens through particularities.

Yet this isn't moral relativism (which, at least as it's manifested in America, is white since only the ones with privilege can get rid of morals). There is a particular principle or person, namely the Logos, who is the reason for a universal order of what is good. The Logos, who is Goodness undivided, is a particular person, and has always been incarnational in its relational particularity with creation. Genocide is universally wrong because the Logos or Reason that underlies and sustains all things is the kind of person in whom there is no hint of genocide. This non-genocidal nature may be expressed variously in diverse cultures, but it is always present regardless of whether we recognize the reality of it or not.

As we've seen, the Trinity shows us the reality of this unity in diversity, of particularity in union. Just as the Jewish Logos finds his union with, in, and as the triune God, while maintaining his unique incarnated personhood (his particularity), so do our particular theologies rooted in our own cultures find their union with and in the Jewish Logos as a member of the triune Godhead. It's through the filling of all the little crevices throughout the material universe by the Jewish Logos that the Logos is incarnated into all particularities, but this is also how the whole of the cosmos is held together, sustained, and finds its unity in the Jewish Logos. This is why such particular indigenized theologies that share in the Jewish Logos can at once maintain integral particularity and at the

---

102. Cone, *Black Theology of Liberation*, 126.

same time, by relationship to the Logos, be connected to one another and able to maintain the Jewish DNA.

In the same way that much of early Christianity could Christianize Hellenistic culture[103] and borrow from various Greek philosophies such as various versions of Platonism, so can Christianity utilize and grow in the native soil of wherever it finds itself planted. Earlier we quoted Justin Martyr's reason why he was a Christian: "I confess that I both boast and with all my strength strive to be found a Christian; *not because the teachings of Plato are different from those of Christ, but because they are not in all respects similar . . .* "[104] In a similar way we can say this about every culture: "I confess to be a Christian, not because the teachings of Plato, Cherokee sages, Lao Tzu, or Lakota elders are different from those of the Jewish Messiah but because they are not in all respects similar." There are of course things incompatible with the Christian faith,[105] but not everything is incompatible; and sometimes a culture that does not recognize Yeshua by name is more Christian than the so-called Christian culture.

Contextualization must happen when Christianity is openly expressed in a culture, and we must be careful to avoid syncretism. But I would argue much of Christianity in America and the West is more a product of syncretism than it is of true contextualization. Westerners have not been careful about contextualization in the areas they think they've been careful, namely their own Northern European culture. This I think is due to the colonial claim made by white European culture that they are the height of humanity and therefore the standard of Christianity. This has led to the syncretism of unhealthy aspects of Western culture with Christianity, and to the downplaying or outright genocide of cultural embodiments from peoples such as the Natives of this land (Turtle Island), when in reality their indigenous cultural values are often more in line with the Jewish Messiah than that of Western culture.

In conclusion, given the permanent Jewish enfleshment of the Logos and that same Logos's characteristic incarnational particularity, by which all things are filled and connected with one another, each people group and its culture, by virtue of the good, true, and beautiful found in its culture because of its share in the Jewish Logos, can express itself truly, while following Yeshua as itself, without distorting the essential Jewishness of the core of our faith, namely Yeshua and his people Israel. How each

---

103. See Wilken, *Spirit of Early Christian Thought*, xvi–xvii.
104. Justin, *First and Second Apologies*, 72. Emphasis added.
105. Racism, colonialism, polytheism, and Gnosticism as just a few examples.

people determines the best way to uphold their own covenantal faithfulness to this Jewish Messiah is, I would suggest, for the people themselves to faithfully decide in consultation with Jewish disciples of Yeshua.

Speak now, oh Lord, our true God, for when you speak, we your flesh, together as one, give birth to your Word, for we are your body, the church.

Conclusion
How Then Shall We Live?

May this book, with my voice, as me, in my place, cry out,
may it disclose things covered, proclaim secrets,
howl what was done, resound forgotten things,
reveal the invisible, pronounce the pretexts,
proclaim of the depths, tell of sins,
strip bare things unseen, show the forms of things hidden.
through it may snares be perceived, stumbling blocks discovered,
may unspeakable things be reproved, the remnants of evils wrung out,
and may your life of grace and mercy reign, O Christ,
And to you, the only Savior, to your Spirit, and the Father, sharing in Essence,
to your united lordship and your ineffable Trinity,
with mystic praise, glory and bowing down,
unto ages,
Amen.[1]

GRIGOR OF NAREK (ARMENIAN ORTHODOX, 945–1003)

IN OCTOBER OF 2021, while in the middle of writing this book, I was discerning God's call to put a pause on writing and work on becoming a

---

1. Grigor of Narek, "Book of Lamentation," 188–89.

person of gentleness and humility, to kill my ego and practice being bold. The Syriac poem *Ode of Solomon* 24 says, "Those who were arrogant in their hearts . . . they were rejected, Because the truth was not with them."[2] In other words, to be arrogant is to lack truth, and therefore if we wish to say anything true, we must strip ourselves of the arrogance within us. It was made clear to me I wasn't doing a great job of this in the way I was writing, and if I were to write a truly prophetic book pointing people towards reorientating to and in Yeshua, I needed to walk the talk; I needed to embody the things I was talking about; I needed to write and live with compassion, mercy, humility, and gentleness, in addition to justice, righteous anger, truth, zeal, boldness, and courage. I needed to write and live theology as prayer. The truly prophetic rebuke and correction, as a call to the people of God to greater faithfulness and allegiance to that God, is one of gentleness, humility, and boldness. Good theology, no matter how good, true, and beautiful, is never arrogant, and it is also always a matter of prayer embodied in our everyday lives.

As I have argued in this book, when someone is truly embodying gentleness they are at one and the same time embodying truth. The extent to which one embodies justice is the extent to which one embodies compassion; truth and gentleness are not at odds with one another, because God is the essence of both virtues, and God is not lacking in love to the same extent that God is not lacking in truth; Yeshua of Nazareth, Messiah God in the flesh, is both *Love and Truth*. Of course I'm sure at some points I have failed in the writing of this book to embody this way of life which God has asked me to practice before continuing to write. Just as a child learning to walk stumbles in that process, part of the process of learning to become gentle, humble, and bold is in making mistakes, indeed in not being gentle, humble, and bold. It's a hard line to learn how to walk, to express one's righteous anger in a productive manner while also trying to be compassionate.

When I began writing this book, I wasn't sure where I was headed, or exactly what this book would turn out to be. It's taken turns and birthed themes I had not thought of originally addressing. What I have found during my years in the deconstructionist movement and liberal Protestant circles, particularly over the course of writing this book, is that much of what is wrong in the deconstructionist movement and in liberal Protestantism can be summed up as white normativity and theological

---

2. *Odes of Solomon*, 53.

colonialism. The book has in some sense turned out to argue that the way forward, the way of recovering from our fundamentalism, is to depart from the dualistic and individualistic womb of the Northern European colonial Enlightenment, the worldview in which we were raised, and in a sense in which we have lived, moved, and had our being. In other words, I have argued in a certain sense we must die and be reborn into a new worldview, a premodern worldview.

That doesn't mean we act like the past 250–500 years didn't occur, or that we will look exactly like what the church looked like in the early third century, nor even that the premodern church was somehow perfect, but it does mean we will live in continuity with the past rather than discontinuity as we are now. It does I think mean a certain kind of parallelism with what came before that sings in harmony with the melody of the past, in resonance. So it doesn't mean we can go back to our childhood, so to speak, or that as a tree we can go back to the stage of being a seed. As we stand now, we are not the same person or tree that existed in the past but something else entirely. We are an apple tree, but the premodern church was and is an olive tree. While we cannot go back in time to once again become the seed of the olive tree, we can remove ourselves from the apple tree and be regrafted into the Jewish olive tree.

At the beginning of this book, I set up our situation as like that of the addict. We are, I have tried to show in some very real sense, recovering fundamentalists, or if we're not in recovery then we are simply fundamentalists actively living in our addiction to modernism. If we wish to be sober and work on our recovery from fundamentalism, then like the alcohol, sex, or drug addict we must withdraw from all forms of fundamentalism. Much of what we've been doing is trying to control and enjoy our addiction, rather than dealing with it by avoiding the use of this substance all together. Just like the alcohol, sex, or drug addict, we cannot try to moderate our intake. We can't simply try to limit ourselves to one drink per week, or one porn flick per month; we must totally cut ourselves off.

Simply going from one kind of fundamentalism to another kind doesn't bring us sobriety or healing. Fundamentalism, or modernism, in either it's liberal Protestant or "conservative" fundamentalist form, is still feeding our addiction. Part of addiction is self-deception and delusion, and it's progressive if not dwelt with openly and honestly. Progressive here means two things: first, it means that if not dwelt with it continually gets worse, not better; second, while the "conservative" side of the modernist coin is often explicit in its racism, when it turns progressive it does a much better job of hiding its colonialism, general racism, anti-Jewish racism, and white normativity, and thus of putting on a false façade deluding itself into thinking it's sober.

Just as we have a perfect storm for rampant and prolific porn addiction in our culture, so to the conditions are ripe for addiction to fundamentalism, or said another way, addiction to Northern European German Endarkenment culture, which views itself as *the* standard, the most *evolved* worldview, whose responsibility is therefore to whiten the world, imposing its assumptions and categories on the Christian faith through theological colonialism. This is our addiction.

Although many of us are unaware of this fact, we simply don't know what we don't know. On the one hand, we've been handed this, spoon-fed it from birth as if it was proper food; it's the water we swim in, and we are fish going about life as best as we know how. On the other hand, the food being fed to us was and is poison, which we are now feeding to our infants; the water we swim in is actually blood, and we're inviting or forcing others to swim in it. How does one give grace to the racist because it's what we were raised in and all we've ever known, while at the same time calling ourselves to repentance with all the justice, truth, compassion, and gentleness that is required for the task? I don't know, but in a sense I think this has been my task in this book. Whether I have succeeded in it will, I suppose, be for the church over time and place to decide.

I've contended we have largely been doing deconstruction poorly, and the way forward is not simply to depart from European modernism, but to reclaim the Jewishness of Christianity and in a sense resource ourselves to a broad premodern orthodox worldview rooted in the Catholic, Eastern, and Oriental Orthodox traditions, much of which are homegrown and rooted in Africa and Asia rather than Europe—although there's also a lot of good stuff from premodern Europe. What this book has fermented into is perhaps the most controversial critique and guide forward I could have written, which wasn't exactly my intention. While it is true I do not write to make people like me—I write because there is a burning fire in my bones and I must let it out—such writing has brought and I am confident will continue to bring me sorrow.

In a sense writing this book has made life difficult and a struggle because I know the veil has been lifted and it is my vocation to help unveil it for others. Realizing theological colonialism, white normativity, and anti-Judaism is at the root of so many of our problems as recovering fundamentalists and as American Christians in general is deeply troubling because now I have a responsibility to help people see this themselves. It is an exercise in placing one's head into the mouth of a lion. Much of what I have said applies to not just the deconstructionist movement I've been a part of, but also to my own denomination and tradition, the Episcopal Church. I've placed my head in the mouth of the lion, and it turns out the lion is my mother. Will my own tear me apart? I suppose only time will tell.

The title of this book indicates the goal has been to show us a way forward, a way of recovering from our fundamentalism, a way towards greater faithfulness to the true, the good, and the beautiful. And that I have attempted to do to the best of my ability by articulating the Christian vision as I understand it to be embodied in the great tradition rooted in the Jewish Messiah. In this sense I've tried to bring us back to the basics of the Christian faith by way of a sort of (re)introduction to the faith. The Syriac Theodore bar Koni once wrote, "Although the matter was laborious, we have forced ourselves to do it, because the benefit of others was more honorable in our eyes than the easing of ourselves, not so that we might boast in this, because theoretical speculation does not belong to us; ours is this: That we labor in collecting."[3] In modernity we hold the sentiment that originality and novelty is the highest good one can obtain in writing, and anything else, for that matter and any kind of indebtedness, is seen as weakness and failure.

I'd like to suggest this is just arrogance and ego rooted in white individualistic constructions of identity. For most of the world today and most of world history (everything outside of Northern Europe in the last few hundred years) it's been the opposite way around. Instead of trying to be original and novel, people attempted, in humility, to show just how they were indebted. They attempted to uplift the tradition that came before them and show how what they were doing was connected to that tradition. My goal has been to emulate this approach and attitude by endeavoring not to be novel but to "labor in collecting" the tradition upon whose shoulders I stand. As such I tried to limit my speculation even while trying to further develop that tradition, deferring to what others had said before me, which is why I have quoted so extensively. Of course my knowledge is limited, and I'm sure as I continue to grow I'll be better able to articulate in part the whole global Christian vision,

---

3. Theodore bar Koni, "Scholion, Memra 10," 131.

although no one person can do this alone; my attempt is but one small puzzle piece. Anything I've left out or underrepresented will have to be forgiven me as I am just one man.

Considering the authority of tradition, Maximus the Confessor once wrote, "I have no dogma of my own, just the common dogma of the Catholic Church."[4] Thus, with Maximus allow me to declare that for what I have written that has not already been revealed to Moses at Sinai, carried forth in the body of the one who is the Revelation of God, who dwells in the womb of Israel, may it be cast out into the outer darkness where there is gnashing of teeth.[5] To the extent I have failed to embody this attitude of Maximus and pre-Northern European modernity, I hope to be corrected and ignored.

Lastly, I have also seen my task in this project as not simply giving different answers to many of our questions, but teaching different questions altogether. In other words, I've seen my task here as a midwife helping to give birth to a new worldview, to a conversion of the imagination. Whether I have succeeded in this endeavor only time will tell, and it is an ongoing project which one would hope will over time manage to improve its ability to work the task at hand. The key to our recovery from addiction to fundamentalism is the treasure found in the earthen clay jar that is the one, holy, catholic, and apostolic church. We need not run from it to find healing—that's been our problem—but we need to go back to that brown Jewish clay jar. Everything we need is already there. The old wine is better. Let us turn with open eyes and see Yeshua the Jew embodied in his people. Amen.

---

4. Maximus the Confessor, *Selected Writings*, 22.

5. In Rabbinic theology all teaching uttered by Jewish sages in the future was already revealed to Moses at Sinai. I would add that since Yeshua is the one who gave the revelation to Moses at Sinai (and himself is that revelation), all that which is true within the gentile Christian tradition was also revealed to Moses at Sinai.

Recommended Resources

Resources for Those Suffering from Addiction:

- For people suffering from sex addiction: Sexaholics Anonymous (https://www.sa.org) and or Sex Addicts Anonymous (https://saa-recovery.org)
- For people suffering from addiction to Alcohol: Alcoholics Anonymous (https://www.aa.org)
- For people suffering from addiction to Narcotics: (https://www.narcotics.com)

Recommended Publishers:

- Gorgias Press
- St Vladimir's Seminary Press
- The Catholic University of America Press
- InterVarsity Press
- Langham Publishing
- Wipf and Stock (and their imprints)

Recommended Organizations:

- Yachad BeYeshua (The Church needs the voices of Jewish Disciples of Yeshua.) (https://www.yachad-beyeshua.org)
- Society for Post-Supersessionist Theology (https://www.spostst.org)

Jewish Christians/Messianic Jews to Read and Listen to:

- Ephraim Radner—Anglican
- Marty Solomon—Christian Church
- Jennifer Rosner—Messianic Jew
- Mark Kinzer—Messianic Jew
- Antoine Levy—Roman Catholic
- Lee Spitzer—American Baptist
- Svetlana Panich—Eastern Orthodox
- Richard Harvey—Messianic Jew
- David Rudolph—Messianic Jew

Non-Christian Jews to Read and Listen to:

- Amy Jill-Levine
- Daniel Boyarin
- Benjamin Sommer
- Paula Frederiksen
- Mark Nanos
- Jonathan Sacks

One may of course survey the bibliography for books, but for the sake of giving a starting point, below I have made a short selection that *may* be less overwhelming.

Readings on the Early Church:

Anatolios, Khaled. *Retrieving Nicaea: The Development and Meaning of Trinitarian Doctrine*. Grand Rapids: Baker Academic, 2011.

Ayres, Lewis. *Nicaea and Its Legacy: An Approach to Fourth-Century Trinitarian Theology*. Oxford: Oxford University Press, 2004.

Bantu, Vince L. *A Multitude of All Peoples: Engaging Ancient Christianity's Global Identity*. Downers Grove, IL: InterVarsity, 2020.

Bantu, Vince, and Nathan Gibson, eds. *Global Christian Texts: Readings in Premodern Christianity from African, Middle Eastern, Asian Languages*. Berkeley, CA: University of California Press, forthcoming.

Barron, Bishop Robert. *Light from Light: A Theological Reflection on the Nicene Creed*. Park Ridge, IL: Word on Fire, 2021.

Behr, John. *Becoming Human: Meditations on Christian Anthropology in Word and Image*. Crestwood, NY: St Vladimir's Seminary Press, 2013.

———. *The Mystery of Christ: Life in Death*. Crestwood, NY: St Vladimir's Seminary Press, 2006.

———. *The Way to Nicaea*. The Formation of Christian Theology 1. Crestwood, NY: St Vladimir's Seminary Press, 2001.

(And really anything by John Behr)

Brock, Sebastian. *The Luminous Eye: The Spiritual World Vision of Saint Ephrem the Syrian*. Kalamazoo, MI: Cistercian, 1992.

Ephrem. *Hymns on Faith*. Translated by Jeffrey T. Wickes. The Fathers of the Church. Washington, DC: Catholic University of America Press, 2015.

———. *Hymns on the Nativity*. Translated by Kathleen E. McVey. The Classics of Western Spirituality. Mahwah, NJ: Paulist, 1989.

Geffert, Bryn, and Theofanis G. Stavrou, eds. *Eastern Orthodox Christianity: The Essential Texts*. New Haven, CT: Yale University Press, 2016.

González, Justo L. *The Story of Christianity*, vol. 1, *The Early Church to the Dawn of the Reformation*. New York: HarperCollins, 2010.

Lubac, Henri de. *History and Spirit: The Understanding of Scripture According to Origen*. Translated by Anne Englund Nash. San Francisco: Ignatius, 2007.

Origen. *Origen: On First Principles: A Reader's Edition*. Translated by John Behr. Oxford: Oxford University Press, 2019.

Palmer, G. E. H., Philip Sherrard, and Kallistos Ware, trans. and eds. *The Philokalia: The Complete Text. Compiled by Nicodemus of the Holy Mountain and Makarios of Corinth*. Vol. 2. London: Faber and Faber, 1981.

(And really any of the five volumes of the *Philokalia*)

Walters, J. Edwards, ed. *Eastern Christianity: A Reader*. Grand Rapids: Eerdmans, 2021.

Wilken, Robert Louis. *The Spirit of Early Christian Thought: Seeking the Face of God*. New Haven, CT: Yale University Press, 2003.

Young, Francis, Lewis Ayres, and Andrew Louth, eds. *The Cambridge History of Early Christian Literature*. Cambridge, UK: Cambridge University Press, 2004.

Readings on Scripture:

Boersma, Hans. *Scripture as Real Presence: Sacramental Exegesis in the Early Church*. Grand Rapids: Baker, 2017.

Gregory of Nyssa. *The Life of Moses*. Translated by Abraham J. Malherbe and Everett Ferguson. Harper Collins Spiritual Classics. New York: Harper One, 2006.

Irenaeus. *On the Apostolic Preaching*. Translated by John Behr. Popular Patristics Series. Crestwood, NY: St Vladimir's Seminary Press, 1997.

Jersak, Bradley. *A More Christlike Word: Reading Scripture the Emmaus Way*. New Kensington, PA: Whitaker House, 2021.

Krestos, Hensa. *Harp of Glory: Enzira Sebhat: An Alphabetical Hymn of Praise for the Ever-Blessed Virgin Mary from the Ethiopian Orthodox Church*. Translated by John Anthony McGuckin. Popular Patristics Series. Yonkers, NY: St Vladimir's Seminary Press, 2010.

Origen. *Commentary on the Gospel of John, Books 1–10*. Translated by Ronald E. Heine. The Fathers of the Church. Washington, DC: Catholic University of America Press, 2010.

Must-Reads:

Basil the Great. *On the Holy Spirit*. Translated by Stephen Hildebrand. Popular Patristics Series. Yonkers, NY: St Vladimir's Seminary Press, 2011.

———. *On Social Justice*. Translated by C. Paul Schroeder. Popular Patristics Series. Crestwood, NY: St Vladimir's Seminary Press, 2009.

Boyarin, Daniel. *The Jewish Gospels: The Story of the Jewish Christ*. New York: New Press, 2012.

Cohick, Lynn H., and Amy Brown Hughes. *Christian Women in the Patristic World: Their Influence, Authority, and Legacy in the Second through Fifth Centuries*. Grand Rapids: Baker, 2017.

Gregory of Nazianzus. *On God and On Christ*. Translated by Frederick Williams and Lionel Wickham. Popular Patristics Series. Crestwood, NY: St Vladimir's Seminary Press, 2002.

Edwards, Dennis R. *Might from the Margins: The Gospel's Power to Turn the Tables on Injustice*. Harrisonburg, VA: Herald, 2020.

Jacob of Serug. *On the Mother of God*. Translated by Mary Hansbury. Popular Patristics Series. Crestwood, NY: St Vladimir's Seminary Press, 1998.

Julian of Norwich. *Revelations of Divine Love*. Translated by Elizabeth Spearing. London: Penguin, 1998.

Rosner, Jennifer M. *Finding Messiah: A Journey into the Jewishness of the Gospel*. Downers Grove, IL: InterVarsity, 2022.

———. *Healing the Schism: Karl Barth, Franz Rosenzweig, and the New Jewish-Christian Encounter*, Bellingham, WA: Lexham Academic, 2021.

Thurman, Howard. *Jesus and the Disinherited*. Boston: Beacon, 1976.

Twiss, Richard. *One Church, Many Tribes: Following Jesus the Way God Made You*. Ventura, CA: Regal, 2000.

———. *Rescuing the Gospel from the Cowboys: A Native American Expression of the Jesus Way*. Downers Grove, IL: InterVarsity, 2015.

Woodley, Randy. *Indigenous Theology and the Western Worldview: A Decolonized Approach to Christian Doctrine*. Grand Rapids: Baker, 2022.

———. *Living in Color: Embracing God's Passion for Ethnic Diversity*. Downers Grove, IL: InterVarsity, 2004.

———. *Shalom and the Community of Creation: An Indigenous Vision*. Grand Rapids: Eerdmans, 2012.

———. "White Supremacy and the Fate of the Earth." *Sojourners*, April 7, 2021. https://sojo.net/magazine/may-2021/white-supremacy-and-fate-earth.

Readings on the Anglican, Catholic and Orthodox Traditions:

Barron, Robert. *Catholicism: A Journey to the Heart of the Faith*. New York: Image, 2014.

Chapman, Mark. *Anglicanism: A Very Short Introduction*. Oxford: Oxford University Press, 2006.

Griffiss, James E. *The Anglican Vision*. Boston: Cowley, 1997.

Louth, Andrew. *Introducing Eastern Orthodox Theology*. Downers Grove, IL: InterVarsity, 2013.

Ware, Kallistos. *The Orthodox Church: An Introduction to Eastern Christianity*. London: Penguin, 2015.

———. *The Orthodox Way*. Yonkers, NY: St Vladimir's Seminary Press, 2018.

White, Thomas Joseph. *The Light of Christ: An Introduction to Catholicism*. Washington, DC: Catholic University of America Press, 2017.

Readings on the Problem of Evil:

Athanasius. *On the Incarnation*. Translated by John Behr. Popular Patristics Series. Yonkers, NY: St Vladimir's Seminary Press, 2011.

Harrison, Nonna Verna, David G. Hunter, eds. *Suffering and Evil in Early Christian Thought*. Grand Rapids: Baker, 2016.

Lewis, C. S. "The Problem of Pain." In *The Complete C.S. Lewis Signature Classics*, 371–433. New York: Harper Collins, 2002.

Oord, Thomas Jay. *God Can't: How to Believe in God and Love after Tragedy, Abuse, or Other Evils*. Grasmere, ID: SacraSage, 2019.

———. *The Uncontrolling Love of God: An Open and Relational Account of Providence*. Downers Grove, IL: InterVarsity, 2015.

Regarding the last two suggestions, I want to make a quick caveat. While Tom Oord and I have reached similar conclusions regarding the doctrine of the uncontrolling love of God, we have different starting points. Tom starts from the framework of Open Theism and Process Theology, whereas I start from a classical theist framework. Due to Tom's Northern European modernist leanings, he is more open to revising the Christian tradition considering new evidence, a fundamentally modernist move. I am more open to seeing the new evidence in light of the Christian tradition and am therefore more likely to side with some aspect of the Christian tradition, particularly as it's embodied pre-Reformation. Tom is an American of Norwegian descent, an ordained elder in the Church of the Nazarene, firmly established in the Wesleyan tradition of Protestantism. I am a Jewish Anglican whose theology leans more Catholic than Protestant, and most heavily towards Eastern and Oriental Orthodoxies.

For what it's worth, Tom and I both value the centrality of love, particularly understood as uncontrolling love, and for that reason I think we tend to jive well. So, while I recommend and endorse Tom's theology of the uncontrolling love of God, and the books in which he discusses them, I think the thrust of his worldview is modernist and from my perspective it is from this orientation that he rejects traditional theism for the novel theologies of Open Theism and Process Theology. Accordingly, I do not endorse his modernist leanings or his Open Theism and Process Theology.

Bibliography

Alvarez, Emilio. *Pentecostal Orthodoxy: Toward an Ecumenism of the Spirit.* Downers Grove, IL: InterVarsity, 2022.
Amma Sarra. *Apophthegmata Patrum.* In *The Book of Mystical Chapters: Meditations on the Soul's Ascent from the Desert Fathers and Other Early Christian Contemplatives,* translated and introduced by John Anthony McGuckin, 16–17. Boston: Shambhala, 2002.
Anatolios, Khaled. *Retrieving Nicaea: The Development and Meaning of Trinitarian Doctrine.* Grand Rapids: Baker Academic, 2011.
Anderson, Paul N. *The Riddles of the Fourth Gospel: An Introduction to John.* Minneapolis: Fortress, 2011.
Athanasius. *On the Incarnation.* Translated by John Behr. Popular Patristics Series. Yonkers, NY: St Vladimir's Seminary Press, 2011.
Augustine, "Homilies on I John 1.12." In *Works of Saint Augustine,* translated by Boniface Ramsey. Hyde Park, NY: New City, 2008.
Aulén, Gustaf. *Christus Victor: An Historical Study of the Three Main Types of the Idea of Atonement.* Translated by A. G. Herbert. London: SPCK, 2010.
Ayres, Lewis. *Nicaea and Its Legacy: An Approach to Fourth-Century Trinitarian Theology.* Oxford: Oxford University Press, 2004.
Azar, Michael G. "Origen, Scripture, and the Imprecision of 'Supersessionism.'" *Journal of Theological Interpretation* 10:2 (2016) 157–72.
Babai the Great. "Book of the Union." Translated by Adam Bremer-McCollum. In *Invitation to Syriac Christianity: An Anthology,* edited by Michael Philip Penn, Scott Fitzgerald Johnson, Christine Shepardson, and Charles M. Stang, 99–101. Oakland: University of California Press, 2022.
Bantu, Vince L. *A Multitude of All Peoples: Engaging Ancient Christianity's Global Identity.* Downers Grove, IL: InterVarsity, 2020.
Barrett, Matthew. *God's Word Alone: The Authority of Scripture.* Grand Rapids: Zondervan, 2016.
Barron, Robert. *Light from Light: A Theological Reflection on the Nicene Creed.* Park Ridge, IL: Word on Fire, 2021.

Barron, Robert, and Brandon Vogt. "Gnosticism, the Enduring Heresy." *Word on Fire* (podcast), episode 222, October 18, 2022. https://www.wordonfire.org/videos/wordonfire-show/episode222/.

Barth, Karl. *Church Dogmatics: The Doctrine of Reconciliation*. Vol. 4, part 1. Edited by G. W. Bromiley and T. F. Torrance. Translated by G. T. Thomson and Harold Knight. Peabody, MA: Hendrickson, 2010.

———. *Church Dogmatics: The Word of God*. Vol. 1, part 2. Edited by G. W. Bromiley and Thomas T. F. Torrance. Translated by G. T. Thomson and Harold Knight. Peabody, MA: Hendrickson, 2010.

———. *Dogmatics in Outline*. Translated by G. T. Thomson. New York: Harper & Row, 1959.

Basil the Great. *On the Holy Spirit*. Translated by Stephen Hildebrand. Popular Patristics Series. Yonkers, NY: St Vladimir's Seminary Press, 2011.

———. *On Social Justice*. Translated by C. Paul Schroeder. Popular Patristics Series. Crestwood, NY: St Vladimir's Seminary Press, 2009.

Bass, Diana Butler. *A People's History of Christianity: The Other Side of the Story*. New York: HarperCollins, 2009.

Bates, David. "The Church Is a Whore?" *Restless Pilgrim* (blog), February 24, 2021. https://restlesspilgrim.net/blog/2021/02/24/the-church-is-a-whore/.

Bates, Matthew W. *Gospel Allegiance: What Faith in Jesus Misses for Salvation in Christ*. Grand Rapids: Brazos, 2019.

———. *Salvation by Allegiance Alone: Rethinking Faith, Works, and the Gospel of Jesus the King*. Grand Rapids: Baker, 2017.

Behr, John. *Becoming Human: Meditations on Christian Anthropology in Word and Image*. Crestwood, NY: St Vladimir's Seminary Press, 2013.

———. *The Mystery of Christ: Life in Death*. Crestwood, NY: St Vladimir's Seminary Press, 2006.

———. "Reading Scripture." *Public Orthodoxy*, December 12, 2017. https://publicorthodoxy.org/2017/12/12/reading-scripture/.

Berry, Wendell. "In Defense of Literacy." In *The World-Ending Fire: The Essential Wendell Berry*, 292–95. Berkeley, CA: Counterpoint, 2017.

———. "Rugged Individualism." In *The World-Ending Fire: The Essential Wendell Berry*, 265–67. Berkeley, CA: Counterpoint, 2017.

———. "Why I Am Not Going to Buy a Computer." In *The World-Ending Fire: The Essential Wendell Berry*, 234–41. Berkeley, CA: Counterpoint, 2017.

Blaski, Andrew James. "Fleshing Out Christ: Origen of Alexandria and the Scriptural Incarnation of the Word." PhD diss., University of Edinburgh, 2016.

Blosser, Benjamin P. *Become Like the Angels: Origen's Doctrine of the Soul*. Washington, DC: Catholic University of America Press, 2012.

Boersma, Hans. "Joshua as Sacrament: Spiritual Interpretation in Origen." *CRUX* 48:3 (2012) 23–40.

Bonhoeffer, Dietrich. *Life Together*. Translated by Jon W. Doberstein. New York: Harper, 1954.

Bouquet, A. C. "Revelation and the Divine Logos." In *The Theology of the Christian Mission*, edited by Gerald H. Anderson, 183–98. Nashville: Abingdon, 1961.

Boyarin, Daniel. *The Jewish Gospels: The Story of the Jewish Christ*. New York: New Press, 2012.

Bray, Gerald. "One God in Trinity and Trinity in Unity." In *The Trinity among the Nations: The Doctrine of God in the Majority World*, edited by Gene L. Green, Stephen T. Pardue, and K. K. Yeo, 18–36. Carlisle, UK: Langham, 2015.

Bibliography

Brianchaninov, Ignatius. *The Arena: An Offering to Contemporary Monasticism*. Madras (Chennai), India: Diocesan, 1970.

Brock, Sebastian. "Introduction." In *On The Mother of God*, by Jacob of Serug, translated by Mary Hansbury, 1–14. Crestwood, NY: St Vladimir's Seminary Press, 1998.

———. *The Luminous Eye: The Spiritual World Vision of Saint Ephrem the Syrian*. Kalamazoo, MI: Cistercian, 1992.

Buren, Paul M. Van. *A Theology of the Jewish-Christian Reality*, part 3, *Christ in Context*. San Francisco: Harper & Row, 1988.

Childers, Alisa. "5 Signs Your Church Might Be Heading toward Progressive Christianity." February 16, 2024. https://www.crosswalk.com/slideshows/5-signs-your-church-might-be-heading-toward-progressive-christianity.html.

Claiborne, Shane. *Irresistible Revolution: Living as an Ordinary Radical*. Grand Rapids: Zondervan, 2016.

Cohick, Lynn H., and Amy Brown Hughes. *Christian Women in the Patristic World: Their Influence, Authority, and Legacy in the Second through Fifth Centuries*. Grand Rapids: Baker, 2017.

Cone, James H. *A Black Theology of Liberation*. Philadelphia: Lippincott, 1990.

"The Coptic Gospel of Thomas." Translated by Thomas O. Lambdin. In *Lost Scriptures: Books that Did Not Make It into the New Testament*, edited by Bart D. Ehrman, 19–28. New York: Oxford University Press, 2003.

Cyprian. "The Unity of the Catholic Church." In *Early Latin Theology: Ichthus Edition*, translated and edited by Stanley Lawrence Greenslade, 119–42. Library of Christian Classics. Philadelphia: Westminster, 1956.

Descartes, Rene. "Discourse on Method." In *Sources of the Western Tradition*, vol. 1, *From Ancient Times to the Enlightenment*, edited by Marvin Perry, 423–26. 8th ed. Boston: Wadsworth, 2012.

"Discourse on the One God." Translation obtained from Li Tang, *A Study of the History of Nestorian Christianity in China and Its Literature in Chinese: Together with a New English Translation of the Dunhuang Nestorian Documents* (Frankfurt am Main: P. Lang, 2002), 156–60. In *Invitation to Syriac Christianity: An Anthology*, edited by Michael Philip Penn, Scott Fitzgerald Johnson, Christine Shepardson, and Charles M. Stang, 365–68. Oakland: University of California Press, 2022.

Doctrina Addai. In *Eastern Christianity: A Reader*, translated and edited by J. Edward Walters, 22–35. Grand Rapids: Eerdmans, 2021.

Edwards, Dennis R. *Might from the Margins: The Gospel's Power to Turn the Tables on Injustice*. Harrisonburg, VA: Herald, 2020.

Edwards, Mark. *Origen Against Plato*. New York: Routledge, 2002.

Ehrman, Bart D., ed. *Lost Scriptures: Books that Did Not Make It into the New Testament*. New York: Oxford University Press, 2003.

Elmer, Duane. *Cross-Cultural Connections: Stepping Out and Fitting In around the World*. Downers Grove, IL: InterVarsity, 2002.

Ephrem the Syrian. *Hymns on Faith*. Translated by Jeffrey T. Wickes. The Fathers of the Church. Washington, DC: The Catholic University of America Press, 2015.

———. *Hymns on the Nativity*. Translated by Kathleen E. McVey. The Classics of Western Spirituality. Mahwah, NJ: Paulist, 1989.

Evagrius Ponticus. "Texts on Discrimination in Respect of Passions and Thoughts." In *The Philokalia: The Complete Text. Compiled by Nicodemus of the Holy Mountain and Makarios of Corinth*, translated and edited by G. E. H. Palmer, Philip Sherrard, and Kallistos Ware, 1:38–52. New York: Farrar, Straus and Giroux, 1983.

Francis of Assisi. "A Prayer Attributed to St. Francis." In *The Book of Common Prayer: And Administration of the Sacraments and Other Rites and Ceremonies of the Church*, 833. New York: Church Publishing, 2006.

Freire, Paulo. *Pedagogy of the Oppressed*. Translated by Myra Bergman Ramos. 50th anniversary ed. New York: Bloomsbury, 2021.

Fujimura, Makoto. *Art and Faith: A Theology of Making*. New Haven, CT: Yale University Press, 2020.

Gavrilyuk, Paul L. *The Suffering of the Impassible God: The Dialectics of Patristic Thought*. Oxford: Oxford University Press, 2004.

González, Antonio. "Trinity as Gospel." In *The Trinity among the Nations: The Doctrine of God in the Majority World*, edited by Gene L. Green, Stephen T. Pardue, and K. K. Yeo, 69–85. Carlisle, UK: Langham, 2015.

González, Justo L. *The History of Theological Education*. Nashville: Abingdon, 2015.

———. *The Story of Christianity*, vol. 1, *The Early Church to the Dawn of the Reformation*. New York: HarperCollins, 2010.

———. *The Story of Christianity*, vol. 2, *The Reformation to the Present Day*. New York: HarperCollins, 1985.

"The Gospel of Peter." Translated by Bart D. Ehrman. In *Lost Scriptures: Books that Did Not Make It into the New Testament*, edited by Bart D. Ehrman, 31–34. New York: Oxford University Press, 2003.

"The Gospel of Philip." Translated by David Cartlidge and David Dungan In *Lost Scriptures: Books that Did Not Make It into the New Testament*, edited by Bart D. Ehrman, 38–44. New York: Oxford University Press, 2003.

Green, Gene L., Stephen T. Pardue, and K. K. Yeo, eds. *The Trinity among the Nations: The Doctrine of God in the Majority World*. Carlisle, UK: Langham, 2015.

Gregory of Nazianzus. *On God and On Christ*. Translated by Frederick Williams and Lionel Wickham. Popular Patristics Series. Crestwood, NY: St Vladimir's Seminary Press, 2002.

Gregory of Nyssa. *Catechetical Discourse*. Translated by Ignatius Green. Popular Patristics Series. Yonkers, NY: St Vladimir's Seminary Press, 2019.

———. *The Life of Moses*. Translated by Abraham J. Malherbe and Everett Ferguson. Harper Collins Spiritual Classics. New York: HarperOne, 2006.

Grigor of Narek. "Book of Lamentation, Discourse 1, Discourse 88." Translated by Jesse S. Arlen. In *Eastern Christianity: A Reader*, edited by J. Edward Walters, 181–89. Grand Rapids: Eerdmans, 2021.

Gupta, Nijay. *15 New Testament Words of Life: A New Testament Theology for Real Life*. Grand Rapids: Zondervan, 2022.

Harakas, Stanley Samuel. *Orthodox Christian Beliefs about the Bible: Real Answers to Real Questions from Real People*. Minneapolis: Light & Life, 2003.

Harper, Lisa Sharon. *The Very Good Gospel: How Everything Wrong Can Be Made Right*. Colorado Springs, CO: Waterbrook, 2016.

Harrison, Nonna Verna. *God's Many-Splendored Image: Theological Anthropology for Christian Formation*. Grand Rapids: Baker, 2010.

Hay, Richard B. *Echoes of Scripture in the Gospels*. Waco, TX: Baylor University Press, 2016.

Herberg, Will. "Judaism and Christianity: Their Unity and Difference." In *Jewish Perspectives on Christianity*, edited by Fritz A. Rothschild. New York: Crossroad, 1990.

Heschel, Abraham Joshua. *God in Search of Man: A Philosophy of Judaism*. New York: Farrar, Straus and Giroux, 1955.

Hesychios. "On Watchfulness." *The Book of Mystical Chapters: Meditations on the Soul's Ascent from the Desert Fathers and Other Early Christian Contemplatives*, translated and introduced by John Anthony McGuckin, 15. Boston: Shambhala, 2002.

Hildegard of Bingen. *Hildegard of Bingen: Scivias*. Translated by Columba Hart and Jane Bishop. The Classics of Western Spirituality. New York: Paulist, 1990.

Hofstede, Geert, Gert Jan Hofstede, and Michael Minkov, eds. *Cultures and Organizations: Software of the Mind*. New York: McGraw-Hill, 2010.

"Homilies on the Gospel Readings for Holy Week." Translated by John C. Lamoreaux. In *Eastern Christianity: A Reader*, edited by J. Edward Walters, 284–90. Grand Rapids: Eerdmans, 2021.

Hughes, Amy Brown. "The Apostle's Creed—Ben Myers and Natasha Kennedy." *On Script* (podcast), March 2, 2022. https://onscript.study/podcast/the-apostles-creed-ben-myers-and-natasha-kennedy/.

Ignatius of Antioch. "The Epistle to the Romans." In *The Apostolic Fathers: Early Christian Writings*, translated by Maxwell Staniforth and revised translation by Andrew Louth, 83–89. New York: Penguin, 1987.

Irenaeus of Lyon. *Against Heresies*. Middletown, DE: Beloved, 2015.

———. *On the Apostolic Preaching*. Translated by John Behr. Popular Patristics Series. Crestwood, NY: St Vladimir's Seminary Press, 1997.

Isaac of Nineveh. *On Ascetical Life*. Translated by Mary Hansbury. Popular Patristics Series. Crestwood, NY: St. Vladimir's Seminary, 1989.

———. "On Gehenna." Translation based on the translation of Sebastian P. Brock. In *Invitation to Syriac Christianity: An Anthology*, edited by Michael Philip Penn, Scott Fitzgerald Johnson, Christine Shepardson, and Charles M. Stang, 185–88. Oakland: University of California Press, 2022.

Ishaq, Hunayn Ibn. "How to Discern the True Religion." Translated by John C. Lamoreaux. In *Eastern Christianity: A Reader*, edited by J. Edward Walters, 304–8. Grand Rapids: Eerdmans, 2021.

Jacob of Serug. *On the Mother of God*. Translated by Mary Hansbury. Popular Patristics Series. Crestwood, NY: St Vladimir's Seminary Press, 1998.

Jersak, Bradley. *A More Christlike God: A More Beautiful Gospel*. Pasadena, CA: Plain Truth Ministries, 2015.

———. *A More Christlike Word: Reading Scripture the Emmaus Way*. New Kensington, PA: Whitaker House, 2021.

"The Jesus Prayer." https://www.christianity.com/wiki/prayer/the-jesus-prayer-lord-have-mercy.html.

Johnson, Luke Timothy. *The Creed: What Christians Believe and Why It Matters*. New York: DoubleDay, 2003.

Julian of Norwich. *Revelations of Divine Love*. Translated by Elizabeth Spearing. London: Penguin, 1998.

Justin Martyr. *Dialogue with Trypho*. Translated by Thomas B. Falls. Edited by Michael Slusser. Selections from the Fathers of the Church. Washington, DC: Catholic University of America Press, 2003.

———. *First and Second Apologies*. Middletown, DE: Beloved, 2018.

Keener, Craig. *The IVP Bible Background Commentary: New Testament*. Downers Grove, IL: InterVarsity, 1993.

King, Martin Luther, Jr. "Letter from a Birmingham Jail." April 16, 1963. https://www.africa.upenn.edu/Articles_Gen/Letter_Birmingham.html.

Kinzer, Mark. *Postmissionary Messianic Judaism: Redefining Christian Engagement with the Jewish people*. Grand Rapids: Brazos, 2005.

———. "Scripture and Tradition." In *Voices of Messianic Judaism: Confronting Critical Issues Facing a Maturing Movement*, edited by Dan Cohn-Sherbok, 29–38. Baltimore, MD: Messianic Jewish, 2001.

Kiraz, George A., ed. *Syriac-English New Testament*. Piscataway, NJ: Gorgias, 2020.

Kombo, James Henry Owino. *Theological Models of the Doctrine of the Trinity: The Trinity, Diversity and Theological Hermeneutics*. Carlisle, UK: Langham, 2016.

Krestos, Hensa. *Harp of Glory: Enzira Sebhat: An Alphabetical Hymn of Praise for the Ever-Blessed Virgin Mary from the Ethiopian Orthodox Church*. Translated by John Anthony McGuckin. Popular Patristics Series. Yonkers, NY: St Vladimir's Seminary Press, 2010.

Kugel, James L. *How to Read the Bible: A Guide to Scripture, Then and Now*. New York: Free Press, 2008.

Lawson, Steven J. "The Invincible Word." In *The Inerrant Word: Biblical, Historical, Theological, and Pastoral Perspectives*, edited by John MacArthur, 319–33. Wheaton, IL: Crossway, 2016.

Levenson, Jon D. *The Hebrew Bible, The Old Testament and Historical Criticism*. Louisville: John Knox, 1993.

Levy, Antoine. *Jewish Church: A Catholic Approach to Messianic Judaism*. Lanham, MD: Lexington, 2021.

Lewis, C. S. *The Last Battle*. Narnia. London: Harper Collins, 1956.

———. "Letter to Mrs. Johnson, November 8, 1952." In *The Collected Letters of C.S. Lewis*, edited by Walter Hooper, vol. 3, *Narnia, Cambridge, and Joy, 1950–1963*. New York: HarperCollins, 2006.

———. *Mere Christianity*. New York: HarperOne, 1980.

———. "Preface." In *On the Incarnation*, by Athanasius, translated by John Behr, 9–15. Popular Patristics Series. Yonkers: St Vladimir's Seminary Press, 2011.

———. "The Problem of Pain." In *The Complete C.S. Lewis Signature Classics*, 371–433. New York: Harper Collins, 2002.

Lindbeck, George. "The Church as Israel: Ecclesiology and Ecumenism." In *Jews and Christians: People of God*, edited by Carl E. Braaten and Robert W. Jenson, 78–94. Grand Rapids: Eerdmans, 2003.

Long, D Stephen. *Theology and Culture: A Guide to the Discussion*. Eugene, OR: Cascade, 2010.

Lossky, Vladimir. *The Mystical Theology of the Eastern Church*. Crestwood, NY: St Vladimir's Seminary Press, 1957.

Louth, Andrew. *Introducing Eastern Orthodox Theology*. Downers Grove, IL: InterVarsity, 2013.

Lubac, Henri de. *History and Spirit: The Understanding of Scripture According to Origen*. Translated by Anne Englund Nash. San Francisco: Ignatius, 2007.

Luther, Martin. *The Essential Luther*. Translated and edited by Tryntje Helfferich. Indianapolis: Hackett, 2018.

MacArthur, John F. "Introduction: Why a Book on Biblical Inerrancy Is Necessary." In *The Inerrant Word: Biblical, Historical, Theological and Pastoral Perspectives*, edited by John F. MacArthur, 11–21. Wheaton, IL: Crossway, 2016.

Maimonides, Moses. *The Guide for the Perplexed*. Translated by M. Friedlander. Originally published 1904. Barnes & Noble Library of Essential Reading. New York: Barnes & Noble, 2004.

Marshall, Joseph M., III. *The Lakota Way: Stories and Lessons for Living*. New York: Viking Compass, 2001.

Martin, James. *The Jesuit Guide to (Almost) Everything: A Spirituality for Real Life*. New York: HarperOne, 2010.

Matthews, Victor H., and Don C. Benjamin. *The Social World of Ancient Israel, 1250–587 BCE*. Grand Rapids: Baker, 1993.

Maximus the Confessor. *Maximus Confessor: Selected Writings*. Translated by George C. Berthold. The Classics of Western Spirituality. Mahwah, NJ: Paulist, 1985.

———. "Two Hundred Texts on Theology and the Incarnate Dispensation of the Son of God." In *The Philokalia: The Complete Text*. Compiled by Nicodemus of the Holy Mountain and Makarios of Corinth, translated and edited by Palmer G. E. H., Philip Sherrard, and Kallistos Ware, 2:114–63. London: Faber and Faber, 1981.

McGuckin, John Anthony. "Introduction." In *The Harp of Glory: Enzira Sebhat: An Alphabetical Hymn of Praise for the Ever-Blessed Virgin Mary from the Ethiopian Orthodox Church*, translated by John Anthony McGuckin, 9–24. Crestwood, NY: St Vladimir's Seminary Press, 2010.

McLaren, Brian D. *The Great Spiritual Migration: How the World's Largest Religion Is Seeking a Better Way to Be Christian*. New York: Convergent, 2016.

Merton, Thomas. *Thoughts in Solitude*. New York: Farrar, Straus and Giroux, 1958.

Metzger, Bruce. *The New Testament: Its Background, Growth, and Content*. New York: Oxford University Press, 2004.

Meyer, Barbara U. *Jesus the Jew in Christian Memory: Theological and Philosophical Explorations*. Cambridge, UK: Cambridge University Press, 2022.

Middleton, J Richard. *A New Heaven and a New Earth: Reclaiming Biblical Eschatology*. Grand Rapids: Baker, 2014.

Mignolo, Walter D., and Catherine E. Walsh. *On Decoloniality: Concepts, Analytics, and Praxis*. Durham, NC: Duke University Press, 2018.

Miller, Robert J., ed. *The Complete Gospels: Annotated Scholars Version*. San Francisco: Harper Collins, 1994.

Mohawk, John C. *Utopian Legacies: A History of Conquest and Oppression in the Western World*. Santa Fe: Clear Light, 2000.

Morris, Joe E. *Revival of the Gnostic Heresy: Fundamentalism*. New York: Palgrave Macmillan, 2008.

Munhall, L. W. "Inspiration." In *The Fundamentals: A Testimony to the Truth*, edited by R. A. Torrey and A. C. Dixon, 2:44–60. Grand Rapids: Baker, 2003.

Murray, Robert. *Symbols of Church and Kingdom: A Study in Early Syriac Tradition*. Rev. ed. London: T. & T. Clark, 2006.

Myers, Ben. *The Apostles' Creed: A Guide to the Ancient Catechism*. Christian Essentials. Bellingham, WA: Lexham, 2018.

Narsai. "On the Canaanite Woman." Translated by Erin Galgay Walsh. In *Eastern Christianity: A Reader*, edited by J Edward Walters, 69–87. Grand Rapids: Eerdmans, 2021.

"A New Student." https://www.passiton.com/your-everyday-heroes/5682-a-new-student.

Nirenberg, David. *Anti-Judaism: The Western Tradition*. New York: Norton, 2014.

Nouwen, Henri J.M. *Life of the Beloved: Spiritual Living in a Secular World.* New York: Crossroad, 1992.

Odes of Solomon. Translation based on *The Odes of Solomon: A Commentary*, translated by Michael Lattke (Minneapolis: Fortress, 2009). In *Invitation to Syriac Christianity: An Anthology*, edited by Michael Philip Penn, Scott Fitzgerald Johnson, Christine Shepardson, and Charles M. Stang, 53–54. Oakland: University of California Press, 2022.

———. "Ode 24." In *Invitation to Syriac Christianity: An Anthology*, edited by Michael Philip Penn, Scott Fitzgerald Johnson, Christine Shepardson, and Charles M. Stang, 52–53. Oakland, CA: University of California Press, 2022.

Olson, Roger. *The Story of Christian Theology.* Downers Grove, IL: InterVarsity, 1999.

Olver, Matthew S.C. "Missed and Misunderstood Jewish Roots of Christian Worship." In *Understanding the Jewish Roots of Christianity: Biblical, Theological, and Historical Essays on the Relationship between Christianity & Judaism*, edited by Gerald R. McDermott, 69–103. Bellingham, WA: Lexham, 2021.

Origen. Edited by Claude Jenkins. "Commentary on 1 Corinthians." *Journal of Theological Studies* 9 (1908) 231–47.

———. *Commentary on the Gospel of John, Books 1—10.* Translated by Ronald E. Heine. The Fathers of the Church. Washington, DC: Catholic University of America Press, 2010.

———. *Commentary on the Gospel of Matthew (Book X).* Translated by John Patrick. In *Ante-Nicene Fathers*, vol. 9., edited by Allan Menzies. Buffalo, NY: Christian Literature, 1896. Revised and edited for *New Advent* by Kevin Knight. https://www.newadvent.org/fathers/101610.htm.

———. *Homilies on Genesis and Exodus.* Translated by Ronald E. Heine. The Fathers of the Church. Washington, DC: Catholic University of America Press, 1982.

———. *Homilies on Isaiah.* Translated by Elizabeth Ann Dively Lauro. The Fathers of the Church. Washington, DC: Catholic University of America Press, 2021.

———. *Homilies on Leviticus: 1–16.* Translated by Gary Wayne Barkley. The Fathers of the Church. Washington, DC: Catholic University of America Press, 1990.

———. *Homilies on the Psalms: Codex Monacensis Graecus 314.* Translated by Joseph W. Trigg. The Fathers of the Church. Washington, DC: Catholic University of America Press, 2020.

———. *Origen: On First Principles: A Reader's Edition.* Translated by John Behr. Oxford: Oxford University Press, 2019.

Pagels, Elaine. *The Gnostic Gospels.* New York: Random House, 1976.

Paul VI, Pope. "Dogmatic Constitution on Divine Revelation: *Dei Verbum*." Promulgated November 18, 1965. https://www.vatican.va/archive/hist_councils/ii_vatican_council/documents/vat-ii_const_19651118_dei-verbum_en.html.

Peeler, Amy. *Women and the Gender of God.* Grand Rapids: Eerdmans, 2022.

Pelikan, Jaroslav. *Credo: Historical and Theological Guide to Creeds and Confessions of Faith in the Christian Tradition.* New Haven, CT: Yale University Press, 2003.

Pietersma, Albert., and Benjamin G. Wright, eds. *A New English Translation of the Septuagint.* New York: Oxford University Press, 2007.

"The Prayers of St. Thomas Aquinas." https://thecatholichandbook.com/the-prayers-of-st-thomas-aquinas/.

Pseudo-Dioscorus of Alexandria. "Encomium of Macarius of Tkoou 7.1—8.16." Translated by Mary K. Farag. In *Eastern Christianity: A Reader*, edited by J. Edward Walters, 344–51. Grand Rapids: Eerdmans, 2021.

Qurrah, Theodore Abu. "That God Is Not Weak." Translated by John C. Lamoreaux. In *Eastern Christianity: A Reader*, edited by J. Edward Walters, 291–96. Grand Rapids: Eerdmans, 2021.

Radner, Ephraim, and David Ney, eds. *All Thy Lights Combine: Figural Reading in the Anglican Tradition*. Bellingham, WA: Lexham, 2022.

Rah, Soong-Chan. *The Next Evangelicalism: Freeing the Church from Western Cultural Captivity*. Downers Grove, IL: InterVarsity, 2009.

"A Reflection on St. Patrick's Prayer." World Vision, March 16, 2018. https://www.worldvision.org/christian-faith-news-stories/reflection-st-patrick-day-prayer.

Richardson, Cyril C., ed. and trans. *Early Christian Fathers*. New York: Touchstone, 1996.

Rohr, Richard. *Falling Upward: A Spirituality for the Two Halves of Life: A Companion Journal*. San Francisco: Jossey-Bass, 2011.

Rosenzweig, Franz. *The Star of Redemption*. Translated by Barbara E. Galli. Madison: University of Wisconsin Press, 2005.

Rosner, Jennifer M. *Finding Messiah: A Journey into the Jewishness of the Gospel*. Downers Grove, IL: InterVarsity, 2022.

———. *Healing the Schism: Karl Barth, Franz Rosenzweig, and the New Jewish-Christian Encounter*, Bellingham, WA: Lexham Academic, 2021.

Sacks, Jonathan. *Essays on Ethics: A Weekly Reading of the Jewish Bible*. Jerusalem: Maggid, 2016.

Schmemann, Alexander. *Introduction to Liturgical Theology*. Crestwood, NY: St Vladimir's Seminary Press, 1986.

Severus of Antioch. "Homily XVIII." In *Severus of Antioch*, translated by Pauline Allen and C. T. R. Hayward, 119. The Early Church Fathers. New York: Routledge, 2004.

Shenoute of Atripe. "I Have Been Reading the Holy Gospels (Discourse 8.1)." Translated by Mary K. Farag. In *Eastern Christianity: A Reader*, edited by J. Edward Walters, 338–43. Grand Rapids: Eerdmans, 2021.

Smith, J. Warren. "Once Again into the Breach." *Firebrand*, September 14, 2021. https://firebrandmag.com/articles/once-again-into-the-breach-returning-to-the-mandate-for-unity.

Sommer, Benjamin. *The Bodies of God and the World of Ancient Israel*. New York: Cambridge University Press, 2009.

Soulen, R. Kendall. *The God of Israel and Christian Theology*. Minneapolis: Fortress, 1996.

Spong, John Shelby. *Why Christianity Must Change or Die: A Bishop Speaks to Believers in Exile*. New York: HarperCollins, 1998.

Stephen, Caroline Emelia. *Quaker Strongholds*. Originally published, Philadelphia: Henry Longstreth, 1891. Project Gutenberg, April 10, 2020. https://www.gutenberg.org/cache/epub/61802/pg61802-images.html.

Swoboda, A. J. *After Doubt: How to Question Your Faith without Losing It*. Grand Rapids: Brazos, 2021.

Theodore bar Koni. "Scholion, Memra 10." Translated by Aaron Michael Butts. In *Eastern Christianity: A Reader*, edited J. Edward Walters, 129–41. Grand Rapids: Eerdmans, 2021.

Therrien, Mark E. *Cross and Creation: A Theological Introduction to Origen of Alexandria*. Washington, DC: Catholic University of America Press, 2022.

Thompson, Marianne Meye. *John: A Commentary*. New Testament Library. Louisville: Westminster John Knox, 2015.

Thurman, Howard. *Jesus and the Disinherited*. Boston: Beacon, 1976.
Tolkien, J. R. R. *The Fellowship of the Ring: Being the First Part of The Lord of the Rings*. Boston: Mariner, 1994.
Torrey, R. A., and A. C. Dixon, eds. *The Fundamentals: A Testimony to the Truth*. 4 vols. Grand Rapids: Baker, 2003.
Tutu, Desmond Mpilo. *No Future without Forgiveness*. New York: Doubleday, 1999.
Twiss, Richard. *One Church, Many Tribes: Following Jesus the Way God Made You*. Ventura, CA: Regal, 2000.
———. *Rescuing the Gospel from the Cowboys: A Native American Expression of the Jesus Way*. Downers Grove, IL: InterVarsity, 2015.
Vincent of Lerins. "Vincent of Lerins on the Role of Tradition." In *The Christian Theology Reader*, edited by Alister E. McGrath, 78–79. 4th ed. West Sussex, UK: Wiley-Blackwell, 2011.
Viola, Frank. *Reimagining Church: Pursuing the Dream of Organic Christianity*. Colorado Springs, CO: David C. Cook, 2008.
Walters, J. Edwards, ed. *Eastern Christianity: A Reader*. Grand Rapids: Eerdmans, 2021.
———. "Introduction." In *Eastern Christianity: A Reader*, edited by J. Edwards Walters, 1–7. Grand Rapids: Eerdmans, 2021.
Ware, Kallistos. *The Orthodox Church: An Introduction to Eastern Christianity*. London: Penguin, 2015.
———. *The Orthodox Way*. Yonkers, NY: St Vladimir's Seminary Press, 2018.
White, Thomas Joseph. *The Light of Christ: An Introduction to Catholicism*. Washington, DC: Catholic University of America Press, 2017.
Wilken, Robert Louis. *The Spirit of Early Christian Thought: Seeking the Face of God*. New Haven, CT: Yale University Press, 2003.
Wood, Jordan Daniel. *The Whole Mystery of Christ: Creation as Incarnation in Maximus Confessor*. Notre Dame, IN: University of Notre Dame Press, 2022.
Woodley, Randy. *Indigenous Theology and the Western Worldview: A Decolonized Approach to Christian Doctrine*. Grand Rapids: Baker, 2022.
———. *Living in Color: Embracing God's Passion for Ethnic Diversity*. Downers Grove, IL: InterVarsity, 2004.
———. *Shalom and the Community of Creation: An Indigenous Vision*. Grand Rapids: Eerdmans, 2012.
———. "White Supremacy and the Fate of the Earth," *Sojourners*, May 2021, https://sojo.net/magazine/may-2021/white-supremacy-and-fate-earth.
Wright, N. T. *The Day the Revolution Began: Reconsidering the Meaning of Jesus's Crucifixion*. New York: HarperOne, 2018.
———. *Surprised by Hope: Rethinking Heaven, the Resurrection, and the Mission of the Church*. New York: Harper One, 2008.
Ya'eqob, Zar'a. "Book of the Trinity." In *Eastern Christianity: A Reader*, translated by Aaron M. Butts and edited by J. Edward Walters, 402–5. Grand Rapids, MI: Eerdmans, 2021.
Zizioulas, John D. *Being As Communion: Studies in Personhood and the Church*. Crestwood: St Vladimir's Seminary Press, 1985.

www.ingramcontent.com/pod-product-compliance
Lightning Source LLC
Chambersburg PA
CBHW070236230426
43664CB00014B/2319